SPOTLIGHT ON
CIVIC COURAGE
HEROES OF CONSCIENCE™

HENRY DAVID THOREAU

AUTHOR OF "CIVIL DISOBEDIENCE"

Heather Moore Ni

D1532110

Rosen
YA™
New York

Published in 2018 by The Rosen Publishing Group, Inc.
29 East 21st Street, New York, NY 10010

First Edition

Library of Congress Cataloging-in-Publication Data

Names: Niver, Heather Moore, author.
Title: Henry David Thoreau : author of "Civil Disobedience" / Heather Moore Niver.
Description: New York : Rosen YA, 2018. | Series: Spotlight on civic courage: heroes of conscience | Includes bibliographical references and index. | Audience: Grades 5–10.
Identifiers: LCCN 2017014242| ISBN 9781538381151 (library bound) | ISBN 9781538381120 (pbk.) | ISBN 9781538381137 (6 pack)
Subjects: LCSH: Thoreau, Henry David, 1817–1862—Juvenile literature. | Authors, American—19th century—Biography—Juvenile literature. | Naturalists—United States—Biography—Juvenile literature.
Classification: LCC PS3053 .N56 2018 | DDC 818/.309 [B] —dc23
LC record available at https://lccn.loc.gov/2017014242

Manufactured in the United States of America

On the cover: This photo of Thoreau was taken in August 1861. In the background is a photo of Walden Pond from the site of the hut where Thoreau moved "to live so sturdily and Spartan-like as to put to rout all that was not life."

CONTENTS

THE MANY HATS OF THOREAU

Some think of Henry David Thoreau as a writer of poems and essays. Others picture a philosopher, abolitionist, and transcendentalist. Still others consider him a scientist or naturalist. Many think he lived a life of simplicity and solitude. And the list goes on. That sounds like more "hats" than a single man could possibly wear, but they are all true, at least in part. Thoreau also made pencils, worked odd jobs, and tutored students. He wore each hat with admirable confidence. Well-known for building a cabin in the woods "to live deliberately," Thoreau made contributions in several fields.

A joke about Thoreau says that throughout his life he was either in jail or at Walden Pond. While that's not actually true, Thoreau's book *Walden* and his essay "Civil Disobedience" are such influential pieces that they sometimes overshadow the full story of his life. What is true is that his determination inspired others to stand up and work with courage and tenacity.

Henry David Thoreau was a man of many talents, multiple interests, and strong convictions. He always had the courage to stand up for what he felt was right.

A Nature Boy Is Born

On July 12, 1817, a second son was born to John and Cynthia Dunbar Thoreau in Concord, Massachusetts. They named him David Henry Thoreau. (He changed his name to Henry David after college.) The household also included older siblings John Jr. and Helen, as well as a younger sister, Sophia.

Henry spent most of his childhood in Concord, although for a few years his father, a shopkeeper, moved the family in hopes of better business opportunities. By 1823, they were back in Concord, where he began a pencil-making business. The pencil factory eventually helped the family financially and would provide employment for Henry later on in life. Cynthia and the family had boarders stay at their home, too, as an additional way to make money.

In 1828, after a few years in Concord's grammar school, Henry attended Concord Academy. He was an excellent student and the academy prepared him for college. Henry's mother also encouraged him to explore and learn about nature, nurturing an interest that would stay with him all his life.

John Thoreau Sr., father to John Jr., Helen, Henry, and Sophia, moved the family several times before settling back in Concord, Massachusetts, and starting a pencil-making factory.

COLLEGE GUY

In 1833, Henry attended Harvard College. Although he was only sixteen, entering college at this age was common then. The family could only afford to send one son to college, so the studious Henry David was selected. John Jr. and Helen, both teachers, contributed money to help support their younger brother's education. (A year of expenses was about $179 at the time.) At Harvard, Henry continued to be a good student, although he complained that the teaching methods focused on "all the branches and none of the roots." Nevertheless, he studied Latin and Greek grammar, mathematics, English, history, and several kinds of philosophy. He learned a number of languages, too.

Thoreau graduated from Harvard in 1837. He left school for a time to teach to earn some money. He also missed some time when he was ill. Nevertheless, he gradated in the top half of his class. Thoreau refused his diploma, though, because he objected to wasting his money on the five-dollar fee.

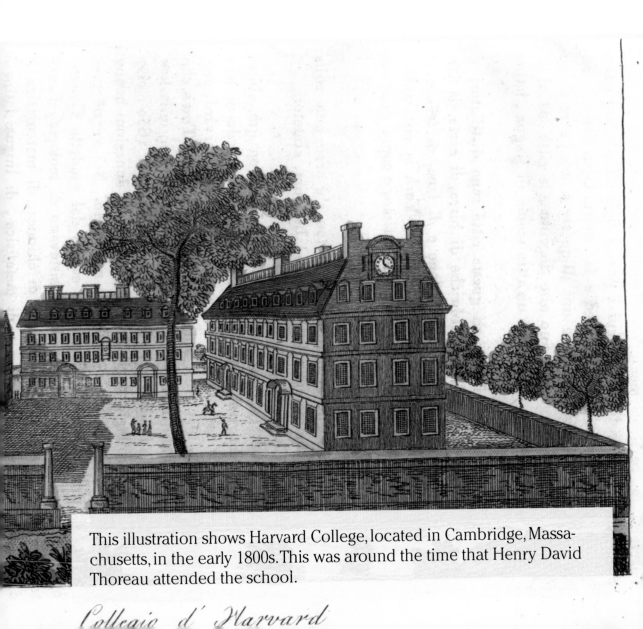

This illustration shows Harvard College, located in Cambridge, Massachusetts, in the early 1800s. This was around the time that Henry David Thoreau attended the school.

Collegio d´ Harvard

WORKING MAN

In 1837, graduates of Harvard usually chose to follow one of four career paths: ministry, the law, medicine, or teaching. Thoreau didn't think he had the right character for any of these options, except teaching. He took a job as teacher back in his hometown of Concord, but he didn't keep it for long. When the supervisor insisted that he use corporal punishment to discipline the students, Thoreau refused. He left after two weeks.

Now without a job, Thoreau considered heading to Kentucky with his brother. Instead, the young men decided to stay in Concord and work in the family pencil factory. Thoreau studied different ways to make the lead black and hard.

His research made the family's pencils the top brand in the country!

Thoreau did not completely abandon the idea of teaching, though. When he did not find another teaching job, he opened his own school in 1838.

Thoreau's research into more efficient pencil-making techniques made the John Thoreau & Co. brand of pencils the best in the United States.

THE THOREAU BROTHERS

When Concord Academy had enough students, Thoreau asked John to help teach. The brothers got along really well at home and as coworkers. Besides teaching, the two young men relaxed and went on vacation together. They went on a boating adventure in September 1839, traveling up the Concord and Merrimack rivers until they reached New Hampshire's Mount Washington.

The Thoreau brothers even ended up proposing to the same girl! Ellen Sewell seems to have captured the fancy of both boys. Thoreau mentions her in his journal and penned a poem about her. Soon after meeting her he wrote, "There is no remedy for love but to love more." Apparently, his brother proposed first, but she refused him. Thoreau, already a wordsmith, proposed in the form of a letter. She refused him, too, evidently because her father wanted her to do so. Thoreau never married and the remainder of his love life is a matter of speculation.

Henry David Thoreau is pictured around 1839, in a painting created by his youngest sister, Sophia. As a young man, he and his brother went on many memorable adventures together.

ENTER EMERSON

Unfortunately, John became too ill to teach in April 1841, so Thoreau closed Concord Academy. He briefly returned to work at the family pencil factory.

Friend and neighbor Ralph Waldo Emerson invited Thoreau to live and work at his home. Thoreau did odd jobs, such as gardening and other tasks around the house. He also tutored Emerson's oldest son, William, in his home on Staten Island while trying to reach out to publishers in New York. Emerson encouraged the young Thoreau to publish poems and essays, including "The Natural History of Massachusetts," which was a step toward his future as a naturalist and environmentalist.

Emerson became a tremendous mentor. He was among the most famous writers and philosophers in America, and his ideas about transcendentalism influenced Thoreau. For the transcendentalists, a life lived successfully meant putting aside material goods and trying to concentrate on the spiritual aspects of life and nature. Emerson believed that "God is in every man."

Ralph Waldo Emerson became a remarkable influence and mentor for Henry David Thoreau, inspiring him to publish his writing as well as providing work for him over the years.

PLANNING WALDEN

In 1842, John Thoreau died unexpectedly. Losing a brother who was such a close friend may have influenced Thoreau's decision to move to the woods. Also, the boarders his mother took in made the family home too busy for a writer who craved solitude. And working at the pencil factory used up energy he wanted for writing. He remembered visiting a friend's cabin retreat and began hatching a plan to build his own.

Emerson gave Thoreau permission to build a cabin on his land in 1845. He found the perfect spot right along Walden Pond and went to work. He bought supplies and recycled an old chicken coop for its wooden boards. By July 4 that year, twenty-seven-year-old Thoreau moved into Walden.

In his newly built home, Thoreau planned to write his first book, *A Week on the Concord and Merrimack Rivers.* (It would be in memory of his brother.) He also hoped to try to live by working only one day a week. The other days he would focus on more transcendental matters. And he wanted to be close to nature there.

Walden Pond struck Thoreau as the idyllic location on which to build a writing retreat when living at home proved too distracting for the young author.

LIVING IN THE "INKSTAND IN THE WOODS"

Thoreau lived on Walden Pond in his "inkstand in the woods" from July 1845 to September 1847. Here, he wrote, he was "living deep and sucking out all the marrow of life."

As a transcendentalist, Thoreau wanted a simple life. He planted a garden to grow most of his own food, such as beans, and otherwise tried to eat fruits and vegetables he could find on the land. Technological advances, such as railroads and the telegraph, fascinated him, but he worried that these advances came at a great cost to nature. He also wrote, "perhaps we are led oftener by the love of novelty, and a regard for the opinions of men, in procuring it, than by a true utility."

This reconstruction of Thoreau's cabin shows the small size of the hut the author built, using recycled materials and his own muscle and sweat. He lived in his tiny home for two years.

Usually, Thoreau spent the bulk of his time reading, writing, rowing, and walking in the woods and fields. He wrote in a journal, including observations about nature (a habit he began in 1837), as well as what he did and what he thought.

Although Thoreau enjoyed solitude at Walden Pond, he joined friends and family in town. He also took a trip to the rugged wilderness of Maine, as depicted here in Frederic Edwin Church's paining of Mount Katahdin.

Thoreau has become known as a recluse over the years, but he actually welcomed visitors to Walden and enjoyed meals in town with his family or the Emersons. (Thoreau may have even brought his laundry to the family home!) He also worked as a surveyor and took on various jobs for people around Concord. He traveled to Maine's Mount Katahdin, where the wilderness was far more rugged than anything he experienced at home.

Later in his Walden stay, he focused his writing more on nature and its study. In 1846, he began writing a lecture to help explain to people in town what he was doing out at the pond. People were curious about how he lived and wanted to know the details of his day-to-day life. His writing eventually resulted in his second book, *Walden*.

After his death, his journals from this time resulted in additional publications: *Excursions*, *The Maine Woods*, *Cape Cod*, and *A Yankee in Canada*.

AFTER WALDEN

In 1847, Thoreau left his writing retreat. He writes in the conclusion of *Walden*, "I left the woods for as good a reason as I went there. Perhaps it seemed to me that I had several more lives to live, and could not spare any more time for that one." After staying with his family for a month, he moved in to help out at the Emerson home. He stayed two years while Ralph Waldo Emerson was touring and lecturing across Europe.

In 1849, Thoreau published *A Week on the Concord and Merrimack Rivers.* He paid for the publication himself, so it must have been disappointing when it only sold about two hundred copies. It was criticized for an absence of structure,

as well as a preachy tone and distinct lack of humor. Thoreau used this as a learning experience and delayed publishing *Walden.* He went through seven drafts of this later book, making changes such as tightening the structure and adding more humor.

Today visitors can enjoy the Emerson home as a museum. For Thoreau, it was a respite after leaving his pond home instead of moving back into his busy family home.

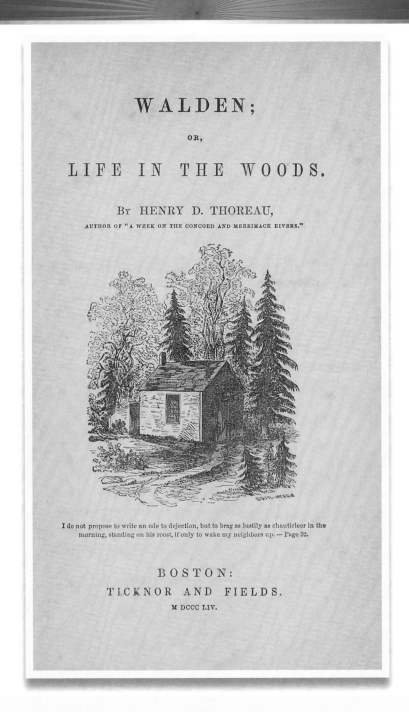

WALDEN;

OR,

LIFE IN THE WOODS.

BY HENRY D. THOREAU,

AUTHOR OF "A WEEK ON THE CONCORD AND MERRIMACK RIVERS."

I do not propose to write an ode to dejection, but to brag as lustily as chanticleer in the morning, standing on his roost, if only to wake my neighbors up. — Page 92.

BOSTON:

TICKNOR AND FIELDS.

M DCCC LIV.

Thoreau's *Walden* was published on August 9, 1854. The cover features an illustration of his "inkstand in the woods." He postponed publication so he could work on editing his writing.

The extra editing was well worth the additional time, effort, and postponed publication. His experience publishing his first book had taught him a lot. *Walden* turned out to be something of a success after it was published on August 9, 1854. Reviewers were mostly positive and sales were good. *Walden* even gained Thoreau a few admirers! It continues to be read and admired to this day.

After Ralph Waldo Emerson came back home from his tour, Thoreau returned to his parents' house, where he rented a room. He went back to work at the pencil factory and supplemented his income with surveying work, with lectures, and by writing for publications such as newspapers and journals.

Thoreau never really made much money, preferring to spend more time walking in the woods, thinking, observing nature, and writing about it all in his journal. He continued revising his other essays in the hopes of getting them published, too.

NOT-SO-DELIBERATE LIVING

Not everyone was taken with *Walden*. In the 1870s and 1880s, especially, critics called him cranky and thought he lived a careless lifestyle. To this day, critics accuse him of hypocrisy and of trying to make himself look good. *Walden* gives an impression of Thoreau living a simple life of complete solitude and spirituality, eating only what food he could grow or find on the land. The book describes the advantages of solitude, but Thoreau had many visitors. He was only about a mile (1.6 km) from Concord and his mother and sisters brought him food. He didn't stay at Walden the whole time, but also went on trips to places such as Maine.

Supporters argue that Thoreau admitted to some of these contradictions in his book. They point out that he exaggerated his experience for artistic reasons, as writers sometimes do. His use of literary elements, such as hyperbole and metaphor, makes his writing stronger. He distills his two-year stint into a series of four basic, simple seasons: summer, autumn, winter, and spring.

Thoreau was hardly living out in the wilderness. He was not far from his family home, seen here, where his mother and sisters baked and cooked food for him.

RESISTANCE AND DISOBEDIENCE

One event during Thoreau's stay at Walden Pond still stands out after all these years: his arrest and night in jail. On a trip into town, Thoreau crossed paths with the Concord jailer and tax collector, who informed the writer that he had not paid a poll tax in several years. Thoreau's nonpayment was no accidental oversight. Thoreau deliberately refused to pay this tax, because it supported the Mexican-American War. He felt that this war was no more than a justification for slavery, which he (as well as his family and other abolitionists) opposed. Thus, Thoreau was sent to jail.

A friend offered to pay the bail to liberate him, but Thoreau refused. He wanted to be an example to the community. But in the end, someone—possibly his aunt—paid his owed taxes before he could object.

Thoreau may have been disappointed that he was only in jail overnight. A single night did not make much of a stand against slavery.

This print shows the Battle of Buena Vista, during the Mexican-American War. Thoreau objected to the war on the grounds that it was just an excuse to expand slavery. He refused to pay the poll tax, which supported the war.

When his arrest resulted in a single
night in jail, Thoreau did what he
did best: he wrote a stinging essay,
"Resistance to Civil Government," now
known as "Civil Disobedience."

So, the frustrated writer took pen to paper and wrote one of his more famous essays, titled "Resistance to Civil Government." It was originally presented as a lecture on January 26, 1848, to the Concord Lyceum. It was published under that same name in 1849, but not many people read it. After his death, it was republished and retitled "On the Duty of Civil Disobedience," better known more simply as "Civil Disobedience."

Thoreau was not opposed to taxes in general. He was in favor of those that supported the upkeep of roads and schools, for example. He wrote, however, that if a law "is of such a nature that it requires you to be the agent of injustice to another, then, I say, break the law." Thoreau did not support any laws that supported slavery.

Some rumors circulate suggesting that Thoreau also penned a poem while behind bars, but none of his poems tackle this topic. He does mention that other prisoners may have written some verse, though.

ARDENT ABOLITIONIST

Thoreau did more than just criticize slavery. He assisted with the Underground Railroad, a network of people who helped slaves escape to the northern United States and Canada. The Thoreau home was part of the Underground Railroad, and his family, especially his mother and sisters, worked actively to thwart slavery. Cynthia Thoreau helped found the Concord Female Anti-Slavery Society.

Thoreau's journal notes helping, hiding, and transporting runaway slaves. He may have accompanied slaves to the next station during his Walden stay and definitely hosted a meeting of the Concord Female Anti-Slavery Society there.

Thoreau became an outspoken opponent of the Fugitive Slave Act, an 1850 law that introduced harsh punishments for anyone who refused to help in the capture of escaped slaves. His "Slavery in Massachusetts" speech commented on the fate of Anthony Burns, a slave who escaped and arrived in Boston, Massachusetts, as a free man in 1854. But his owner came for him, and Burns was captured and sent back to Virginia after a trial. This infuriated many Massachusetts abolitionists, Thoreau included.

THE ESCAPE ON SHIPBOARD.

ARREST IN BOSTON.

DEPARTURE FROM BOSTON.

THE SALE.

THE ADDRESS.

AUCTION

Anthony Burns was a topic of Thoreau's "Slavery in Massachusetts" essay. This portrait of Burns is surrounded by scenes from his life.

Abolitionist John Brown's raid on Harpers Ferry was intended to motivate slaves to rise up and rebel. Thoreau defended his controversial act in his essay, "Plea for Captain John Brown."

Though it was later published, "Slavery in Massachusetts" began as a speech in Framingham, Massachusetts, on July 4, 1854. Thoreau shared the stage with the abolitionists Sojourner Truth, Wendell Phillips, and Lucy Stone, as well as William Lloyd Garrison, who organized the event. In the speech, Thoreau said, "The law will never make men free; it is men who have got to make the law free."

Of all his anti-slavery work, Thoreau's defense of the abolitionist John Brown was probably the most controversial. On October 16, 1859, Brown headed a raid on a federal arsenal in Harpers Ferry, Virginia (now West Virginia). Rather than inspiring a slave rebellion, as he had intended, Brown was captured, tried, and hanged. Thoreau's speech, "Plea for Captain John Brown," in 1859 was widely published in the press. In it he praised Brown and described him as a "transcendentalist above all, a man of ideas and principles."

Simple, Natural Living

After leaving Walden Pond, Thoreau continued writing; he also gave lectures, published, and always kept a sharp eye on politics. More importantly, he continued to live a modest life, in part because he felt it helped him see everything more clearly.

He also kept up his interest in nature. In his journal, he continued to write his observations of the natural world around Concord, with detailed records about the flora and fauna of the area. He walked almost every morning and, as he had at Walden, he took detailed notes about plant life cycles, water levels of the local bodies of water, and temperatures. His writing was concise and even considered scientific, although he was a self-taught naturalist.

Thoreau certainly did not limit himself to writing about nature in the Concord area. He wrote *The Maine Woods,* based on several trips to that wild, northern state, and traveled to New Hampshire; Cape Cod, Massachusetts; Canada; and Minnesota. Eventually, Thoreau's nature writing helped inspire the environmental movement.

Just because he left his Walden cabin behind did not mean that Thoreau also left his interest in nature behind. He was often seen walking through Concord's woods and fields, taking notes.

THE FATAL COLD

Back in college, Thoreau had begun what would be a lifelong battle with lung issues. He was out in the woods counting tree rings on December 3, 1860, when he caught a cold. His cold quickly developed into bronchitis, and his efforts to get well over the next two years eventually failed. He was only forty-four years old when he died of tuberculosis. The last words of Henry David Thoreau are said to have been "Moose … Indian."

His sisters and friends made sure his words remained alive by publishing some of his work. Over the years, his words became more popular.

Thoreau's Walden Pond cabin was dismantled in 1849, but in 1862 fans began coming to the spot where it once stood. They left stones in a cairn, or memorial mound. Finally, in 1940, Roland Robbins excavated the site of the little house and built stone pillars to mark its place.

After losing a battle with tuberculosis, Thoreau was laid to rest on December 3, 1860, in Concord's Sleepy Hollow Cemetery.

POWERFUL PROSE

Henry David Thoreau may have enjoyed solitude, but he clearly wrote and worked for civil liberties, as we can see in his abolitionist writing and Underground Railroad activities. Thoreau inspired many other pillars of civil courage, including Russian writer Leo Tolstoy and Indian spiritual leader and nationalist Mahatma Gandhi.

Thoreau also inspired Martin Luther King Jr., who first read "Civil Disobedience" as a college freshman. King wrote, "I became convinced that noncooperation with evil is as much a moral obligation as is cooperation with good. No other person has been more eloquent and passionate in getting this idea across than Henry David Thoreau."

Concord was a small town teeming with literary talent. Writers such as Emerson, Nathaniel Hawthorne, and Margaret Fuller also lived and wrote there. But Henry David Thoreau's civic courage made him a singular artist. His powerful prose inspired many, whether environmentalists,

Henry David Thoreau's iconic words mark the area at Walden Pond where he spent two short but significant years of his life, reading, writing, and making a stand against slavery.

transcendentalists, or abolitionists. His willingness to write and act for the civil rights of others continues to win him admirers to this day.

GLOSSARY

abolitionist Someone who is against slavery and wants to end it.

boarder A person who pays money to live in a room in another's house.

corporal punishment A type of physical discipline, which can include flogging or hitting with a cane.

distill To take the most essential meaning or parts of something.

fauna The animals living in a specific place, time, or habitat.

flora The plants living in a specific place, time, or habitat.

hyperbole Declarations that are deliberately exaggerated and not meant to be taken literally.

infuriate To make someone mad.

justification A defense of someone's actions as right or reasonable.

lyceum An old-fashioned term for a literary institution, hall for speeches, or education space.

mentor Someone who is a dependable counselor, usually with ample experience.

metaphor A literary element in which a word or phrase is used in place of another to emphasize their similarities (but not to be taken literally).

poll tax A tax of a certain amount that adults are required to pay, often connected to voting.

prose Written language that is not in the form of poetry.

recluse Someone who lives alone and often avoids other people.

spiritual Having to do with the soul or spirit rather than material things.

stint A certain amount of time.

surveyor Someone who observes and keeps records of the land in a certain area.

tenacity Determination or ability to hold onto something.

transcendentalism A philosophy in New England that viewed the world as either material or spiritual.

The Henry David Thoreau Herbarium

Harvard University Herbaria & Libraries

22 Divinity Avenue

Cambridge, MA 02138

Website: http://botlib.huh.harvard.edu/libraries/Thoreau.htm

This collection of Henry David Thoreau's botanical specimens includes biographical information, size, material type, and more.

Thoreau Farm

PO Box 454

341 Virginia Road

Concord, MA 01742

Email: info@thoreaufarm.org

Website: http://thoreaufarm.org

Facebook: @ThoreauBirthplace

Twitter: @ThoreauFarm

Also known as the "Minott House," the birthplace of Henry David Thoreau is run by the nonprofit Thoreau Farm Trust. They seek to provide an inspiration for "living deliberately, practicing simplicity, and exploring new ideas for positive change."

The Thoreau Society, Inc.

341 Virginia Road

Concord, MA 01742

(978) 369-5310

Email: info@thoreausociety.org

Website: http://www.thoreausociety.org

Facebook: @TheThoreauSociety

Instagram: @thoreausociety

Twitter: @ThoreauSociety

The Thoreau Society seeks to encourage interest in and education about Thoreau's life, writing, heritage, and "his place in his world and in ours, challenging all to live a deliberate, considered life."

The Walden Woods Project

The Thoreau Institute at Walden Woods
44 Baker Farm Road
Lincoln, MA 01773
(781) 259-4700
Website: https://www.walden.org
Facebook: @TheWaldenWoodsProject
Twitter: @TheWaldenWoods
Instagram: @thewaldenwoodsproject
The Walden Woods project seeks to preserve and conserve the land that Henry David Thoreau loved so well. They also endeavor to protect his writing and legacy through research, education, and advocacy.

WEBSITES

Because of the changing nature of internet links, Rosen Publishing has developed an online list of websites related to the subject of this book. This site is updated regularly. Please use this link to access this list:

http://www.rosenlinks.com/CIVC/Thoreau

FOR FURTHER READING

Burleigh, Robert. *If You Spent a Day with Thoreau at Walden Pond.* New York. NY: Christy Ottaviano Books, 2012.

Caravantes, Peggy. *Self-Reliance: The Story of Ralph Waldo Emerson (World Writers).* Greensboro, NC: Morgan Reynolds, 2011.

Coddington, Andrew. *Henry David Thoreau* (Great American Thinkers). New York, NY: Cavendish Square, 2017.

Harding, Walter. *The Days of Henry Thoreau.* Rev. ed. Princeton, NJ: Princeton University Press, 2016.

Kirk, Andrew. *Understanding Thoreau's "Civil Disobedience"* (Words that Changed the World). New York, NY: Rosen Young Adult, 2011.

Mooney, Edward F. *Excursions with Thoreau: Philosophy, Poetry, Religion.* New York, NY: Bloomsbury Academic, 2015.

Olson, Steven P. *Henry David Thoreau: American Naturalist, Writer, and Transcendentalist.* New York, NY: Rosen Publishing, 2006.

Smith, Corinne Hosfeld. *Henry David Thoreau for Kids: His Life and Ideas, with 21 Activities.* Chicago, IL: Chicago Review Press, 2016.

Smith, Harmon L. *My Friend, My Friend: The Story of Thoreau's Relationship with Emerson.* Amherst, MA: University of Massachusetts Press, 1999.

Thoreau, Henry David. *Walden, and On the Duty of Civil Disobedience* (First Avenue Classics). Minneapolis, MN: First Avenue Editions, 2014.

BIBLIOGRAPHY

Andres, Barry. "Henry David Thoreau." Unitarian Universalist History & Heritage Society. March 30, 2014. http://uudb.org/articles/henrydavidthoreau.html.

Calliope Film Resources. "Thoreau, Civil Disobedience and the Underground Railroad." 2001. http://www.calliope.org/thoreau/thurro/thurro3.html.

PBS. "Henry David Thoreau." *American Experience*. 1999. http://www.pbs.org/wgbh/amex/brown/peopleevents/pande04.html.

Poetry Foundation. "Henry David Thoreau 1817–1862." 2017. https://www.poetryfoundation.org/poems-and-poets/poets/detail/henry-david-thoreau.

Purdy, Jedediah. "In Defense of Thoreau: He May Have Been a Jerk, but He Still Matters." *The Atlantic*. October 20, 2015. https://www.theatlantic.com/science/archive/2015/10/in-defense-of-thoreau/411457.

Schulz, Kathryn. "Pond Scum: Henry David Thoreau's Moral Myopia." *The New Yorker*. October 19, 2015. http://www.newyorker.com/magazine/2015/10/19/pond-scum.

Solnit, Rebecca. "The Thoreau Problem." *Orion Magazine*. Retrieved March 21, 2017. https://orionmagazine.org/article/the-thoreau-problem.

The Thoreau Society. 2015. http://www.thoreausociety.org.

The Walden Woods Project. 2017. https://www.walden.org.

Witherell, Elizabeth, with Elizabeth Dubrulle. "Life and Times of Henry David Thoreau." Retrieved March 1, 2017. http://thoreau.library.ucsb.edu/thoreau_life.html.

INDEX

ABOUT THE AUTHOR

Heather Moore Niver writes and edits all types of books for all types of kids. She has written biographies about Sojourner Truth, Ruth Bader Ginsberg, and Ponce de Leon, just to name a few. Niver lives, writes, and edits in New York State, mere hours away from Henry David Thoreau's old sauntering grounds at Walden Pond in Concord.

PHOTO CREDITS

USING COMPUTERS

THIRD EDITION

USING COMPUTERS

D. G. DOLOGITE

Baruch College, City University of New York

PRENTICE HALL, Englewood Cliffs, New Jersey 07632

Dologite, D.G. (Dorothy G.)
  Using computers / D.G. Dologite — 3rd ed.
    p. cm.
  Includes index.
  ISBN 0-13-928508-3:
    1. Computers. 2. Computer software. I. Title.
  QA76.D64 1992   91-34662
  004 — dc20   CIP

FOR:

All students who are "using computers,"
especially Kim and Brent, Nicky, Chris,
Matt, Brad, Kathleen, MaryBeth, Chrissy,
JoJo, Barbara, Michael and Mary Jean,
Joanna and Barry, Jennifer, Thomas,
Emily and Kevin, Lindsey, Matthew,
Andrew and Jenny

Editorial/production supervision: bookworks
Interior design and cover design: Jerry Votta
Prepress buyer: Trudy Pisciotti
Manufacturing buyer: Robert Anderson
Page layout: Debbie Toymel
Photo research: Teri Stratford
Photo editor: Lorinda Morris
Cover photo: Francekevich/The Stock Market

© 1992, 1989 by Prentice-Hall, Inc.
A Division of Simon & Schuster
Englewood Cliffs, New Jersey 07632

Printed in the United States of America

10 9 8 7 6 5 4 3 2 1

ISBN 0-13-928508-3

Prentice-Hall International (UK) Limited, *London*
Prentice-Hall of Australia Pty. Limited, *Sydney*
Prentice-Hall Canada Inc., *Toronto*
Prentice-Hall Hispanoamericana, S.A., *Mexico*
Prentice-Hall of India Private Limited, *New Delhi*
Prentice-Hall of Japan, Inc., *Tokyo*
Simon & Schuster Asia Pte. Ltd., *Singapore*
Editora Prentice-Hall do Brasil, Ltda., *Rio de Janeiro*

Overview

Contents   vii
Letter to the Student   xiii
Letter to the Instructor   xiv
Acknowledgments   xix

Contents

12 Programming   321

MODULE III: Special Topics

13 Artificial Intelligence   347

Letter to the Student

Dear Student:

This book was written for you. It is designed to help you learn about computers.

As the title suggests, you are especially encouraged to *use* computers. That is the best way to know them well. They are sturdy machines that will let you experiment as long as you like. (If your school has a computer lab, you will probably have restrictions about how long you can use a computer at any one sitting.)

There are so many ways that a computer can help you accomplish current and future tasks. Examples include producing written assignments, like term papers (using word processing), to preparing a company's annual budget (using an electronic spreadsheet).

Be open-minded about exploring the rich storehouse of programs available. Programs are also called "software" or "applications." They make the computer perform useful tasks, such as word processing. There is an endless variety of software available to support school, work, home, and even entertainment purposes.

Hopefully you will be motivated to pursue a study of computers beyond this book. Chapter 1 offers some ideas about how to do this.

If there is any topic concerning this book that you would like to express an opinion about, I would like to hear from you at the following address:

D.G. Dologite
Box 513
Baruch College of the City University of New York
17 Lexington Avenue
New York, NY 10010

I hope that this book enriches your study of computers.

Best regards,

D.G. Dologite

Letter to the Instructor

Dear Instructor,

The Third Edition of *Using Computers,* and its supplementary package, are designed to provide the support you need for teaching an introduction to computers course.

Your welcome input has been invaluable in preparing this Third Edition of *Using Computers.* The main revision you wanted, which helped to mold this new Edition, was a focus on "essentials" without being "lightweight." Students can learn key concepts and important terminology without being burdened with unnecessary detail. Yet his book avoids the shallow coverage of too few concepts found in other "essentials" textbooks.

Approach to How This Book is Organized

This Third Edition of *Using Computers* approaches content the way most instructors teach this course. It organizes the study of computers, as diagrammed in Figure A, in a pyramid manner. The first two chapters, in the pyramid analogy, lay the foundation on which the rest of the book is built.

Since most students today begin their computer education through individual use of personal computers, a single-user perspective dominates the early chapters. As identified in the figure below, the study progresses from learning about personal computer hardware in Chapter 3 to learning about the main

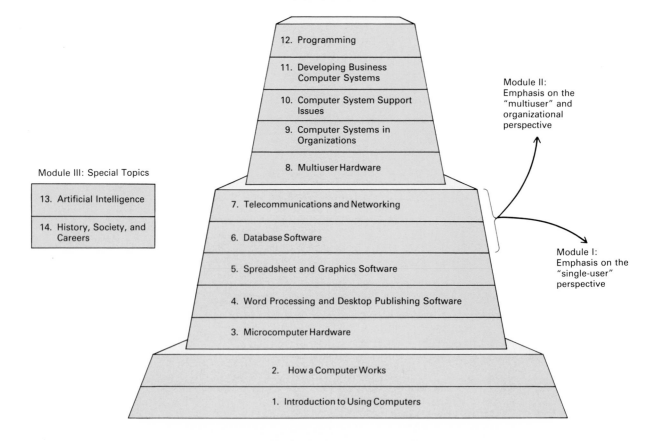

types of software that individuals use, in Chapters 4-7, word processing, spreadsheet, graphics, database management systems, and telecommunications.

As the previous figure shows, two chapters serve as a connecting bridge between "Module I: The Single-User Perspective" and "Module II: The Multiuser Perspective." They are Chapters 6 and 7. That is because database, as well as telecommunication and networking software, provide the foundation for almost all multiuser computing in organizations.

Multiuser computing systems are more complex than single-user systems. They often are built on hardware that supports many users at once. So Chapter 8 covers "Multiuser Hardware."

After hardware, the focus spirals up the pyramid to software in Chapter 9, "Computer Systems in Organizations." The focus here is that organizations with many users doing many different jobs tend to use many different kinds of software.

How software gets into use in an organization is treated as a separate issue. Some organizations, especially smaller ones, buy it and may involve every employee in some phase of rolling it out into the organization. This is the focus of Chapter 10, "Computer System Support Issues."

By contrast, larger organizations build the software they need from scratch. First, they decide what they need and design it, which is the focus of Chapter 11, "Developing Business Computer Systems." Then they follow the design to write, or code, programs, which is the focus of Chapter 12, "Programming."

But Chapters 11 and 12 have a broader appeal. They should interest anyone who covers computer software development or programming, whether from a single-user or multiuser perspective.

The last two chapters in the book make up Module III: Special Topics. They cover themes that round out any comprehensive study of computing. Chapter 13 covers two artificial intelligence themes—knowledge-based systems, which are also called expert systems, and robotics. The final Chapter 14 covers

- The history of computers
- Social issues in computing
- Careers in the computer area

Course "Fit." This approach provides a sequencing of chapters that either eliminates or minimizes the need to do "surgery" in order to make the book "fit" the course.

All material can be covered in one term, with or without a microcomputer lab segment. This provides maximum flexibility for course design, even for those who want to build in a programming segment. For them, *Using BASIC* is available as a separate supplement.

Student Viewpoint. The Third Edition of *Using Computers* carries on a successful tradition of being written from the student reader's point of view. Reviewers of this Third Edition have found the text "very readable" and the tone "engaging." It is designed to encourage, rather than intimidate, a student.

This book will help students on the road to becoming computer literate. But more importantly, it will help promote an understanding of basic concepts that can be applied to competently handle any computing task at hand.

Exciting New Free Courseware

Free to adopters and their students is exciting new courseware that makes *Using Computers* unique. It distinguishes this book as having an instructional package that has no peer. Also, "hands-on exercises" are right in the book in Appendix C for students to use the software, which includes

1. Telecommunications simulation
   - Log-on procedure (with ID and password security)
   - Electronic mail
   - Electronic bulletin board
   - Electronic news service
2. Knowledge-based, or expert, systems
3. Accounting
   - Income and expense transaction processing

Instructors can now effortlessly demo software for students that they formerly could only talk about. Also, students now can "experience," through hands-on exercises, what this software is really like. Contact your Prentice Hall representative if you have not already received the software.

A fourth item, "multimedia computing demonstration," is also available to adopters.

New Content

Content in every chapter is updated. It continues to give *Using Computers* a "state-of-the-art" reputation that adopters have always enjoyed. Some high-interest topics explored are

- Multimedia Computing (chapters 1, 5)
- Graphical user interface (chapter 2)
- Object-oriented databases (chapter 6)
- Electronic data interchange (EDI) (chapter 7)
- Downsizing computer systems (chapter 8)
- Mission-critical systems (chapter 9)
- Executive information systems (chapter 9)
- Workgroup computing (chapters 1, 9)
- Computer-aided software engineering (CASE) (chapter 11)
- Object-oriented programming (chapter 12)
- Knowledge-based (or expert) systems (chapter 13)
- Neural networks (chapter 13)

More coverage is provided on ethics and globalization, which accommodates AACSB recommendations. This enables instructors effortlessly to update their courses because these two important topics are integrated into the text. Students will be challenged by the ethic views addressed and stretched to consider the global issues in computing. Selected examples of each are

Ethics
- Computer virus issues (chapter 2, Case Study)
- Database information privacy issues (chapter 6, Case Studies #1 and #2)
- Electronic mail snooping issues (chapter 7, Case Study)
- Knowledge-based or expert systems failure issues (chapter 13, Focus On)

Globalization
- New international code to replace ASCII (chapter 2, Focus On)
- Financial systems across borders (chapter 10, Focus On)

- Global data privacy issues (chapter 6, Case Study #2)
- Telecommunications global standards (chapter 7)

New content is also evident in many new Case Studies as well as Focus On inserts included in this edition.

Supplements

A complete package of supplementary materials has been assembled to support students and instructors using this book. They include

Free to students and instructors/adopters:

- *New York Times "student supplement" newspaper.* It contains recent articles chosen by the author to complement computer topics in the book. These articles bring classroom topics to life and help to expand students' knowledge beyond the textbook and into the world we live in.
- *A Buyer's Guide to Computers and Software.* This booklet provides tips to aid students make an educated purchase of computers and software.

For purchase by students:

- *Student Study Guide and Workbook*
- *Microcomputer lab manuals.* A variety of lab manuals are offered in prepared or "customized" format. At this writing, prepared manuals are available singly or in combination for: DOS, WordPerfect, Lotus, Quattro, dBASE, Paradox, and Microsoft Works. (A full-version of Microsoft Works is provided free to schools that make a quantity purchase of the Microsoft Works lab manual.)
- *Using BASIC,* by D.G. Dologite and R.J. Mockler

Free to instructors/adopters:

- *A diskette* of a "multimedia computing demonstration" for students to do "hands-on exercises" or for instructors to demonstrate.
  —Telecommunications
  —Knowledge-based (or expert) systems
  —Accounting
- *Instructor's Guide* that provides for every chapter a chapter overview, both a summary and detailed outlines, teaching notes, answers to review questions and much more.
- *Color transparencies*
- *New York Times* complimentary subscription for the first semester after the book adoption.
- *ParSYSTEM Testing.* This PC-based test system is menu-driven, provides on-line help, accepts all question types (including essay and questions with graphics), includes word processing capabilities or allows importing test items, and provides automatic scoring of every student test. It allows students to take a test on-line, if desired, and can provide student feedback reports with correct answers and textbook references. The system also interfaces with a SCANTRON optical reader.
- *Telephone Test Preparation Service.* With one call to 1-800-842-2958, Prentice Hall will provide test preparation and typing on bond paper or ditto master. Within 48 hours of the request, a personalized exam and separate answer sheet will be returned to the instructor.

- *Video Library.* A variety of quality video options are available, including the
  —Annenberg Video Series: 26 modules on "The New Literacy: An Introduction to Computers."
  —Video Professor Series: 21 hands-on tutorials that provide step-by-step instructions for many software packages.
  —ABC News Video Library: Various selections possible from programs for which Prentice Hall has exclusive college distribution rights, including Nightline, 20/20, World News Tonight, and Business World.
- A diskette of all BASIC programs in the *Using BASIC* supplement, as well as an Instructor's Guide for the supplement.

Your comments on this book, supplementary package, or the introductory course they support are always welcome. Please write to

D.G. Dologite
Baruch College of the City University of New York
Box 513
17 Lexington Avenue
New York, NY 10010

Best regards,

D.G. Dologite

THE NEW YORK TIMES and PRENTICE HALL are sponsoring A CONTEMPORARY VIEW: a program designed to enhance student access to current information of relevance in the classroom.

Through this program, the core subject matter provided in the text is supplemented by a collection of time-sensitive articles from one of the world's most distinguished newspapers, THE NEW YORK TIMES. These articles demonstrate the vital, ongoing connection between what is learned in the classroom and what is happening in the world around us.

To enjoy the wealth of information of THE NEW YORK TIMES daily, a reduced subscription rate is available in deliverable areas. For information, call toll-free: 1-800-631-1222.

PRENTICE HALL and THE NEW YORK TIMES are proud to co-sponsor A CONTEMPORARY VIEW. We hope it will make the reading of both textbooks and newspapers a more dynamic, involving process.

Acknowledgments

Appreciation is gratefully extended to:

- The following companies for furnishing software and other materials for research: Aldus Corporation, Ashton-Tate, Banner Blue Software, Inc., Borland International, DacEasy Inc., Datastorm Technologies, Inc., Decision Ware, EXSYS, Inc., IBM Corporation, Information Builders, Inc., Lotus Development Corporation, Matrix Software Technology Corp., Micrografx, Microsoft Corp., Paperback Software, Polytron, Quarterdeck Office Systems, QW Page Associates, Inc., RightSoft, Inc., Software by Seidman, Software Garden, Inc., Software Publishing Corp., WordPerfect Corporation.

- Developers or contributors of software that is included on the disk accompanying this book: Bruce Daniels, Vantanee Hoontrakul, Instant Replay Corporation, Paperback Software, Inc., Nancy Ward, Wordtech Systems, Inc.

- Contributors of material for the end-of-chapter case studies, Focus On boxed inserts, and opening vignettes: *Business Week*, Cahners Publishing Company, CMP Publications Inc., Consumer Software Inc., CW Publishing Inc., International Computer Programs Inc., Peed Corporation, *The Chronicle of Higher Education*, *The New York Times*, *The Wall Street Journal*, *Time Magazine*, William Morrow and Company Inc., Yourdon Press, Ziff Davis Publishing Co.

- Manuscript reviewers for this book or portions of it that appeared in previous editions: colleagues and students at Baruch College—City University of New York, including B. Loerinc Helft, Samuel Ryan, David Stephan, William Ferns; Marie-Claire Barthelemy, Norwalk Community College; Margaret P. Cline, Western Kentucky University; Rosann Webb Collins, University of North Carolina; John A. Cross, Indiana University of Pennsylvania; Ray Fanselau, American River College; John W. Fendrich, Bradley University; J. Patrick Fenton, West Valley College; Richard T. Fernald, Midlands Technical College; Madison K. Finley, Dutchess Community College; Frank Greene, Ventura College; Elaine Haight, Santa Monica College; Cindy Howry, Collin County Community College; Peter L. Irwin, Richland College; Cynthia J. Kachik, Santa Fe Community College; Richard Lee Kerns, East Carolina University; William W. Lau, California State University, Fullerton; Kenneth E. Martins, University of North Florida; James A. Nelson, New Mexico State University; Kay V. Nelson, North Idaho College; Mary Jane Peters, Jacksonville State University; Albert M. Polish, Macomb Community College; David A. Valdez, Dona Ana Branch Community College; and Melanie Wolf-Greenberg, California State University, Fullerton.

- Research and student assistants for helping to construct this manuscript. First among them is Nancy Ward, who served as chief researcher, draftsperson, and production assistant. Her efforts supported this entire project. Others are Mark Aune and Bruce Daniels.

- All the people at Prentice Hall and its contractors who have nurtured this book from its inception, especially Dennis Hogan, President, Regents/Prentice Hall; P.J. McCue and Ted Werthman, Acquisitions Editors; Jerry Isenga, Accusoft Systems Inc., Software Developer; bookworks, Production Editor; Debbie Toymel, Layout Artist, and the talented and energetic staff in sales whose feedback provided encouragement as well as material for improving the present edition, especially Kate Moore and Julie Hildebrand.

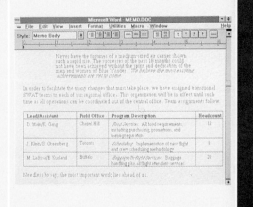

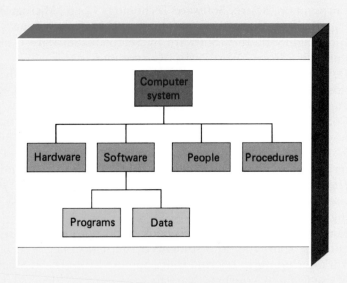

Introduction to Using Computers

AFTER READING THIS CHAPTER, YOU SHOULD BE ABLE TO

- Give examples of how individuals use computers
- Give examples of how computers are used to automate activities in organizations
- Identify sources where computer topics can be explored further

Computer literacy requires analytical thinking. This means understanding some basic concepts and applying that understanding to the task at hand.

For example, a student who knows how to do a procedure to save a file in a word processing program but doesn't understand what a file is will have trouble when faced with saving a file in another program. But a student who understands what a file is can easily learn the different ways different programs save those files.

You don't need a lot of fancy computer hardware to start on the road to computer literacy. You do need imagination.

T he goal of this book is to enable students of computers to become computer literate as well as computer competent. This means that at the completion of this book and the related course, students will have a working vocabulary of computer terms and concepts. It also means that students will be able to apply their understanding of fundamental concepts to the computer task at hand.

Most students begin their computer education through some encounter with a microcomputer. The microcomputer is probably the most significant productivity tool of our time. Anyone who does not learn to harness its capability will be functioning at a disadvantage.

Figure 1-1 illustrates typical microcomputers, which are widely called *personal computers* (the two terms are interchangeable in this book). Small shops and individuals can use such computers as easily and cheaply as can large companies.

This chapter begins by looking at different kinds of computers and basic computer concepts. Then it explores how computers are being used today by individuals and by workgroups of individuals in organizations. Individuals who use computers are frequently called *end-users,* or simply *users*.

FIGURE 1-1
Typical personal computers: an Apple
Macintosh (top) and an IBM
PS/2 (bottom)

Display —
System unit —
Floppy disk drive —
Keyboard —
Mouse pointer (an alternative to typing) —
3½ inch floppy disks —

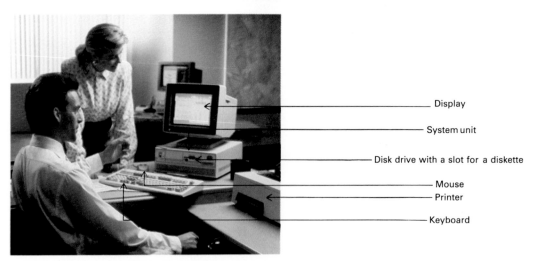

— Display
— System unit
— Disk drive with a slot for a diskette
— Mouse
— Printer
— Keyboard

The chapter next identifies places to look for additional information about computers. A final section explains how this book is organized.

To draw attention to concepts that are important, certain terms in this book are emphasized with bold typeface. Normally, a definition is provided for all boldfaced terms. But in this chapter no attempt is made to provide formal definitions of all boldfaced terms. Instead, it is more important to grasp the general "flavor" of these emphasized introductory concepts. Most of the terms used are repeated and defined later in this book.

COMPUTER DISTINCTIONS

A traditional classification of computers is

- **Microcomputers** (small computers)
- **Minicomputers** (medium-sized computers)
- **Mainframe computers** (large computers)

Figure 1-2 provides a brief comparison of these computers from the perspective of typical users and uses.

At one time it was easy to tell one computer from the other. But technology has been narrowing the gap rapidly in terms of capability. For example, a small desktop **personal computer,** technically called a microcomputer, is as powerful today as a mainframe of 20 years ago.

Computers that can support several users at once, as diagramed in Figure 1-3, are called **multiuser computers.** In such an environment, everyone shares one centrally located main computer unit, which usually is called a **processor.**

At one major beverage company, for example, a large mainframe processor

FIGURE 1-2

BRIEF COMPARISON OF COMPUTERS

TYPE	TYPICAL USERS AND USES
General	
Microcomputer	One user; personal and business or professional use
Multiuser microcomputer Minicomputer Mainframe	Many users; business and other uses often requiring a large collection of commonly used files
Special	
Supercomputer	Many users; research, scientific, and business use; handles very large files of information or data at extremely fast speeds

is located on the seventh floor of the headquarters building. Employees can link their personal computers to the company's mainframe regardless of where they are located. This gives them access to organizational information stored by the central computer.

FIGURE 1-3
Comparison of single-user and multiuser computers

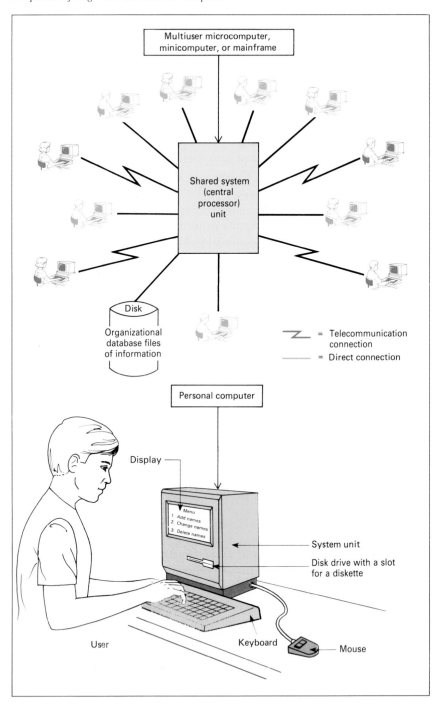

IMPORTANCE OF SOFTWARE

Hardware is the physical part of a computer. It contrasts with **software,** which is the nonphysical part. Software is another term for the **programs** that tell hardware what to do. Without software, hardware is useless.

Software can be compared to music residing on compact discs or cassette tapes. A music lover may want a certain song by a certain vocalist and so buys a disc or tape to have a copy of it. In a similar way, a copy of desired software is acquired by buying it most commonly on a diskette, like the one shown in Figure 1-1. An example of software is a word processing program that helps a computer user to produce letters and reports. Anyone who wants to do automated word processing buys a diskette with a copy of a desired word processing program on it.

Sometimes the software that users buy is called **application software.** As the term implies, this software *applies* a computer to a specific user task. The list in Figure 1-4 gives an example of the breadth of computer application software.

Typical reasons given for acquiring a computer include the following applications:

- To improve personal productivity, for example, by automating letter and other document production (with a word processing program)
- To improve file storage and searches (with a file or database management program)
- To access computer files of information at another location (with a telecommunication program)

One person may have all these reasons for using a computer. Such a person

FIGURE 1-4

APPLICATION SOFTWARE

Where Covered in This Book	Examples
Module I (from a single-user perspective)	Word processing Spreadsheet Graphics
	File and database management systems Telecommunications (linking of computers)
Module II (from a multiuser or organizational perspective)	Accounting-based systems Industry-specific systems Management information systems Decision support systems Executive information systems
Module III (special topics)	Knowledge-based or expert systems Robot systems

would use many different kinds of application programs or software. Only one computer, however, is necessary. The programs would all work on the same computer hardware.

Individuals and smaller organizations usually buy ready-made, or **packaged, programs** or **software** for their microcomputers and minicomputers. Generally, they do their computing without the aid of computer professionals.

By contrast, large organizations generally have a computer department staffed with computer specialists and programmers. This professional staff creates some of the organization's main programs that help to run the business.

WHAT IS A SYSTEM?

Anyone studying computing finds the word *system* used over and over again. The word generally refers to interrelated items considered as a unit. In a **computer system,** the interrelated terms, as diagrammed in Figure 1-5, are

- Hardware
- Software
- People
- Procedures

If any of these ingredients is ignored, computing is usually a failure.

In addition to selecting hardware, users must knowledgeably select software. Then they must learn how to use the software or train someone else to use it. Often new software means new ways of doing things or new procedures to follow. Who decides what information goes into the computer? Where does the information come from? What happens when errors occur? Who should have access to programs?

To stress the interrelated nature of all elements that make computing possible, hardware and software suppliers often attach the term *system* to product names:

FIGURE 1-5
Interrelated items in any computer system

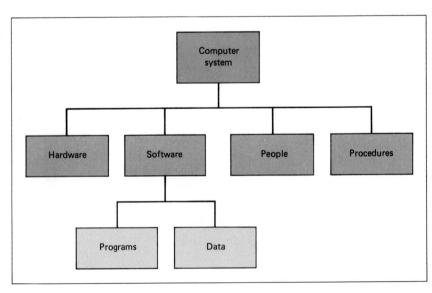

Type	Examples of Product Names
Hardware	IBM System 390
	Unisys System 80
Software	Business Graphics System
	Micro Data Base System

In these cases, hardware generally consists of many interrelated equipment parts. Likewise, the software consists of a collection of interrelated programs.

The word *system* is also often used to classify hardware and software categories:

Type	Examples of Category Names
Hardware	Microcomputer systems
	Minicomputer systems
	Mainframe systems
Software	Word processing systems
	Database management systems
	Accounting systems

Knowing that *either* software or hardware is at the heart of any computer-based "system" encountered eliminates some of the confusion caused by the term *system*.

COMPUTER USES AND USERS

It is enlightening to explore how individuals and organizations use computers. The following sections provide examples. They are grouped into the two main categories that are the focus of this book:

- Single-user perspective
- Multiuser perspective

SINGLE-USER PERSPECTIVE

Individuals use computers mainly to improve their personal productivity. A student, a sales manager, and a reporter are no different from anyone else who tries to make every minute of the workday count. The following examples focus on the software, some of which is identified in Figure 1-6, that these individuals use. In all cases, computers are regarded as a tool to help boost personal performance.

Student

Students find computers helpful when preparing written reports. Reports are prepared with a **word processing program.** The program improves personal productivity by allowing a user to type text and electronically revise it. This includes moving paragraphs around. Once the typed document looks right, it can effortlessly be printed. Figure 1-7 shows what a computer screen looks like while preparing text.

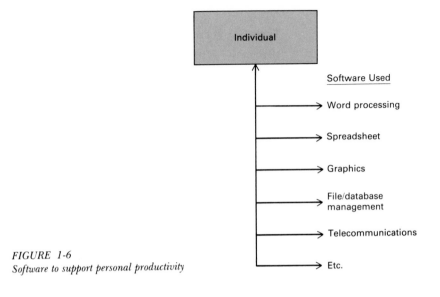

FIGURE 1-6
Software to support personal productivity

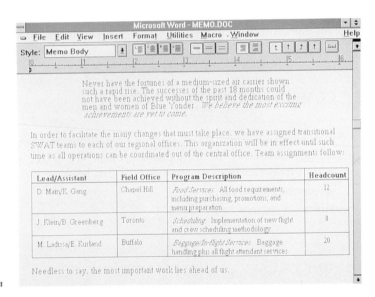

FIGURE 1-7
*Sample display screen when
using a word processing program*

Another type of software used by students is a spreadsheet program. A **spreadsheet program** is used to automatically calculate rows and columns of numbers. Some business school students find spreadsheets helpful for analyzing the financial profiles of companies they investigate.

Anyone can use a spreadsheet to maintain a personal budget. The one in Figure 1-8 shows a simple student budget for two semesters. The spreadsheet program automatically calculates all totals, as well as the difference amount. The student must type in everything else.

A spreadsheet program makes it easy to explore alternatives. For example, the student may want to see what figures will "look like" if there is an increase in tuition. By changing only the tuition amounts, affected totals and difference amounts are automatically revised.

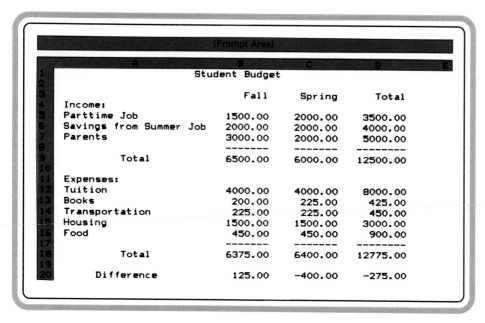

FIGURE 1-8
A student budget prepared with a spreadsheet program

Sales Manager

A sales manager for a video distributor also uses packaged programs to help improve personal productivity.

A word processing program is used to create memos for the sales staff, as the example in Figure 1-9 illustrates. The staff sells the company's products to local video stores and other retailers.

A spreadsheet program is used to help calculate numbers for decision making. Figure 1-9 shows a spreadsheet used to examine sales of five categories of video tapes in four regions. If changes are made to any sales figure, new totals are automatically computed.

The sales manager can easily change the spreadsheet into a graphic. Computer **graphics programs** can convert spreadsheet numbers into easy-to-understand charts and make images for presentations. For example, the graphic in Figure 1-9 was created from the spreadsheet sales numbers for the first three video categories in the same figure.

The manager also uses a *file* or *database management* package to create files of

- Sales representatives
- Potential major customers
- Business contacts

As its name implies, a **file** or **database management program** helps users to set up, maintain, and manipulate data. Data reside in computer *files* that usually consist of many uniform *records,* as shown in the example in Figure 1-10.

```
                              MEMO

      TO: All Sales Staff Representatives
    FROM: Greg Ward, Sales Manager
    DATE: February 23, 199X
 SUBJECT: Sales results for year ended December 31, 199X

    ------------------------------------------------------------------

 Congratulations!  Last year was a record-breaking one for all
 four sales regions.  I know how hard everyone worked and it paid
 off.

 A close look at the final sales figures show that the Southern
 region had a tremendous increase in both total sales and sales
 growth last year.  Let's all _




 B:\MEMO                                      Doc 1 Pg 1 Ln 3.67" Pos 3.9"
```

Word processing

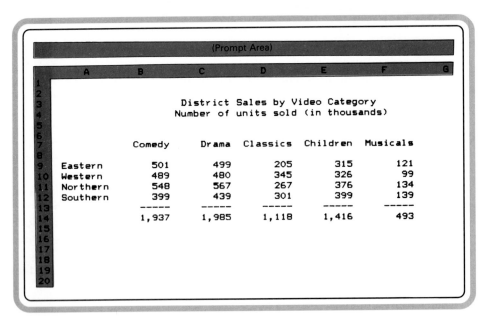

Spreadsheet

FIGURE 1-9
Three common personal productivity packages

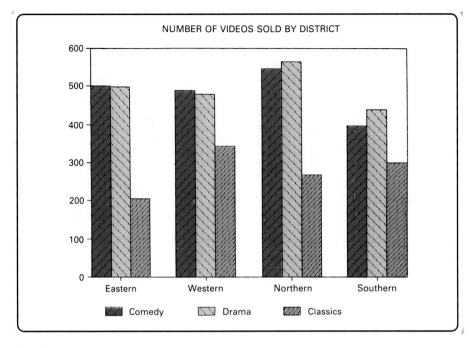

NUMBER OF VIDEOS SOLD BY DISTRICT

Comedy   Drama   Classics

FIGURE 1-9 (cont.)

Graphics

Reporter

A reporter for a local television station also depends on a computer to maintain a high level of personal productivity. Like the student and the sales manager, the reporter uses word processing and other common packaged programs.

The word processing program is used to prepare news stories. A spreadsheet program is used to prepare budgets for each major story project. A file manager

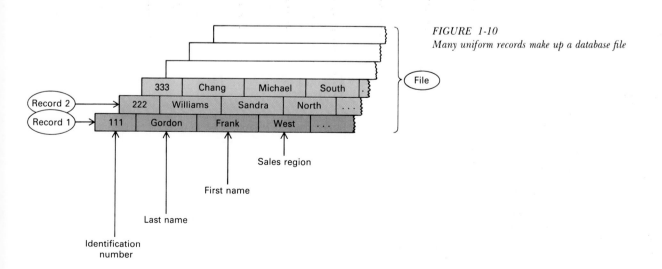

FIGURE 1-10
Many uniform records make up a database file

Record 2 — 222 Williams Sandra North ...
Record 1 — 111 Gordon Frank West ...
333 Chang Michael South .

File

Sales region

First name

Last name

Identification
number

package helps to keep expense records as well as records of people to contact for news stories.

When away from the office, the reporter also uses a **telecommunication program.** It enables telephone use from anywhere in the world, so that one computer can exchange information with another. This is useful for sending finished news stories or even expense records to the main office computer.

MULTIUSER PERSPECTIVE

In contrast to the previous section's view of the single-user's perspective of computing, this section focuses on the multiuser perspective. This is the perspective of the organization that has many individuals all doing computing, sometimes on a single computer, at the same time.

Figure 1-11 indicates the types of support provided by computers in organizations. For ease of understanding, this book divides organizational uses into

- "Front-office" support
- "Back-office" support
- Management and control support

Front-office computer systems support the goals, or critical mission, of an

FIGURE 1-11
Typical support software for organizations

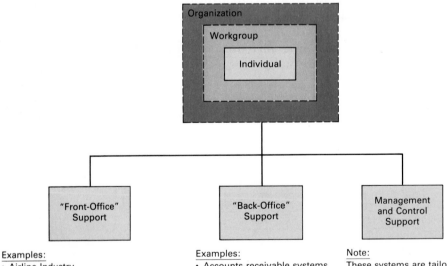

organization. In a credit card company, for example, one goal is to provide instant credit authorization to customers for purchases. So a computer program that supports evaluating customers' credit purchases is a front-office system. This task is critical to the successful mission of the organization.

Back-office computer systems, on the other hand, are often accounting-based tasks or other routine volume processing tasks. Typical back-office examples include processing volumes of employee paychecks or monthly statements of account (bills) to customers.

But many formerly back-office tasks, like processing orders, have changed. Rows of clerks no longer sit at rows of computer keyboards and displays entering the time-delayed orders. Instead, orders are captured at the point of sale using computer support. As the first example illustrates, the efficiencies offered by today's inexpensive computers are blurring the distinctions between back-office and front-office computer systems in organizations.

Organizations usually also have management and control support systems. This software filters selected information from front- and back-office systems as well as from other sources. The filtered information is used to monitor and control organizational activities as well as to support management decision making.

The following sections provide representative examples of multiuser computing in organizations. Examples are in the sporting goods supply, retail clothing, and health care areas.

FOCUS ON: *Multimedia Computing*

A student at a college in Ohio attends a biology class on the principles of genetics. At several points the student interrupts the teacher and asks for further explanations. No one else in the class is disturbed or held up because there is no class—this is one-on-one instruction performed by a multimedia computer.

A multimedia computer is one that has the capability to process various types of "media"—that is, text, graphics, still images, animated images, video, audio, and special effects—on the same computer at the same time.

An architect leads a customer on a walking tour of a new building. The customer requests changes in several areas—even deciding to add two more floors. The architect smiles, because the building has not yet been built—the two have been walking around inside a "virtual reality" on the architect's multimedia computer.

This is not the future. This is today. These examples and others already exist either in production or trial cases—thanks to the growth of multimedia computing.

Of course, a lot of change must occur before multimedia becomes normal for most users. For example, computer displays will routinely have to show video-quality images and text at the same time.

The Year 2001

By the beginning of the next century, personal computers are likely to be true "information appliances" that carry audio, video, and text simultaneously.

In that world, multimedia may well be the established means of communication. For example, personal computers are expected automatically to scan the news media for information their users have requested and assemble custom-designed electronic newspapers daily.

Supplier

A sporting goods supply company equips its field sales representatives with portable, or *laptop,* computers, such as the one shown in Figure 1-12. The laptops are used for entering customer orders at the customer office, which is at the *point of sale.*

The portable computers are outfitted with telecommunication software. This enables representatives to send orders directly to the home office's minicomputer. The minicomputer returns notice of item availability, as well as an estimated delivery date, before the representative leaves the customer's office. The supplier finds that such operations give it an edge over competitors.

In addition to order entry, the sporting goods company uses computers to support

- Billing customers for items ordered (often called accounts receivable)
- Paying suppliers for goods it distributes (often called accounts payable)
- Recording all business activity in general ledger accounts

All these support systems provide additional information to manage and control the organization.

Retailer

A chain of women's retail clothing stores uses personal computers as cash registers, as shown in Figure 1-13. The computers are custom painted black and have a cash drawer and printer below the countertop. A credit card reader attaches to the keyboard.

The personal computers are linked to a central minicomputer in each store.

FIGURE 1-12
Using a portable computer for "on-the-road" computing

Portable computer

FIGURE 1-13
Personal computers help to run a retail business.

The minicomputer controls all merchandise prices, discount offers, and inventory changes.

Periodically, each store's minicomputer telecommunicates summary information to the distant corporate mainframe computer. Information is used for corporate management and control systems.

Health Care Provider

One of the largest health care providers places modified computers in patients' rooms. Physicians use the computers to record patients' conditions and to enter drug prescription orders. A linked computer in the hospital's pharmacy displays prescription orders as they are received and prints prescription bottle labels. The pharmacy's drug inventory records are also automatically reduced. For drugs that fall below a certain inventory level, a new purchase order is automatically created.

Security procedures are built into all computer entry and use procedures. This controls the possibility of misuse. Security procedures are normal at health care organizations and generally anywhere many users have access to common computers and files.

Workgroups

In organizations, individuals often belong to a workgroup such as the hospital pharmacy, sales department, manufacturing department, or product development team. Modern workgroup members are linked, or networked, together, usually in a *local-area network.* In a **local-area network,** as diagrammed in Figure 1-14, a high-speed cable or line connects computers. Everyone on the line can share computer files, exchange mail electronically, and do a variety of other things using the software listed in Figure 1-15.

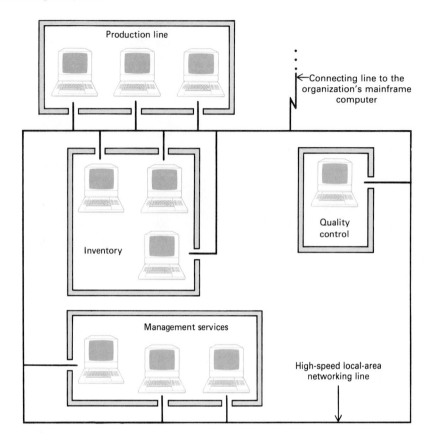

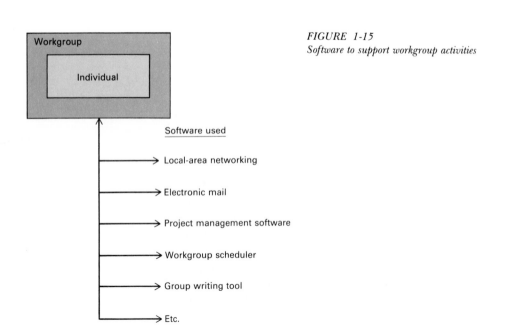

FIGURE 1-15
Software to support workgroup activities

BECOMING INFORMED

Many sources exist to help anyone studying computers to become more informed. They include books, magazines, user groups, shows, exhibitions, and conferences.

Books

Many books focus on learning about computer hardware and how to operate some of the hundreds of program packages available. The card catalog of the library is an ideal source of books on computing topics. Books are also sold in retail computer stores.

Magazines

One of the best sources of information is computer magazines. Most are available at local computer stores. One useful general publication is *PC/Computing*.

Many magazines are dedicated to specific computer products. They assume a reader is somewhat familiar with the products endorsed and include the following:

Magazine	Product
MacWorld	Apple Computer products
PC Magazine	IBM products
PC World	IBM products

Other magazines aim at a computer literate reader but are not product specific. Some are

Computerworld
Byte
Infoworld
PC Week
Datamation

User Groups

Local community **user groups** hold monthly meetings where people can swap computer problems and share solutions. Groups usually have speakers at monthly meetings.

Members often contribute software to the group. It is offered free to other members, except for the cost of distribution. It is called **public domain software** or **shareware,** and it frequently travels from group to group. Much of it is not commercial quality and is of interest only to programmers and hobbyists.

Today, organizations of all sizes sponsor their own user groups. Members look for common and shared solutions to buying, tutorial classes, and other concerns.

Public user-group information is often available from local computer stores.

Shows, Exhibitions, and Conferences

Computer shows, exhibitions, and conferences are often held on local, regional, and national levels. They are a good way to see a collection of the latest computer hardware and software. Some events have all-day workshops and tutorials.

Lists of computer shows, exhibits, and conferences are often available in local newspapers, computer magazines, and from computer stores.

Other Sources

Some public telecommunication services sponsor electronic conferences and bulletin boards about computer topics. Chapter 7, "Telecommunications and Networking," discusses how these electronic information services work.

Computer hardware and software suppliers make free literature available to anyone who requests it. Computer magazines often have convenient postcards inserted for requesting free literature from these suppliers.

The medical, printing, construction, wholesale, retail, and other industries inform members of computer-related topics. They do this through industry-specific magazines, associations, and conferences. No better contact exists for a new computer user than someone in a similar industry who already is an experienced computer user.

ORGANIZATION OF THIS BOOK

Studying computers with this book will help to provide a solid foundation for computer literacy and competency. This study is organized, as diagrammed in Figure 1-16, in a pyramid manner.

The study begins with this general introduction in Chapter 1, followed by an examination of how computers work in Chapter 2. These two chapters provide the foundation for the rest of the book. They represent, in the pyramid analogy, laying the foundation on which the rest of the book is built.

Since most people today develop computer skills through individual use of personal computers, a single-user perspective dominates the early chapters. As identified in Figure 1-16, the study progresses from learning about personal computer hardware in Chapter 3 to learning about the main types of software that individuals use, which include

- Word processing and related software, such as desktop publishing (Chapter 4)
- Spreadsheets and graphics (Chapter 5)
- File and database management systems (Chapter 6)
- Telecommunications (Chapter 7)

As Figure 1-16 shows, two chapters serve as a connecting bridge between Module I: "The Single-User Perspective" and Module II: "The Multiuser Perspective." They are Chapters 6 and 7. That is because database, telecommunication, and networking software provide the foundation for almost all multiuser computing in organizations.

Multiuser computing systems are more complex than single-user systems.

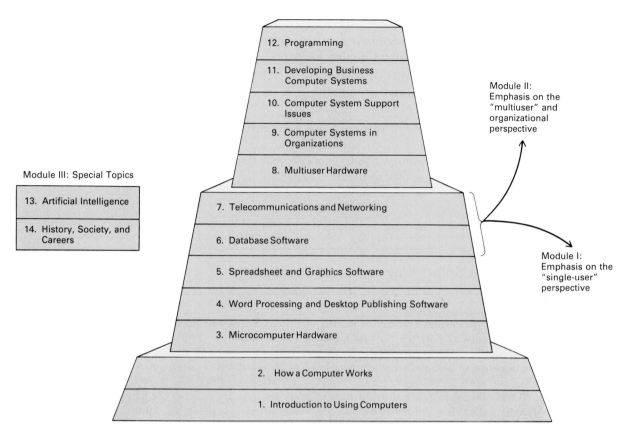

FIGURE 1-16
How this book is organized

They often are built on hardware that supports many users at once. So Chapter 8 covers "Multiuser Hardware."

After hardware, the focus climbs up the pyramid to software in Chapter 9, "Computer Systems in Organizations." Organizations with many users doing many different jobs tend to use many different kinds of software.

How software gets into use in an organization is a separate issue. Some organizations, especially smaller ones, buy it and may involve every employee in some phase of rolling it out into the organization. This is the focus of Chapter 10, "Computer System Support Issues."

By contrast, larger organizations build the software they need from scratch. First, they decide what they need and design it, which is the focus of Chapter 11, "Developing Business Computer Systems." Then they follow the design to write, or code, programs, which is the focus of Chapter 12, "Programming."

But Chapters 11 and 12 have a broader appeal. They should interest anyone who becomes involved in computer programming, whether from a single-user or multiuser perspective. All new computer programs, or software, are built following procedures covered in these chapters.

The last two chapters in the book make up Module III: "Special Topics." They cover themes that round out any comprehensive study of computing.

Chapter 13 covers two contemporary artificial intelligence themes in computing—knowledge-based systems, which are also called expert systems, and robotics. The final Chapter 14 covers

- The history of computers
- Social issues in computing
- Careers in the computer area

A study of this book will help anyone on the road to becoming computer literate. But more importantly, a careful study of this book will promote an understanding of basic concepts that can be applied to competently handle any computing task at hand.

CASE STUDY: *The Smart Way to Learn Computing*

Any new job brings feelings of anxiety—without the added pressure of having to learn how to use a computer. But Lisa Figoli faced both situations when she began working at National Semiconductor. Figoli was given a computer and told to "get computing." The department had no formal training but had standardized on a few programs, such as one for word processing.

"I was told I'd be using word processing and they gave me this big book to learn it. My boss spent a few minutes with me to get me started," recalls Figoli. "But the book was ridiculous."

First-Time Users.   Computers can be intimidating for many of the reasons the preceding case illustrates, especially for the first-time user "required" to use one. Unfortunately, many companies minimize the importance of training people in the rush to "computerize."

For starting out, getting help from someone with experience can speed learning immensely. When you're just familiarizing yourself with the computer, for example, someone can show you how to insert a disk, power up, and begin entering information in a minute's time. Trying to figure out the same things yourself, if you're a beginner, can take a lot longer and make your first experience with computers frustrating.

If you are already putting your computer to good use, you've probably found yourself in the position of unofficial teacher to friends and associates still new to the personal computing game. That is exactly the position Jackie Crews, a manager at McCormack and Dodge, found herself in after she acquired her first personal computer.

Experienced User.   "I've had some friends call me who are absolutely terrified of using a personal computer," says Crews. She attributes this, in part, to their not having experienced anything quite like it before. "They have this compulsion to try to learn everything they can. They do things like make lists of the commands and try to memorize them." In fact, your time can often be better spent understanding how a computer or program works than memorizing procedures.

Computing or Skiing.   Then there is the question of how much time to invest in learning a given program. The amount of time for mastery is going to vary depending on the program itself and your own capacity for, and interest in, learning it. As a general rule of thumb, one analyst suggests you should get enough grasp of a program to be able to use it productively if you spend a weekend learning it—with about the same intensity you approach a ski weekend.

But don't fear. There is hope for those who would rather go skiing on weekends than curl up to a manual about a word processing program. Training courses and computer-based tutorial programs are available. However, the usefulness of such courses and materials varies greatly.

Even the best instruction is only a partial solution. Nobody is going to teach you everything there is to know about computing and how you should best use your personal computer.

Lisa Figoli, who had to learn word processing on her own as part of her job, found her own solution. A trip to the bookstore resulted in the purchase of a handy reference book for learning the word processing program. She was also aided by a series of training disks that came with the book. As she discovered, the smart way to learn computing is the way that best suits you.

SHORTCUTS FOR EASIER LEARNING

1. *Try to grasp universal concepts.* Loading a program into memory and saving files to disk are concepts common to all programs. Program-specific commands will be learned more readily once you understand common operations.

2. *Don't presuppose complexity.* A fear among some people new to computing is that they won't be able to learn because they aren't "computer-oriented" or "math-oriented." But relatively few of the popular programs require extensive mathematical knowledge or training. Word processing surely doesn't.

3. *Be as good as you have to be.* You don't have to be a computer expert—or even an expert of a particular application—to make good use of a program. To perform certain complex operations in some programs, try opening the manual and simply follow the procedures without trying to memorize them. If you use any function enough, you'll remember it.

4. *Conquer the keyboard.* If you're going to be doing a lot of word processing work, it becomes a priority to be at ease with the keyboard. A number of low-cost computer-based programs teach typing. If you don't know how to type, everything you do on the computer is going to seem awfully slow compared to those who do.

5. *Diagnose your own errors.* The phrase "garbage in, garbage out" dates back to the early days of computers. But it can be applied just as readily today. Just as software, or the set of instructions that programs a computer, gives the hardware its smarts, so will giving bad or false information make any computer look dumb. User error is the most frequent cause of a problem.

6. *Look for on-screen help.* Most early computer enthusiasts learned how to use their computers the hard way, by plowing through difficult, often poorly organized manuals or user guides. That's no longer necessary. Today "help" screens are available and easily accessible in most programs.

7. *Find the right program.* If you find that a program is too difficult to learn and help is not readily available, try a different one. Many relatively easy-to-use programs cover the most common applications—word processing, spreadsheet, file or database management, graphing, and telecommunications—well enough so they'll accomplish much of what most people want to do. Don't buy the most complicated (and expensive) programs unless you know you will really need them.

DISCUSSION QUESTIONS

1. Defend the statement "For most of us, becoming an expert is not the primary goal in computing; it is developing enough understanding to get the job done."

2. Because few employers provide the uninterrupted, relaxed time necessary to learn how to use a computer, what advice would help a potential job hunter?

CHAPTER SUMMARY

- People who use computers are frequently called *end-users*, or simply *users*.
- A traditional classification of computers is: *microcomputers* (small computers), *minicomputers* (medium-sized computers), and *mainframes* or *mainframe computers* (large computers).
- A small desktop-sized *personal computer* is technically called a microcomputer.
- A *multiuser computer* supports several people simultaneously, with everyone sharing one central computer unit, or *processor*.
- *Hardware* is the physical part of a computer.
- *Software* is another term for the *programs* that tell the hardware what to do. Without software, hardware is useless.
- *Application software* applies a computer to a specific user task.
- A *packaged program* or *software* is ready-made, or ready-to-use, software.
- A *computer system* consists of interrelated hardware, software, people, and procedures.
- Four common programs to improve personal productivity are word processing, spreadsheet, graphics, and file or database management.

- A *word processing program* allows a user to type text and electronically make changes.
- A *spreadsheet program* is used to automatically calculate rows and columns of numbers. *Graphics programs* can convert spreadsheet numbers into easy-to-understand charts and make images for presentations.
- A *file* or *database management program* helps users to set up, maintain, and manipulate data.
- A *telecommunication program* enables using a telephone so that one computer can exchange information with another.
- Organizational uses of computer systems are categorized as front-office, back-office, and management and control support.
- Examples of organizational computer use are entering point-of-sale customer orders and placing personal computers in hospital rooms to enter patient information directly into computer files.
- In a *local-area network*, a high-speed cable or line connects computers in order to share a company's computer files, among other tasks.
- Sources to learn more about computers include books, magazines, user groups, shows, exhibitions, and conferences.

SELECTED KEY TERMS

Computer system
File or database management
  program
Graphics program
Hardware
Local-area network
Mainframe computer

Microcomputer
Minicomputer
Multiuser computer
Packaged program or software
Personal computer
Program

Public domain software
Software
Spreadsheet program
Telecommunication program
User group
Word processing program

REVIEW QUESTIONS

1. What is a traditional classification of computers?
2. Describe the difference between a personal computer and a multiuser computer.
3. Contrast hardware and software.
4. What are packaged programs?
5. Identify the four interrelated components of a computer system.
6. Give examples of how single users improve their personal productivity with computers.

7. For what is a file or database management program used?
8. For what is a telecommunication program used?
9. Give examples of how computers are used in organizations.
10. How is a local-area network used in organizations?
11. Identify sources to help a person learn more about computers.

EXERCISES

1. *C. Davidson Case.* After Charles Davidson bought a microcomputer, he found many computer publications that were of interest. Instead of subscribing to all of them, he asked you to investigate which ones are available at the library.
   a. Make a list of all the computer periodicals available in your library.
   b. Classify the periodicals according to the following categories:
      General publications
      Product-specific publications
      Computer-literate-audience publications
   c. Examine one periodical from each category and identify article topics that overlap across publications.
   d. Pick one topic and read it in all three publications. Make a summary of your investigation that specifies for each article
      • Publication examined and article title
      • A short summary with a list of things you did not understand.

   Indicate which of the three publications you found to be the most helpful and explain why.

2. *C. Davidson Case.* Mr. Davidson liked your library investigatory work and asked you to do another project. This involves finding out about the local computer user group.
   a. Visit a local computer-user-group meeting. Write a report on what happens there. Make a list of what you did not understand.
   b. At the end of your computer study, review the list to see how many items you can answer yourself.

3. Visit a local computer show, exhibition, or conference. Make a written or oral report about your field trip. Include in the report
   a. Hardware you liked the best and why
   b. Software you thought was especially interesting and why

4. Research the use of computers in organizations. Look first at computer magazines. You may also find useful articles in *Businessweek, The Wall Street Journal,* and other published sources. Prepare a report on the different organizational computer uses you find.

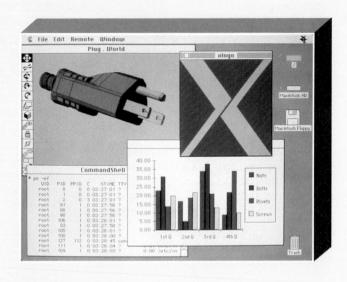

2

How Computers Work

AFTER READING THIS CHAPTER, YOU SHOULD BE ABLE TO

- Explain the fundamentals of how computers work
- Describe what an operating system does
- Identify three categories of operating systems

Standards are taken for granted where they exist. For example, we don't think twice about the fact that we can plug any telephone into the wall and call anywhere—even on the other side of the world. But in the recent past we have accepted that data on an Apple Macintosh computer wouldn't make any sense to an IBM-compatible computer sitting next to it.

The day is fast coming when computers, like telephones, will be able to communicate and work with each other regardless of who manufactured them.

I n order to understand what is necessary to make different computers work together, it helps to understand what goes on "under the hood" of *all* computers.

The first half of this chapter discusses fundamental concepts like input, processing, and output. The second half focuses on *operating systems*. An operating system is a special kind of computer program that makes input, processing, and output possible.

Since input, processing, and output occur on a computer, which is also called *hardware*, this chapter must be considered one half of a two-part chapter sequence. The next chapter covers hardware.

INPUT, PROCESSING AND OUTPUT

Input and **output** are computer jargon for putting something into a computer and getting something out. Between input and output, as shown in Figure 2-1, **processing** occurs to transform input into output.

For example, the owner of an apartment building may input, or type, a command to find tenants who have overdue rent balances. During the processing stage, the tenant file on the disk is searched. Every tenant record is examined to see who has a past due balance. As records meeting the search requirement are found, they are output or displayed. It all happens at lightning speed.

If it is necessary to add $20 to tenant Jackson's monthly rent, the apartment building owner must first input, or type, 20. The output is to the disk file. The Jackson record on the disk file then has a changed rent amount.

Storage

As Figure 2-2 shows, processing occurs inside a computer using both memory and a central processing unit. But the computer's *memory* is only a temporary

FIGURE 2-1
Fundamental computer input,
processing, and output operations

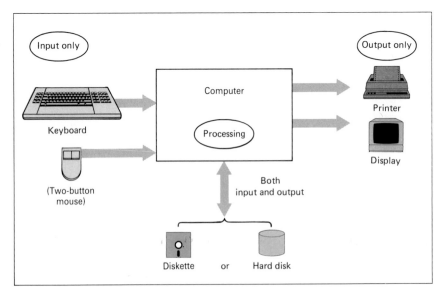

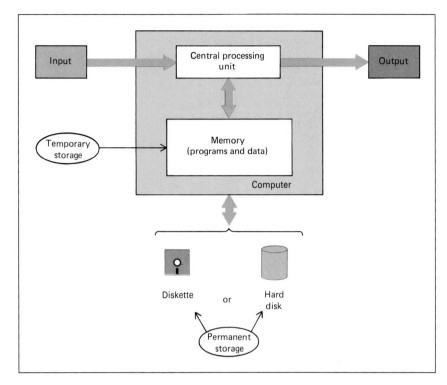

FIGURE 2-2
A computer's memory is only a temporary workspace for programs and
data, which are permanently stored on disk

workspace or storage area. It is used only when the computer power is on. When
the power goes off, everything in memory disappears.

This is why a computer session starts by first loading programs from disks.
Disks provide permanent storage for programs and files of data. Programs are
loaded into memory from disks to give the *central processing unit,* which is equivalent to the computer's brain, something to work on, or "process."

Bits and Bytes

Everything in a computer's memory is represented by an on or off electronic
pulse. This two-state limitation is called a **binary system,** as indicated in Figure
2-3. One *b*inary dig*it* is called a **bit.**

To overcome the limitation and to store meaningful information, several
electronic pulses are grouped together. The computer industry standardized on
a group of seven, as shown in Figure 2-4.

Whenever an A is typed on the keyboard, for example, what really gets sent
to the computer's memory for processing is 1000001. A special check bit, called
a parity bit, is first added to each 7-bit grouping, which results in a total of 8
bits. Eight bits equal one **byte** (pronounced "bite").

The computer industry calls this bit arrangement the *A*merican *S*tandard
*C*ode for *I*nformation *I*nterchange, or **ASCII** (pronounced "as-key"). While
ASCII code dominates microcomputer and minicomputer hardware, another
code is found with mainframes. It is called *E*xtended *B*inary *C*oded *D*ecimal

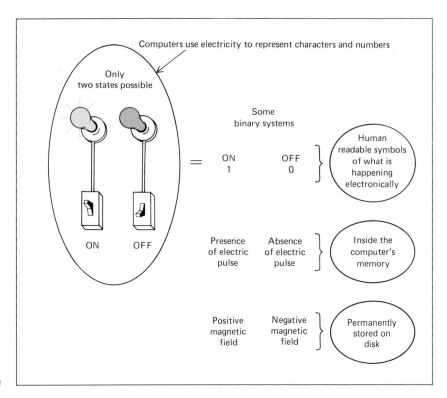

FIGURE 2-3
The two-state limitation of representing data with electricity

EXAMPLES OF 7-DIGIT BINARY CODES

Character	7-Bit Code
A	1000001
B	1000010
C	1000011
D	1000100
E	1000101
F	1000110
0	0110000
1	0110001
2	0110010
3	0110011
4	0110100
5	0110101

FIGURE 2-4

*I*nterchange Code, or **EBCDIC** (pronounced "eb-see-dick"). A chart of ASCII and EBCDIC codes is given in Appendix A.

An 8-bit byte is the fundamental unit computers work with. The chart in Figure 2-5 compares the bit and byte relationship.

Computer memory and disk storage capacity are usually quoted in bytes. For example, a personal computer may be sold with 2 megabytes of memory. This means that memory can hold approximately 2 million characters or bytes. Generally, the higher the byte capacity, the more powerful the product.

BITS AND BYTES

Units	Composed of	Number of Characters It Can Store
bit	1 or 0	none
byte	8 bits	1
Kbyte	1,024 bytes (or 1,000 bytes rounded)	1,024
640 Kbytes	640,000 bytes	640,000
Mbytes	1,000,000 bytes	1,000,000
Gbytes	1 billion bytes	1 billion
Tbytes	1 trillion bytes	1 trillion

Abbreviations:
K = kilo, a thousand
M = mega, a million
G = giga, a billion
T = tera, a trillion

FIGURE 2-5

FOCUS ON: *A Standard for All Languages*

A group of leading computer companies announced an ambitious effort to develop a universal digital code that could be used by computers to represent letters and characters in all the world's languages. The new code is known as Unicode.

If the code were to become a worldwide standard, it would be easier for people in different countries to communicate by electronic mail. The code would also make it easier for software companies to develop programs that could work in different languages.

Easier Communication

Right now, for instance, an American computer system often cannot understand the codes used by a French computer to represent accented characters. So a message sent electronically from France to the United States might arrive without the accents or with mistaken characters.

But with the new code, any computer anywhere could understand and display everything from French accents to Chinese ideographs, not to mention letters in Bengali, Hebrew, Arabic, and other languages.

Unicode would represent letters and symbols by a sequence of 16 zeros and ones, instead of 8, allowing for 65,536 different combinations. That is enough to give each character used in all the living languages of the world its own unique sequence, with enough combinations left over to eventually include obsolete scripts like cuneiform and hieroglyphics as well.

The proposed code still faces hurdles. The group needs to attract support from foreign companies, and an international standards organization is developing a competing code. Using 16 bits instead of 8 to represent each character would also mean that computers would require more memory and disk storage capacity.

Problems could also arise in achieving compatibility between computers using Unicode and those using older codes.

INSIDE A DISK

Computer input and output are commonly stored on disks. Five-and-¼-inch disks have a cardboard jacket with a hole in the middle, as shown in Figure 2-6. Smaller, 3½-inch disks have rigid plastic jackets. These portable disks are also called *diskettes*.

The jacket covers a thin disk housed inside it. The disk material feels like a thin layer of recording tape used in tape recorders. It is covered with invisible magnetized areas that the computer can read. The magnetized areas represent program instructions and data to the computer.

Everything stored on a disk is called a *file*. A disk usually holds only two types of files:

- **Program files,** which are usually purchased from a computer store or other outlet (example: a word processing program file)
- **Data files,** which are usually created by the user (example: a business-letter file created with a word processing program)

Purchased programs come with disks. The main contents of a *program* or *software package,* as shown in Figure 2-7, are

- One or more disks that contain the program files (usually, one program uses a collection of files)
- A **User Guide,** or manual, with instructions about how to use the program

The *User Guide* contains instructions about how to put a disk into the computer disk drive, like the drive shown in Figure 2-7. It explains what happens

FIGURE 2-6
Cutaway view of a 5¼-inch disk

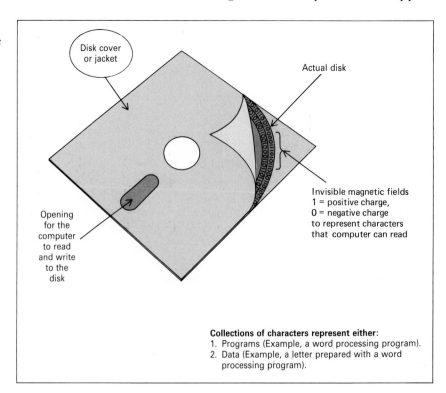

Disk cover or jacket

Actual disk

Invisible magnetic fields
1 = positive charge,
0 = negative charge
to represent characters
that computer can read

Opening
for the
computer
to read
and write
to the
disk

Collections of characters represent either:
1. Programs (Example, a word processing program).
2. Data (Example, a letter prepared with a word processing program).

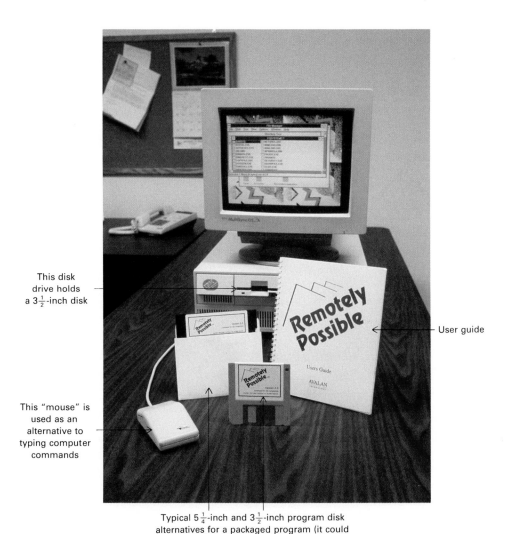

This disk
drive holds
a $3\frac{1}{2}$-inch disk

User guide

This "mouse" is
used as an
alternative to
typing computer
commands

Typical $5\frac{1}{4}$-inch and $3\frac{1}{2}$-inch program disk
alternatives for a packaged program (it could
be a word processing or other package; this one
is a telecommunications package)

FIGURE 2-7
A software package bought from a retail store contains a User Guide
and one or more program disks.

after the computer power is turned on and the first menu appears on the screen.
It details what each menu option is for and what typing, mouse movements, or
other action a user is expected to do.

OPERATING SYSTEM

The **operating system** is a special program that manages everything that
happens inside the computer. In some ways it acts like a traffic cop, controlling
the direction and flow of activity over the proper electronic roadways. For ex-

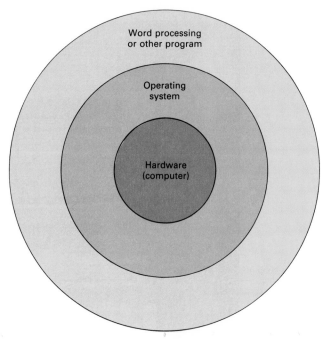

FIGURE 2-8
The operating system acts as a buffer between user programs, such as word processing, and computer hardware.

ample, it monitors a computer's mouse or keyboard movements to detect when information is being *input.* It sends *output,* like reports and other documents, to the printer. It also transfers files between disks and memory for *processing.*

It is convenient to think about the operating system as a buffer between whatever program is being used, such as word processing, and computer hardware, as diagrammed in Figure 2-8.

Most microcomputer users relate the term "operating system" with **DOS** (rhymes with "floss"), for **Disk Operating System.** It comes in a package just like the one in Figure 2-7. DOS, or any other operating system, prepares hardware to accept whatever program is to be used.

MS-DOS is the most popular operating system for microcomputers. MS stands for Microsoft, the company that designed the software. When IBM put MS-DOS on its Personal Computer, IBM called it **PC-DOS.** DOS is considered an industry standard because of its widespread use on millions of microcomputers.

The operating system needs to work very closely with a computer's hardware. For this reason, each type of computer hardware traditionally has its own operating system. Examples in the microcomputer area include

Operating System	Designed to Support
DOS or some variation of DOS	IBM Personal Computer and compatible machines
Finder or some variation of Finder	Apple Computer Company's machines

Three of the operating system's major management tasks are described in the following sections. They are

- Memory—how to divide it
- Input and output—how to get data into and out of memory
- Execution—how to do one program step at a time

Memory Management

One task of an operating system is to allocate use of a computer's memory, also called random access memory (RAM).

Figure 2-9 illustrates how one operating system, in this case DOS, manages 16 million bytes of memory. Some of it holds the operating system itself. But most memory is reserved for user programs and data.

As an example, a user might load a word processing program from a disk into memory. The memory manager assigns an area for it, as diagrammed in Figure 2-10. If the user wants to revise an old letter, a copy of the old letter is also loaded from the disk into memory. Figure 2-10 shows that data, in this case, the old letter, is placed into an area of memory that is separate from the program.

Two types of memory are commonly used by DOS programs:

- Conventional memory
- Extended memory

Conventional Memory.   Figure 2-9 shows that *conventional memory* ranges from 0 to 1 million bytes. The upper limit is technically 1,024,000 bytes. However, it is normally rounded to 1,000,000 bytes and referenced as 1 megabyte, or 1 Mbyte. Most programs reside in this region.

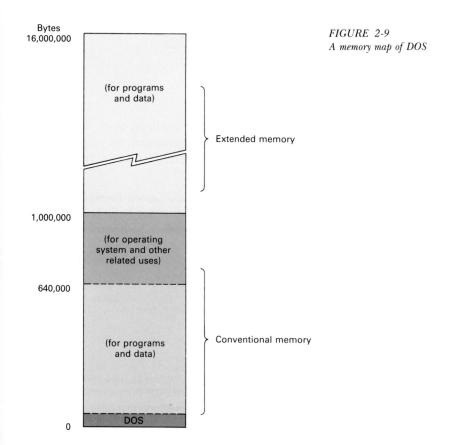

FIGURE 2-9
A memory map of DOS

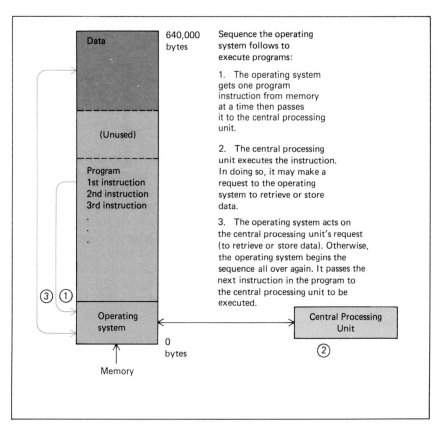

FIGURE 2-10
Programs and data are placed in separate areas of memory. The sequence of program execution is outlined.

When DOS originally was developed, the idea of 1 million bytes of memory on a personal computer seemed like an inexhaustible amount. As program size grew, however, memory needs also grew. So ways were devised to "trick" DOS into using memory areas above 1 megabyte.

Extended Memory.   *Extended memory* is the name given to memory that extends beyond 1 megabyte. It is accessed by programs that have built-in *DOS extenders*. As the name implies, **DOS extenders** provide a bridge between extended and conventional memory areas.

The spreadsheet program Lotus 1-2-3, Release 3 is an example of a DOS-extended program. It requires 640,000 bytes of conventional memory as well as 384,000 bytes of extended memory.

As DOS evolves along with new hardware technology, memory management schemes will evolve and change as well.

Input and Output Management

Another job of the operating system is to manage transfers between memory and hardware. Transfers occur every time a program sends or receives data with hardware such as a mouse, keypad, disk drive, display screen, printer, or other connected device.

In the word processing example, the input/output manager handles getting the old letter file from the proper storage slot on the correct disk. Once the letter is retrieved, it is placed into the memory area which the memory manager assigned.

Execution Management

A third function of the operating system is to execute, or run, programs in memory. In this case, the execution manager acts like the conductor of a symphony orchestra, directing the program, one instruction at a time, through the computer.

As an example, when the word processing program needs the old letter file, the execution manager halts program processing until the input/output manager retrieves the file. If the file is found, it continues processing. If the requested file does not exist, the execution manager switches to an error routine to notify the user of the problem.

All three operating system management functions work seamlessly together. This discussion artificially separates the functions to provide some insight to the activity going on "under the hood."

CATEGORIES OF OPERATING SYSTEMS

Major differences in how operating systems work are evident in single-tasking, multitasking, and multiuser computer environments.

Single Tasking

A **single-tasking operating system** accommodates one user and is used only on microcomputers. A user can do only one thing at a time, such as a word processing task.

Early DOS versions are the best known of the single-tasking operating systems. The equivalent single-tasking operating system for Apple computers is called Finder.

Operating systems, as well as other programs, are sold by version number, such as DOS 4.0 or DOS 5.0. The version number reflects different upgrades or improvements to the software, as evident in Figure 2-11.

When an operating system is traded up to a new version, all of a user's application programs should be usable on the new version. This is called **compatibility.** Otherwise, it means trashing all old programs. Users with heavy investments in packaged programs and training do not willingly change to an incompatible operating system.

Multitasking

Microcomputer operating systems evolved from single-tasking to multitasking versions. **Multitasking operating systems** can run, or can simulate running, several programs at once.

Multitasking operating systems typically use windows, such as the ones shown in Figure 2-12, to display all the tasks that are active at the same time. A **window**

Evolution of multitasking operating systems and environments

For Apple Computers

(Original) Single-tasking   Multitasking

Finder – – – – – – – – – – – – – – – – – –→ MultiFinder ⟶ System 7 ⟶ ......

For IBM and Compatible Computers

(Original) Single-tasking   Multitasking

DOS 1 ⟶ DOS 2 ⟶ DOS 3 ⟶ DOS 4 ⟶ OS/2⟶........................
                                                            or
                                                            DOS 5⟶.....................
                                                            or
                                                            Older DOS versions plus Windows,
                                                            DESQview, or other add-on
                                                            "window" multitasker

FIGURE 2-11   **For many computers**   Unix

FIGURE 2-12
Multitasking's common
"look and feel"

A. MultiFinder operating system on an Apple computer

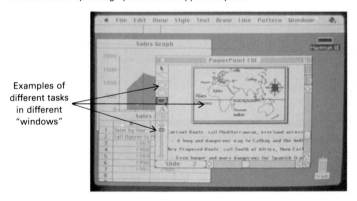

Examples of
different tasks
in different
"windows"

B. OS/2 operating system on an IBM PS/2 computer

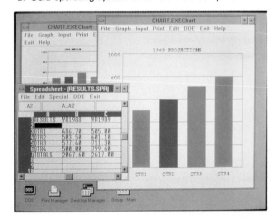

C. Windows program on an IBM-compatible computer with DOS

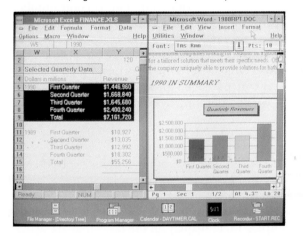

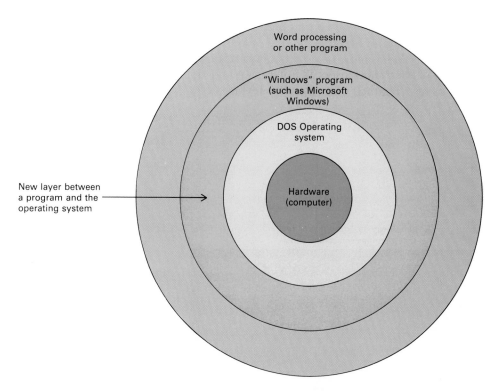

New layer between
a program and the
operating system

FIGURE 2-13
Multitasking with a separate
"windows" program

is one area of a divided display screen. A user can create a document with a word processor in one window, examine a spreadsheet in another, and create a chart with a graphics program in a third.

Multitasking on microcomputers is done two ways, with

- Multitasking operating systems. Examples are IBM's *Operating System/2,* or *OS/2,* and Apple Computer's *System 7.*
- **"Windows" programs.** They add a multitasking capability to single-tasking operating systems (an example is Microsoft's Windows, which works with DOS). Windows programs are sometimes called *operating environments.* They are sold like any other packaged program. They add a new layer of software between DOS and any program desired, as diagrammed in Figure 2-13.

Graphical User Interface.   A graphical user interface, as shown in Figure 2-14, is common in modern multitasking. A **graphical user interface,** or **GUI** (pronounced "gooey"), has symbols and a mouse selection device as an alternative to typing commands on a keyboard. Figure 2-15 shows more of the symbols and other elements found in a typical graphical user interface.

As evident, *user interface* refers to the communications that occur between a user and a computer. The two dominant user interface styles are graphical- and character-based, as shown in Figure 2-14. The character user interface typically requires typing on a keyboard. The graphical user interface, by contrast, requires a *point and click* sequence using a mouse. The sequence to select a menu item, for example, requires moving the arrow, or mouse pointer, on the screen to the menu item. Then a click on the mouse button indicates the selection.

Programs written with a graphical user interface have a common "look and feel." Apple Computers was the first to popularize this style with its Macintosh computers. Today most new programs are designed with a graphical user interface. Studies show users like it better and do more productive work than when using a character-based user interface.

FIGURE 2-14
Comparison of user interfaces

A. Example of a graphical user interface

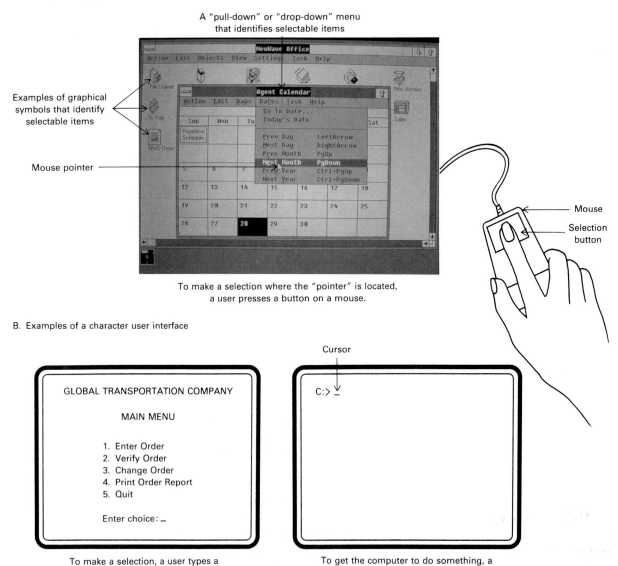

B. Examples of a character user interface

The following all assume that the mouse or screen pointer is dragged, or moved, to the area of concern.

1. **MAIN MENU CONTROL BOX**
   Click on the mouse button to open main menu; double-click to close.

2. **MINIMIZE BUTTON**
   Click to shrink window.

3. **MAXIMIZE BUTTON**
   Click to expand window to full size.

4. **WINDOW BORDERS AND CORNERS**
   Drag mouse at any point to resize windows.

5. **GROUP ICON**
   Double-click to open window containing program (also called application) icons.

6. **PROGRAM ICON**
   Double-click to run a program.

7. **DROP-DOWN (OR PULL-DOWN) MENU**
   Highlight options and click mouse, or type the underlined letter. Keyboard-equivalent commands are listed to the right of options.

8. **MENU OPTION**
   Click to select.

9. **MENU OPTION WITH ELLIPSIS**
   Click to display a pop-up "dialog box" or submenu.

10. **RESTORE BUTTON**
    Click to restore window to previous size.

11. **VERTICAL SCROLL BOX**
    Use to move window contents up and down.

12. **SCROLL ARROWS**
    Click to view one new line of information.

13. **SCROLL BOX**
    Drag mouse up and down to scroll; box shows relative position of view in window.

14. **HORIZONTAL SCROLL BAR**
    Use to move window content left and right.

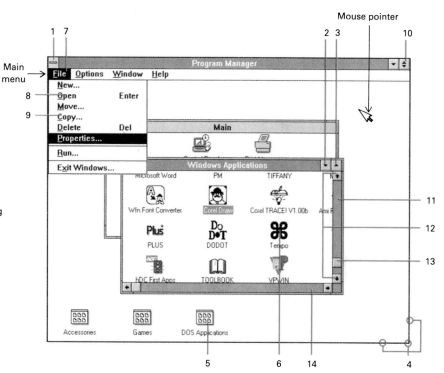

FIGURE 2-15
Elements associated with a graphical user interface

Unix. **Unix** is another multitasking operating system for personal computers that is different from all others. The difference is that it works on many vendors' computer hardware. For example, versions of Unix are available for Apple and IBM-compatible computers, as well as a host of other computers, from microcomputers to mainframes. This hardware flexibility makes Unix appealing to many users.

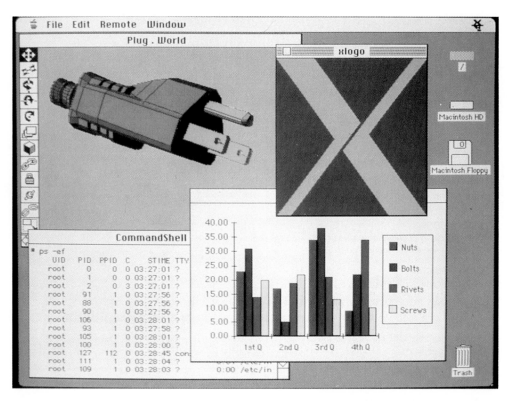

FIGURE 2-16
Example of a graphical user interface
with the Unix operating system

While the original Unix operating system was not easy to use, graphical user interfaces now make it easier. As shown in Figure 2-16, programs written to run on newer versions of Unix resemble the look and feel of other user interface graphical-based programs.

Unix is not only a multitasking operating system, it is also a *multiuser* operating system, which is the third category of operating systems.

Multiuser

A **multiuser operating system** provides services to many users who share one computer. This book reserves major multiuser considerations for discussion in the next module, "The Multiuser Perspective."

UTILITY PROGRAMS

A wide range of utility programs are packaged with operating systems. **Utilities** are a collection of small separate programs that mainly help perform disk housekeeping chores.

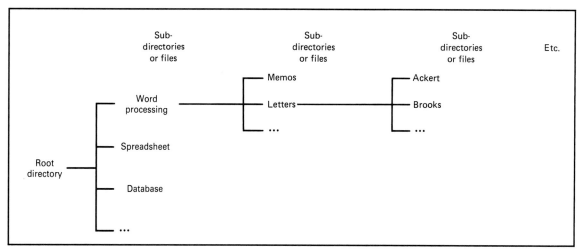

FIGURE 2-17
Examples of a tree directory plan for files stored on a disk

Some of the first utilities a user of a microcomputer system learns are as follows:

- *Format.* **Formatting** prepares a blank disk to make it usable by a computer. It is similar to marking streets before building a housing development. The operating system checks for unused slots before it can save a file.
- *Diskcopy.* This utility copies all files on one disk to another disk. This is useful to make backup copies of disks. Users typically store originals in a safe place away from the computer and use *working copies* of disks for regular use.
- *Copy.* This utility copies one file instead of an entire disk.
- *Directory.* The directory utility is used to display a list of files stored on a disk. Experienced computer users have many subdirectories, as shown in the directory plan in Figure 2-17. Each subdirectory is a refinement of the one before it.
- *Erase.* This utility deletes unwanted files. Utility packages are sold that help to recover erased files.

A large number of separately sold utility packages, such as those listed in Figure 2-18, are available for personal computers. They contain many additional disk housekeeping capabilities.

FIGURE 2-18
Examples of utility packages

A SAMPLER

Mace Utilities
MacTools Deluxe
Magellan
Norton Utilities
PC Tools Deluxe

CASE STUDY: *The Threat of Computer Viruses*

Computer security experts routinely warn users about vandals and mischief-makers who deliberately plant destructive programs, called *computer viruses*, in computer systems. Computer viruses are so named because they parallel in the computer world the behavior of biological viruses.

How a Virus Program Spreads

  1. A programmer creates a program that can secretly bind to another program or a computer operating system and copy itself.

2. The program is placed on a disk or hidden in a program sent to an electronic information service, or electronic "bulletin board," where information is exchanged by computer over telephone lines.

3. When an unknowing user inserts the disk in a computer or retrieves data containing the virus program from another computer by telephone, a new computer is infected.

4. Once inside the new computer, the program copies itself onto a new disk or the computer's hard disk.

5. Later, the program is activated according to instructions originally embedded within it by the programmer. It might be set off on a certain date or after making a certain number of copies of itself. The instructions can be as simple as displaying a message or as destructive as the erasure of all the data stored in the computer.

A virus program can copy itself into the computer's master software, or operating system, without calling attention to itself. From there, the program can be passed to additional disks inserted in the computer. Someone who took an "infected" disk from one computer and used it in another could unwittingly allow the virus program to enter the second machine.

Depending on the intent of the creator, the virus program might cause a harmless message to appear on the computer's screen. Or the program could easily be more damaging, erasing computer files, altering data, or causing the computer to shut down.

A senior consultant at Lehigh University's Computing Center has seen hundreds of IBM personal computer users' disks erased by a runaway virus launched by a computer vandal.

Lehigh has developed its own "vaccine," a program that checks a disk and, if it finds a virus, writes over that part of the disk.

Computer security experts say many users would do well to consider acquiring a commercially available vaccine program. It can go a long way toward protecting disks as well as peace of mind. But none are complete answers, and none guarantee that the buyer won't fall victim to the next round of cleverness in this escalating germ warfare.

DISCUSSION QUESTIONS

1. Discuss the statement "Computer viruses represent a clear and present danger to anything stored on a computer's disks."
2. One computer virus was created by brothers who owned a computer store. They were angry because purchasers of computer packages gave away illegal copies of their programs. This denied the brothers legitimate sales of software packages. The virus they planted destroyed files only for users of the illegal copies. Discuss the ethical issues concerning the brothers' motives; the software package buyers who distributed free software to friends; and the friends who took the free software.

CHAPTER SUMMARY

- *Input* is computer jargon for putting something in a computer. *Output* means to get something out. Between the two, *processing* occurs to transform input into output.

- Computer *memory* offers only a temporary workspace or storage area. That is why users begin a computer session by loading memory with programs and data from disks.

- Everything inside the computer's memory is represented by a *binary system* of on or off electronic pulses.

- A *bit* is one binary digit. Eight bits are called a *byte*.

- A *byte* is the fundamental unit with which a computer works.

- *ASCII* is an acronym for *American Standard Code for Information Interchange*. It is a 7-bit code that is a computer industry standard for microcomputers and minicomputers.

- Disks contain two types of files: *program files* (an example is a word processing file) and *data files* (an example is a business letter created with a word processing program).

- A purchased *program* or *software package* typically contains disks of program files and a *User Guide* of instructions for how to use the programs.

- An *operating system* is a special program that manages everything that happens inside a computer.

- *DOS* stands for *Disk Operating System*. It is the most popular operating system for IBM-compatible microcomputers.

- An operating system enables user programs to run on a computer by managing memory, input and output, and program execution.

- Two types of memory managed by a microcomputer's operating system are *conventional memory* and *extended memory*.

- *Conventional memory* is base memory located in the first 1 million bytes (1 Mbyte) of a computer's memory area. *Extended memory* extends beyond 1 Mbyte and is accessed by programs with built-in *DOS extenders*.

- A *single-tasking operating system* accommodates one user solving one task at a time and is used only on microcomputers. DOS (for IBM-compatible computers) and Finder (for Apple computers) are two single-tasking operating systems.

- *Multitasking operating systems* can run several application programs at once. IBM's Operating System/2 (OS/2) and Apple's MultiFinder are multitasking operating systems.

- A *window* divides a screen into areas to display multiple tasks in progress. For example, one window may display a word-processed letter, while a second window may show a table created with a spreadsheet program.

- A *windows program*, also called an operating environment, adds a multitasking capability to a single-tasking operating system.

- *Graphical user interfaces* have graphic symbols and a mouse input device as an alternative to typing commands on a keyboard.

- A *multiuser operating system* provides services to many users who share one computer. *Unix* is a multiuser operating system for microcomputers as well as other computers.

- *Utilities* are a collection of programs that mainly help perform disk housekeeping chores.

- Five common utilities are format a disk, copy a disk, copy a file, examine file directory content, and erase a file.

SELECTED KEY TERMS

ASCII	Input	Program files
Bit	Multitasking operating system	Program or software package
Byte	Multiuser operating system	Single-tasking operating system
Data files	Operating system	Utilities
Disk operating system (DOS)	Output	Window
Graphical user interface	Processing	Windows program

REVIEW QUESTIONS

1. Draw a diagram to show the relationship of input, processing, and output.

2. Compare bits and bytes.

3. Identify two types of files typically found on a disk. Give an example of each type.

4. What are the contents of a typical purchased software package?

5. What is an operating system? Identify three functions performed by a microcomputer operating system.

6. What is the most popular operating system for IBM-compatible computers?

7. Compare single-tasking and multitasking operating systems.

8. What is a window?

9. Identify characteristics of a graphical user interface.

10. What are utilities? Describe three of them.

EXERCISES

1. Use articles from computer magazines to write a report on the evolution of the DOS or Finder or Unix operating system. What role do you think the operating system will play 5 years from now?

2. Locate and run a computer-disk-based tutorial for learning DOS or another operating system. Make an outline of the steps in the learning sequence followed. Prepare an oral or written report about what you have learned and how you learned it.

3. Read three recent articles about microcomputer multitasking operating systems. All three articles could be about one operating system or several. For each operating system, list the features available. If several are used, compare the features offered.

4. Choose a graphical user interface program to demonstrate to the class. Illustrate how the graphic symbols and other elements are used to perform tasks and manipulate the appearance of the screen. For example, show how to enlarge a window, scroll items in a window, and choose items from drop-down menus.

3

Microcomputer Hardware

AFTER READING THIS CHAPTER, YOU SHOULD BE ABLE TO

- Identify the basic input, output, and processing hardware components of a business-use microcomputer
- Differentiate between various microcomputer hardware standards
- Initiate a systematic evaluation of microcomputer hardware to make a buying decision

More than a decade into the personal computer revolution, tens of millions of people are still far more comfortable scribbling on a pad than typing on a computer keyboard.

A few computer makers sell computers with a simple solution to the problem: they get rid of keyboards altogether and allow users to write on a touch-sensitive screen with a pen. Their writing is converted, not quite instantly, into neat rows of glowing computer type, which can be intermingled with careful electronic sketches or digitized doodles, then printed out in type just as is done on an ordinary personal computer.

The battery-operated, notebook-sized machines are called "pen computers," "stylus systems," or "smart paper."

Some say this way to communicate with computers may be even less intimidating than the "mouse" pointing devices that were invented to make personal computers more inviting. The technology could, in a few years, make a computer the size of a writing tablet approachable to people who do not type and who refuse to go near anything that clacks and beeps, as many of today's personal computers do.

FIGURE 3-1
An IBM personal computer

T his chapter is about **hardware**, the physical part of a computer. Figure 3-1 illustrates some of the basic hardware components of a business-use personal microcomputer. Components include the keyboard, display, printer, disk drive, and system unit. They are all discussed in this chapter. Discussions of hardware related to communications, graphics, and desktop publishing applications are reserved for separate chapters in this book.

The discussion begins by examining the evolution of microcomputer hardware. It concludes with hardware-buying evaluation considerations.

Informed buyers determine the software needed *first* and select the hardware *second*. Software discussions occupy most of the chapters in this book. To understand the software discussions, it helps to be familiar with hardware fundamentals.

MICROCOMPUTER HARDWARE EVOLUTION

The first commercial microcomputer appeared in 1974. It was offered in kit form and was called the Altair. By 1977, Apple Computer, Radio Shack, and Commodore were selling completely assembled microcomputers, which were also called personal computers.

Microcomputers did not attract business users until 1979, when the first electronic spreadsheet program, *VisiCalc*, appeared. The program ran only on the Apple II microcomputer. It was the first time a software program was responsible for the sale of computer hardware.

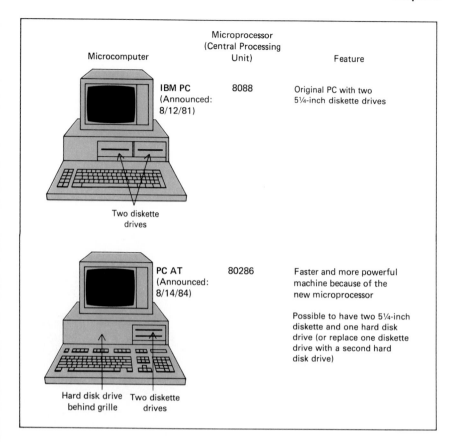

Microcomputer	Microprocessor (Central Processing Unit)	Feature
IBM PC (Announced: 8/12/81)	8088	Original PC with two 5¼-inch diskette drives
PC AT (Announced: 8/14/84)	80286	Faster and more powerful machine because of the new microprocessor

Possible to have two 5¼-inch diskette and one hard disk drive (or replace one diskette drive with a second hard disk drive) |

FIGURE 3-2
Two microcomputers in the IBM PC family

The Apple personal computer was eclipsed in the early 1980s by the IBM Personal Computer (PC). Two major microcomputers in the IBM PC family are shown in Figure 3-2.

Today there are many brands of personal computers available. The majority are compatible with the IBM PC. **Compatibles**, or **clones**, is the term used to identify non-IBM personal computers that can run software designed for IBMs. Clone manufacturers usually advertise that their products are "IBM compatible." Figure 3-3 shows a sampling of the hundreds of personal computers available today.

IBM's successor to the Personal Computer line is the **Personal System/2** (a short form is PS/2). It was introduced in 1987. Figure 3-4 shows one of the computers, a floor-standing version, from this line. Other models in the PS/2 line, such as the Model 50, resemble the original desktop PC.

An example of a computer from Apple's popular Macintosh line appears in Figure 3-5. It is one of many types of desktop and portable computer models that are available in the personal computer market.

The following sections cover the components in a typical microcomputer system that are evaluated when buying a computer:

- Input hardware, which refers to the keyboard and other devices
- Output hardware, which refers mainly to displays and printers
- Storage hardware, which refers to diskettes and hard disks
- Processing hardware, which refers to microprocessor chips and related hardware

A SAMPLER

PRODUCT	MODEL
Desktop Models	
Apple	Macintosh IIsi
	Macintosh LC
Compaq	Deskpro 486
Dell	System 310
IBM	Personal System/2 Series
Zenith	Z-386
Portable Models	
Apple	Macintosh Portable
Compaq	Portable 386
IBM	Personal System/2
	Model P70 386
NEC	ProSpeed 386
Sharp	PS-5541
Tandy	11FD

FIGURE 3-3
Examples of Personal Microcomputers

FIGURE 3-4
The IBM Personal System/2 Model 80,
a floor-standing microcomputer

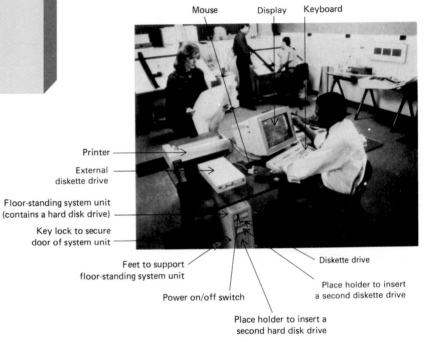

Mouse   Display   Keyboard

Printer

External
diskette drive

Floor-standing system unit
(contains a hard disk drive)

Key lock to secure
door of system unit

Feet to support
floor-standing system unit

Diskette drive

Place holder to insert
a second diskette drive

Power on/off switch

Place holder to insert a
second hard disk drive

FIGURE 3-5
The Apple Macintosh IIsi microcomputer

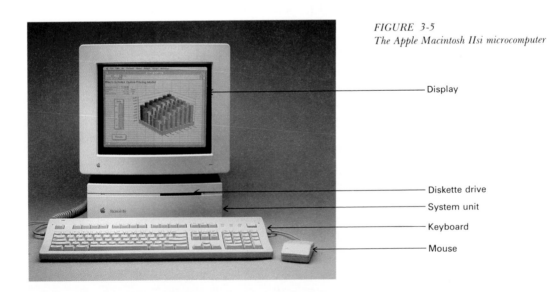

Display

Diskette drive

System unit

Keyboard

Mouse

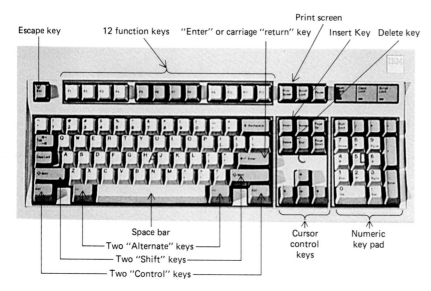

Escape key   12 function keys   "Enter" or carriage "return" key   Print screen   Insert Key   Delete key

Space bar
Two "Alternate" keys
Two "Shift" keys
Two "Control" keys

Cursor control keys   Numeric key pad

FIGURE 3-6
Typical keyboard with function keys,
numeric keypad that incorporates cursor
control keys, and auxiliary keys

KEYBOARD INPUT

A **keyboard** is the traditional way to get input into a computer. The keyboard that comes with some microcomputers resembles the one shown in Figure 3-6. Part of it looks like a familiar typewriter keyboard. This similarity helps to shorten the learning curve for those new users who already know how to type even a little.

The separate **numeric keypad** is for speeding data entry in numeric-oriented applications. The **cursor control keys**, also called **arrow keys**, are another separate bank of keys. They allow cursor manipulation. The **cursor** is the tiny underscore, often set to blinking, on the display, as shown in Figure 3-7. It always indicates the position where the next typed character will appear. It is usually found after a **prompt**, which is a message for some user action. It indicates a keyboard entry is needed, such as to select a numbered choice from a menu of text editing options.

Another group of keys are the **function keys**. They are also called *program function keys* and are referenced as F1 or PF1, or whatever number applies. Programmers call them *soft keys* because their functions are controlled by software.

For example, one word processing package uses the F8 key to underline text and the F10 key to save text. Another application uses the same keys differently, which can get confusing. To help remember function key assignments, some users attach labels to keys as reminders. Software applications that use function keys extensively often provide cardboard *keyboard templates* that overlay function keys and have a place to write memory-jogging labels for function key actions.

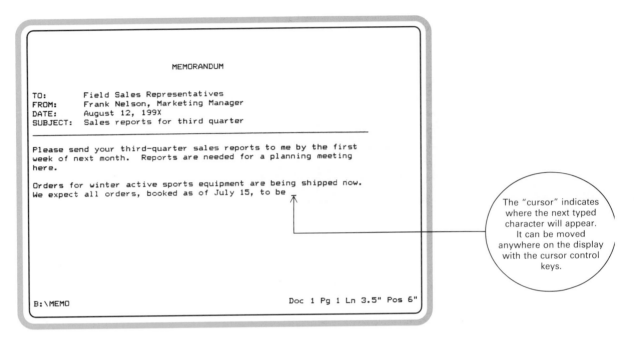

FIGURE 3-7
A cursor as it appears in a word processing memo

Keyboard Alternatives

Alternatives to keyboarding include a *mouse, touch-sensitive display, light pen, scanner,* and *voice.* All require specialized software to integrate with a given computer and application.

A **mouse** is a pointing device that functions much like the cursor control arrow keys. As the mouse is physically moved around the desktop, a mouse *pointer* on the display moves.

In Figure 3-8, the pointer is directed at an item in the menu bar. Selecting any menu item requires a click of the mouse's button. At the moment, the pointer indicates selection of the "justify" function to alter text on the display. The menu that appears next is called a *pull-down,* or *drop-down, menu* because it appears only in response to the selection at the top from the menu bar.

A **touch-sensitive display**, as shown in Figure 3-9, is another alternative to a keyboard for entering data into a computer. It is activated by touching the screen and blocking light beams. This generates an electronic signal that is interpreted by the software. Some futurists predict that the touchscreen will replace the mouse for professional and occasional users. It is already an important input device in educational and graphic applications.

Another keyboard alternative is a **pen input system**. Figure 3-10 shows a railroad employee using a pen input system to complete a screen-displayed form. The electronic stylus, or pen, is placed on the specially coated display screen. The pen's location is sensed by the computer, and it activates the appropriate processing. Southern Pacific Transportation Company expects this new technology to help eliminate billing errors caused by traditional paperwork problems.

Manufacturers of pen input systems currently are developing the ability to convert hand-drawn characters into computer-readable form. Programming a computer to recognize the various patterns of handwritten characters is a huge

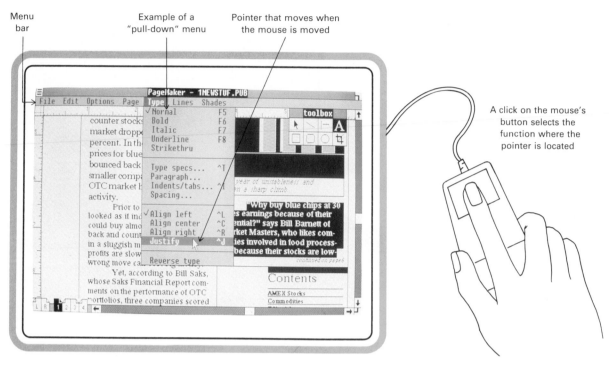

Menu bar

Example of a "pull-down" menu

Pointer that moves when the mouse is moved

A click on the mouse's button selects the function where the pointer is located

FIGURE 3-8
Using a mouse to make menu selections

FIGURE 3-9
A touch-sensitive display

FIGURE 3-10
Using a pen-based computer to record train information

FIGURE 3-11
A hand-held scanner

task. It is available now for very limited, specialized applications. Eventually this technology could have a major impact on how people enter information when working with word processing, spreadsheet, and other software.

Another input device is a scanner, such as the example shown in Figure 3-11. **Scanners** convert text, drawings, and photographs from a printed page to a form that a computer can interpret and process. Scanners come in both hand-held and desktop models.

Voice recognition, another alternative to keyboards, uses a microphone to input sound, as shown in Figure 3-12. It remains limited in its ability to interpret human words accurately and requires large amounts of computer memory to process.

Most voice systems available today are speaker dependent: each operator must train the system to recognize his or her voice pattern. This involves repeating words or phrases three or more times. The words are digitized and stored as data on disk. Later, when a word is spoken as a command to the computer, its sound pattern must match one of those previously stored. After a match, the program continues to perform whatever it was designed to do. For example, with a word processing document, a user can speak commands such as "bold," "underline," or "check spelling."

FIGURE 3-12
Using voice-recognition input

More innovative, special-purpose input devices also exist. For example,
- Braille keyboards and large-type display screens enable visually impaired persons to use computers.
- "Eye-tracker" devices, such as the one shown in Figure 3-13, enable physically impaired persons to "point" to locations on a computer screen with their eyes.
- Devices with a mouthpiece connected to a headset allow paralyzed persons to input data by puffing air into the mouthpiece.

FIGURE 3-13
An "eye-tracker" input device

Video camera mounted under display tracks the position of the eye's pupil and translates this into "pointing" to menu selections or other choices

FOCUS ON: *Hand-Held Computers Cut Paperwork*

Frito-Lay Inc. has given hand-held computers to all of its 10,000 delivery people. The data they collect feed a system that helps manage many of the company's operations.

The devices help delivery people, too. Don Staeck, who handles a 61-store route in New Jersey for Frito-Lay, used to spend hours doing paperwork—writing orders, invoices and sales reports. Now, with a palm-sized computer, he can enter orders at each store in a minute or two, running through a programmed product list complete with prices. The machine plugs into a printer in his truck to produce an itemized invoice. At day's end, it generates a sales report and,

data from some 34,000 hand-held computer scanners used by its drivers and other personnel.

Police in Newark, N.J., began using radio-powered hand-held computers last summer, entering license plate numbers of parked cars to check for drivers with traffic violations. It found them. Through December, the department booted or towed 1,633 cars and collected $526,000 from fines and fees paid by unlucky owners.

Sifting Through Data

Some management experts warn of risks. One

Hand-held computers at work

through a hookup in the local warehouse, transmits it in seconds to company headquarters in Dallas.

Strategic Innovation

Hand-held computers aren't perfect, of course. They're expensive, have small screens, have keyboards that are tough to master, and are heavy, weighing a pound or two.

Still, companies value their capabilities. "It is an absolutely critical strategic innovation," says Roger A. Podwoski, a vice president at Federal Express Corp. The company tracks parcels with

is that companies will "robotize" field workers by demanding they collect increasing amounts of data. Companies may also go astray by failing to filter properly the wealth of information hand-held computers can gather. "Too much data can cause you to make incorrect decisions," says James I. Cash, a professor of Harvard Business School.

Charles S. Feld, a Frito-Lay vice president, says the company is completing a computerized "executive information system" to fully exploit the information gathered from hand-held and other devices. Says Mr. Feld, "We have reshifted our energies to solving problems instead of figuring out that we have problems."

DISPLAY OUTPUT

One of the typical devices for viewing computer-processed output is a TV-like **display**, which is also called a **monitor**.

Display Terminology

Monochrome monitors or displays present only one color, usually green, amber, or white, against a solid background on the screen. They are the least expensive display choice.

Monochrome displays usually have *high resolution.* **Resolution** refers to the number of distinguishable points or dots on the display. The higher the resolution, the more precise the image.

One manufacturer divides its screen into 1,024 columns by 768 rows for graphics applications. This gives the screen 786,432 points, or pixels. **Pixel** is a term for one *pic*ture *el*ement. Through appropriate software, each pixel can be turned on or off. Each can also be assigned a color.

Text, on the other hand, is usually displayed in 80 columns by 25 rows, as shown in Figure 3-14. The greater the number of pixels forming each individual text character, the more solid each character appears on the screen. For text, as for graphics, more pixels mean sharper images.

Color monitors have become the monitor of choice for most personal computer users. They are often called *RGB monitors.* The acronym RGB stands for red, green, and blue. **RGB monitors** use a refined color separation technology to produce high-quality color images.

Display Connection

In some cases, a separate piece of hardware enables the display to "talk to" the computer. The hardware is called a number of things, such as a **display**, **graphics**, or **video**

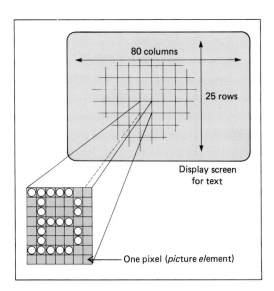

FIGURE 3-14
Text displays divide a screen into 80 columns by 25 rows.

"Pins" to seat the controller
board into an "expansion slot"
in the system unit

FIGURE 3-15
An example of a controller board

- **Controller board**
- **Adapter**
- **Card**
- **Interface**
- **Circuit board**

An example of a controller board is given in Figure 3-15. It must be inserted, as shown in Figure 3-16, into a slot in the computer's system unit. The *system*

FIGURE 3-16
Inserting a controller board into an
expansion slot in the system unit

Cover of system unit

Keyboard

Display

Controller board being
inserted into an
"expansion slot"
in the system unit

System unit
pulled out
from its cover

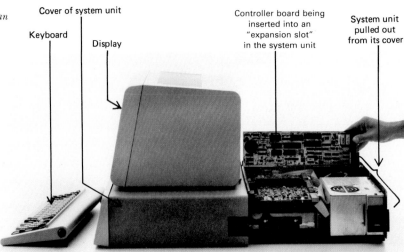

unit of a computer houses its main electronic circuitry. A cable physically connects the display to the controller board once it is "seated" in the computer's system unit.

Controller boards are a common way to attach so-called peripheral devices such as displays, printers, and disk drives to the computer's system unit. All controller boards look similar, regardless of their function.

The display controller board must match one of several available graphic "standards" supported by the computer. Graphic standards are discussed in Chapter 5.

While some computers require a controller board to connect the display to the system unit, others do not, notably the PS/2 computers. They have the necessary circuitry already built in.

Flat-Panel Displays

Flat-panel displays often come on small portable computers, like the one shown in Figure 3-17. The most popular portable display technology used is the familiar *liquid crystal*, such as that used in an ordinary wristwatch.

Flat-panel displays eliminate the bulk associated with standard *cathode-ray tube (CRT)* technology used in ordinary television sets and computer displays. Some experts expect flat-panel to replace CRT displays before the end of the 1990s.

PRINTED OUTPUT

Not all computer output is displayed. A good deal of it is also printed. Microcomputer printers can

- Print text at a speedy 800 characters per second
- Produce characters of perfect quality
- Dazzle with color graphics
- Cost less than a portable typewriter

FIGURE 3-17
A portable computer with a flat-panel display

Unfortunately, no one printer has all these characteristics. Trade-offs are inevitable, which requires some planning.

A first step is to decide what primary job the printer will be used for. Will it print mainly text or graphic images? Is color needed? Where will printed documents be used? Printed material sent outside the company has to be of a higher quality than that sent inside the company. Most companies like to project a quality image to customers and others through their printed material.

Next, printing speed and volume have to be established. Choices include printing material at slow characters-per-second to faster lines-per-minute speeds. Typical speed requirements come from estimating the lines of printing done each workday and dividing by a printer's speed. The result gives the time necessary to complete a printing task. Tasks should be finished in the time planned for them, or the printer is too slow for the job.

In many cases the computer cannot be used for anything else while printing is going on. If printing takes 3 hours, the computer cannot be scheduled for any other use. But programs are available that allow printing and other tasks to occur simultaneously.

Still another consideration is software and printer interfacing: Will they "talk" to each other? Printers have specific commands that move margins, change line spacing, and the like. Most software packages list the printers with which they work. For the most part, popular software works with popular printers.

Once the necessary planning of printer quality, speed, and interface is completed, it remains to compare the main printer types, dot-matrix and laser printers.

Dot-Matrix Printers

For flexible printing requirements, from rough drafts to company correspondence and graphics, users often get a **dot-matrix printer**. These printers form characters with dots arranged in a matrix, much like the pixels on a display. Characters are produced by software-controlled pins that are activated against an inked ribbon, as shown in Figure 3-18.

Dot-matrix printers are noisy, but they are fast and usually inexpensive.

An example of a dot-matrix printer's capability appears in Figure 3-19. Graphics mix with ordinary text of various type styles. Printing is controlled entirely by software.

Today's dot-matrix printers, which are called **near-letter-quality printers**, produce both rough-draft- and letter-, or correspondence-, quality output. High-

FIGURE 3-18
(A) A dot-matrix printing head. (B) Building a solid-looking character. These dots show the letter B being formed by a dot-matrix printer after one pass and after multiple passes.

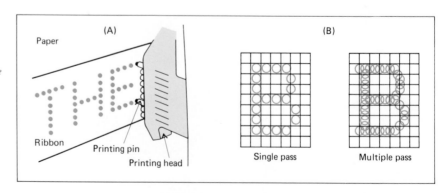

Example of
graphic
capability

Example of
four different
type styles

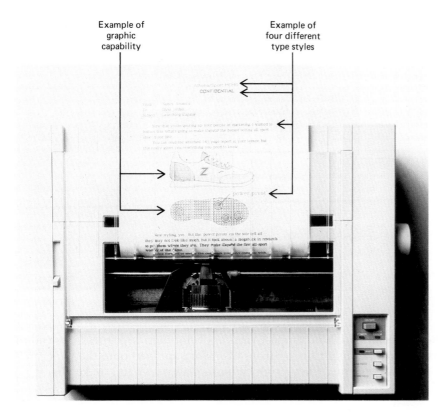

FIGURE 3-19
Print possibilities with a dot-matrix
printer

quality print is accomplished with repeated printhead passes and various pinhead arrangements, such as those shown in Figure 3-20. Specifications for one example printer include the following:

Quality	Dot Matrix	Speed in Characters Per Second
Letter	18 × 48	100
Rough draft	9 × 7	290

Some dot-matrix printers have color capabilities. Their ribbon contains bands of different colored ink. The printer changes color by raising or lowering the ribbon to strike the desired color band. Such color typically is not high quality.

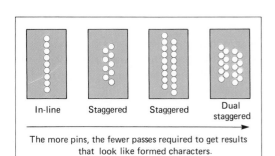

FIGURE 3-20
Examples of dot-matrix pinhead layout

Laser printer

FIGURE 3-21
A laser printer

Ink-jet printers are a nonimpact version of dot-matrix printers. Instead of a matrix of pins hitting a ribbon, drops of ink are sprayed onto the paper in a specified character array. They produce high-quality text and make almost no noise. They also offer color.

Laser Printers

Laser printers, such as the one in Figure 3-21, print on paper like ordinary copy machines. Internally a **laser printer** projects a beam of laser light to form character images on a rotating drum. The images are covered with ink, like copy toner, before they are transferred to plain paper.

Laser printers can produce images that resemble not just typewriter quality, but professional typeset quality. An example of this print quality appears in Figure 3-22. It is a quality favored by companies that do their own in-house desktop publishing.

A summary of typical personal computer printer choices appears in Figure 3-23. Laser printers are the most expensive choice.

STORAGE

Computers lose everything in memory when the power is shut off. To preserve both programs and data from destruction, computers come equipped with disk drives for more permanent storage. The drives house disk storage media.

Drives and Disks

Many personal computers come with two built-in disk drives, much like those in Figure 3-1. A **disk drive** is a unit that houses, and physically provides access to, disks during use by a program.

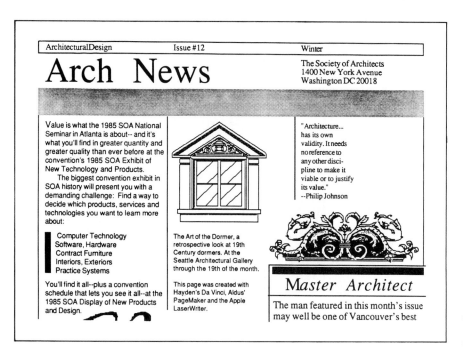

FIGURE 3-22
This newsletter is an example of laser-quality printing

FIGURE 3-23

SOME PERSONAL PRINTER CHOICES

Printer Type	Example of Speed
Dot-matrix	18–800 characters per second
Ink jet	30–300 characters per second
Laser	6–28 pages per minute

Disk drives work with portable disks, called diskettes or floppy disks, or built-in disks, called hard disks. **Disks** are magnetic storage media for data and programs. They contain an invisible coating which is stamped during use with positive and negative fields, represented by 1's and 0's as shown in Figure 3-24. Groups of 1's and 0's make up the coded characters of programs or data. All can be erased and reused.

A read/write head in the disk drive, which is similar to one in a record player, is positioned over a specific track of the disk. Once positioned, it can either read information stored there or write it.

Diskettes

Diskettes are small portable computer storage media. They can be carried anywhere. By contrast, hard disks are mounted inside the disk drive and generally cannot be separated from the disk drive itself. Once a diskette is placed, by hand, inside a disk drive slot, it works the same as a built-in hard disk.

An example of a 5¼-inch diskette appears in Figure 3-25. It is shown along with a 3½-inch diskette.

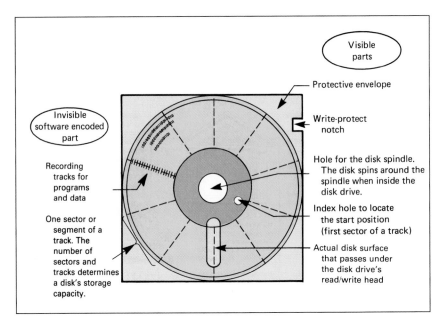

FIGURE 3-24
Diskette

If a user glues a label over the *write-protect notch* of a 5¼-inch diskette, it signals the disk drive not to accept write-overs which would destroy stored data. It is good practice to write-protect original copies of program disks to avoid inadvertently erasing the programs stored there. A 3½-inch diskette has a hole that opens to signal write-protection is in force.

A double-density 5¼-inch diskette holds 360,000 characters or bytes. A high-

FIGURE 3-25
As the size of a diskette decreases, its storage capacity continues to grow

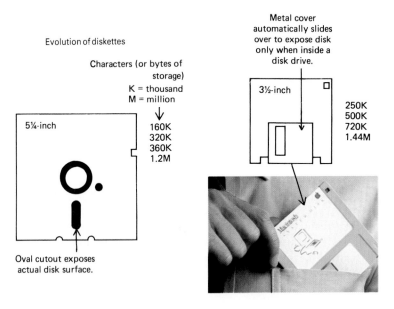

density 5¼-inch diskette holds 1,200,000 characters. By contrast, a high-density 3½-inch diskette holds 1,440,000 characters.

Hard Disks

Hard disks, also called fixed disks, are faster and more expensive than diskettes. They are built right into the disk drive and normally cannot be removed. One model offers over 2.5 billion characters of storage. This amount supports large files of a company's customers, orders, inventory, and other data. It is capable of supporting the storage needs for many users at once as a group file server on a local-area network.

Hard disks do not eliminate the need for a diskette drive, which serves as a transfer device to get purchased software onto the hard disk. Most software currently is sold on diskettes.

Figure 3-26 shows a cutaway photo of a hard disk drive. Disk platters are rigid metal. An access arm moves to the track where requested data are located, and its read/write head takes over. Data are automatically read or written in response to program commands.

Removable hard drives offer the opportunity to move data to other physical locations. This is useful especially for off-site storage of data for security purposes.

Like internal hard drives, removable drives can fail, or "crash," and destroy precious data and programs stored on them. For this reason, disk backup is vital. Only a safely stored duplicate, or **backup copy** of a disk, can restore the data lost on a damaged disk.

More often than not, backups are required because of simple human error. An entire disk or just one file might inadvertently be erased. If the erased file contains a mailing list that took two weeks to enter, and no backup exists, the entire effort must be repeated. This is the usual kind of problem that makes backing up disks a vital concern to computer users.

One of many ways to back up a hard disk is with a **tape cartridge**, as shown in Figure 3-27. File backup onto diskettes, the common alternative to tape backup, is time consuming and error prone because of the need to use many disks to do the job.

FIGURE 3-26
A cutaway photo of a hard disk drive

Hard disk platter

Movable access arm with read/write head

Front panel (only part visible to a user on some systems)

Personal computer
system unit

Backup tape cartridge drive

FIGURE 3-27
*Tape cartridge is often used on personal
computers to back up hard disk files*

Tape cartridge

Diskette
drive

FIGURE 3-28
*This 5¼-inch optical disk stores 680
million characters*

Optical Disks

Optical disks, like the one shown in Figure 3-28, are another personal computer storage medium. They come in three varieties.

One type of optical disk is an erasable optical disk. It has the potential to replace hard disks with such added benefits as

- Providing vastly improved storage capacity
- Offering the potential to combine data, video, and audio information in a single medium
- Permitting the removal of a disk from its drive, which simplifies data backup and security procedures and encourages the collection of databases

A second type is a WORM (write once, read many times) disk. While data can be written to the disk by a personal computer, they cannot be erased. The lack of erasability can be an advantage. A WORM disk containing bank records, for example, provides an indestructible audit trail. It makes the disk ideally suited to office storage systems.

The third type is called a CD ROM (compact disk read-only memory). Since a CD ROM is pressed at the factory, information cannot be recorded on it by a personal computer. This makes it unsuitable as an ordinary disk storage medium. Instead, CD ROMs are used to distribute large commercial databases and reference materials. As an example, *Microsoft Bookshelf* includes a dictionary, a thesaurus, a world almanac, and Bartlett's *Familiar Quotations*.

SYSTEM UNIT

The **system unit**, as shown in Figures 3-1, 3-4, and 3-5, is the housing unit for components that perform the actual processing in a microcomputer. The following main components work together to do the processing:

Relative size of
a microprocessor chip,
also called an
integrated circuit (IC) chip

Actual
chip

Carrier

A microprocessor chip
in its carrier

Pins to socket
the integrated
circuit chip to
a system or other
controller board

FIGURE 3-29
A microprocessor chip

- *Central processing unit (CPU)*, also known as a *microprocessor*
- *Random access memory (RAM)*, also known as *memory*
- *Read-only memory (ROM)*

Chips

All these components are **integrated circuit (IC) chips**, as shown in Figure 3-29, which illustrates a central processing unit (CPU) or microprocessor chip. Chips engineered for special purposes are manufactured by etching thousands of electronic components onto a tiny surface of silicon. Silicon is a compound made from sand. Sometimes the chip is called a *silicon*, or *semiconductor, chip*.

After a chip is manufactured, it may be placed and concealed inside a plastic housing, called a **carrier**. The carrier has tiny pins that stick out underneath to plug it into a controller board. The controller board shown in Figure 3-15 has dozens of special-purpose chips on it. Pins connect chip circuitry to the electronic roadways, called **buses**, that are etched into the controller board. Figure 3-30 illustrates a closeup of chips and buses on a controller board.

The main controller board inside the system unit is called a **system board** or **motherboard**. It supplies all the electrical connections for the computer's components. Figure 3-31 shows a system unit and its components which are anchored to the system board.

Expansion slots provide a place to connect controller boards to the system board. Connector pins, like those in Figure 3-30, connect any add-on controller board to the system board.

Microprocessor

The **central processing unit (CPU)**, also called a **microprocessor**, is the "brain" of the computer. It does the processing in the three-part input-processing-output cycle of a computer's operations. It works hand-in-glove with special software called the operating system, which is discussed in Chapter 2. Operating system software is programmed to work directly with a specific microprocessor chip or family of chips, such as those identified in Figure 3-32.

As Figure 3-29 shows, the central processing unit may consist of one tiny thumbnail-sized chip. Its small size earns it the name "micro" processor. This tiny "engine" drives the entire computer.

FIGURE 3-30
An "add-on" controller board populated
with integrated circuit chips

Top view of an
integrated circuit
chip "carrier"
socketed onto
a controller board

Closeup view of
electronic
"roadways" called
"buses"

Connector pins to
attach the controller
board to one of
the system unit's
expansion slots

FIGURE 3-31
A bird's-eye view of a personal
computer's system unit

A. Power supply
B. Read-only memory (ROM) chips
C. Central processing unit (CPU) chip
D. Disk drive
E. Expansion slots (most are empty)
F. Random access memory (RAM) chips
G. System board (motherboard) covers
    floor of system unit
H. Controller board (plugged into an
    expansion slot)

Front of disk drive panel

EXAMPLES OF MICROPROCESSOR MANUFACTURERS AND PRODUCTS

Manufacturer	Product	Size in Bits	Personal Computers That Use the Chip
Intel	8088	16	IBM Personal Computer
	80286	16	IBM Personal Computer AT
	80386	32	IBM Personal System/2 Models 70 and 80
	80386SX	32	AST Premium 386/SX
	80486	32	IBM Personal System/2 Models 90 and 95
MOS Technology	6502	8	Apple II
Motorola	68000	32	Apple Macintosh Classic
	68010	32	AT&T Personal Computer 7300
	68020	32	Apple Macintosh LC
	68030	32	Apple Macintosh IIsi

FIGURE 3-32

80386-based computers are called 32-bit computers because the 80386 microprocessor chip processes information 32 bits at a time. They are more powerful than computers that process only 8 or 16 bits at a time. The number of bits a computer processes is a classic way to chart the rapid advances in computer technology. One *Computerworld* ad sums up the evolution this way: "If the auto industry had done what the computer industry has done in the last 30 years, a Rolls-Royce would cost $2.50 and get 2 million miles per gallon."

A major design goal of the 80386 microprocessor was to be **downward** or **backward compatible**, which is the ability to run applications designed for older microprocessors without alteration. It does this in what is called its **real mode**, which mimics an old 8088 microprocessor. This includes a limitation to address only 1 megabyte of memory, as listed on the comparison chart in Figure 3-33. Traditionally, this means running only one old DOS application at a time.

But the 80386 was evolutionary and introduced two other modes of operations, the protected mode and the virtual 86 mode. **Protected mode** makes multitasking, the ability to execute concurrently two or more tasks, possible. *Protection* refers to preventing two or more applications from trespassing into each other's territory. Protected mode can address up to 4 gigabytes (billions of bytes) of memory. Operating System/2 (OS/2) runs in this mode.

Virtual 86 mode duplicates real mode, but does it many times over. Instead of one DOS application, a user can run many of them. This mode allows a user to continue to use all old software with a master control program such as Windows.

Memory

Programs and data must reside in **random access memory (RAM)**, also simply called **memory**, before they are processed by the central processing unit.

Memory is temporary storage. If the computer power is turned off, every-

EVOLUTION OF A MICROPROCESSOR

	MICROPROCESSOR: INTEL MODEL NUMBER		
	8088	80286	80386/486
Clock speed (in megahertz, millions of clock cycles per second)	4.77 MHz	10–16 MHz	16–33+ MHz
Operating system optimized for the microprocessor	DOS	OS/2	Windows program with DOS
Multitasking	No	Yes	Yes
Processes data at one time	16 bits	16 bits	32 bits
Memory size (bytes it can work with, or "address," directly)	1 megabyte (although DOS addresses only 640 kilobytes)	16 megabytes	4 gigabytes
Virtual memory size (bytes it can address indirectly; "virtual" memory uses the disk as a substitute for real memory)	None	1 gigabyte	64 terabytes

Note:
  Kilobyte = One thousand bytes, or 1 Kbyte
Megabyte = One million bytes, or 1 Mbyte
 Gigabyte = One billion bytes, or 1 Gbyte
 Terabyte = One trillion bytes, or 1 Tbyte

FIGURE 3-33

thing in it is lost. That is why programs and data are permanently stored on disks. Whenever a program is needed, a copy of it is first loaded from a disk into memory and then processed.

The amount of memory needed depends, in part, on the largest program to be resident there. A program's memory requirements are published with software packages.

Every byte in random access memory, as the name implies, is randomly addressable. The central processing unit can instantly access any one of the locations that a program resident there may require. Each location stores eight bits, or the equivalent of one character.

Unlike random access memory, **read-only memory (ROM)** offers permanent storage. It consists of a few special-purpose chips on the system board. They come preprogrammed with instructions that do not disappear when the power is turned off. Usually read-only memory contains utility programs that

- Put images on the screen
- Give the keyboard keys their special control capabilities
- Start the computer

Starting the computer from scratch is referred to as a **cold boot**. The phrase comes from an old expression to "pull yourself up by your bootstraps." Read-only memory contains the *bootstrap program*. A **warm boot** refers to restarting a program with the machine already powered on.

STANDARD ARCHITECTURES

In computing, the term **architecture** refers to the overall design of how a computer is built to handle its input-processing-output functions. With the introduction of IBM's Personal System/2 line, microcomputers took on some of the characteristics of their older minicomputer and mainframe cousins. It was the start of a new standard architecture in microcomputers.

Expansion slots are called *micro channel connectors* in the PS/2 line. They borrow the name "channel" from the mainframe world. In a mainframe, channels connect various components, such as disk and communication controllers, to the central processing unit. Each mainframe *controller* is a separate specialized computer in its own right. Each is designed to off-load some of the processing burden from the central processing unit (CPU).

This same architecture is implemented, in a more miniaturized way, in the newer microcomputers, as evident in Figure 3-34. The new **Micro Channel Architecture (MCA)** allows other processors, in addition to the central processing unit (CPU), to coexist and perform various processing tasks. Every micro channel processor controls its own "private" resources that are located on its own controller board. Each also has a chance to access "public" resources, such as disk storage and printers, through the micro channel bus.

Some of the possibilities using the Micro Channel Architecture include

• *Multiuser computing*, which allows more than one user to share the computer's resources

FIGURE 3-34
Diagram of the micro channel connector slots filled with optional controller boards

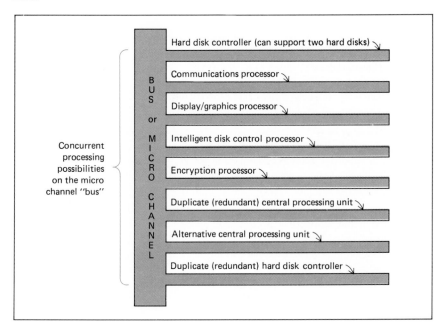

- *Fault-tolerant computing*, which kicks in a duplicate hardware component the instant a failure is detected in a primary component
- *Parallel processing*, which harnesses the power of several coprocessors for a single computing task

By comparison, the older PC AT standard, called the **Industry Standard Architecture** or **ISA**, is limited. It does not support multiple microprocessors. Another difference is the rate at which the two standards move data through the computer. ISA shifts 8-bit or 16-bit blocks of data at the rate of 2.5 to 3.5 million bytes per second. By contrast, MCA transfers 32-bit chunks at 20 million bytes per second. This makes MCA capable of handling heavier input/output traffic, such as that found in networks and multiuser environments.

As an alternative to IBM's Micro Channel Architecture, major manufacturers developed **Expanded Industry Standard Architecture**, or **EISA**. EISA is very similar to MCA, with a 32-bit data bus and the capability for multiple processors and multiuser computing. The main difference is that EISA is compatible with the older ISA standard. This means that PC controller boards can be removed from old computers and used in EISA slots on newer hardware.

Some industry observers maintain that most users do not need the extra speed and power provided by the newer 32-bit standards. They contend that the older PC or ISA standard is not in danger of disappearing any time soon.

FIGURE 3-35

HARDWARE EVALUATION CHECKLIST

PART ONE: GENERAL CONDITIONS

General

Is hardware compatible with the personal computer business-use standard?
Is it easy to use?
Are a large number already in use?
Are current users happy with the hardware?
Is the *User Guide* easy to follow?
Are the manufacturer's reputation and length of time in business significant?
Is the warranty period reasonable?
Is a diagnostic self-test available?
Are delivery and related costs reasonable?
Is the delay between order placement and delivery acceptable?

Installation

Who does the hardware installation at the user site?
Are required power supply and number of outlets in place?
Are other supplies, like cables, known and available?

Maintenance

Is service provided by the hardware manufacturer or another company with a good service reputation?
Are acceptable service contracts available, such as on-site, carry-in, or other options?
Are local user references about service favorable?
Is loaner hardware provided if a service emergency arises?

HARDWARE EVALUATION CHECKLIST (Continued)

PART TWO: SPECIFIC HARDWARE

System Unit

Is the microprocessor chip used considered state of the art?
Are memory increments possible (in what increment size and cost per increment)?
Are enough expansion slots provided (number available, number required for basic
    functions, number of disk types and drives supported, number of printers supported,
    number of communication ports supported)?

Keyboard

Does it have a familiar key arrangement?
Does it include a numeric keypad and programmable function keys?
Are keyboard alternatives available?

Display

Is the screen size of the display acceptable?
Does the display screen have an antiglare surface?
Are the color and resolution satisfactory?

Printer

Does print quality meet or surpass requirements?
Is speed satisfactory?
Is it compatible with the other hardware and software to be used?
Does it accept continuous-form and single-sheet paper?
Does it handle desirable paper sizes (minimum/maximum dimensions)?
Does it print copies (maximum possible)?
Does it handle graphics?
Does it produce color graphics?
Are character styles adequate?
Are changing paper and ribbon easy to do?
Is the noise level acceptable, or is a noise shield available?

Disk

Is disk storage capacity adequate?
Are backup devices available with software included?

FIGURE 3-35 (Continued)

EVALUATION

The Hardware Evaluation Checklist in Figure 3-35 can guide a systematic
evaluation and selection of personal computer hardware. The first part helps to
evaluate general concerns, such as hardware cost and maintenance. The second
part helps to evaluate specific hardware components, such as the system unit.

CASE STUDY: *Buying a Personal Computer*

I have made no attempt to recommend any specific computer: even if I could magically pick the best personal computer in the world (which would be difficult without knowing what you intend to use it for), it would probably be replaced by a better computer in a very short time.

Though I won't tell you what you should buy, I can give you some general guidelines that should be helpful.

Ask For Help.   Many people feel terribly alone when they venture into a computer store to buy their first machine. This is understandable, but not really necessary. You should be able to find several sources of information to help you make a wise choice. Friends, teachers, and business colleagues are probably the best source of information. They can tell you about their experiences and give you advice about how your specific needs would best be met by a personal computer.

Visit your local magazine shop and buy a handful of popular computer magazines. Look for a *Consumer Reports* evaluation of popular computers. Check the newspaper for information about computer shows, conferences, or fairs that may be appearing in your city.

Let the Buyer Beware.   You've probably learned over the years to be slightly suspicious of used car, real estate, insurance, and other salespeople. There is no reason why you should be any more trusting of the salespeople in the retail computer store from which you will probably buy your first personal computer. *Always remember: salespeople are in business to sell a consumer product*, not to provide a solution to your particular problem.

Never Buy Your First Computer from a Mail-Order Company or from a Discount Dealer.   Mail order is *terrific* if you know exactly what you want and if you don't expect to need any help or service after the sale. If you are buying your first computer, I would suggest that you go straight to a retail outlet that is willing to spend a lot of time answering your questions both before and after you buy your computer. This doesn't mean that you should unilaterally trust the answers you get from the salespeople in these stores, either—but at least you can ask them questions!

Many of the discount stores participate in what's known as the "gray market." They buy merchandise at distress-level discounts from reputable computer stores that find themselves stuck with excess inventory. If you buy your computer from a "discount house" like Wacky Willie's Wild and Wooly Camera, Stereo, Computer, and Lawn Care Shop, you may find yourself in great trouble if you need repair work done. Wacky Willie won't want to do it. If your warranty is still valid, he'll suggest that you send your computer back to the manufacturer. It means that you won't see it for a month or two. If you take your ailing computer to the repair shop of your local computer repair store, you'll find that the already high labor charges have been tripled for all computers purchased from Wacky Willie—or you may find that they simply refuse to touch it.

Don't Concentrate on the Hardware Features. Find Out What Software You Want First; Then Find Out What Hardware Will Accept That Software.   The most important thing is to determine what kind of software you need *first*, and then choose your hardware *second*. Most of the popular software packages will run on virtually any personal computer, but some of the more exotic ones will not.

DISCUSSION QUESTIONS

1. Before buying a personal computer, how can one take advantage of buying experience that already exists?

2. What are some sound shopping tips to give a first-time personal computer buyer?

CHAPTER SUMMARY

- The basic hardware components of a business-use personal computer include *keyboard, display, printer, disk drives*, and *system unit*.

- The first *microcomputer*, or *personal computer*, appeared in 1974.

- When other manufacturers make personal computers that can run software designed for the IBM PC, their products are called *compatibles* or *clones*.

- IBM's *Personal System/2 (PS/2)* succeeds the IBM PC and represents a new generation of computers—and potentially a new standard.

- A *keyboard* is the traditional way to get input into a computer.

- Alternatives to keyboarding include a pointer device called a *mouse, touch-sensitive displays, pen input systems, scanners*, and *voice*.

- TV-like screen *displays*, or *monitors*, are the normal device for viewing computer-processed output.

- *Controller boards* are a common way to attach devices such as displays, printers, and disk drives to the computer's system unit.

- Before buying a printer, preplanning print quality, speed, and software interface requirements is necessary.

- The main personal computer printer types are *dot-matrix* and *laser*.

- A *disk drive* is a unit that houses, and physically provides access to, disks during use by a program. *Disks* are magnetic storage media for data and programs. They can be either portable *diskettes* or *hard disks*.

- An *optical disk* is a high-capacity personal computer storage medium.

- The *system unit* is the housing unit for components that perform the actual processing in a microcomputer, such as the central processing unit, random access memory, and read-only memory. These components are *integrated circuit (IC) chips*. They reside inside the system unit on the *system board* or *motherboard*.

- A *microprocessor* is a miniature *central processing unit (CPU)* on a single integrated circuit chip. It is the "brain" of a microcomputer.

- *Random access memory (RAM)* is the place in the computer where programs and data must reside before they are processed by the central processing unit. RAM is temporary, or volatile, storage.

- *Expansion slots* provide a place to connect controller boards to the system board.

- *Read-only memory (ROM)* offers permanent storage. It contains utility programs that do not disappear when the power is turned off.

- *Architecture* refers to the overall design of how a computer is built to handle its input-processing-output functions. *Micro channel architecture (MCA)*, in IBM's PS/2 line, allows other processors, in addition to the central processing unit (CPU), to co-exist and perform various processing tasks such as *multiuser computing, fault-tolerant computing*, and *parallel processing*.

- The older PC standard is called *Industry Standard Architecture (ISA)*. A newer standard that is similar to MCA is the *Expanded Industry Standard Architecture*, or *EISA*. Unlike MCA, EISA is compatible with ISA.

- A systematic hardware evaluation considers general cost and maintenance factors, as well as specific technical detail about hardware, like display size and disk storage capacity.

SELECTED KEY TERMS

Architecture	Compatibles	Disk drive
Central processing unit (CPU)	Controller board	Diskette
Clones	Disk	Display

Dot-matrix printer
Expansion slots
Hard disk
Hardware
Integrated circuit (IC) chips
Keyboard
Laser printer

Memory
Micro Channel Architecture (MCA)
Microcomputer
Microprocessor
Mouse
Optical disk
Personal computer (PC)

Personal System/2 (PS/2)
Random access memory (RAM)
Read-only memory (ROM)
Standards
System board
System unit

REVIEW QUESTIONS

1. What are the basic components of a business-use personal computer?

2. What are clones?

3. Give examples of alternatives to keyboarding for getting information into a computer.

4. What is a controller board?

5. Before making a printer purchase, what planning is necessary? Why?

6. Describe the two main types of printers used with microcomputers.

7. Compare diskettes, hard disks, and optical disks.

8. What is a system unit? A system board?

9. What is a microprocessor? Is it the same as a microcomputer?

10. Describe the difference between random access memory (RAM) and read-only memory (ROM).

11. How are controller boards connected to the system board?

12. Define the following terms:
   a. Architecture
   b. Micro Channel Architecture (MCA)
   c. Industry Standard Architecture (ISA)
   d. Expanded Industry Standard Architecture (EISA)

13. Identify at least four items that should be carefully investigated when evaluating personal computer hardware for purchase.

EXERCISES

1. Learn what hardware your microcomputer lab has installed. The components and examples listed below can serve as a guide:
   a. System unit manufacturer (examples: IBM, Apple)
   b. System unit model (examples: Personal Computer, Macintosh)
   c. Display manufacturer (examples: IBM, NEC)
   d. Keyboard arrangement in relation to the example shown in Figure 3-6 (examples: function keys on left, cursor control keys incorporated into numeric keypad)
   e. Alternative input devices (example: mouse)
   f. Printer manufacturer (examples: IBM, Epson)

   This information is often visible on individual hardware components. If not, ask a lab consultant or ask to see the *User Guide* or *User Manual* for the hardware component in question.

2. To become more familiar with your hardware, examine the various *User Guides* or *User Manuals* that come with components. Your micro lab prob-

ably makes them available for student use. Find answers for the following:
   a. Microprocessor chip used for the central processing unit and size (bits it can process at one time)
   b. System unit clock speed (in megahertz)
   c. Memory or random access memory (RAM) storage capacity
   d. Diskette drives
      • Number installed
      • Disk size (example: 3½-inch, 5¼-inch)
      • Disk storage capacity (example: 1.2 megabytes)
   e. Hard disk drives
      • Number installed
      • Disk size
      • Disk storage capacity
   f. Display
      • Type (digital or analog)
      • Size of screen
      • Color range

g. Expansion slots
  - Number available
  - Number used—and for what (example: one for display and one for expanded memory)
h. Printer
  - Type (example: dot matrix)
  - Width (example: 80 columns)
  - Speed (example: 120 characters per second)
  - Capabilities (examples: condensed type, graphics)

3. Use this chapter as a guide to develop a list of hardware for your "ideal" microcomputer. Then shop at local computer stores for a microcomputer that meets your ideal requirements. Use the hardware evaluation guidelines in Figure 3-35 for shopping assistance. Find two or three candidate systems and compare them in a chart that covers the hardware components mentioned in Exercise 2. Be sure to include price in your comparisons. Based on an analysis of the results, write a short report explaining which hardware candidate you would buy and explain why.

4. Many diskette-based tutorials are available that can help you "Get to Know Your Hardware." If any are available in your micro lab, ask to run one. It should come with instructions for use, from power on to power off.

TMS 8 point

TMS 10 point

TMS 12 point

HELV 8 point

HELV 10 point

HELV 12 point

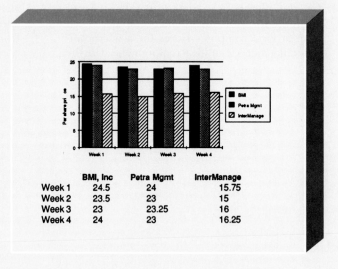

	BMI, Inc	Petra Mgmt	InterManage
Week 1	24.5	24	15.75
Week 2	23.5	23	15
Week 3	23	23.25	16
Week 4	24	23	16.25

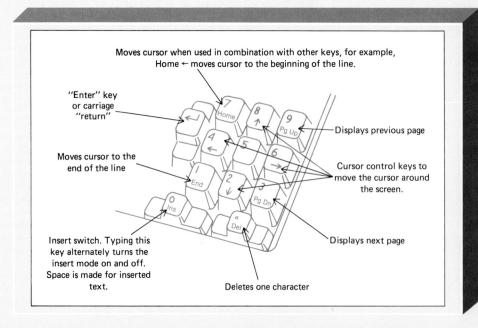

4

Word Processing and Desktop Publishing Software

AFTER READING THIS CHAPTER, YOU SHOULD BE ABLE TO

- Describe word processing software features
- Identify phases in a document's life cycle
- Describe desktop publishing and the steps necessary to create a page layout
- Initiate an evaluation of a desktop publishing system and a word processing package

---

Say you load your new copy of *WordWhiz* onto your personal computer and start to work. As you do your work over the first week or two, *WordWhiz* notices that you typically write three kinds of documents. The simplest are one-page letters. They have the date and formal inside address at the top, a "Dear so-and-so:" salutation and the usual Sincerely, John Doe at the bottom of the page.

The second style is simply a multipage letter based on the same "look" you like in one-page letters. And the third style you often use is what we'll call a report, with tight margins all round and centered boldfaced headings dropped in from time to time.

So after a few weeks, as you start a new document, *WordWhiz* decides it's probably one of those one-page letters. The screen comes up with the margins in place.

As you keep typing, it becomes clear the letter will spill over to two or more pages. Now *WordWhiz* identifies this as an example of that second type of work, and automatically inserts page headers with the style you prefer.

But what if you had at one point in this exercise hit *WordWhiz's* keystroke code for centering a heading? *WordWhiz* would have instantly realized this wasn't a letter at all, but one of those reports it had noticed you sometimes write. And it would have automatically rejiggered margins and made the other changes needed to reformat to that standard.

That kind of truly smart word processor, finally using the computer's capacity to act as an *intelligent machine*, is only a bit over the horizon.

N one of the current word processing packages, nor many of the next crop, are terribly intelligent. All extend the old typewriter metaphor, sometimes very powerfully; but none go very far beyond giving the user a faster, more muscular typewriter. In other words, they don't use the power of the computer for much beyond mechanizing the work, leaving the *approach* to that work much the same.

According to many studies, more personal computer users own a *word processing* package than any other application. This chapter explores the phases a word processing document passes through. It also looks at word processing features and package evaluation guidelines.

In many ways, preparing an effective and attractive written document is more of an art than a science. But *desktop publishing* software helps to make the job substantially easier. The second part of the chapter walks through the step-by-step procedure involved in using page composition software. Page composition software is the main ingredient in most desktop publishing systems.

The chapter concludes with a discussion of desktop publishing system evaluation considerations.

WORD PROCESSING CHARACTERISTICS

A **word processing package** provides for the automated manipulation of words in a document. It requires as much upfront work as doing the job manually. Someone has to create the words to be processed. Whether these words form a contract, a letter, or a manuscript, typing them into the computer is not much different from typing the same document on a typewriter.

It may require, in fact, learning a new command language. Even if the application is part of an integrated package with common commands throughout, learning word processing features and vocabulary, as shown in Figure 4-1, is preliminary to use.

The payoff comes when changes are needed. The ability to print a fresh original document after typing a few changes immeasurably reflects on productivity. Time saved can be spent on other tasks.

Because of the ease of producing revised drafts, changes to upgrade documents can be made more freely. Proofreading is reduced to just the changes. This encourages revision to produce even better crafted documents.

Standard word processing is divided into five phases related to a document's life cycle, as follows:

Phase in Document Life Cycle	User Action
1. Create a document	Type text on keyboard
2. Edit a document	Make corrections
3. Format a document	Insert print instructions
4. Print a document	Start printing
5. Save a document	Use document/file handling functions

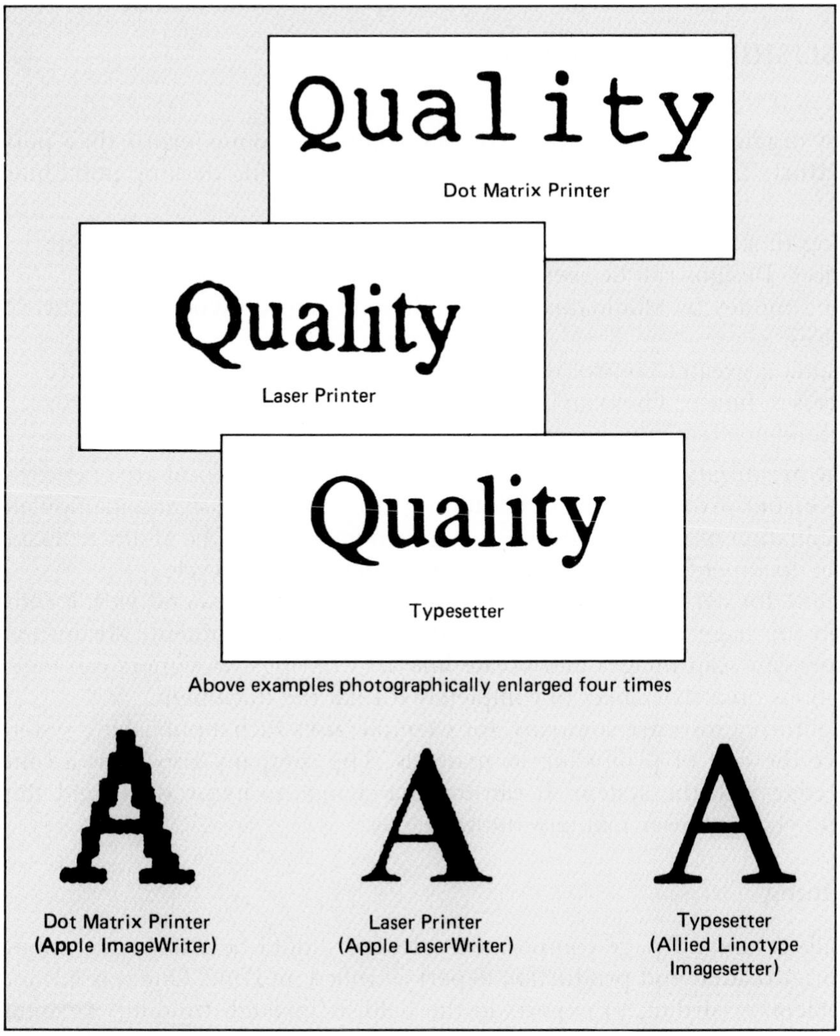

Quality

Dot Matrix Printer

Quality

Laser Printer

Quality

Typesetter

Above examples photographically enlarged four times

A   A   A

Dot Matrix Printer   **Laser Printer**   **Typesetter**
(Apple ImageWriter)   **(Apple LaserWriter)**   **(Allied Linotype**
                                                                  Imagesetter)

FIGURE 4-32
Samples show the comparative quality of output from a dot-matrix
printer, a laser printer, and a typesetter.

typesetter. A **typesetter** (also called phototypesetter or imagesetter) is machinery that uses photographic processes to produce a page image on photosensitive paper for reproduction.

Many typesetters are equipped to read a document file produced by microcomputer page composition software. Because of this, the quality of a finished document can be upgraded without any additional effort except to print it on a typesetter.

Some typesetting services accept a page layout file that is sent by modem.

The magic that enables a document file to drive a typesetter as easily as it drives a laser printer is called a **page description language (PDL)**. A PDL is a system for coding document files in order to make the files acceptable to laser printers, typesetters, or any other device that can read the coded PDL file. File coding is done automatically by most page composition packages.

PUBLISHING: THE MODERN METHOD

Many organizations have acquired microcomputers to modernize their publishing effort. The benefits they hope to realize from using desktop publishing include

- Saving time by eliminating the communication delays of using outside services. Designs can be seen almost instantly instead of in days.
- Saving money by eliminating the purchase of outside type and layout services.
- Regaining greater control of publishing projects by moving the entire process in-house. They can better meet deadlines and use trial and error to stimulate creativity.

Some organizations use page composition software on a local-area network. It allows anyone involved in the publication effort to view, adjust, and manipulate any combination of text and graphics. A group member can be at any workstation. The document can be at any stage of its development cycle.

Writers, for example, can enter text at their workstations and view it composed on the page as it will appear in the completed document. Meanwhile, illustrators can scan images and create line art drawings. Designers can enter specifications on a style sheet to completely format the document.

A California software company, for example, uses such a publishing system to reduce the cost of producing its manuals. The company also gains a competitive edge with the system. It can make a change to its products and ship them with changed user manuals the same day.

Training

Ideally, a user of page composition software should be a designer, editor, writer, proofreader, and production expert all rolled into one. One way around this problem, according to experts in the field, is through training. Training should at least cover the basics of design and how to use page composition software.

All trainers seem to agree that mastering the basics of good visual communications is essential. Otherwise, a document's message may be confusing and unappealing.

EVALUATION

Any desktop publishing evaluation begins by asking questions such as these:
- What kind of documents are to be created with the desktop publishing system?
- What is the average length of the documents?
- What are the time and costs to produce documents using the current production process?
- What type of improvements over the present production method can be achieved?

PAGE COMPOSITION SOFTWARE EVALUATION CHECKLIST

- Is the package WYSIWYG (what you see is what you get), which combines text and graphics on the screen and prints pages that match (or nearly match) the screen version?
- Does it provide both automatic and manual hyphenation and justification?
- Can the package import word processing files with format characteristics intact?
- Does text automatically wrap around a graphic and continue to the next column, page, or assigned location?
- Can most popular graphics files be imported?
- Can graphics be cropped and resized?
- What tools are available for creating lines, boxes, and so on?
- Are templates available? Can new layout templates or style sheets be created?
- Is hardware required at an affordable price?
- Are training and support available?

(Figure 10-9, General Software Evaluation Checklist, is necessary to complete this evaluation.)

FIGURE 4-33

With answers in hand, it is then necessary to evaluate available software and hardware. The main software component in most cases is a page composition package. An evaluation checklist, such as the one in Figure 4-33, is drawn up to support the software search. It focuses on topics covered in this chapter.

Equally important is the hardware evaluation. Some companies sell turnkey desktop publishing systems, such as the one shown in Figure 4-22. Systems usually come with a microcomputer, a laser printer, and a scanner.

CASE STUDY: *Setting Up for Desktop Publishing*

As its best records charge up the pop music charts, Arista Records sends out weekly fliers to dealers around the country. The fliers keep dealers informed of the recording artists' concert tours and chart ratings. But when Arista released several records in one week from several of its major artists, the record maker wasn't able to generate fliers fast enough. Designers in Arista's Creative Services department found themselves staying until 8 or 10 o'clock at night waiting for type to come back from the company's in-house typesetters.

Needing a quick and efficient way to produce fliers, Creative Services invested in a desktop publishing system. While it met the goals of speed and efficiency, setting it up turned out to be more work than staff members anticipated.

"We learned that in order for the page composition package to work with the typesetting equipment we have, we needed to upgrade the software," said Millie DeFino, administrative assistant of finance and administration. That meant paying $600 on top of the $695 already spent. But shortly after the new software arrived, the program's publisher declared bankruptcy. On the recommendation of an outside consultant, Arista switched to a more established page composition package.

"Then we couldn't print," recalled DeFino. "At first we thought it was the printer. We went crazy hooking it up and taking it apart. When we realized there was nothing wrong with the printer, we called the software vendor. The problem was something called handshaking. We had to put another command in the system file. It took us a week to figure all this out."

DeFino also says, "I couldn't get used to the mouse. My hand is too heavy. I have to develop that touch." Now Amy Finkle, an assistant in the Creative Services department, produces the fliers as well as promotional literature enclosed with record albums sent to radio stations. "Her job is getting bigger and bigger," explains DeFino.

DISCUSSION QUESTIONS

1. Arista discovered that buying a desktop publishing system, plugging it in, and expecting to produce documents immediately was a problem. What kind of advice do you think would have helped Arista to go about setting up for desktop publishing in a more realistic way?

2. Do you think Arista could have avoided buying software from the first (bankrupt) vendor? Why?

CHAPTER SUMMARY

- A *word processing package* provides for the automated manipulation of words in a document.

- Word processing requires as much up-front work as doing the job manually. The payoff comes when changes are required.

- The five phases of a word-processed document's life cycle are create, edit, format, print, and save a document.

- *Editing* a document means to revise or correct it.

- *Function keys* are a separate part of the keyboard that perform various tasks, depending on the software used.

- *Search and replace* are the functions used to find a word or phrase in a word-processed document and replace it with another word or phrase.

- *Formatting* concerns a document's appearance on the printed page.

- *Macros* permit the recording of keystrokes under one name and playing them back exactly as they were recorded.

- Creating *personalized form letters* involves setting up two files: a primary form letter file and a secondary file. They are merged in processing, which is often called a *mail-merge* application.

- A *spelling checker* matches words in a document with words in its dictionary for mismatches.

- A *grammar* or *style checker* picks out errors a spelling checker would ignore, such as selected spellings (for example, cannot), archaic words, and awkward usage.

- When evaluating word processing packages, it is important to consider the end product desired. Other considerations are the desirability of a "what you see is what you get" display and the speed and convenience of basic editing tasks.

- An *outline processor* helps to organize thoughts on a screen in outline form. Hierarchic outline levels can be expanded or collapsed as desired.

- A *text-based data manager* allows a user to write notes marked with keywords for later search, retrieval, and organization.

- *Hypertext* is an electronic system for organizing and presenting information nonsequentially.

- *Desktop publishing* refers to the use of microcomputers and other hardware, as well as software, to produce documents for publication purposes.

- A *page composition package* replaces a drafting table, scissors, and glue with electronic assembly of text and graphics.

- The four steps necessary to assemble a page layout electronically are: prepare text and graphic files, develop a document format, bring in graphic and text files to the page layout, and print.

- A *format* defines the appearance of a document in terms of its number of columns and other standing design elements.

- A *font* is a complete set of characters in one typeface and size. A *typeface* is a designed set of characters with a name.

- A *typesetter* is machinery that uses photographic processes to produce a page image on photosensitive paper.

- A *page description language (PDL)* is a system for coding document files in order to make the files acceptable to laser printers, typesetters, and other devices.

SELECTED KEY TERMS

Desktop publishing	Hypertext	Page description language (PDL)
Editing	Macro	Search and replace
Font	Mail merge	Spelling checker
Format	Master pages	Text-based data manager
Formatting	On-line help	Typeface
Function keys	Outline processor	Typesetter
Grammar checker	Page composition package	Word processing package

REVIEW QUESTIONS

1. Identify the five phases in a word processed document's life cycle.

2. What is search and replace used for?

3. Give an example of how a macro can enhance word processing productivity.

4. Compare spelling with grammar checker packages.

5. Diagram how to create personalized form letters with a word processing mail-merge application.

6. What are three important guidelines when evaluating word processing packages?

7. Compare outline processors with text-based data management packages.

8. What is hypertext?

9. What is desktop publishing?

10. What is a page composition package used for?

11. Briefly describe the steps necessary to assemble a page layout electronically.

12. What is a page description language?

EXERCISES

1. *Brighton Company Case.* Assume that the Brighton Company marketing manager has asked you to research recent computer periodicals and to prepare a report on the most appropriate word processing package for general department use. All except one in the department are hunt-and-peck typists. They will need to produce
   • Company memos
   • Customer correspondence
   • Marketing reports (five pages maximum)
   Budget is no problem. The report should compare three word processing packages. Use the evaluation checklist in Figure 4-14 as a guide to desirable features. Pick one package that you think is the best for Brighton's marketing department personnel. Justify your recommendation.

2. *Brighton Company Case.* A full evaluation of a word processing package for the Brighton Company project requires a hands-on test of the package.

   Assume whatever word processing package that you have access to is a candidate package. Use the document in Figure 4-1 as the test document to evaluate how well the word processing package can perform all the features illustrated. Write a report on the results of this test.

3. *Alton College Case.* Assume that you are a student assistant in the registrar's office at Alton College. The registrar asks you to research and recommend the purchase of a suitable page composition package. The office's publishing needs are mainly for long, text-intensive documents, such as a schedule of courses and classes for each term, and various shorter documents. Examine package reviews in current microcomputer periodicals and make a comparative report of two suitable packages. End the report by recommending the one that would be the better purchase, and justify your recommendation.

(

Victory Sportshoe
Administration Expenses

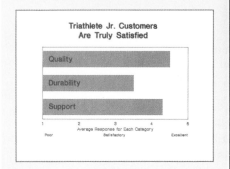

Triathlete Jr. Customers
Are Truly Satisfied

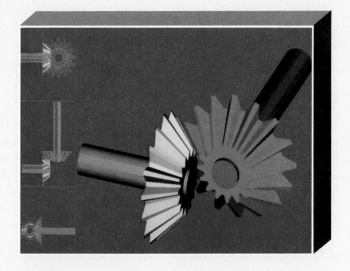

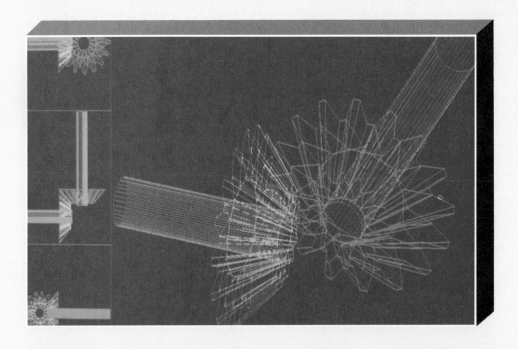

5

Spreadsheet and Graphics Software

AFTER READING THIS CHAPTER, YOU SHOULD BE ABLE TO

- Identify spreadsheet software uses and features
- Describe uses for business graphics packages as well as for painting, imaging, and computer-aided design packages
- Initiate evaluations of spreadsheet and graphics packages

"I can't see the forest for the trees," Michael Lomar thinks to himself more than once after looking at a spreadsheet. Mr. Lomar is a dairy specialist for a large food broker in the southwest. He regularly attends annual meetings with presidents of the clients he represents. "My job is basically sales," says Lomar. "In sales, you need every aid you can get, so charts become tools of the trade."

The numbers that make up Mr. Lomar's charts are compiled from industry and sales data he keeps in spreadsheet files. But he has learned that masses of numbers sometimes hide important facts and figures. That is why he converts his spreadsheets into graphical form.

Most of Lomar's attention is directed toward finding the correct graph style and making sure the data are clear. For instance, Lomar has learned that to show detailed statistics, he should use a line chart instead of a bar chart. Then to give a graph a professional, typeset look, he uses his software's optional features to create labels and headings.

One thing Lomar has discovered, however, is that no matter how professionally done the charts may be, some people distrust charts entirely. "This person figures you've gone to a lot of trouble to make this chart, so you must be trying to manipulate the data," says Lomar. "They still need to see the spreadsheet numbers."

M r. Lomar is one of many business professionals who use spreadsheet and graphics software to analyze data and display the results.

The first part of this chapter "walks through" how a decision maker uses an electronic *spreadsheet* to help solve number-oriented problems. In doing so, it illustrates this computer age tool's impact on improving personal productivity. Spreadsheet features, problems, and guidelines for evaluation are also examined.

Since business users increasingly turn to visual charts or graphics to analyze volumes of numbers, the second part of this chapter examines graphics software. Users do not have to be graphic artists to create professional-looking graphs.

This section reviews both *analytic* and *presentation business graphics* packages. It also covers painting, imaging, and computer-aided design software, as well as multimedia and guidelines for evaluating graphics software.

SPREADSHEET CHARACTERISTICS

An electronic **spreadsheet** is a convenient tool to explore problems that can be defined numerically in row-and-column format. It is an automated version of the traditional pencil-and-paper method of analyzing numeric data.

To compare manual and automated techniques of problem analysis, suppose that a marketing manager at Interstate Distributing Company prepares a table of sales projections for one of the company's sports lines of baseball bats. Figure 5-1 shows the table using conventional scratch pad, calculator, and pencil.

Now suppose that an electronic spreadsheet is used to do the projections. What differences would there be? The answer is that initially, except for numbers in the total column, none. In other words, the burden of developing the planning model is the planner's. Primary numbers in the spreadsheet have to be manually entered into the computer. In addition, the planner must precisely define relationships between numbers on the spreadsheet.

In Figure 5-1, totals reflect the result of units times price. The relationship of the two columns is important to the spreadsheet. It gets typed into the computer as a simple $A \times B = C$ formula. The formula stays hidden while a result flashes on the computer's screen.

FIGURE 5-1
Scratch pad spreadsheet prepared
with a pencil and a calculator

	PRICE	UNITS	TOTAL
B-BAT-1	12.75	100	12.75
B-BAT-2	10.98	200	2196
B-BAT-3	7.75	360	2790
		G-TOTAL	6261

This ability to memorize entered relationships gives the electronic spreadsheet its power. Whenever changes affecting stored relationships are made, the program instantly recalculates and redisplays updated values.

To use an example, assume that the marketing manager wants to know what effect there will be on totals if sales of baseball bats, type 3, fall to 300 units. With an electronic spreadsheet, typing the number for the new units is all that is needed. Instantly the total and grand total appear updated. This immediate feedback to "what if" questions makes an electronic spreadsheet a powerful, flexible analysis tool.

CREATING A SPREADSHEET

Looking over a planner's shoulder, one observes how to enter a spreadsheet on the computer. The opening screen looks like Figure 5-2, a blank spreadsheet with labeled columns and rows.

The spreadsheet program used could be any one of many available. This one happens to be Lotus 1-2-3. All commands described relate to this particular example.

Figure 5-2 illustrates only a small portion of what often is an enormous sheet of electronic paper. Undisplayed columns and rows can be scrolled into the display area by pressing the cursor control or "arrow" keys.

At the intersection of column A and row 1, called **coordinate** or **cell** A1, is the cell pointer. The **cell pointer** indicates which cell is currently activated or being considered for use.

To enter the spreadsheet shown in Figure 5-3, the planner moves the cell pointer to cell A2. After typing B-bat-1, he moves to the next cell, and the next, for the following two entries.

At the top of column B, he types in a column description. In cell B2, and

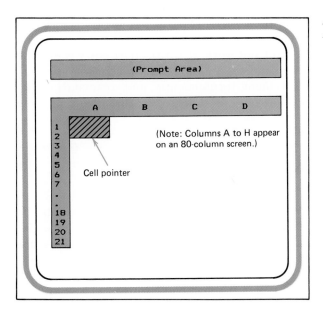

FIGURE 5-2
First screen of a typical spreadsheet

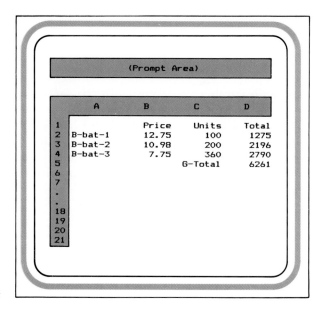

	A	B	C	D
		Price	Units	Total
1				
2	B-bat-1	12.75	100	1275
3	B-bat-2	10.98	200	2196
4	B-bat-3	7.75	360	2790
5			G-Total	6261
6				
7				
.				
.				
.				
18				
19				
20				
21				

(Prompt Area)

FIGURE 5-3
A spreadsheet of sales projections

the next two cells, he types prices. He repeats the procedure for column C. He concludes column C with the label G-Total.

Descriptive labels, numbers, or formulas can be typed into any cell. Column D requires the entry of formulas to calculate total amounts. Totals are the result of price multiplied by units.

So the planner types the formula to multiply cell B2 (price) by cell C2 (units), and the result appears instantly in D2. The formula, meanwhile, remains in the computer's memory as cell information and is not displayed.

The last item in the total column is the sum of all the items above it. Special functions such as summation make it easy to instruct the spreadsheet to add the column.

The spreadsheet entry is complete. To make it look a bit neater, a **command** is entered to right-justify labels. From a **menu bar** of command names in the prompt area, as shown in Figure 5-4, the **menu pointer** highlights the available choices. It requires pressing the enter key to indicate a command selection. Other commands include ones to save a spreadsheet on a disk as a file for later use or to print a spreadsheet on paper.

As in word processing, the up-front work of spreadsheet entry is often as labor intensive as doing the job manually. In addition, a planner has to learn about cell and menu pointer movement, formula entry, and commands from a *User Guide*. While the learning effort requires time, it does not require previous computer experience.

"WHAT IF" QUESTIONS

The payoff for all the initial effort comes in asking "what if" questions. To get a response to the "what if" question posed earlier requires only changing the number of units for baseball bats, type 3, from 360 to 300. Totals across and down instantly display the reduced figures.

A planner might consider exploring whether a price-cutting strategy is worth pursuing. "What if" the price of type 1 baseball bats drops to $11.99, causing

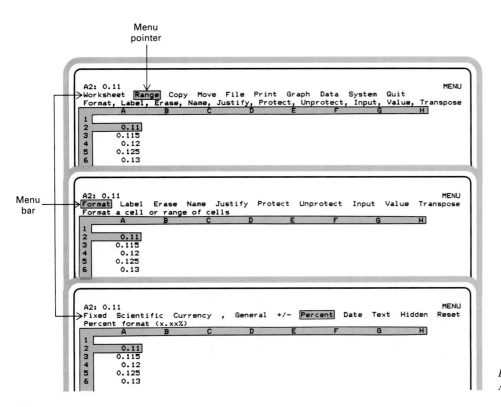

FIGURE 5-4
A menu bar and pointer

sales to climb to 150 units? Entering the new dollar and sales figures quantifies this assumption. The instantly available bottom line recommends that the strategy is worth more serious investigation.

One planner calculates quarterly sales on the basis of a growth rate from a base figure. The spreadsheet is shown in Figure 5-5. By changing the growth-

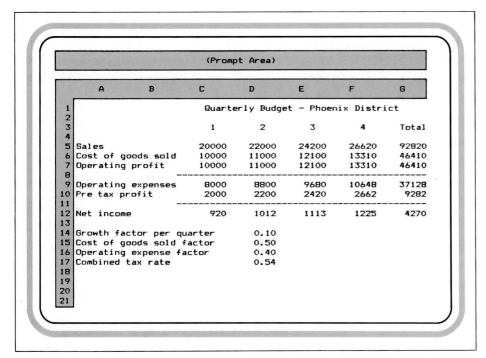

FIGURE 5-5
A spreadsheet of a quarterly budget

rate figure, the program automatically recalculates projected sales for each period. All expense and profit figures are also automatically changed.

But a spreadsheet is capable of more complex analyses. One investment manager uses it to create 5-year income statements for real estate ventures. The statements are based on about 50 revenue and cost assumptions. Any change in assumptions takes only seconds to recalculate.

PRODUCTIVITY FEATURES

Spreadsheet packages, such as those listed in Figure 5-6, share a basic set of features or commands. All help to enhance a user's personal productivity.

A **copy** feature, in particular, automatically duplicates cells across a range of rows or columns. A business forecaster preparing a 10-year plan, for example, enters figures for only the first year's column. With a few keystrokes, subsequent columns replicate the same or incremented figures in a matter of seconds. This copy feature is a great timesaving device when preparing more elaborate spreadsheets.

Equally useful are features to *insert, delete,* or *move* entire rows and columns. They can be especially helpful when a spreadsheet is finished and it is discovered that an important calculation was omitted.

A **format** feature controls the way spreadsheets are displayed. Formatting specifications might include
- Expand the width of a column
- Put two decimal places in numbers
- Position information in a column flush with the right or left margin, or centered
- Show negative numbers with a preceding minus sign, surrounded by parentheses, or displayed in red

A host of other possibilities exist to define the format for individual cells, columns, rows, or blocks of cells.

Users working with large spreadsheets find the *split-screen window* feature helpful. A vertical **split screen**, as shown in Figure 5-7, juxtaposes different

FIGURE 5-6
Examples of spreadsheet software packages

A SAMPLER

Stand-Alone Packages

Lotus 1-2-3	PFS: Professional Series
MacCalc	Quattro Pro
Microsoft Excel	Wingz For OS/2

Integrated Packages with a Spreadsheet (plus other software)

Enable/OA	SmartWare II
Integrated 7 Advanced	The Office
Microsoft Works	WordPerfect Office

	(Prompt Area)	

	A	B	C	D	E		J	K
1			Phoenix	Chicago	Boston	1	Atlanta	L. A.
2						2		
3	Sales		92820	55420	60000	3	60000	74500
4	Cost of goods sold		46410	24939	31200	4	30000	35015
5	Operating profit		46410	30481	28800	5	30000	39485
6	------------------					6	------------------	
7	Operating expenses		37128	23276	24000	7	27000	26075
8	Pre tax profit		9282	7205	4800	8	3000	13410
9	------------------					9	------------------	
10	Net income		4270	3314	2208	10	1380	6169
11						11		
12						12		
13	Break-even point		0.50	0.55	0.48	13	0.50	0.53
14						14		
15	Factors used:					15		
16	Manufacturing cost		0.50	0.45	0.52	16	0.50	0.47
17	Operating expenses		0.40	0.42	0.40	17	0.45	0.35
18	Combined tax rate (all)			0.54		18		
19						19		
20						20		
21						21		

FIGURE 5-7
A spreadsheet with a vertically split screen

sections of a spreadsheet. This can be valuable for comparative analysis. Horizontal splits are also possible.

A related feature, often called *titles*, locks in a row or column on the display. The secured title area, usually at the top or left edge of the screen, remains in place regardless of which rows or columns are selected for viewing.

Most spreadsheets can also be protected against unauthorized use or changes. A **protected spreadsheet** locks in ranges of cells that do not need updating. The cursor moves from one unprotected cell to another whenever the return key is typed. It simplifies updating the spreadsheet. It also helps to prevent accidental changes.

Built-In Functions

The availability of **built-in functions**, like summation, further support a user's personal productivity. Functions are equivalent to prepared formulas. They eliminate the need to create common formulas from scratch. In addition to *sum, average,* and *count*, generally *minimum* and *maximum* are available. Financial functions, such as *internal rate of return* and *net present value*, are also common. Many include statistical functions like *variance, standard deviation,* and *frequency distribution*. A small list of some available functions appears in Figure 5-8, which shows the common SUM function being selected with a mouse.

The spreadsheet in Figure 5-8 uses a mouse to move the pointer to list choices. Hitting the mouse button selects whatever function the pointer is resting on. By contrast, other spreadsheets require typing the "@" key to signal a function selection, followed by the function name, such as @SUM.

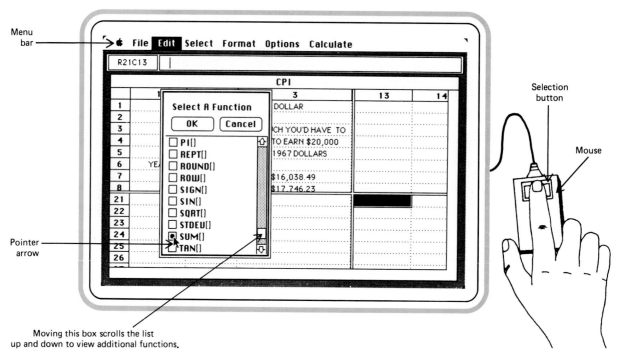

Menu bar

Selection button

Mouse

Pointer arrow

Moving this box scrolls the list
up and down to view additional functions.

FIGURE 5-8
Selecting the SUM function from a list of available functions. The list
pointer arrow is moved by the mouse.

Macros

To create a sophisticated spreadsheet for reuse by others requires a spreadsheet with a macro capability. A **macro** capability means a programming capability, as shown in Figure 5-9. Programmers and experienced spreadsheet users do not find such macro creation intimidating. After a programmer prepares the master spreadsheet, called a **template**, it is copied for circulation to users.

A user types only a keystroke or keyword to activate a macro. This is why macros are sometimes called "the typing alternative." They allow a user to replace a block of keystrokes with a simple key entry.

More spreadsheet packages are allowing the effortless creation of macros. As shown in Figure 5-10, one has a menu item called "Macro" and another called "Set Recorder." By selecting both menu items, every keystroke is translated into the program's macro language and saved for later reuse. The user never has to learn the macro language, because the macros are automatically created. Sample macros created by the "recorder" appear in the "sample macros" window of Figure 5-10. The recorded macros created a loan amortization spreadsheet. An example of a completed loan amortization spreadsheet appears in Figure 5-11.

Templates

A *template* is a spreadsheet without actual numbers or data. All the formulas and data relationships are in place, ready to calculate as soon as there is something other than zeros to enter. The loan amortization schedule shown in Figures 5-

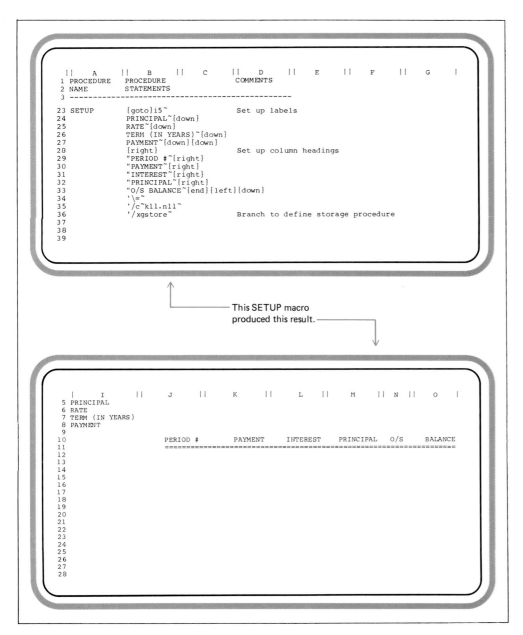

```
   ||   A    ||    B    ||   C    ||    D    ||   E    ||   F    ||   G    |
 1 PROCEDURE  PROCEDURE                COMMENTS
 2 NAME       STATEMENTS
 3 -----------------------------------------------
23 SETUP      {goto}i5~                Set up labels
24            PRINCIPAL~{down}
25            RATE~{down}
26            TERM (IN YEARS)~{down}
27            PAYMENT~{down}{down}
28            {right}                  Set up column headings
29            "PERIOD #~{right}
30            "PAYMENT~{right}
31            "INTEREST~{right}
32            "PRINCIPAL~{right}
33            "O/S BALANCE~{end}{left}{down}
34            '\=~
35            '/c~k11.n11~
36            '/xgstore~                Branch to define storage procedure
37
38
39
```

↑ This SETUP macro
produced this result. ↓

```
   |   I    ||    J    ||    K    ||    L    ||   M    ||  N  ||   O    |
 5 PRINCIPAL
 6 RATE
 7 TERM (IN YEARS)
 8 PAYMENT
 9
10               PERIOD #     PAYMENT    INTEREST   PRINCIPAL  O/S   BALANCE
11               ===========================================================
12
13
14
15
16
17
18
19
20
21
22
23
24
25
26
27
28
```

FIGURE 5-9
A hand-coded macro named SETUP

9 and 5-11 is a template. A blank one is always ready to be used to enter new loan information.

Internally developed templates have two advantages. One is that they are used to standardize company policies and methods. For example, copies of the loan amortization template are used by all loan officers at a bank. Because of this, management knows that loan negotiations will all be based on the correct amortization formula in the template.

The second advantage of a template is that it captures expertise that can be

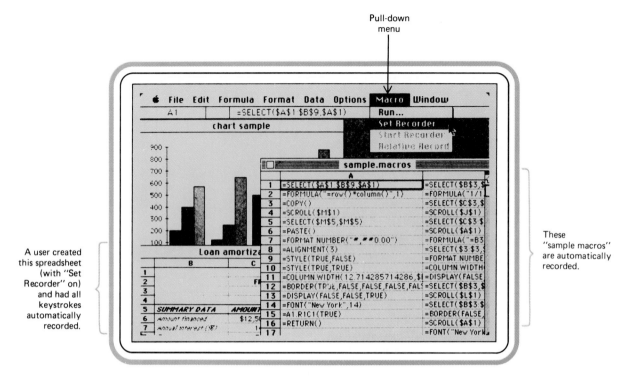

Pull-down menu

A user created this spreadsheet (with "Set Recorder" on) and had all keystrokes automatically recorded.

These "sample macros" are automatically recorded.

FIGURE 5-10
Creating macros automatically by selecting "Set Recorder" from the menu

shared. In a large organization all managers may not know how to handle a certain aspect of a quarterly report. A template can capture this expertise so that it can be passed around. As a result, it automatically raises the general level of competence in the organization.

Commercially sold templates are available in areas such as finance, real estate, and science.

FIGURE 5-11
Completed loan amortization spreadsheet

```
       |   I    ||     J    ||   K    ||    L    ||    M    || N ||    O    |
 5  PRINCIPAL        10,000.00
 6  RATE                 15.00
 7  TERM (IN YEARS)       1.00
 8  PAYMENT             902.58
 9
10                     PERIOD #     PAYMENT    INTEREST   PRINCIPAL   O/S    BALANCE
11                     ===========================================================
12
13                                                                          10,000.00
14                       1.00       902.58      125.00      777.58           9,222.42
15                       2.00       902.58      115.28      787.30           8,435.11
16                       3.00       902.58      105.44      797.14           7,637.97
17                       4.00       902.58       95.47      807.11           6,830.86
18                       5.00       902.58       85.39      817.20           6,013.66
19                       6.00       902.58       75.17      827.41           5,186.25
20                       7.00       902.58       64.83      837.75           4,348.50
21                       8.00       902.58       54.36      848.23           3,500.27
22                       9.00       902.58       43.75      858.83           2,641.44
23                      10.00       902.58       33.02      869.57           1,771.87
24                      11.00       902.58       22.15      880.43             891.44
25                      12.00       902.58       11.14      891.44                .00
26                     -----------------------------------------------
27                                10,831.00      831.00   10,000.00                .00
28                     ===========================================================
```

ADVANCED FEATURES

As spreadsheet users become more experienced, they often demand increased functionality. These users find some advanced spreadsheet features, such as those listed next, a requirement.

- **Consolidation:** Allows consolidating, or combining, data from several spreadsheets of the same format into a "master" spreadsheet. The master spreadsheet automatically reflects changes made in subordinate spreadsheets.
- **File linking:** Automatically updates common cells in multiple spreadsheets. Although called *file* linking, this feature dynamically connects individual *cells*. A linking formula causes a "target" cell in an inactive spreadsheet to be updated when changes are made to a "source" cell in an active spreadsheet.
- **Database access:** Accesses and manipulates data stored in database files.
- **Advanced graphics:** Provides various graphics features, including three-dimensional graphs and painting and drawing capabilities. Another feature allows combining a spreadsheet and a related chart in a single display, as shown in Figure 5-12.
- **Spreadsheet publishing:** Transforms spreadsheets into high-quality presentation materials with the addition of shading, boxes, lines, and type styles.

A typical spreadsheet is two-dimensional, since it is composed of rows and columns. By contrast, a **three-dimensional spreadsheet**, as shown in Figure 5-13, has rows, columns, and pages. For example, if there are five departmental managers in an organization, each department budget would be on a separate page, representing a third dimension to a consolidated summary. Another common organization is budget category (first dimension, or rows), time category (second dimension, or columns), and departments (third dimension, or pages).

Some spreadsheets allow more than three dimensions. Each dimension is considered a subset of a single multidimensional spreadsheet.

FIGURE 5-12
A spreadsheet displayed with a related graph

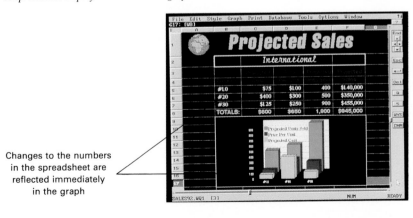

Changes to the numbers in the spreadsheet are reflected immediately in the graph

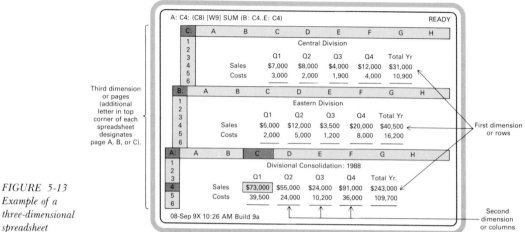

FIGURE 5-13
Example of a
three-dimensional
spreadsheet

FOCUS ON: *Designing a Spreadsheet*

Designing a good spreadsheet requires the kind of care and thought normally devoted to writing a fine letter. Just as a good word processor cannot produce a good writer, a good spreadsheet program cannot produce a good spreadsheet developer. There is no technological fix for sloppy thought or poor expression.

A well-designed spreadsheet consists of three fundamental sections: (1) the Introduction, which tells the reader what is about to appear; (2) the Initial Data and Special Formulas Section, which presents the raw material of the model; and (3) the Model Section, where the spreadsheet performs its work on the numbers.

The Introduction Section

The top of the model introduces readers to the model:

- The *title line* identifies critical information. The title should be short and memorable.
- The *description* declares the purpose. A strong description statement briefly states the goal of the model and how it is achieved.
- The *table of contents* maps the spreadsheet's organization.

Other desirable elements in the Introduction Section include *directions* on how to use the model and *references* of where important ideas in the spreadsheet model came from.

The Initial Data and Special Formulas Section

Initial data are the numbers that are known when creating the model. They should be clearly labeled and conveniently arranged. Storing these data in a separate section makes it easier to ask "what if" questions that depend on varying the initial data. It also makes changing the initial data easier than if the data were hidden in formulas in the Model Section.

It is also the responsibility of this section to explain what assumptions are embedded in formulas from the Model Section.

One of the most serious errors in spreadsheet modeling is that of burying a raw number—a constant, a factor, or a rate—in a formula. Such a raw number should *never* be submerged in a formula. Such a number must be forced to the surface and clearly labeled in the Initial Data and Special Formulas Section.

The Model Section

This section holds the spreadsheet model itself.

These guidelines are not intended to set rigid standards of design. They are intended to encourage careful spreadsheet construction.

	A	B	C	D	E	F	G
1							
2			Introduction Section				
3	Title:	INCOME STATEMENT PROJECTION					
4	Date:	February 22, 1992					
5	Author:	L. Taylor					
6	Description:	Make a five-year income statement projection based on growth					
7			percentages. Begin with gross sales, subtract cost of goods				
8			sold, taxes, and selling, general, and administrative expenses				
9			to find profit after taxes.				
10							
11	Contents:		(each section is a named range)				
12		INTRO	Introduction: Title, description, contents, and map (first section)				
13		INITIAL	Initial data and beginning assumptions (middle section)				
14		MODEL	Income statement projection (last section)				
15							
16							
17			Initial Data and Special Formulas Section				
18							
19	Initial data, beginning assumptions, and special formulas:						
20		Thousands of dollars	Units of measurement				
21		1992	Starting year				
22		2%	Gross sales growth				
23		5%	Labor growth				
24		7%	Materials growth				
25		5%	Overhead growth				
26		18%	Selling, general, and administrative				
27			(SG&A) rate				
28		3%	Tax rate				
29		2%	Returns and allowances rate				
30	Returns and Allowances = Gross sales * (Returns and allowances rate)						
31	Selling, general, and						
32	administrative (SG&A) expense = (SG&A rate) * Net sales						
33	Taxes = (Tax rate) * Profits before taxes						
34							

Model Section

INCOME STATEMENT PROJECTION

	1992	1993	1994	1995	1996
Gross sales	3985.00	4303.80	4648.10	5019.95	5421.55
Less returns and allowances	79.70	86.08	92.96	100.40	108.43
Net sales	3905.30	4217.72	4555.14	4919.55	5313.12
Less labor	859.17	902.13	947.23	994.60	1044.33
materials	702.95	752.16	804.81	861.14	921.42
overhead	1288.75	1353.19	1420.85	1491.89	1566.48
Cost of goods sold	2950.87	3007.47	3172.89	3347.63	3532.23
Gross profit	1054.43	1210.25	1382.25	1571.92	1780.88
Selling, general, and administrative expense	702.95	759.19	819.93	885.52	956.36
Profit before taxes	351.48	451.06	562.33	686.40	824.52
Taxes	105.44	135.32	168.70	205.92	247.36
Profit after taxes	246.04	315.74	393.63	480.48	577.16

ADD-ON PRODUCTS

Add-ons or **add-ins**, in the software industry, are packages created to add value to other, more widely used, packages. In the spreadsheet market, most of this software is written to add value to the Lotus 1-2-3 package.

Many add-on packages are actually *patches* to improve weaknesses in the original product. In many cases, the value they add eventually gets incorporated into the original product.

Add-ons generally fall into the following categories:

Category	Comment
Database management	To view and edit database files from within a spreadsheet program.
Documentation	To attach brief notes to spreadsheet cells and produce support documentation.
File utilities	To compress spreadsheet files for storage, create backup files, increase usable memory, and recover corrupted or lost spreadsheet files.
Graphics	To enhance or add graphic features.
Macro recorders	To simplify macro creation.
Printing utilities	To rotate a spreadsheet 90 degrees for printing horizontally on one continuous sheet of paper.
Report writers	To format a spreadsheet into a polished report complete with page header and footer lines on multiple pages with margins and mixed type styles.
Word processors	To provide text editing features in the familiar spreadsheet environment.

Another type of add-on is usually sold as a template and enhances a spreadsheet with specific functionality. For example, one package adds accounting capabilities, with modules for General Ledger, Payroll, Accounts Receivable, and other functions. This type of package is ideal for a small business that does not want to get involved with accounting software. Other templates are available to write budgets and perform risk analysis for finance, insurance, real estate, and agriculture areas, among others. Templates that assist in tax preparation are also common.

RELATED ISSUES

Many organizations *standardize* on a single spreadsheet package. **Standardizing** means that all employees who need a package use the same one. It simplifies data sharing. Data sharing is accomplished, in some cases, by swapping a disk with a copy of the spreadsheet file of interest on it. Standardizing also enables an organization to benefit from volume discount buying, common training, and support.

If several different spreadsheet packages are in use, a **file conversion** or *translation* feature is usually necessary to share data. The *conversion* feature *exports* a copy of the file in a format for use on a foreign spreadsheet. The foreign spreadsheet may have to use an *import* function to retrieve the file and convert it into its native format before it can be used. Common formats for spreadsheet file exchanges include:

File Format	Comment
DIF (Data Interchange Format)	A general file exchange format
ASCII (American Standard Code for Information Interchange format)	A general file exchange format
WKS and WK1	Lotus 1-2-3 file formats

Spreadsheet files translated into ASCII, for example, also can be used in many word processing projects. The import of an ASCII file into a spreadsheet, however, usually requires some work to make it usable by the program.

Spreadsheets are also used on local-area networks, minicomputers, and mainframes. When two or more people have access to a centralized spreadsheet, it is known as a **multiuser spreadsheet package**.

All users of such a package may be able to change a copy of a spreadsheet, but they cannot save their changed copy unless they rename it. This is known as **file locking**. Only the designated "owner" of the spreadsheet has permission to destroy it by saving a new spreadsheet in its place. A file-locking feature ensures that everyone is working from the same spreadsheet data. In addition, it places control for the spreadsheet numbers with a single source.

Increasingly, organizations of all sizes are saving spreadsheet data items in centralized databases. Whenever a user wants to see the data in a spreadsheet, it is made available in the user's preferred spreadsheet format. In such cases, spreadsheet items are treated the same as other database items, which are discussed in Chapter 6.

SPREADSHEET EVALUATION

Before acquiring a spreadsheet package, individual requirements that must be met by the application should be specified. The Spreadsheet Evaluation Checklist, given in Figure 5-14, helps identify requirements and provides a systematic tool for the evaluation process.

Such checklists are best used as a point of departure for more intense analyses. This is especially true if an acquisition involves a new computer that will be used to run more than the spreadsheet package.

Although most spreadsheets perform the same functions, packages differ significantly in style. Style choice is between spreadsheets that are one of the following:

- *Mouse oriented* with pull-down menus (as evident in Figure 5-8)
- *Keyboard oriented* with menu bars and commands (as evident in Figure 5-4 and related figures)

Some practice is needed to get the right hand-eye coordination to move the

---

SPREADSHEET EVALUATION CHECKLIST

Are the maximum number of rows and columns adequate?

Is the maximum cell size adequate?

Is the recalculation speed adequate?

Is it possible to turn off automatic recalculation?

Are built-in functions adequate?

Is formatting adequate?

Can spreadsheets be linked or consolidated?

Can files be transferred into and out of the program?

Are split-screen windows provided?

Is password protection possible?

Does the spreadsheet have a preferred mouse or keyboard orientation?

Does it have a macro capability?

Are business graphics supported?

Are multidimensional spreadsheets supported?

(Figure 10-9, General Software Evaluation Checklist, is necessary to complete this evaluation.)

FIGURE 5-14

FIGURE 5-15
Examples of financial modeling software packages

A SAMPLER

Micro
_____

Business Wits
Encore!Plus
Financial Wonder
IFPS/Personal
Javelin Plus
MicroSIMPLAN

Mainframes
_____

IFPS/Plus
CA-Strategem
SAS/ETS Software
SIMPLAN
System W
System/36 Strategic
  Profit Model II

pointer with a mouse. Many who have tried it like the power and convenience that this style brings to spreadsheet work.

Keyboard-oriented spreadsheets have similar menu bars. They require pressing an arrow key to reach and activate a menu option. Some experienced users skip the arrow key alternative and enter commands directly. In most cases, commands are activated with a single character, for example, "C" activates column width, and "F" activates format.

FINANCIAL MODELING PACKAGES

Many computer consultants recommend to users who outgrow spreadsheet packages that they move up to a financial modeling package, such as one of those listed in Figure 5-15. A **financial modeling package** is used to handle problems that have more dimensions and complex formulas than can easily be handled by the present generation of spreadsheet packages.

For example, one feature commonly available in financial modeling packages allows "executing formulas backwards," as one user describes it. This feature is called *goal seeking*.

To give an example, assume that a spreadsheet user has a common formula, such as Profits = (Unit Price × Number of Units Sold) − Expenses. Whenever unit price is changed, profits change. But what if the spreadsheet user wants to know the unit price necessary to achieve a specific profit? Spreadsheets traditionally have not handled going backward to show what the supporting numbers would have to be in order to produce a specific desired result.

Financial modeling software has its origin in mainframe software. It has

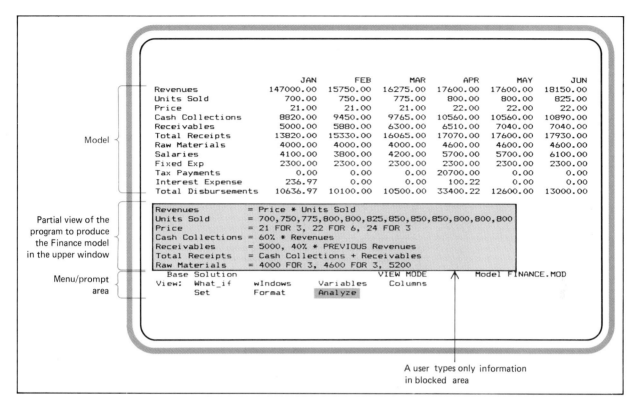

	JAN	FEB	MAR	APR	MAY	JUN
Revenues	147000.00	15750.00	16275.00	17600.00	17600.00	18150.00
Units Sold	700.00	750.00	775.00	800.00	800.00	825.00
Price	21.00	21.00	21.00	22.00	22.00	22.00
Cash Collections	8820.00	9450.00	9765.00	10560.00	10560.00	10890.00
Receivables	5000.00	5880.00	6300.00	6510.00	7040.00	7040.00
Total Receipts	13820.00	15330.00	16065.00	17070.00	17600.00	17930.00
Raw Materials	4000.00	4000.00	4000.00	4600.00	4600.00	4600.00
Salaries	4100.00	3800.00	4200.00	5700.00	5700.00	6100.00
Fixed Exp	2300.00	2300.00	2300.00	2300.00	2300.00	2300.00
Tax Payments	0.00	0.00	0.00	20700.00	0.00	0.00
Interest Expense	236.97	0.00	0.00	100.22	0.00	0.00
Total Disbursements	10636.97	10100.00	10500.00	33400.22	12600.00	13000.00

Model — (labels the upper block)

Partial view of the program to produce the Finance model in the upper window

```
Revenues         = Price * Units Sold
Units Sold       = 700,750,775,800,800,825,850,850,850,800,800,800
Price            = 21 FOR 3, 22 FOR 6, 24 FOR 3
Cash Collections = 60% * Revenues
Receivables      = 5000, 40% * PREVIOUS Revenues
Total Receipts   = Cash Collections + Receivables
Raw Materials    = 4000 FOR 3, 4600 FOR 3, 5200
```

Menu/prompt area

```
      Base Solution                      VIEW MODE        Model FINANCE.MOD
View: What_if      wIndows     Variables     Columns
      Set          Format      Analyze
```

A user types only information in blocked area

FIGURE 5-16
Split-screen view of a model and program produced by a financial modeling package that runs on microcomputers and mainframes

been available for years to financial specialists at large corporations. Corporations either bought the software, sometimes at a cost of over $100,000, or paid a hefty fee for its use (over telecommunication lines) to a computer time-sharing service bureau.

But the line between financial modeling and spreadsheet packages is starting to blur. More and more of the functionality once found in financial modeling packages is appearing in spreadsheet packages.

Even though the output from a financial modeling package looks like a spreadsheet, the cells are not active. They can be changed only by writing a program. A program is also necessary to load cell content, as the example in Figure 5-16 shows. To spreadsheet users, this requires an adjustment. Working on a cell-by-cell basis is replaced with programming on a line-by-line basis.

Many large organizations maintain a staff of technical support specialists who are knowledgeable about programming. They are trained to help users, and they usually design and program models for top-level decision makers.

Because decision makers are the main consumers for this type of software, both financial modeling and spreadsheet packages are often called *decision-support tools*. Such modeling tools are at the heart of any computer-based decision-support system, which is usually found in large organizations. Decision-support systems are discussed in Chapter 9, "Computer Systems in Organizations."

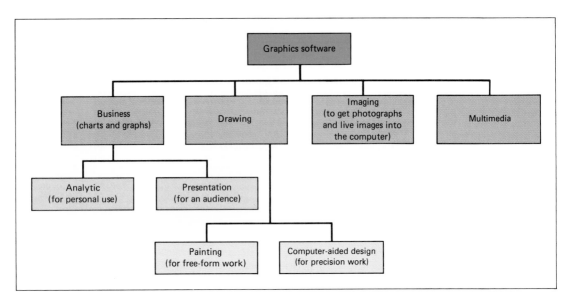

FIGURE 5-17
Categories of graphics software packages
for personal computers

GRAPHICS

Masses of numbers in a spreadsheet sometimes hide important trends and patterns. To reveal the facts underlying all the figures, many users convert their spreadsheets into a graphic format.

Using graphics for personal data analysis is called **analytic graphics**. This type of graphics feature is built into most spreadsheet packages. Sprucing up the same graph for presentation to others often requires different software called a **presentation graphics** package. Some even use painting and image processing packages.

The second half of this chapter examines the wealth of graphics software available. First it looks at **business graphics**, which is the general classification for analytic and presentation graphics, as shown in Figure 5-17. Then after a review of free-form painting packages, image processing software, and multimedia systems, the chapter concludes with a look at computer-aided design (CAD) packages.

ANALYTIC GRAPHICS

Analytic graphics are commonly used for personal data analysis. They help a decision maker analyze a problem, discern a trend, assess relationships, or study any of many other decision-related possibilities. The software produces charts that usually are viewed as *soft copy* on a display only by the spreadsheet

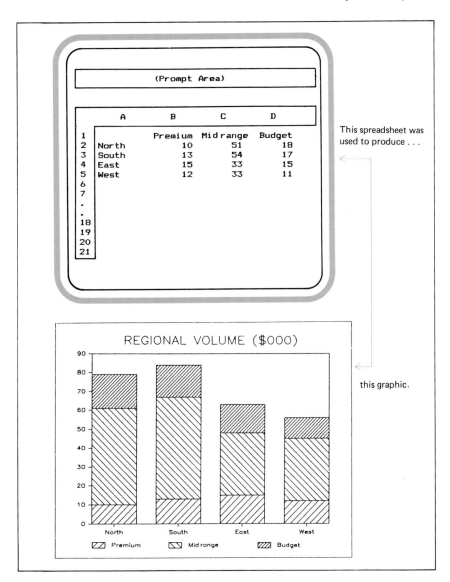

FIGURE 5-18
A spreadsheet converted into a graphic that is printed on a dot-matrix
printer

creator. If a printed or *hard copy* is desired, a standard dot-matrix personal printer
is adequate. It gives black-and-white hard copy that is useful for reference, like
the example in Figure 5-18.

With the graph shown in Figure 5-18, for example, a decision maker can
see how figures "look." In this case, they are for a new line of baseball bats that
are sold in three qualities: top-of-the-line or premium, midrange, and budget
categories. The vertical bars instantly highlight differences in how each sales
region is performing in relation to others.

When the decision maker revises the spreadsheet, changes are instantly
reflected in the graph.

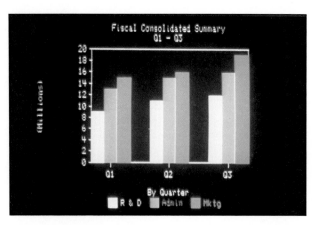

(a)

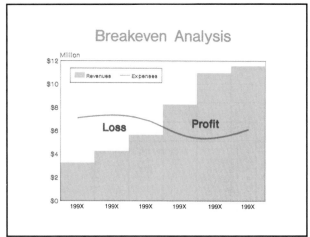

(b)

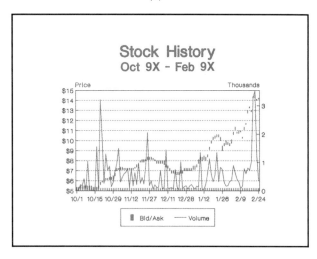

(c)

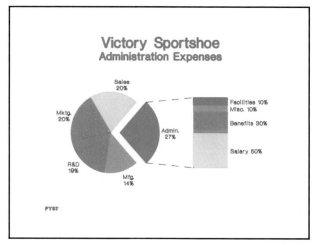

(d)

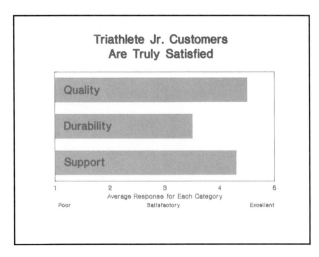

(e)

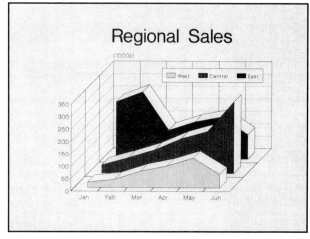

(f)

FIGURE 5-19
Examples of computer-generated presentation graphs

PRESENTATION GRAPHICS

While analytic graphics serve many decision-making needs well, sometimes users require presentation-quality graphics for

- Reports
- Business meetings
- Customer presentations

Presentation quality usually means refined colored charts, such as the ones in Figure 5-19. They have none of the "computerese" feel of the chart in Figure 5-18.

To get presentation quality usually requires an investment in more software and hardware. Presentation graphics packages, such as those listed in Figure 5-20, can cost a few hundred dollars. Graphics output devices, which include plotters like the one shown in Figure 5-21, add to the total cost. **Plotters** do more than print paper charts. They also print on plastic sheets, called *overhead transparencies,* for use in an overhead projector.

Conclusions from a Wharton Business School study convince some companies to make an investment in graphics. The study showed that an audience is twice as likely to be persuaded by a presentation with visuals than without them. It indicated that speakers with visuals appeared better prepared as well as more professional and persuasive.

Other studies show that when visuals are used, an audience remembers about 90 percent of the information compared to only 10 percent without them.

On the other hand, packages come with warnings not to overdo it. Bad

A SAMPLER

Chartmaster
Draw Applause
DrawPerfect
Freelance Plus
Harvard Graphics
Micrografx De-
  signer
Pixie
Powerpoint

FIGURE 5-20
Examples of business graphics software packages

FIGURE 5-21
A typical plotter used for printing presentation graphics

SELECTED PRESENTATION GRAPHICS GUIDELINES

Keep graphs uncluttered.
Keep them brief.
Make only one point with one graphic.

Pie Charts

Use to emphasize the relationship of the parts
  to the whole.
Consider pulled-out slices for special emphasis.

Bar Charts

Use for data arranged in segments (by month,
  year, etc.)
Use vertical or horizontal bars.
Show complex facts clearly by using multiple
  or segmented bars.

Line Graphs

Use to display trends or continuous data.
Select baseline and scale for maximum
  effectiveness.

Word Charts

Use keywords only.
Use bullets and color to highlight key points.
Break up information to make a series of graphs
  (a progressive or "build" series). Use color to show the new line
  added to each chart. Do not try to enhance
  word charts with graphic decorations.

FIGURE 5-22

FIGURE 5-23
Segmented bar chart created
with graphics software

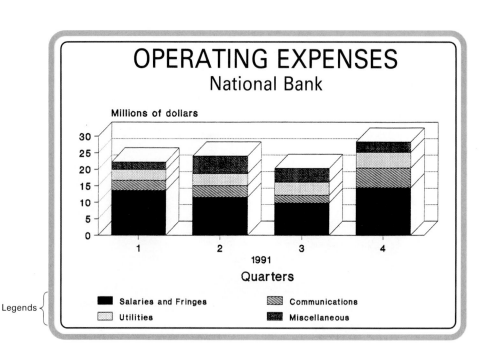

132

graphics can do more harm than good if they are oversimplified and irrelevant to the points being made. The list in Figure 5-22 covers some guidelines about creating presentation graphics.

Creating Graphs

A graphics package was used to create the stacked bar chart in Figure 5-23. It was designed and produced in about 15 minutes.

To create the chart, a user enters data into the Bar/Line Chart Data form shown in Figure 5-24. Data are entered directly into the form on the computer screen. They can also be imported from a spreadsheet file, among other options.

As evident from Figure 5-24, data entry requires four separate pages. On

FIGURE 5-24
Two of several screens used to define chart appearance

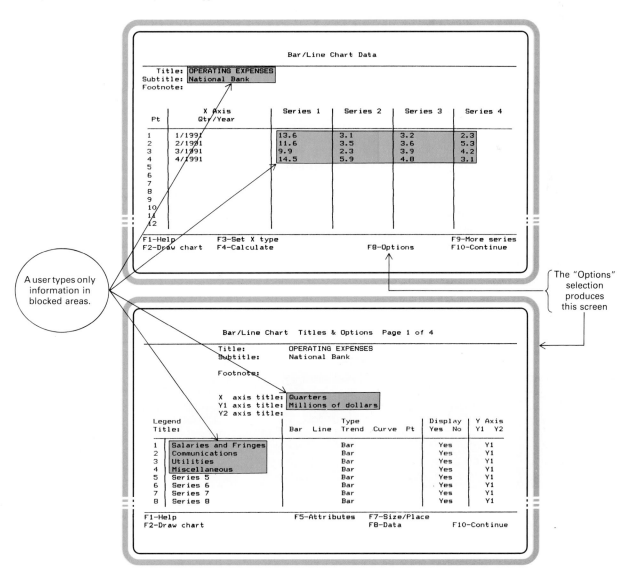

page 1, the user enters the titles and sets preferences that affect each bar on the chart. Pages 2 to 4 give options to alter the look and style of the bars, customize the graph background, and position the legends.

From any page, it is possible to *preview* the chart on the screen. **Previewing** allows a user to examine and revise things like color, fill patterns, and other selections.

While defining the graph's appearance, a user often chooses the *default* options. **Defaults** are preselected items in graphics and other types of software. For example, the creator of this chart chose to accept the default colors for the chart. But the three-dimensional effect was a default exception to give a more professional look to the graph.

In graphics software, defaults reflect a trend toward predefined chart templates or models designed by graphics experts. Chart templates specify the chart type, color schemes, type style, and label positions. A user has only to supply the specific data and text in order to produce custom, professional-looking charts. Users are also free to alter the settings and manipulate the graphics to suit their own tastes.

When finished defining options and satisfied with the result, a user sends the graphic to the plotter for a printed copy.

COLOR DISPLAY HARDWARE

Previewing is done on a high-resolution red-green-blue (RGB) monitor, or color display. All displays adhere to one of several **graphics standards**, some of which are identified in Figure 5-25.

Essentially, there are two groups of standards. The newer group belongs to the **analog graphics standards**. The older group belongs to the **digital graphics standards**.

Digital and analog technologies can be compared to an ordinary light switch

FIGURE 5-25
Resolution and colors in different graphics standards

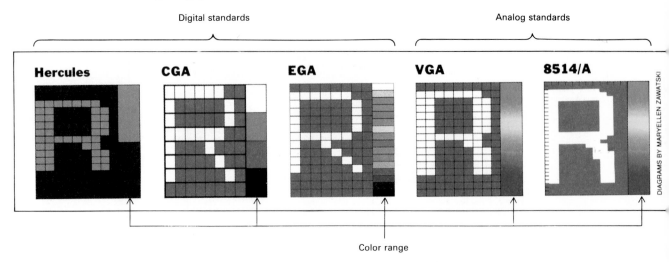

Digital standards — Analog standards

Hercules   CGA   EGA   VGA   8514/A

DIAGRAMS BY MARYELLEN ZAWATSKI

Color range

and a light dimmer. The light switch is a digital device. It is either on or off. There is no in-between variation.

This contrasts with a dimmer, which is an analog device. Turning the dial on the dimmer produces any number of in-between shadings of light. The wide range of light variations parallels the color possibilities available with the analog display.

A dominant characteristic of the analog standard is the ability to display a large number of colors simultaneously. By contrast, the digital graphics standard can display only a small range of colors simultaneously.

So-called *multiscan monitors* or *multisync monitors* accept a range of graphics standards from various graphics controller or display boards. They cost more than other types of displays. Graphics controller or display boards often double the cost of acquiring a graphics capability.

OTHER GRAPHICS HARDWARE

Once a graphic is displayed, it might be sent to a color plotter. An eight-pen plotter, like the one shown in Figure 5-21, produces a color chart in a few minutes. Producing a batch of charts often ties up the plotter and graphics workstation for hours.

To create slides for presentation requires different hardware, as shown in Figure 5-26. The hardware consists of a 35-millimeter camera attached to a recording device. It converts the computer image to the camera image. A separate shoe-box-sized piece of equipment is used to mount the film, produced by the recorder, on plastic mounts.

For companies without access to slide-making equipment, there are graphics packages that have built-in telecommunications links to overnight slide service bureaus. Users can transmit their charts without leaving the graphics program and receive professional-looking slides the next day.

SLIDE SHOWS

Some companies and individuals have eliminated slides by creating a slide show on a personal computer. A professional trainer at a major consumer electronics company, as an example, uses the *slide-show* feature in a graphics package for training purposes. When training classes are small, viewers sit around the personal computer display, which is used as a projection device. If the audience is large, the display plugs into a direct-connect projection device.

A **slide show** is a list of picture files stored on disk. To create a slide show, the trainer types the name of one or more files where graphics are stored. The slide sequence and length of time a slide should remain on the display must be indicated. A special fadeout or dissolve effect, to separate one graphic from the next, can be specified.

The slide show can be set to run automatically. The trainer can also manually advance slides or reverse them at the touch of a key.

Such a slide-show capability is becoming commonplace in presentation graphics packages. It is also available in stand-alone packages.

The package also includes *clip art*. **Clip art** refers to prestored symbol libraries ready for electronic cutting and pasting into any chart, as shown in Figure 5-

FIGURE 5-26
Computer-generated slides

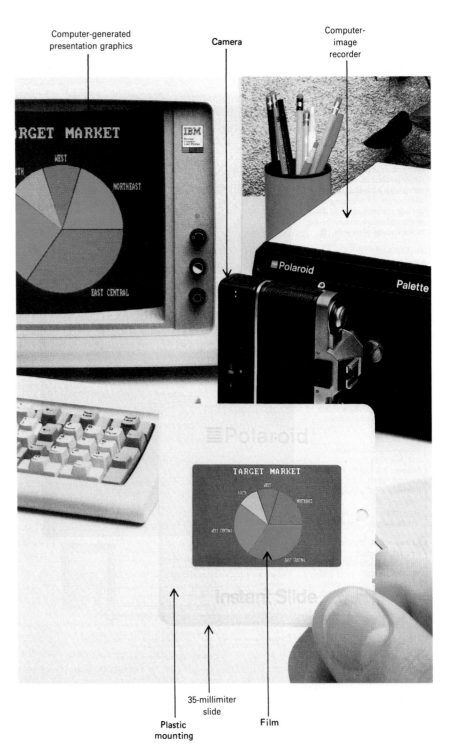

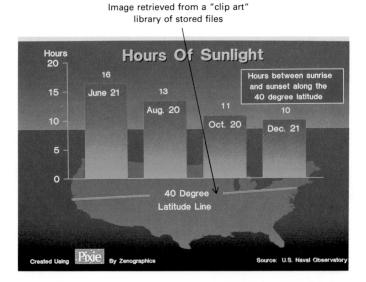

FIGURE 5-27
A graphic enhanced with a clip-art image

27. Some packages offer prestored images of world famous figures and have a "straight from the art department" look.

EVALUATING PRESENTATION GRAPHICS

A list of criteria to help evaluate business graphics appears in Figure 5-28.
Serious graphics shoppers take their most complex chart for a hands-on test of candidate software and hardware and do an "eyeball" examination of the results.

FIGURE 5-28

BUSINESS GRAPHICS EVALUATION CHECKLIST

Are standard bar, pie, and line charts available?
Can data be input automatically from popular programs?
Can data be input directly from a keyboard?
Are all other required charts provided, for example, word charts, organization charts, scatter charts, combination charts, three-dimensional charts?
Are enhancement features available, for example, free-form drawing, animation, slide shows, symbol libraries, text styles, and size options?
Can the software drive the specific graphics hardware products required, including color displays, plotters, printers, cameras, digitizers, and large-screen projectors?
Are image quality and speed requirements met or exceeded?

(Figure 10-9, General Software Evaluation Checklist, is necessary to complete this evaluation.)

Graphic output, on whatever device desired, should meet personal image quality standards for

- Smooth line and edge definition (avoiding a jagged or stair-stepped appearance)
- Solid area fills (free of streaks and voids)
- Accurate colors

In addition, evaluating the speed of graphic printing helps to determine if one chart takes 5 or 20 minutes to produce. The hard-copy device used may lock the computer out of use for other work.

PAINTING

Ever since the Apple Macintosh personal computer appeared with the attractive MacPaint package, the appeal of electronic painting has surged ahead. Some regard **electronic painting**, where the display is used like a canvas, as enormous fun but not very useful.

Others think differently. One person is a partner in a small, eight-person ad agency in North Carolina. She uses a painting program to create, for example, an ad for a shoe manufacturer. "The way the ad looks is directly influenced by something you can do with painting software," she claims. "We had the idea to show lots and lots of shoes with the caption 'What are all those tongues wagging for?' So we drew one and then used the COPY capability to make a whole collection of them on screen. We must have saved a day's work on that one ad alone."

With most painting software, such as the one used in Figure 5-29, icons symbolizing artist's tools border part of the screen. Tools are selected by a click of the mouse button. Other items, such as tool size and color, are selected the same way.

As Figure 5-29 shows, one of the outstanding features of painting software is the ability to clean up a drawing at the dot level. To improve detail, a **zoom** or *magnify* function causes an enlarged dot-by-dot pattern of a drawing section

FIGURE 5-29
Sample artwork using a painting package

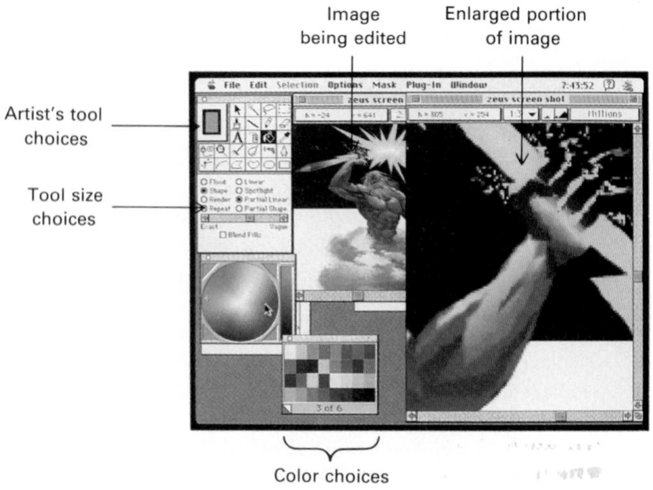

Image being edited

Enlarged portion of image

Artist's tool choices

Tool size choices

Color choices

to display. The success or failure of dot insertions or deletions can be watched in the insert screen.

Painting packages are being used in business to create ads, letterheads, company insignias or logos, and a host of other original projects. Some use them to spruce up business announcements, mailers, promotions, newsletters, and in-house publications.

Imaging Systems

Imaging systems complement painting packages. Instead of a painted image, a photograph can be used. To get an image into the computer requires additional hardware. This usually includes a scanning device, as discussed in Chapter 3, to *digitize* an image into a series of computer-readable dots. Each dot is then stored as a binary digit and manipulated just like any other computer data. Things that can be digitized include

- Maps
- Company logos
- Floor plans
- Signatures
- Live pictures
- Videocassette-recorded images

Images can be stored in black and white or color.

Figure 5-30 shows digitized photographs inserted in database records for personnel and real estate applications.

The Smithsonian Institution uses an imaging system for storage and retrieval of its sensitive, decaying archival materials. Hewlett-Packard, the computer manufacturer, uses a similar imaging system to help illustrate technical manuals.

MULTIMEDIA

Multimedia systems can combine all the graphics options discussed here, plus others, to create powerful presentations. The term **multimedia** refers to presentations that combine computer text and graphics with audio and video, which is all controlled by computer.

One multimedia presentation could, for example, include full-motion video, freeze frames from a video source such as a video camera or videodisk player, voice, music or other sounds, text, and graphics which can be animated. *Animation*, or continuous movement graphics, can be as simple as a bar chart that grows before the viewer's eyes or a complicated walkthrough of how beer is made.

The hardware and software collected to create multimedia presentations often includes

- A 386-based or better microcomputer
- A color monitor
- An erasable optical disk drive
- A multimedia controller board for digital sound, graphics, and motion video
- An **authoring system**, such as IBM's Audio Visual Connection (AVC), which is software for creating multimedia presentations
- A multitasking operating system, such as Windows or OS/2

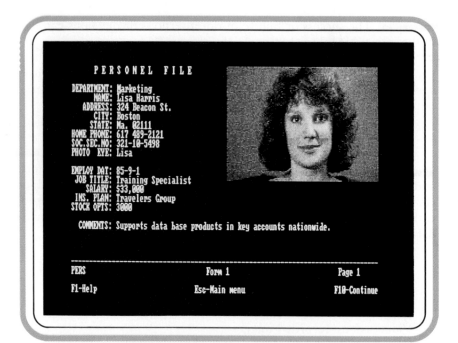

Personnel
record

Real estate
record

FIGURE 5-30

Photographs added to the database records with an imaging system

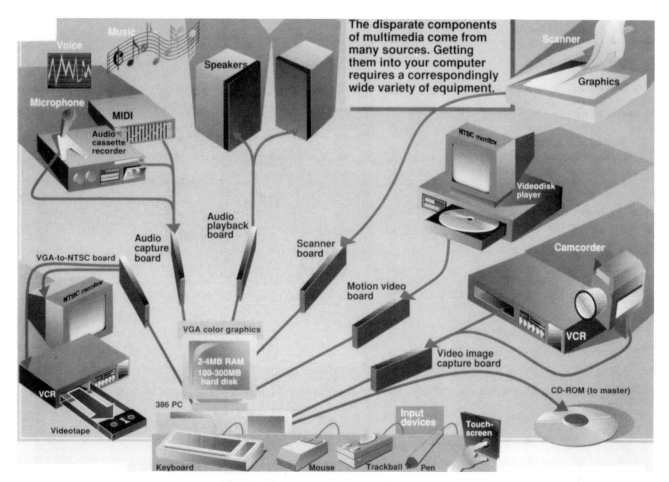

FIGURE 5-31
Multimedia hardware components

This list reflects only the *minimum* requirements. Figure 5-31 shows some other input and output components of a multimedia system. In addition, painting and drawing packages may be essential, if they are not already included in the authoring system software.

Multimedia presentations can be assembled in different ways. Figure 5-32 shows two approaches. One, in the top screen, shows the program code for a presentation. Line 1 of the program, "play shadow1," causes a digitized sound-track to begin and reach full volume over a 3-second interval. The other lines of program code similarly tell the computer what actions to take.

The bottom screen in Figure 5-32 shows a panel of icons used in a different approach to building a multimedia presentation. The icons represent the different elements of the presentation and are combined and arranged into "scenes" as appropriate.

Initial implementations of multimedia have been for training, education, and business meeting purposes, as well as monitoring and controlling operations,

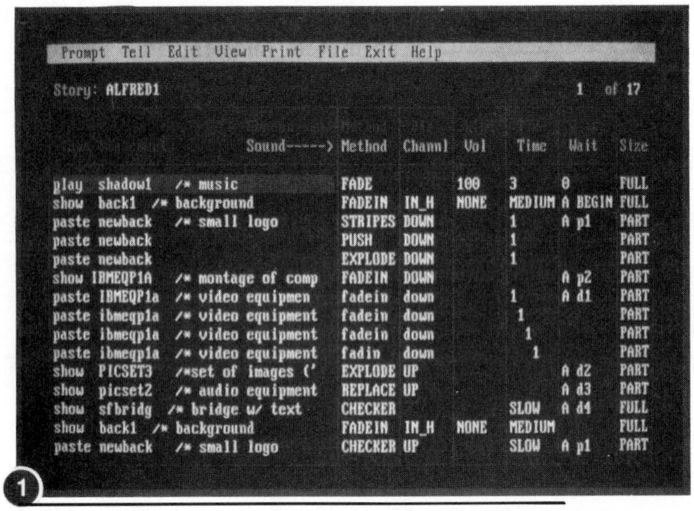

FIGURE 5-32
Two approaches to developing multimedia presentations

as shown in Figure 5-33. Most industry observers expect the potential of multimedia to be much more far-reaching. They imagine, for example, an experienced surgeon appearing in an on-screen window to coach a medical student in a simulated heart-transplant operation. In another example, a noted historian takes students on an interactive sight and sound tour of world famous ruins while students remain right at their desks.

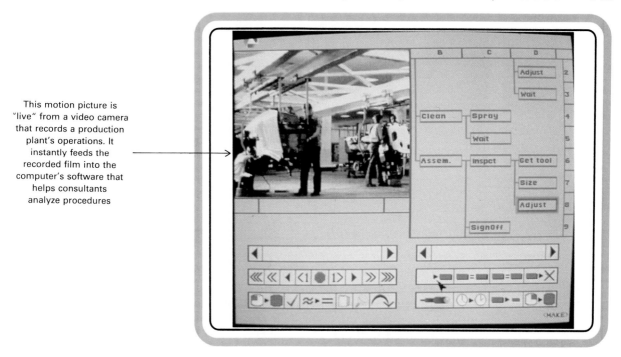

This motion picture is "live" from a video camera that records a production plant's operations. It instantly feeds the recorded film into the computer's software that helps consultants analyze procedures

FIGURE 5-33
A multimedia monitoring and control application

COMPUTER-AIDED DESIGN

Computer-aided design (CAD) packages, such as those listed in Figure 5-34, are used to create and manipulate precision-drawn objects. Professionals whose jobs involve drawing precise objects and assembling them into composite designs include

- Architects
- Civil, mechanical, electrical, and electronics engineers
- Landscape designers
- Theatrical designers
- Television and film animators
- Furniture and jewelry designers
- Model makers
- Illustrators and artists

These and other professionals who must draw objects, move them around, take them apart, and put them back together again might productively use a computer-aided design package.

A SAMPLER

Anvil-5000
AutoCAD
DesignCAD
Easy CAD
Personal Designer
VersaCAD/386

FIGURE 5-34
Examples of computer-aided design software packages

Object-Oriented versus Bit-Mapped Images

The difference between a CAD package and a painting package lies in how an image is produced and stored. A CAD package produces **object-oriented images**. They are stored as mathematical formulas that describe an object's shape.

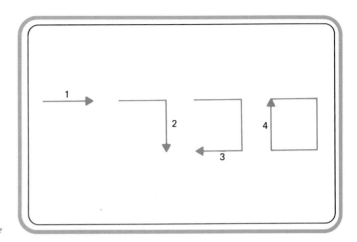

FIGURE 5-35
Creating an object-oriented image

The formula follows the path, as evident in Figure 5-35, that an imaginary pencil point takes to produce the shape, such as a square.

Painting packages, on the other hand, store **bit-mapped images**. The location of each dot making up an image is recorded by the software. The entire screen image is stored with one screen pixel represented as one or more bits of data.

Design Example

To design the floor plan shown in Figure 5-36, an architect uses a computer-aided design package. It displays a menu down the right side of the screen. He begins by setting the grid to any scale, such as 1 inch equals 1 foot. It helps to

FIGURE 5-36
A multilayered architectural plan prepared with a CAD package

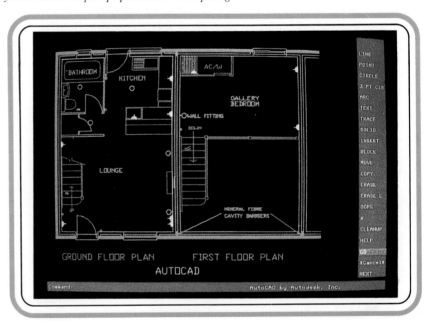

Layer 1

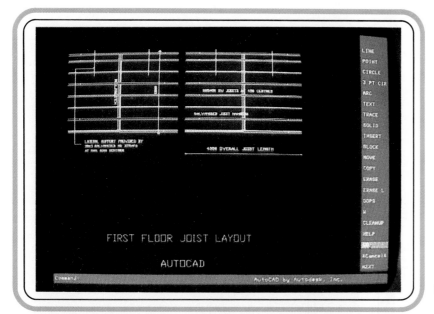

Layer 2

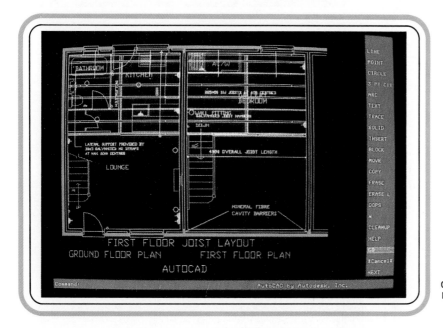

Combined
Layers 1 and 2 *FIGURE 5-36*
(Continued)

keep his floor plan scaled exactly to size. The faint grid appears in the background.

To draw a line on the screen, he simply locks in the beginning and ending points with clicks of the mouse button. The line automatically snaps to the closest grid line in perfect alignment.

Drawing a circle involves locating the circle's center point and another point on the circle itself. After the points are indicated, the circle instantly appears.

The architect often reuses drawings previously designed and stored in a **symbol library**, which is also called an *object library*. They include drawings of a staircase and a window.

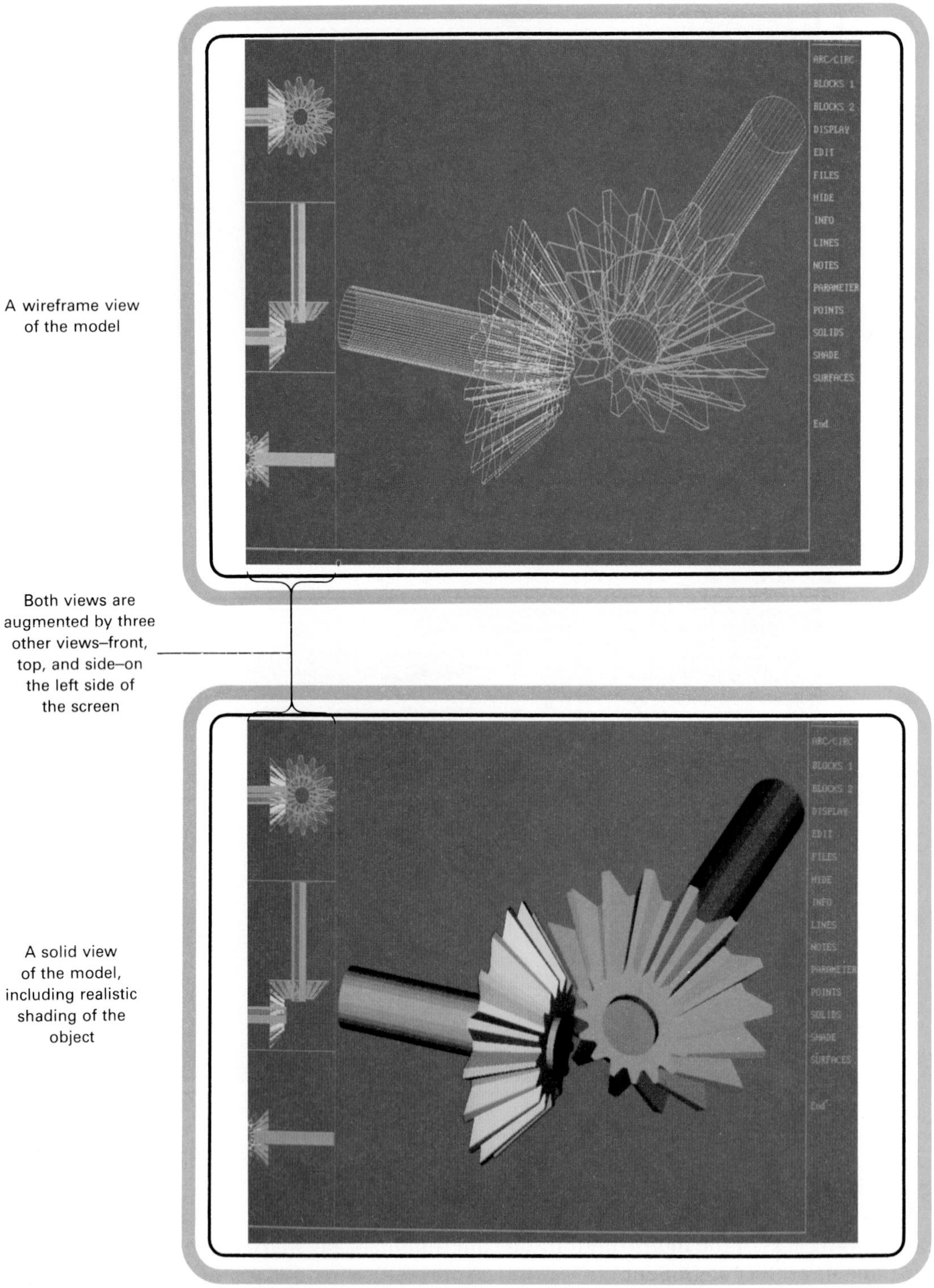
A wireframe view of the model
Both views are augmented by three other views–front, top, and side–on the left side of the screen
A solid view of the model, including realistic shading of the object
ARC/CIRC
BLOCKS 1
BLOCKS 2
DISPLAY
EDIT
FILES
HIDE
INFO
LINES
NOTES
PARAMETER
POINTS
SOLIDS
SHADE
SURFACES
End

FIGURE 5-37
Three-dimensional views provided by a CAD package

He also can place, sketch, shrink, scale, and rotate any symbol on the screen. Joining symbols creates new images for storage in the symbol library.

The floor plan in Figure 5-36 is composed of multiple layers. Copies of layers are printed in different colors for presentation to clients.

Three Dimensions

Another designer, an automotive engineer, uses a different CAD package. It enables her to define three-dimensional images. Like the example in Figure 5-37, a wireframe model is built first. It represents an object as a see-through collection of lines and curves in three-axis, or *X-Y-Z* coordinate, space. To accomplish this, the engineer defines not only the length and width dimensions of her working grid, but depth as well. This differs from the architect's package, which requires only *X* and *Y* coordinates.

A finished three-dimensional solid model of the wireframe image is shown in the second screen in Figure 5-37. Hidden lines are removed, and shading formulas are applied to produce a lifelike model.

Some benefits users of CAD packages claim include the following:
- The clarity, precision and accuracy of a CAD-generated drawing is far superior to that of a manually produced drawing.
- Multiple copies of similar or identical drawings are easily produced.
- Changes mandated by clients and engineers can easily be accommodated.
- Drawing objects to scale is simpler.
- Using library objects not only saves time but also standardizes details from drawing to drawing.

CASE STUDY: *Avoiding Spreadsheet Disaster*

While the spreadsheet affords tremendous productivity gains, it also may cause problems. The reason is simple: the computer's remarkable power to get more work done faster also creates the opportunity to make more mistakes and multiply them more rapidly.

Spreadsheet Sharing.   Errors can creep into calculations in many ways. A common mistake occurs when one person tries to adapt a spreadsheet built by another, perhaps without fully understanding the model's structure. In doing so, the second user may change or overwrite a crucial formula, introducing an error into the calculations. With luck, the error will be obvious. Occasionally, though, the error escapes detection.

Sharing spreadsheets can have another pitfall, says Rick Richardson, partner with Arthur Young & Co. in New York. "When individuals come up with a great template and share it with others, they often end up performing a staff function—training and coordinating the others who want to adopt the spreadsheet. They lose whatever productivity gain the spreadsheet helped achieve in the first place."

Formal Policies.   Accounting firms, attuned as they are to financial controls, developed some of the earliest formal spreadsheet policies and procedures. Arthur Young, for example, treats spreadsheet templates like computer programs: each requires a manual.

Corporations are following the accountants' lead in instituting spreadsheet controls.

As an example, at General Instrument Corp., all spreadsheets must be accompanied by a written narrative explaining how the model works. "There was some initial resistance on the part of some people," says Johnathan Yarmis, a personal computer analyst. "They said writing documentation would take away their initial productivity gains." Yarmis challenged them by betting that if he examined five of their spreadsheets, he could find mistakes in at least two of them. Several people took Yarmis up on the challenge—and lost.

Other Problems.   Brian Smolens, product manager for accounting software at Entre Computer Centers of Vienna, Virginia, finds another problem exists. "Lotus 1-2-3 is very seductive. Once people learn it they want to use it for everything. Many companies," he says, "may be pushing spreadsheet software to accomplish tasks that other programs can do better."

A FEW SPREADSHEETS TIPS

1. *Use templates.*   Setting up a basic model of a spreadsheet and saving a copy of the model with no data (template) will allow you to use the model again and again without wasting time re-creating it. Just load the file holding the template you've created, key in the data, and save the resulting spreadsheet under a unique name.

2. *Include cross-checks.*   A good spreadsheet model should calculate important values more than one way to cross-check the results.

3. *Experiment.*   It's easy to change values and watch the results. Do it often and you will get a better feel for spreadsheet software. Substitute some wildly optimistic or pessimistic values for your assumptions. You may gain insight into the way your model works that wouldn't come out under normal circumstances.

DISCUSSION QUESTIONS

1. "Dependence on spreadsheet programs can leave an organization vulnerable if a template designer leaves the company or is temporarily unavailable." Why could this statement be true?

2. Describe organizational spreadsheet problems and solutions.

CHAPTER SUMMARY

- Electronic *spreadsheets* are convenient tools to explore problems that can be defined numerically in row-and-column format.

- *Cells* hold numbers, labels, and formulas. They are activated by the presence of a *cell pointer* that is moved around the display by cursor control arrow keys or by a mouse.

- To ask a "what if " question requires typing a new amount in a cell. Totals across and down instantly display the changed figures.

- Spreadsheet features that enhance a user's personal productivity include an ability to *insert, delete, move, copy,* and *format* a cell, range of cells, or entire rows or columns.

- *Built-in functions* are equivalent to prepared formulas. They eliminate the need to create common formulas from scratch, like sum, average, count, minimum, and maximum.

- A *macro* is a block of program code. Only a keystroke or keyword is used to activate the program code.

- A spreadsheet *template* is a spreadsheet without numbers or data. It is often created with macros in it to simplify the work of template users.

- A *three-dimensional spreadsheet* allows for the organization and analysis of spreadsheet data by whatever criteria are appropriate, such as budget category, time period, and departments.

- *Add-ons*, or *add-ins*, in the software industry, are packages created to add value to other, more widely used, packages. Add-on packages available for the Lotus 1-2-3 package, for example, include macro recorders, printing utilities, and others.

- A *multiuser spreadsheet* is a centralized spreadsheet that allows many users access at once.

- Criteria used to evaluate spreadsheets include style, cell capacity, and ease of file transfer.

- A *financial modeling package* is used to handle problems that have more dimensions and complex formulas than can easily be handled by a spreadsheet package.

- *Business graphics* include analytic and presentation graphics.

- *Analytic graphics* are used for personal data analysis. They help a decision maker to analyze a problem, discern a trend, assess relationships, or investigate any of many other decision-related possibilities.

- *Presentation graphics* are used for presentation to others. They have a refined, versus "computerese," look.

- *Plotters* are hardware that print presentation graphics on paper or plastic sheets, called overhead transparencies.

- *Previewing* allows a user to examine and revise a graphic before printing a final copy of it.

- *Defaults* in many software packages are preselected items that simplify data entry.

- Many *graphics standards* exist for color display hardware.

- *Slide-show software* is an alternative to more expensive slide presentations.

- *Clip art* refers to prestored *symbol libraries* that hold images ready for electronic cutting and pasting into any graphic.

- Criteria used to evaluate graphics software include types of charts available, image quality, compatibility of hardware and software, and other details.

- *Painting* software allows for the free-form creation of images used to create ads, letterheads, logos, and a host of other original projects.

- *Imaging* software allows for the digitization of a photograph, or any printed (and sometimes live) images.

- *Multimedia* presentations combine computer text and graphics with audio, video, and other technologies which are all controlled by computer.

- *Computer-aided design (CAD)* software is used to create and manipulate precision-drawn objects.

SELECTED KEY TERMS

Add-ons	Copy	Painting software
Analytic graphics	Defaults	Plotter
Bit-mapped image	Financial modeling package	Presentation graphics
Built-in functions	Format	Previewing
Business graphics	Graphics standards	Slide show
Cell	Imaging software	Spreadsheet
Cell pointer	Macro	Symbol library
Clip art	Multimedia	Template
Computer-aided design (CAD)	Multiuser spreadsheet	Three-dimensional spreadsheet
Coordinate	Object-oriented image	Zoom function

REVIEW QUESTIONS

1. Describe some characteristics of electronic spreadsheets.

2. What is a cell? How is a cell pointer used?

3. Describe how to ask a spreadsheet "what if " questions.

4. Identify three common spreadsheet productivity enhancement features.

5. What are built-in functions? Give examples.

6. Differentiate between a macro and a template.

7. What are add-on packages? Give some examples.

8. List criteria to consider when evaluating spreadsheet software.

9. When is a financial modeling package useful?

10. Differentiate between analytic and presentation graphics.

11. Explain the terms defaults and previewing.

12. List criteria to consider when evaluating business graphics software.

13. Describe uses for painting, imaging, and computer-aided design software.

14. What is multimedia?

EXERCISES

1. *Phoenix District Case.* Assume that you are the corporate financial officer in charge of designing a "fill-in-the-blanks" spreadsheet template for all district offices. Use the Phoenix District spreadsheet in Figure 5-5 as a prototype of the result you want from each district.
   a. Which cells would be field protected?
   b. Which cells would contain formulas?
   c. Which cells would contain fixed numeric information?
   d. Which cells would require "fill-in-the-blanks" manual entry?

2. Try to arrange a demonstration of a mouse-oriented and a keyboard-oriented spreadsheet. If possible, try to hands-on test them yourself. Make a determination about which style is easier to learn. Explain your reasons in a report.

3. *Lark Enterprises Case.* Lark Enterprises wants to develop an in-house graphics capability. The company needs both appropriate hardware and software. You are asked to do a computer periodical literature search and write a report about your preliminary findings for the following:
   a. A graphics package that is designed for novice users who intend to create business charts and graphics, especially spreadsheet-based charts. Use the evaluation checklist in Figure 5-28 as a guide. If possible, do a hands-on test, or get a demonstration, of the recommended software.
   b. Hardware that supports the software and includes a color display and an inexpensive flatbed plotter.

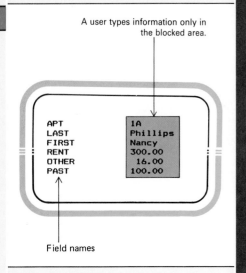

A user types information only in the blocked area.

APT	1A
LAST	Phillips
FIRST	Nancy
RENT	300.00
OTHER	16.00
PAST	100.00

Field names

A SAMPLER

File Express
FileMaker
PFS: Professional File
Q&A
Rapid File
Reflex

CONTENT OF EACH TENANT RECORD

Apartment number
Tenant last name
Tenant first name
Rent amount
Other charges amount
Past due amount

```
  Layout   Fields   Bands   Words   Go To   Print   Exit            12:19:44 pm
[········1·········2·········3·················5········6········7·········
Page      Header   Band

Page No. 999
MM/DD/YY

APT  LAST               FIRST          RENT      OTHER       PAST

Report    Intro    Band
Detail             Band
XXX XXXXXXXXXXXXXX XXXXXXXXXX 99999.99 99999.99 99999.99
Report    Summary  Band
                             99999.99 99999.99 99999.99
Page      Footer   Band




  ────────────────────────────────────────────────────────────────

Report   C:\dbase\<NEW>          Band 1/5        File:Tenant
              Add field:F5  Select:F6  Move:F7  Copy:F8  Size:Shift-F7
```

Database Software

AFTER READING THIS CHAPTER, YOU SHOULD BE ABLE TO

· Describe how to develop a database application
· Identify ways to access database files
· Initiate an evaluation of database software

Some believe we've created a data world in which information goes in but does not always come out. We've found enough ways to put information in: scanners, pen-based systems, mice, voice systems, electronic mail messages, and on and on. There is one problem with so much "more" going in: How are we supposed to get out the exact bits and pieces of information we need?

There is renewed interest in the problem of getting out specific pieces of all the "more" that goes into computers. The goal is to create database management systems that allow a user to define what kind of information is relevant to him or her. The user creates a sort of filter and priority system, which sorts through the information contained in all those hundreds and thousands of databases. Instead of getting a huge load of data dumped onto the computer (like downloading the entire *Wall Street Journal*), the user receives a sifted version based on rules about what is important, relevant, and desired.

The whole idea is to look at the computer retrieval system as an intelligent clerk or librarian. The more this assistant knows about what you're looking for, the closer it can come to getting you exactly the information you need.

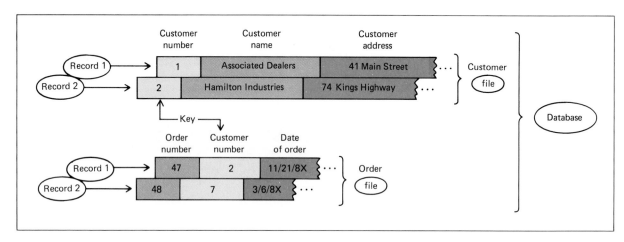

FIGURE 6-1
A collection of related files is called a database. A file consists of records.

Some users prefer to get only the information needed. Others prefer to browse a bit on their way to get the information needed. A computer-literate user of database management system software can have it both ways.

This chapter begins with a step-by-step walkthrough of how database software is used on a personal computer. In this case, an application is created for keeping a file of tenants who live in an apartment building. The file becomes the foundation of a plan to automate a business.

A **database** is a collection of related files, as shown in Figure 6-1. A **file** is a collection of one or more similar records about one subject.

Either a file manager or database management system package could be used for the tenant application described in the first part of this chapter. Simple packages are called **file managers**. They work on one file at a time. More elaborate packages are called **database management systems (DBMS)**. They can work on several files at one time.

The chapter describes how the tenant file begins as a file manager application and grows into a database management system application. This process highlights features that distinguish file manager from database management system packages.

The chapter identifies ways to access the data stored in database files. Also covered are guidelines to evaluate a database package and related database issues.

FIGURE 6-2
Examples of file manager software packages

A SAMPLER

File Express
FileMaker
PFS: Professional File
Q&A
Rapid File
Reflex

FILE MANAGERS

File manager packages, such as those listed in Figure 6-2, work on only one file at a time. They can be thought of as a single-file segment of a database management system package. Anyone who has ever had to make an organized list of anything would find them useful. A purchasing manager of a wholesale distributing company uses one to store the names of suppliers from whom he

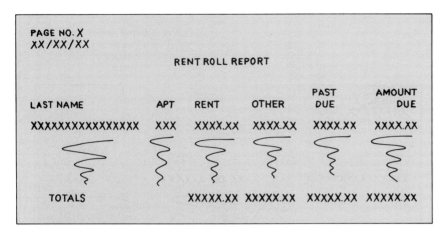

FIGURE 6-3
A rough hand-drawn layout of the Rent Roll Report

buys merchandise. A personnel assistant at a bank uses one to store lists of the bank's job titles and salary ranges. Others use file managers to store mailing lists, customer name and address lists, employee lists, and office equipment control lists, among many other things.

An apartment building owner wanted to computerize a list of tenants in her building. Instead of a file manager package, she bought a database management system package because she felt her needs eventually would outgrow a simple file manager. Nonetheless, she started slowly and used the database software as if it were an ordinary file manager.

All file management software, including file managers and database management systems, help a user to

- Create a file
- Add records to the file
- Search the file
- Sort the file
- Produce reports

But what data should be stored in the file? One approach to an answer is to use a two-step procedure, as follows:

1. Draw a *layout* of the printed list or report wanted
2. Use the report as a guide for what data should be stored in the file

Step 1: Draw a Layout

One desired report from the tenant application is a monthly list of tenants called a Rent Roll Report, as shown in Figure 6-3. The report acts as a control sheet when rent checks arrive. Checks are manually logged in on the report.

Drawing an image of the report, called a **report layout**, is straightforward. Something similar is currently prepared by hand each month.

Step 2: Use the Report to Set Up Files

The next step requires setting up what the file will contain. The two-step approach uses the report content as a guide to what data should be stored in the file.

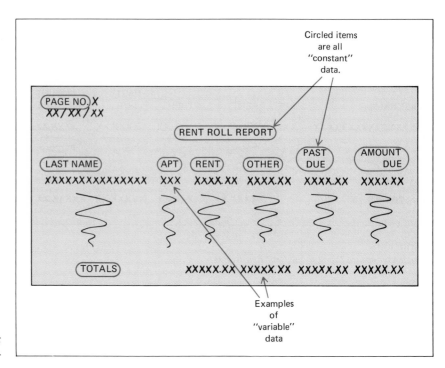

FIGURE 6-4
Constant data never change;
variable data always change.

It requires circling for deletion all the *constant data* contained in the report, as shown in the example in Figure 6-4. **Constant data**, like headings, do not change from report to report. They are not included in the file.

Uncircled items are *variable data*. **Variable data** can change each time the report is run.

Variable data can be split into primary and secondary data. Any variable that can be computed from other variables is considered **secondary data**. In Figure 6-4, the secondary data are totals. For example, amount due is the number that results from adding three primary data items: rent amount, other charges amount, and past due amount.

Primary data cannot be computed. They are the usual items included in a file, such as the items identified in Figure 6-5. Six pieces of information are needed about each individual. The tenant's first name is included in anticipation of using the full tenant name on other reports.

Figure 6-4 shows repetitious variables, which are date and page number. Most software generates these variables automatically, so they are also deleted.

To summarize this second step, the procedure used to get the record content for the file is to use the report layout and

1. Eliminate constants
2. Eliminate computed secondary data elements
3. Eliminate generated data elements (such as date and page numbers)

What is left are data for the file's record content. This simple method suffices for many personal computer applications.

With the record content and report layout in place, database software can be used as a tool to create a custom application.

FIGURE 6-5

CONTENT OF EACH TENANT RECORD

Apartment number
Tenant last name
Tenant first name
Rent amount
Other charges amount
Past due amount

Create the File

A screen like the one in Figure 6-6 helps to define what each *record* will look like in the tenant file. A **record** is divided into slots, called *fields*, to hold data. A **field** is one data element of a record. The column headings on the Rent Roll Report are used as field names.

If a field contains data that will not be used in numeric calculations, it is considered a *character* type. If a field contains a number that will be used in arithmetic calculations, it is a *numeric* type.

In Figure 6-6, a Y for yes in the "index" column tells the software that the field is a key field in the record. For example, the APT (apartment number) field is the key to answer a question about "which tenant lives in apartment 2B."

Once the record fields are established, an automatic data-entry form, like the one in Figure 6-7, appears. Each tenant record is typed into such a screen form. Once all records are completed, the tenant file can be searched.

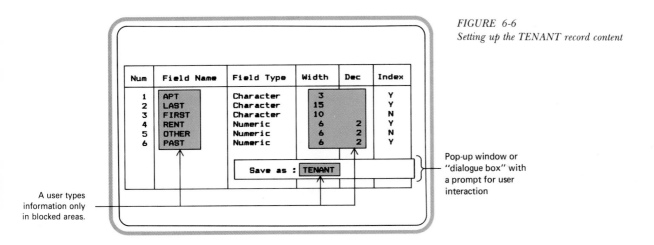

FIGURE 6-6
Setting up the TENANT record content

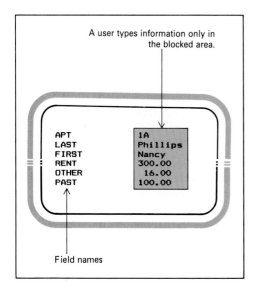

FIGURE 6-7
The first record filled with data

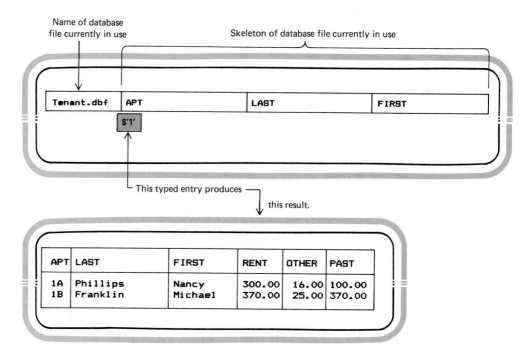

FIGURE 6-8

A query to temporarily filter the database file to select only records that have a "1" in the APT field

Search the File

The term **query** is database jargon for searching a file for records that meet specific criteria. The software's query capability can be used to ask, for example, which tenants live on the first floor in the building. This query requires the entry of a $'1' under the APT (apartment number) field, as shown in Figure 6-8. Figure 6-8 presents a skeleton of the tenant record. Only a few fields fit on the display. Hitting the tab key causes the other three fields to scroll into the display area.

The $ means "ignore all characters in the field," except for the character in quotes. This query creates a filter that sifts the database file. It selects only records that have a "1" in the apartment number field. Almost instantly the answer appears on the display.

This style of database searching is called **query by example (QBE)**. It is characterized by filling inquiry conditions into empty slots under displayed field information. Three other examples of query by example are shown in Figure 6-9.

The examples in Figure 6-10 show a second way to do searches. This **command mode** requires that a user type programlike instructions to produce any desired result. It requires a mastery of commands and command syntax. It is not appropriate for inexperienced users.

A variation of the command mode is called **structured query language (SQL)**, as illustrated in Figure 6-11. Increasingly, structured query language is becoming a kind of database access standard to exchange files with other database software.

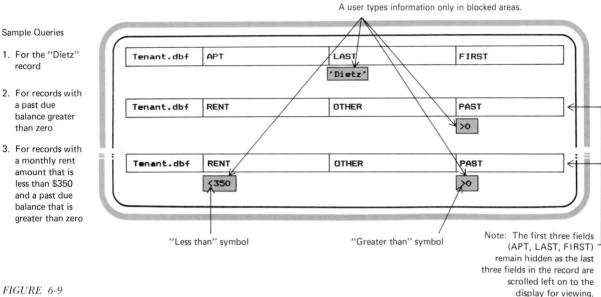

Sample Queries

1. For the "Dietz" record

2. For records with a past due balance greater than zero

3. For records with a monthly rent amount that is less than $350 and a past due balance that is greater than zero

FIGURE 6-9
Three query by example (QBE) file searches

Generally a user does not have to learn the structured query language (SQL) syntax. Instead, a simpler query by example (QBE) request may be keyboarded. The QBE request is then automatically converted by the software to an SQL request for the actual data retrieval. The data can be retrieved from a micro-

FIGURE 6-10
Examples of searching a file using commands

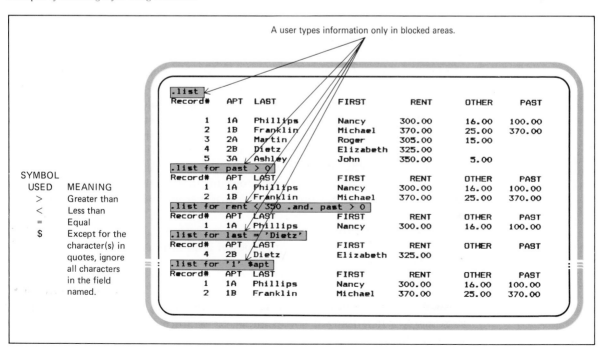

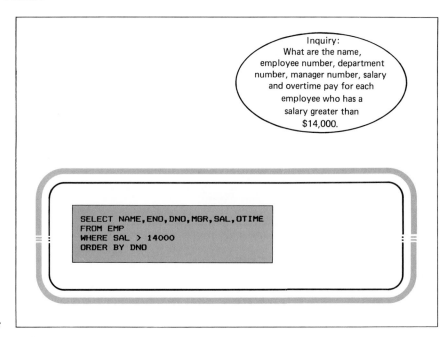

FIGURE 6-11
Structured query language style

computer, mainframe, or minicomputer database, as long as it provides a standard SQL exchange facility. This way most users never deal with the structured query language at all, even though the database, in effect, handles structured query language requests.

A third way to query database files is with **natural language**. It enables a user to query a database in plain English. A natural language package may be add-on software to some database packages and built into others.

A natural language package interprets a request based on an internal dictionary. One package has a built-in root dictionary of 600 items. A user can add more words and is restricted only by available disk space.

A dictionary might contain, as an example, the words job, occupation, work, and position. It can be told that they all mean the same thing when used in an inquiry. Words can also be defined as the result of computation or data manipulation. As an example, profit might be defined as "sales minus expenses."

Loading the dictionary is a one-time effort. A user must tell the program in which file and field to look to find every dictionary item.

If a new item is encountered during an inquiry, the dictionary can be expanded immediately. In effect, it "learns" new information as it is used. This ability to learn is a characteristic of programs that display artificial intelligence. Learning, in this case, is simply the result of loading more terms to expand the internal dictionary.

It is anticipated that natural language programs will mature over time and simplify the use of many different types of applications.

Sort the File

Database packages can also **sort** records, or place them into any alphabetic or numeric order desired. For example, to produce the sorted records shown in Figure 6-12, a user has only to instruct the software to sort on the RENT

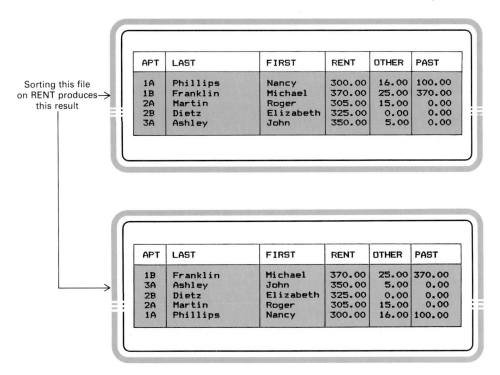

Sorting this file on RENT produces → this result

FIGURE 6-12
Example of sorting a file that requires four selection keystrokes

field in descending order. Similarly, other fields can be sorted in either ascending or descending order.

Database software traditionally produces a new file of the sorted records and leaves the original file in place. This can quickly result in a number of files with duplicate records.

To eliminate the problem of duplicate records, some database software maintains only one master file with as many *views* of it as desired. A **view** is nothing more than a sort or search request (query), saved in a special query file. The special view/query file can be reused anytime desired. When a query is rerun, all data is as current as the most recent update to the master file.

Indexing

Special **index files** created by database software also provide a service function. They speed up querying a master file. An index file is much like an index to a book. Readers often do not read through an entire book to find a particular item. They look up the item in a shorter index, note the page number, then turn to the page in the book. It is more efficient than searching through the entire book to find something.

As shown in Figure 6-6, the tenant file is indexed on the last name and other key fields. A **key field** is usually any important lookup item in a record. Each key field automatically generates a separate index file. An index file contains only the key field and a pointer to indicate where the full record is located in the master file.

Whenever a master file is updated, index files are automatically updated by the software. So index fields are always synchronized with their master file.

Create a Report

The database package used to create the tenant application has a "Quick Layout" option, as shown on the screen in Figure 6-13. The automatically generated report layout provides all the *bands* necessary to describe a simple report. As apparent, all report layout information comes from the tenant record content shown in Figure 6-6.

The automatically generated layout represents a good portion of the original report layout design shown in Figure 6-3. In many instances, such a quick layout is adequate for printing and displaying simple reports.

But in this case, to realize the original report layout design requires some typing. For example, the report title, RENT ROLL REPORT, must be typed into the Header Band on Figure 6-13. A new field must also be added. It is called AMOUNT DUE and contains a calculated number made up of three primary data items: monthly RENT + OTHER charges + PAST due balance.

Some other header revisions include deleting FIRST and moving APT to the second column. As a result of these changes, the Detail Band is automatically adjusted. The Detail Band controls the format of every tenant record printed in the main body of the report.

After some alterations to the Report Summary Band, such as totaling the columns, a test-run printing of the report shows some spacing could be improved. After a few changes, the application produces a Rent Roll Report that looks like the one in Figure 6-14.

With surprisingly little effort, the monthly chore of Rent Roll Report preparation has been transferred to the computer. No program code had to be written

FIGURE 6-13
This report layout was generated automatically from the record content
shown in Figure 6-6.

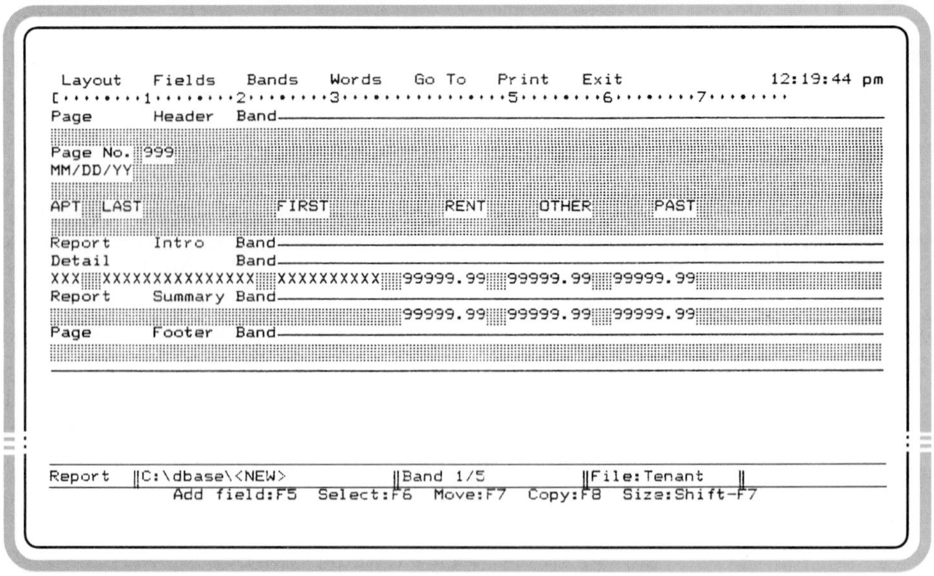

```
Page No.      1
05/27/9X
                        RENT ROLL REPORT

LAST NAME      APT      RENT      OTHER      PAST      AMOUNT
                                            DUE          DUE


Phillips       1A      300.00     16.00    100.00     416.00

Franklin       1B      370.00     25.00    370.00     765.00

Martin         2A      305.00     15.00      0.00     320.00

Dietz          2B      325.00      0.00      0.00     325.00

Ashley         3A      350.00      5.00      0.00     355.00

*** Total ***
                      1650.00     61.00    470.00    2181.00
```

FIGURE 6-14
A report prepared without programming using a database package

to get the report. It is produced with the standard report generation feature built into database software. **Report generator** is the term used to describe this feature of software that produces custom reports without programming.

Database packages provide various report options. An important one is the automatic calculation of the average, minimum, or maximum for a column or row of numbers.

Transfer Files

Most software provides commands to transfer files into and out of a package. It is usually a simple task to transfer database files, for example, into a word processing package. This is often done to personalize correspondence with database information.

One nonprofit organization needed to transfer a word processing file into its database package. It originally put a simple mailing list on a word processing package. As the list grew, it became desirable to have the greater file management capabilities offered by the database package. So the list was transferred from the word processor into the database package. The organization could then transfer the resulting sorted file back to the word processing package to create a variety of customized form letters.

FIGURE 6-15
Examples of database management software packages

DATABASE MANAGEMENT SYSTEM

Sometimes a user's requirements extend beyond the capabilities of file manager software. In these instances, a database management system (DBMS) package, such as one of those listed in Figure 6-15, is often used.

The following section discusses additional features found in DBMS packages. They are mainly

- An ability to link or relate several fields to each other through a key field, as shown in Figure 6-16 (some sophisticated file managers *simulate* this feature)
- A built-in language to program special application requirements

DBMS packages require more skill to use than file managers. Some individ-

A SAMPLER

Clipper
DataEase
dBASE
FoxPro
Informix-SQL
Oracle for Macintosh
Paradox
PC/FOCUS
R:Base

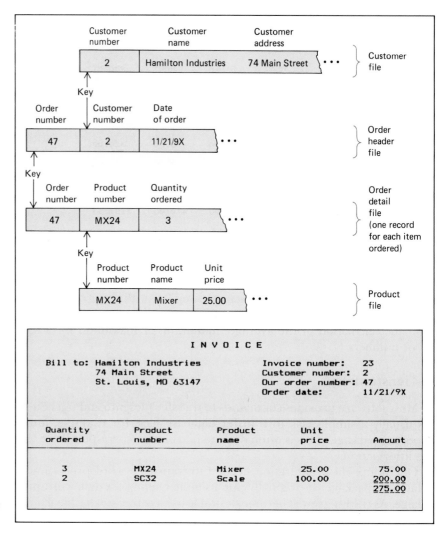

FIGURE 6-16
*Using data from four linked files
to create one customer bill*

uals and companies hire consultants with experience in DBMS packages to help them use the software.

Relate Files

The apartment building owner expected the feature to relate files would eventually be necessary. For example, she planned to maintain a separate file to monitor lease expirations. To get a Lease Expiration Report, she would need to relate the lease file to the tenant file.

In order to visualize how files could relate to each other, it is often best to examine examples. The one illustrated in Figure 6-16 shows an ordinary situation where four files are used to create one customer bill. One file relates to another in a linked chain.

Many packages require typing an *example* in the field common to both linked files. Figure 6-17 shows how this could be accomplished with the tenant and lease files. The example can be anything, as long as it is identical in both linked files.

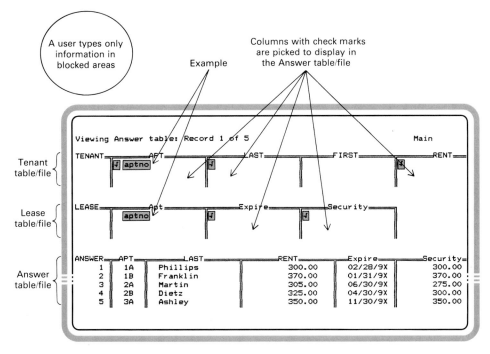

FIGURE 6-17
Using an example to show
how to link two files
(called tables)

DBMSs that provide for relating files, or linking files to each other through a key field, are called **relational database management systems (RDBMSs)**.

Many database applications start simply and grow as needed. This is one of the benefits of a relational database management system. Because data file manipulation is so flexible, it can handle integrating new requirements.

Multiple-File Design

To set up and maintain a smooth-running relational DBMS with several related files requires good file design. The several files used to create the invoice in Figure 6-16 are well designed. They were created by following two basic rules, illustrated in Figure 6-18, which are

1. Eliminate any repeating groups of fields

2. Eliminate fields that do not depend entirely on the key field

The example in Figure 6-18 shows how a bad file design is converted into a good file design. To avoid repeating groups of fields, the order detail is removed to become a separate record type. Each detail record now creates one row on an invoice.

The second change makes product descriptive information a separate file. This information depends more on product number as a key than on order number. The extracted data also become a separate record type.

Experienced relational DBMS users always keep files organized by the "one-file, one-subject" concept. Four examples of subject files appear in Figure 6-16:

- Customers
- Order header
- Order detail
- Products

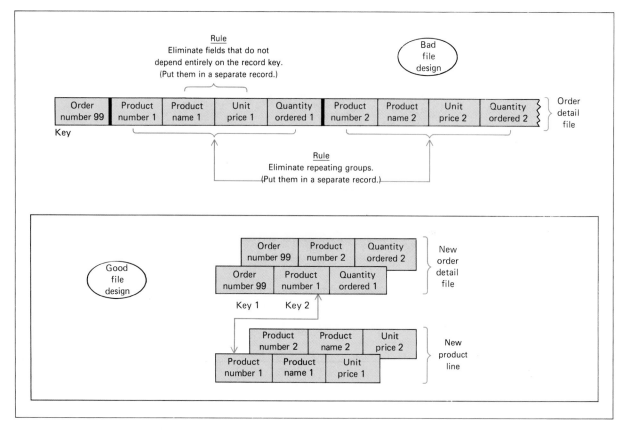

FIGURE 6-18
Splitting one long record into two smaller records

Smaller records help to keep files free of update problems, which include record

- Additions
- Changes
- Deletions

For example, if the unit price is wrong for product number 1 in Figure 6-18, it must be changed in only one place, the product file. Every order detail record that references it has access to the current data. But if files remain poorly designed, every order with product number 1 would have to be located and individually changed. It creates an update nightmare.

The rules just covered are part of what is called **normalizing files**. Relational DBMS designers rigorously follow the rules, as do aware database users.

DBMS Program Language

A built-in DBMS programming language gives any user complete application design flexibility. The price for this flexibility is to learn how to use the programming language. Program languages built into DBMS packages are often called *very-high-level languages* (VHLL), or **fourth-generation languages (4GLs)**. The other three generations progress from machine language, to assembler language, to ordinary *high-level languages* (HLL), like BASIC and COBOL. Examples of these are found in Chapter 12, "Programming."

Figure 6-19 gives an example of the program language code from one DBMS

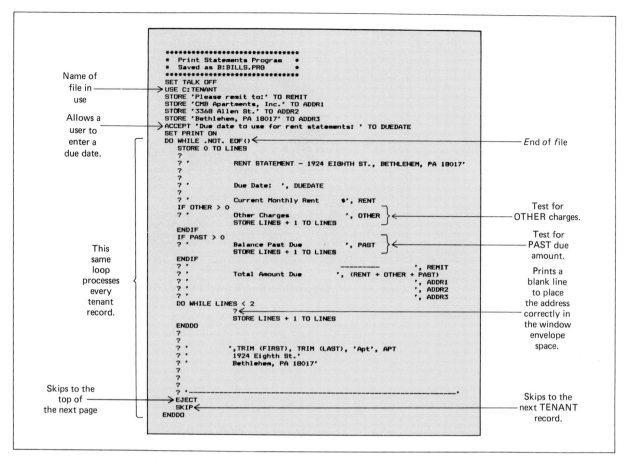

```
*******************************
*  Print Statements Program   *
*  Saved as B:BILLS.PRG        *
*******************************
SET TALK OFF
USE C:TENANT
STORE 'Please remit to:' TO REMIT
STORE 'CMB Apartments, Inc.' TO ADDR1
STORE '3368 Allen St.' TO ADDR2
STORE 'Bethlehem, PA 18017' TO ADDR3
ACCEPT 'Due date to use for rent statements: ' TO DUEDATE
SET PRINT ON
DO WHILE .NOT. EOF()
   STORE 0 TO LINES
   ?
   ? '              RENT STATEMENT - 1924 EIGHTH ST., BETHLEHEM, PA 18017'
   ?
   ? '         Due Date:  ', DUEDATE
   ?
   ? '         Current Monthly Rent      $', RENT
   IF OTHER > 0
   ? '         Other Charges              ', OTHER
                STORE LINES + 1 TO LINES
   ENDIF
   IF PAST > 0
   ? '         Balance Past Due           ', PAST
                STORE LINES + 1 TO LINES
   ENDIF
   ? '                                   ---------  ', REMIT
   ? '         Total Amount Due         ', (RENT + OTHER + PAST)
   ? '                                           ', ADDR1
   ? '                                           ', ADDR2
   ? '                                           ', ADDR3
   DO WHILE LINES < 2
         ?
                STORE LINES + 1 TO LINES
   ENDDO
   ?
   ?
   ? '         ',TRIM (FIRST), TRIM (LAST), 'Apt', APT
   ? '         1924 Eighth St.'
   ? '         Bethlehem, PA 18017'
   ?
   ?
   ? '_____'
   EJECT
   SKIP
ENDDO
```

Labels on figure:
- Name of file in use
- Allows a user to enter a due date.
- This same loop processes every tenant record.
- Skips to the top of the next page
- End of file
- Test for OTHER charges.
- Test for PAST due amount.
- Prints a blank line to place the address correctly in the window envelope space.
- Skips to the next TENANT record.

FIGURE 6-19
The DBMS program language code used to produce the rent statement in Figure 6-20

package. The coded program, when run on a computer, produces the printed rent statement shown in Figure 6-20.

Anyone with a talent for programming could use such a program language to create any kind of application design that depends on a record-oriented database.

Form Generator Example

Newer versions of DBMS software packages include a **form generator**, which eliminates the need to program output, such as rent statements, from scratch. Instead, output can be automatically generated.

An example of how the same rent statement is produced using a form generator is shown in Figure 6-21. In some ways, it resembles using the report generator used to create the Rent Roll Report. But the major difference is that

- The report generator assumes every record in a file will be *one line* in the report.
- The form generator assumes every record in a file will be *one page* by itself.

The form generator begins with a blank screen that requires a user to paint the form desired. **Screen painting** is a term used to describe placing words or graphics on a screen to create a desired layout that can be saved and reused as desired.

167

RENT STATEMENT - 1924 EIGHTH ST., BETHLEHEM, PA 18017

Due date: 09/25/9X

Current Monthly Rent $ 300.00
Other Charges   16.00
Balance Past Due   100.00   Please remit to:
                           _____
Total Amount Due   416.00   CMB Apartments, Inc.
                                                       3368 Allen St.
                                                       Bethlehem, PA 18017

┌ ─ ─ ─ ─ ─ ─ ─ ─ ─ ─ ─ ─ ┐
│ Nancy Phillips Apt. 1A │
│ 1924 Eighth St.   │
│ Bethlehem, PA 18017   │
└ ─ ─ ─ ─ ─ ─ ─ ─ ─ ─ ─ ─ ┘

FIGURE 6-20
A rent statement using data from the first record in the TENANT file

FIGURE 6-21
A "screen painted" form layout of the rent statement

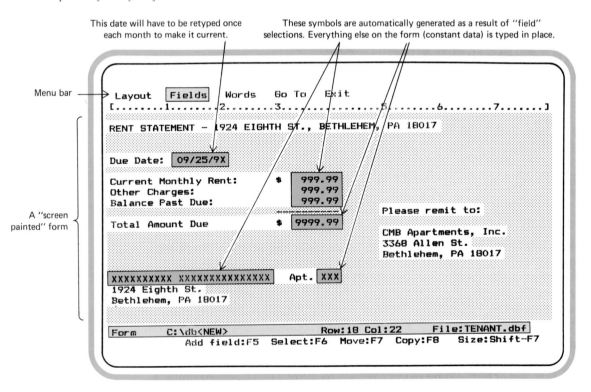

This date will have to be retyped once each month to make it current.

These symbols are automatically generated as a result of "field" selections. Everything else on the form (constant data) is typed in place.

FOCUS ON: *Object-Oriented Databases*

Now that users have become comfortable with relational database management systems (RDBMSs), an alternative approach to handling information, object orientation, begins to grab attention.

In a RDMBS, data are typically arranged by rows and columns in tables. By contrast, in an object-oriented database (OODB), data are arranged by objects in a hierarchy.

RDBMSs store data in the form of character strings and numbers. This model works well for personnel records, general ledger systems, and

onds worth of voice," says Paul Leach, Apollo Fellow at Hewlett-Packard's Apollo Systems Division. "These are data types that are too big and too varying in length among themselves to translate easily into a tabular row and column format."

Joe Forgione, Data General's director of distributed applications architecture, observes that, "Most real-world information is in the form of objects. Objects are a more natural, intuitive way of structuring information than tables, especially when you're dealing with complex and multimedia-based data."

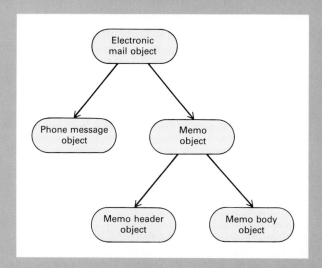

other applications based on numbers and characters. "RDBMSs have more substantial ability than OODBs, for now, when it comes to accessing large, tabular pieces of common information," says Burt Rubenstein, director of technical enhancements at Bull HN Information Systems, Inc.

By contrast, OODBs come out ahead of RDBMSs when dealing with complex data relationships. "RDBMSs get bent out of shape if you want them to store things like a 10-megabyte graphic image, 100 megabytes of video, or 15 sec-

Forgione says, "Objects, as self-contained, modular pieces of information, lend themselves to being distributed around networks." But there is a price for such flexibility, he adds. "You need an object directory that knows such things as which machines objects are on, who is using them, and who is authorized to obtain which objects. The use of networked OODBs can lead to potential problems unless the information is well managed."

EVALUATION

Where a microcomputer user is concerned, perhaps no packaged software is as difficult to evaluate as a DBMS. Perhaps none could benefit a user as much.

When looking for a suitable DBMS package, it helps to have specific requirements. Details such as the number of files needed and the number of records in each file should be known. Such general requirements can eliminate some packages from the search.

Many database packages provide features to validate automatically the accuracy of data as it is entered. Typical data-entry checks that might be desirable include

- This is a mandatory field; data must be entered before proceeding.
- This field must contain numeric data only.
- Only specific values are allowed in this field, such as CA, NY, or TX (for California, New York, and Texas).

The graphics capabilities of different packages also should be investigated. Some special-purpose DBMSs can store graphic images along with data. Such software is useful, for example, for a real estate sales company to store floor plan diagrams with descriptions of properties.

To determine a package's suitability, a hands-on test is desirable. The test should involve creating a file of sample data and performing queries and creating reports. This type of test helps to solve the problem of which packages are suitable.

A Database Software Evaluation Checklist, like the one in Figure 6-22, gives a systematic approach to the evaluation process.

RELATED ISSUES

Computer users in organizations frequently have contact with databases other than those they build themselves. The final section of this chapter looks at these other types of databases. In addition, database security issues are addressed.

Types of Databases

Among the common types of databases, as shown in Figure 6-23, that a person may come in contact with during a professional career are the following.

Type	Description
1. **Personal databases**	People store *personal databases* for their own individual use on their own personal computers. Such databases may include word processing documents, spreadsheets, and files created with a microcomputer DBMS package.
2. **Central databases**	A *central database* contains an organization's main operational databases and some user databases. It is stored in a central location for many users to access.

DATABASE SOFTWARE EVALUATION CHECKLIST

General

Can the package work with several files at once (a relational database management system package) or only one file (a file manager package)?
Is there a built-in programming language?
Is formal training required to use the package?
Are special features provided, like graphics?
Is there an on-line help facility?
Are there security checks to prevent unauthorized file access?

Create the Database

Can a custom data-entry form be designed on the screen?
Are data checks provided, like upper- and lower-range limits?
Are duplicate records allowed in a file?
Is indexing provided?
Are field types like date and dollar amounts provided?
Can a record be inserted in the middle of a file?
Can a deleted record be recalled?

Database Query

Can queries be saved for reuse and be revised if needed?
Are automatic features like count, mean, minimum, maximum, variance, and standard deviation available?
Is a natural language package available to simplify queries?

Generate Reports and Forms

Are reports automatically formatted?
Can reports and forms be screen painted?
Can formats be saved and modified?
Are all query features enabled when generating reports and forms?

Limitations

What is the maximum number of files per database, files available at one time, character size per record, records per file, fields per record, characters per field?
What is the largest calculated number possible?

(Figure 10-9, General Software Evaluation Checklist, is necessary to complete this evaluation.)

FIGURE 6-22

The **operational databases** support the day-to-day transactions and business activity of an organization. For example, in a bank's case, they contain customer checking, savings, and installment loan records.

Centrally controlled **user databases** support the decision-making efforts of individuals in an organization. They often contain:

- Extracts from operational databases
- Extracts from external on-line databases

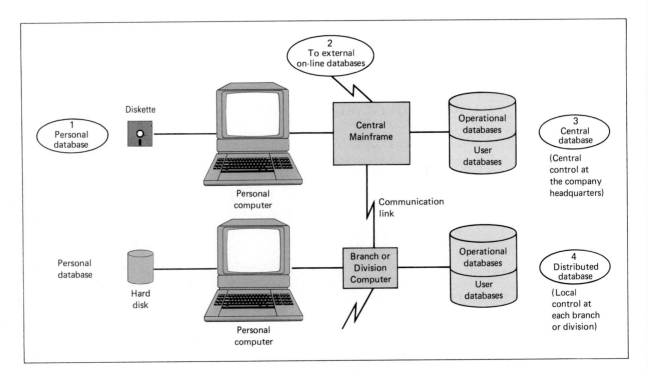

FIGURE 6-23
Common types of databases in use by large organizations

3. **External on-line databases**   Individuals as well as organizations pay fees to subscribe to public and private on-line database services. The services provide useful economic and other information to support decision making. They are discussed more fully in Chapter 7, "Telecommunications and Networking."

4. **Distributed databases**   *Distributed* or *local databases* reside at an organization's subsidiaries and are linked to a centralized computer by communication lines. For example, bank branches may keep only local customers on their local databases. Each subsidiary retains one part of a total organizationwide database. This is an effective way to distribute a database in banking as well as other industries.

Data Security

Whenever more than one person has daily access to a database, security may be enforced at several levels.

One security measure automatically makes the creator of a new DBMS file its owner. Only the owner can grant authority to others to retrieve, add, change, or delete data in the file.

Another feature provides for shielding data from users who should not have access to all data. This involves creating a separate **view**, or file, that contains only those fields that a user needs. Sometimes passwords and IDs are needed for access to certain databases or even to certain sensitive fields.

Database backup and recovery procedures exist to restore files in the event of a system crash. They involve a complex logging and checking procedure that is an entire subsystem within the DBMS. These procedures occur "under the hood" and are unobservable by a user.

Another subsystem provides control to avoid problems if two users try to update one record at the same time. The process is called **record locking** or **lockout** when one user is put on hold until the record is free for reuse.

CASE STUDY #1: *Where the Public Draws the Line*

Everyone's catching database fever, and the consequences can be severe.

Employers are running credit and criminal history checks of employees to assess trustworthiness. Landlords can now access a database to learn if a tenant has ever filed a complaint against a former landlord. Doctors can check to see if a patient has brought a malpractice suit against another doctor.

Although these databases are notoriously inaccurate, they are used to make decisions affecting people at critical junctures of their life.

The good news is that consumers are catching on. They're learning that information about them is being bought, sold, and exchanged by the private sector and the government, and they're beginning to insist on the opportunity to say no to disclosing private information for profit.

Consumers are demanding privacy protection in the development of information products and services, and the industry is responding. Privacy is emerging as a critical factor that can determine the rise or fall of certain products.

The decision by Equifax and Lotus to abandon Lotus Marketplace is a case in point. The product is a database that would have contained names, addresses, buying habits, and income levels of 80 million households. Much of the information came from Equifax's consumer reporting databases. Outraged that such a vast amount of personal information was to be available without their permission, thousands of people insisted that their name be removed from Lotus Marketplace. The product was abandoned in direct response to intense and widespread opposition to the product.

In withdrawing the product, the companies conceded that the privacy problems could not be fixed.

DISCUSSION QUESTIONS

1. Describe your reaction to a targeted mailing that arrives at your door and begins: "Congratulations, Ms. Jones, on your new raise. You'll be needing it since you've just bought a new home and a car and had a baby last year. Wondering how you'll afford your third trip to Barbados? Or how you're going to pay that huge mortgage? Have we got a deal for you!"

2. What would you include if you were to help write a data privacy law?

CASE STUDY #2: *Privacy versus Marketing: Europe Draws the Line*

A single incident highlights the problems of doing business across borders when countries have contrasting notions of privacy.

Two years ago, Fiat managers in France were all ready to transmit personnel records to their home office in Turin, Italy. But this simple action hit an unexpected snag. Citing the private nature of the data—salaries and performance reviews—the French government halted transmission. It relented only after Fiat's management promised to follow France's strict data-privacy law in Italy.

Since the late 1970s, seven European Community (EC) nations have enacted a patchwork of data-protection laws. But some member countries have passed none.

The European Commission, the EC's executive branch, is pushing a single privacy standard. The EC's proposal would

- Prevent companies from keeping personal data or ID numbers without the person's OK
- Let consent be withdrawn at any time and permit damage suits if such privacy rights are infringed
- Require file-keepers to set up a security system to bar unauthorized access

- Ban electronic profiles of individuals based on what they buy or do through computer networks
- Ban transmission of data to countries without similar protections

U.S. companies say the proposal would impede them in many ways. Companies operating in the EC would be barred from sending data to any country, maybe even the United States, without what the EC deems "adequate" protections. Some fear that would let the commission control much of the world's information flow. So many U.S. businesses see the rules as "unworkable," says the director of EC affairs for the U.S. Council for International Business.

Opportunity.   In defense, Ulla Ihnen, an EC lawyer, says the new rules are simply designed to prevent abuses in countries without privacy laws. The EC directive "provides an opportunity to tighten and reexamine our own privacy laws," says Janlori Goldman, who directs the American Civil Liberties Union's privacy-and-technology project.

DISCUSSION QUESTIONS

1. Compare the similarities and differences of the privacy fears in this case study with those in the first case study in this chapter.

2. Would you approve the EC proposal? Defend your answer.

CHAPTER SUMMARY

- A *database* is a collection of related files. A *file* is a collection of one or more similar records about one subject.
- *File manager* packages work on only one file at a time.
- File management software helps a user to create a file, add records to it, search and sort it, and produce reports.
- *Primary data* cannot be computed. They usually are included in a file. *Secondary data* can be computed from primary data. They usually are not included in a file.
- A *record* is divided into slots, called *fields*, to hold data. A *field* is one data element of a record.
- *Query* is a database term for searching a file of records that meet specific criteria.
- *Query by example (QBE)* searching is characterized by filling inquiry conditions into empty slots under displayed field information.
- The *structured query language (SQL)* style of database inquiry is characterized by typing inquiry commands in a structured format.
- *Natural language* enables a user to query a database using plain English.
- A *sort* puts records into any alphabetic or numeric order desired.
- An *index file* provides a service function to speed query responses in a master file.

- A *key field* is any important lookup item in a record.
- A *report generator* produces custom reports without programming.
- Two features that distinguish a *database management system (DBMS)* from a file manager package are (1) an ability to relate several files to each other through a key field and (2) a built-in language to program special application requirements.
- A *relational database management system (RDBMS)* links files to each other through a key field.
- The process of creating smaller, more manageable files from unorganized larger ones is called *normalizing files.*
- *Fourth-generation language* is the name given to program languages built into DBMS packages. They are more efficient to use than third-generation languages, like COBOL or BASIC.
- A *form generator* produces custom forms without programming.
- *Screen painting* is placing words or graphics on a screen to create a desired layout that can be saved and reused as desired.
- When evaluating a DBMS package, it is helpful to have specifications like the number of files and records required, among other details.
- Four types of databases found in organizations are *personal databases, central databases, external on-line databases,* and *distributed databases.*

- Database security is enforced in several ways. For example, creators become owners of files. They can grant and revoke file use to others.

- *Record locking* or *lockout* prevents two users from trying to update one record at the same time.

SELECTED KEY TERMS

Database
Database management system (DBMS)
Field
File
File manager
Form generator
Fourth-generation language
Index file

Key field
Natural language
Normalizing files
Primary data
Query
Query by example (QBE)
Record
Record locking

Relational database management
  system (RDBMS)
Report generator
Screen painting
Secondary data
Sort
Structured query language (SQL)

REVIEW QUESTIONS

1. What is a database? A file?

2. List the things a user can do with file manager packages.

3. Why is a primary data element different from a secondary data element? Which one is included in a database file?

4. What is a record? A field?

5. Describe the main characteristics of the database inquiry styles known as query by example and structured query language.

6. What benefit does natural language provide?

7. Give an example of a file sort.

8. What purpose does an index file serve?

9. What is a report generator?

10. What features distinguish a database management system package from a file manager package?

11. How does a relational DBMS link files together? Give an example.

12. Why are database files "normalized"?

13. What is the name given to program languages that are built into DBMS packages?

14. When evaluating a database package, what kind of detail is helpful?

15. Identify four types of databases found in organizations.

16. Give an example of how database security can be enforced.

EXERCISES

1. *Apartment Building Case.* Assume that you have been asked to research a DBMS package purchase for the tenant application described in this chapter. Examine all the DBMS articles you can that appeared over the last three months. Write a report about your research. Identify two DBMSs that you would recommend evaluating further and explain why you chose the two.

2. *Apartment Building Case.* Selecting a DBMS package for the tenant application described in this chapter requires a closer evaluation. Assume that whatever DBMS package you have access to is a candidate package. Locate a copy of the package's *User Guide* and find answers to questions on the Database Software Evaluation Checklist in Figure 6-22. Prepare a report on the results of this evaluation.

3. *Metro Consultants Case.* Metro Consultants is a financial consulting firm. Due to the highly sensitive nature of its business, database security is a priority concern. The company has hired you to research security measures and make a recommendation about how it can best protect its files. Examine computer periodicals to determine how companies are confronting security problems. Prepare a report that ends with your recommendation to Metro, and justify your recommendation.

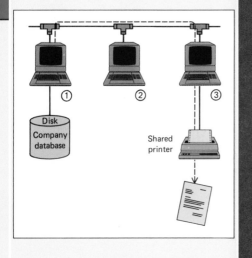

7

Telecommunications and Networking

AFTER READING THIS CHAPTER, YOU SHOULD BE ABLE TO

· Identify the software and hardware necessary for computer telecommunications

· Describe services available to telecommunicators, such as electronic mail, bulletin boards, on-line databases, and computer conferencing

· Distinguish between local-area and wide-area networks

Thomas Golub works with a record company in New York that produces sales catalogs listing the company's records. The catalog preparation process begins when he downloads record information from the company's mainframe into his personal computer. Then software converts the data to a form that the catalog's typesetter can use.

Catalogs have to be accurate. Missing entries mean lost sales, and duplicate entries mean expensive and time-consuming typesetting changes.

Forwarding the corrected file to the typesetter company used to involve the hit-or-miss task of coordinating transmission times. Worse, Golub had to monitor the transfer. So he installed a two-line telecommunication system using a desktop computer.

Now the typesetter company can retrieve catalog data when it is ready, and Golub no longer has to monitor the transfer. His two-line system ensures that the typesetter gets through, even if he is communicating with the mainframe on the other line.

Telecommunications, *data communications*, and *teleprocessing* are some of the terms used to refer to the communication of information, including text, graphics, video, and voice, over a distance using computers.
Personal computer users dramatically increase the value of their computers by using them for such communication services as

- Sending electronic or voice mail
- Maintaining electronic message centers or bulletin boards
- Participating in computer conferences
- Interrogating on-line databases in a public "on-line library" that contains information of interest to business and professional people

This chapter begins with a discussion of the hardware and software necessary to use a personal computer for telecommunications. Then it describes some of the many services just listed. These services are all available on either a public or private basis using computers of all sizes.

The chapter next discusses local-area networks. They facilitate group communications and serve as the backbone of an automated office.

The chapter concludes with a discussion of wide-area networks. They typically require the use of the established telephone system or other media. They allow computer communications over greater distances than possible with local-area networks.

The network discussions provide a bridge to the Module II chapters, which concern multiuser and organizational computer issues.

PERSONAL COMPUTER COMMUNICATIONS

This first section examines how individuals commonly use their personal computer for telecommunications, especially to take advantage of public communication services. It begins with the hardware required to telecommunicate.

Modem

To send electronic mail to the company's sales people, the sales manager of a sporting goods distributing company first had to equip his personal computer for communications. He had to buy a *modem* for linking his computer to a telephone line.

A **modem** modulates digital signals (from a computer) into analog (or telephone) signals, in order to communicate data. "Modem" is short for *mo*dulate and *dem*odulate. *Modulation* is a process that takes discrete digital computer signals of 1's and 0's and endows them with sound to go through the telephone network, as shown in Figure 7-1. Telephone signals are called *analog* signals. Analog signals are *demodulated* back to digital computer signals on the receiving end.

Figure 7-1 illustrates use of an external modem. This one is small enough to fit under a telephone, although some "pocket" modems designed for laptop computers are only about 1 by 2 inches.

The modem is connected to the telephone wall outlet. It is also connected to the computer's **serial port**, at the back side of the system unit. The connecting cable is often called an **RS-232 cable**, or a *serial cable*. The cable carries bits,

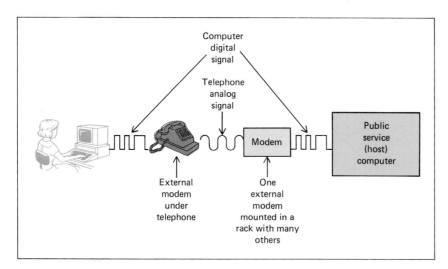

FIGURE 7-1
Computer communications using modems

which are released from the computer's memory in a serial fashion, one digit after another, to the modem.

A less expensive **internal modem** eliminates an extra piece of hardware on the desktop. As shown in Figures 7-2 and 7-3, it is a special-purpose controller board. It fits into a personal computer's expansion slot on the system board. A cable connects the controller board with the telephone wall outlet.

FIGURE 7-2
Components of an internal modem kit

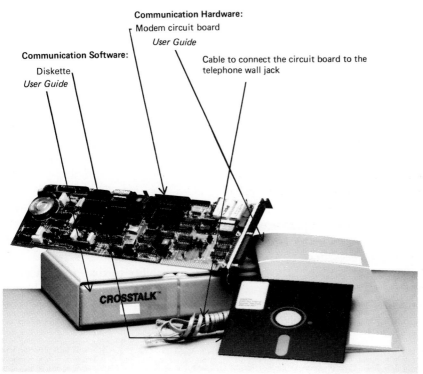

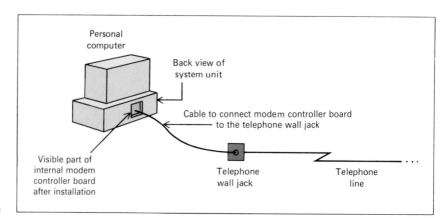

FIGURE 7-3
An installed internal modem

FIGURE 7-4
Examples of modems

A SAMPLER

VENDOR	MODEM PRODUCT
Controller Board Internal Modems	
ATI Technologies	2400etc/i
Hayes Microcomputer	V-series Smartmodem 9600B
IBM	IBM Personal System/2 Internal Modem/A
Intel PCEO	Classic
Practical Peripherals	Practical Modem
Zoom Telephonics Inc.	Zoom/Modem
Stand-Alone External Modems	
General DataComm Inc.	Desktop 596
Hayes Microcomputer	Smartmodem
Prometheus Products	Promodem Plus
Racal-Vadic	2400VP
US Robotics	Courier 2400e
Ven-Tel Inc.	9600 Plus II

FIGURE 7-5
Examples of communication software packages

A SAMPLER

Carbon Copy Plus
Co/Session
CrossTalk
pcAnywhere
ProComm Plus
Relay Gold
Smartcom III

A sampler of modems, as well as communication software, appears in Figures 7-4 and 7-5. The software packaged with modems is what does the "computer-to-computer talking." The modem is just a service device to get the signals from one computer to the other.

One feature of communication software is an ability to dial automatically whatever telephone number is desired. *Auto-dial* phone numbers must be recorded in the software's *dialing directory*, like the one shown in Figure 7-6. The phone numbers of several electronic mail services have been entered in the directory.

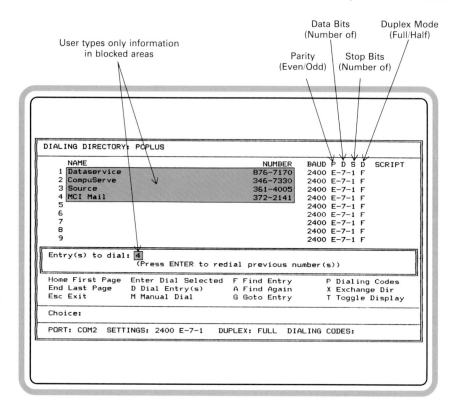

FIGURE 7-6
A sample dialing directory

LINKING COMPUTERS

Before data communication can take place, compatibility must exist between computers. The settings shown in Figure 7-6 were preset because they are the common settings used for personal computers. A brief summary of what they mean helps to understand what is going on "under the hood" during communication exchanges:

Communication Setting	Meaning
2400	This is the **bits-per-second (bps)** rate, or number of bits that theoretically can be sent over a communication line per second. Common rates for personal computers are 1200, 2400, and sometimes 9600. Modems that can send data at higher bits-per-second rates are more commonly found in mainframe installations. Sometimes the bits-per-second rate is called the *baud* (pronounced "bawd") rate.
E	E stands for "even." If, as in Figure 7-7, all the "one;" bits in a character add up to an even number, like two, then a zero is placed in the parity bit slot before the character is sent. The *parity* bit provides a

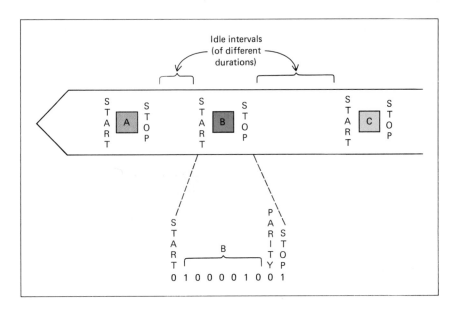

FIGURE 7-7
Standard asynchronous (character-by-character) communication

low level of error checking. If the addition results in an odd number, such as 3, then a 1 is added in the parity slot to "even" out the 1 bits. At the receiving end, should the parity bit not be even, it signals a transmission error.

7   Sets the number of bits that make up one character. Seven is the number of bits in an ASCII character (the ASCII characters are given in the chart in Appendix B).

1   Sets the number of stop bits that concludes the transmission of one character.

These settings reflect the most common way personal computers communicate. It is called **asynchronous communication**. The term asynchronous means "not synchronized." It highlights the fact that single characters are transmitted with a random idle period between characters.

Asynchronous communication is also referred to as the "asynchronous protocol." **Protocol** is the telecommmunication industry's term for a set of rules or procedures established and followed by cooperating devices. To communicate successfully, transmitting and receiving computers must follow the same set of rules, or protocols.

The final setting in the dialing directory in Figure 7-6 is the duplex transmission mode. In **half-duplex transmission**, only one computer can send data at a time. Both computers, usually a personal computer and a host computer, can send data simultaneously in a **full-duplex transmission** mode. In this case, the setting is "F" (full).

With the software set and the modem power turned on, the sales manager is ready to communicate. He first types "4" to auto-dial the electronic mail service. He can hear sounds from his modem as the software "dials" the phone number.

The telephone ringing sound on the remote end is also audible. When the phone is answered, the high-pitched tone heard is the modem's frequency *carrier* sound. Typing a carriage return in response to the tone establishes a link between the two computers. While the tone disappears, the line remains active for the duration of the communication session.

Log-On and Public Services

With the telecommunication link established, the remote computer takes control and prompts a user to *log-on*. A **log-on**, or sign-on, sequence validates a communicator to a host computer. It generally includes a request for a billing account number and a password. Both are stored on the public service company's database when a subscriber originally signs up to use the service.

Public service subscriptions are available at local computer retail stores and from other sources. Sometimes **public communication services** are called *videotex* services and provide, among other options

- Electronic and voice mail
- Bulletin board services
- Computer conferencing
- On-line databases

After log-on, available service options appear in a menu, like the one in Figure 7-8.

FIGURE 7-8
A sample menu for a public communication service

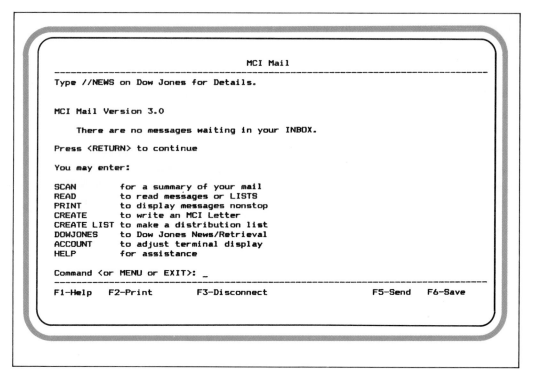

```
                              MCI Mail
-----------------------------------------------------------------------
Type //NEWS on Dow Jones for Details.


MCI Mail Version 3.0

    There are no messages waiting in your INBOX.

Press <RETURN> to continue

You may enter:

SCAN          for a summary of your mail
READ          to read messages or LISTS
PRINT         to display messages nonstop
CREATE        to write an MCI Letter
CREATE LIST   to make a distribution list
DOWJONES      to Dow Jones News/Retrieval
ACCOUNT       to adjust terminal display
HELP          for assistance

Command <or MENU or EXIT>: _
-----------------------------------------------------------------------
 F1-Help   F2-Print        F3-Disconnect            F5-Send   F6-Save
```

FIGURE 7-9
An electronic mail service menu of options

ELECTRONIC MAIL

To eliminate telephone tag with field sales representatives, the sales manager uses electronic mail. Telephone tag results when one party calls another, who is not available, and leaves a message to return the call. Often the returned call finds no one in and results in another meassage. And so it goes, wasting time, money, and effort.

The sales manager prefers **electronic mail**, often referred to as **E-mail**, which is the transfer of messages by electronic methods. When logged-on to the service, the display looks like the one in Figure 7-9. He types SCAN to quickly review received mail. Mail can be exchanged only by subscribers or sponsors of subscription accounts.

After typing READ to see a specific piece of mail, he is asked for its disposition. He can file or delete a letter, create a reply, forward it to another subscriber, or execute a combination of available options.

To send mail requires typing CREATE and the recipient's account number. When the letter is finished, it is possible, among other options, to

- Request an acknowledgment that the letter is received
- Send a copy to another subscriber
- Save a copy

Electronic mail has distinct advantages over alternative messaging methods. It is faster than the postal service and faster and less expensive than courier services. There are drawbacks, though. Unsolicited junk mail pops up as it does in conventional mail. There are also security threats and user training time and costs to be considered.

Some organizations that provide electronic mail services are listed in Figure 7-10.

Uploading and Downloading

Bringing any computer file, like a letter, from a remote computer into one's own computer is called **downloading** a file. Conversely, sending a file to another computer is called **uploading** a file. A transfer takes only a few seconds for short files.

Many users prepare all documents for mailing at a personal computer. Then they upload them as a file transfer to their own electronic mailbox. In a final step, they forward mail to recipients' mailboxes. The efficiency of a file transfer is important, since billing is based on connect time.

Private Service

A personal computer can be dedicated to function as a private electronic mail service. Most communication software packages provide this capability.

To accept mail, a personal computer must be in a ready state with an *auto-answer* feature enabled through the telecommunication software. To send mail, it can auto-dial and transfer files at designated times to designated phone numbers. In problem cases, it can retry to send mail until a successful transmission is achieved.

It is now common for organizations to have private electronic mail services on their internal networks to facilitate office communications. In one management consulting company, staff members spend most of their time working with clients outside the office. The company's private mail system helps to maintain communication between office and staff members. Anyone can send messages to selected individuals or to a distribution list of selected people on the system.

Voice Mail

Voice mail is an alternative to electronic mail. In **voice mail** systems, a *voice digitizer* measures sound frequencies and assigns them values that can be stored as 1's and 0's. To play back voice mail, a *voice synthesizer* reads digital signals and converts them back to sound, as shown in Figure 7-11.

A voice mail controller board, similar to an internal modem, is placed in a personal computer's expansion slot. The board is connected to a telephone which serves as the input and output device. A central computer controls voice traffic in digital mail systems.

RELATED TELECOMMUNICATION USES AND SERVICES

A variety of other telecommunication uses and services related mainly to messaging or communicating include bulletin board systems, computer conferencing, videoconferencing, remote computing, and fax transmission. Each is briefly described below.

A SAMPLER

Bitnet
BRS
CompuServe
Dialog
EasyLink
GEnie
MCI Mail
The Source

FIGURE 7-10
Examples of public electronic mail services

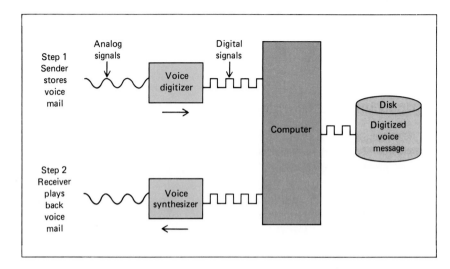

FIGURE 7-11
Voice mail systems use voice digitizing and synthesizing.

Electronic **bulletin board system (BBS)** messages are available for *any* caller to view, unlike voice or electronic mail messages which are sent to specific recipients. In addition, bulletin board system callers are free to add their own messages.

The electronic bulletin board at one public service is divided into about 75 categories. Categories correspond to user interests and include law, photography, astrology, and computer groups.

Some companies maintain bulletin boards on public service systems and some maintain private systems. For example, a medical products manufacturer set up a private bulletin board service for customers to place orders, leave technical questions, and participate in question-and-answer forums. Dedicated bulletin board service computers can run around the clock on "automatic pilot." In this *unattended mode*, the computer takes messages and exchanges files without human intervention.

Another related telecommunication service is **computer conferencing** or **teleconferencing**. This is a *restricted* form of a bulletin board system for informal exchanges among conference participants. Computer conferencing does not require participants to be in designated places at predetermined times. It also provides a printed "progress track" of all exchanges by all conference participants.

A more advanced form of conferencing is videoconferencing. **Videoconferencing** allows conferees in different locations to meet with both sound and picture. The hardware required to set up a videoconference includes a television, a camera, and a codec. *Codec* (compression/*de*compression) devices convert video signals into digital signals to transmit over ordinary telephone lines. The signals are decompressed at the receiving end and turned back into video signals.

Figure 7-12 shows a videoconference session. The local site conferees can communicate with participants at the remote site, as well as send graphics and other information on a second conference screen.

In one innovative use of this technology, prison health personnel videocon-

Remote site
Conferees

Remote site
graphic

Conferees

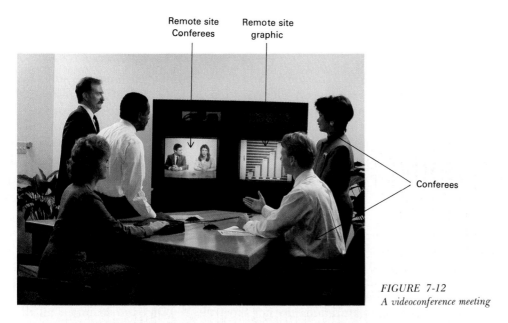

FIGURE 7-12
A videoconference meeting

ference with medical specialists so prisoners do not have to be taken off-site for treatment.

Related to conferencing techniques is **remote computing**, which links two computers together so that both keyboards are active and both screens show the same thing. It enables collaboration on a project, such as a builder and a client working in different cities on an evolving building design. Remote computing also allows a user to operate one computer from another distant computer. A traveler with a portable computer, for example, could use remote computing from a hotel room to operate a desktop computer back at the office, which may be across the country.

Also in the message exchange category is the *facsimile*, or *fax, machine*, such as the one shown in Figure 7-13. Fax systems can transmit both text and graphics

Telephone

FIGURE 7-13
Facsimile (fax) machine

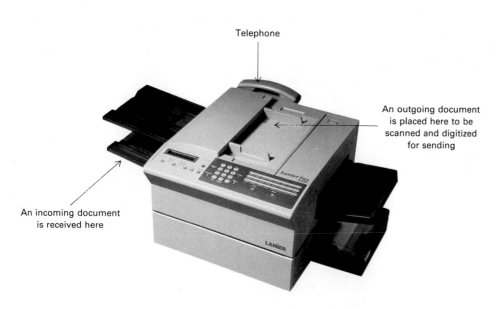

An outgoing document
is placed here to be
scanned and digitized
for sending

An incoming document
is received here

over ordinary telephone lines. As a document is placed into the sending device, it is scanned and digitized. On the receiving end, the fax machine reproduces a paper copy of the scanned image. The entire transmission usually takes less than one minute.

An alternative to purchasing a stand-alone facsimile machine is to add a fax board to a personal computer. These boards, which are similar to an internal modem, are considerably less expensive than fax machines. With a PC fax board, both a scanner and a printer are also required to send and receive fax documents.

ON-LINE DATABASES

In addition to electronic mail, or any of the other message exchange–type systems, most users set up telecommunications to link into on-line database services. **On-line database services**, such as those listed in Figure 7-14, provide collections of information, called *on-line databases*, which are stored in computer files and are available to telecommunication subscribers for a fee. Since most individuals and organizations do not have the resources to maintain all the databases of information they desire, on-line databases provide a valuable service.

Categories

On-line database services can be divided into three categories:

· Financial
· General business/research
· Special purpose

The Dow Jones News/Retrieval is the best known of the financial services. Some of its offerings include

· Price quotes from the New York Stock Exchange, American Stock Exchange, and the over-the-counter market
· Full text of the *The Wall Street Journal*

One service dominates the general business-research category. It is DIALOG Information Services, which has over 250 databases in the areas of

FIGURE 7-14
Examples of organizations that provide on-line database services

A SAMPLER

On-Line Service	Service Supplier
Bechtel	Bechtel Information Services Inc.
BRS	BRS Information Technologies
CompuServe	CompuServe Inc.
Dialog	Dialog Information Services
Dow Jones News/Retrieval	Dow Jones & Co. Inc.
EasyLink	Western Union
MAID	MAID Systems Inc.
Telescan	Telescan Inc.
The Source	The Source Telecomputing Corp.

A SAMPLER

- *Donnelly Demographics.* Demographic data, such as age, sex, race, industry, occupation, education, housing, and income from the U.S. census.
- *EconBase.* Government statistical data for economic forecasting and general business planning from 1948 to the present.
- *Encyclopedia of Associations.* Detailed information on several thousand trade associations, professional societies, labor unions, fraternal and patriotic organizations, and other types of groups.
- *Harvard Business Review.* Abstracts and some full text of articles published in the *Harvard Business Review* magazine from 1971 to the present.
- *ABI/Inform.* Abstracts of articles from 800 major publications in business management and administration.
- *Computer Database.* Comprehensive summaries of computer-related articles and publications from over 500 international sources spanning telecommunications, hardware, software, and services.
- *D&B—Dun's Market Identifiers.* Directory of over 2.2 million public and private companies with 5 or more employees, listing address, products, sales, executives, corporate organization, subsidiaries, industry information, sales prospects.
- *ASI (American Statistics Index).* Summaries of government reports covering social, economic, and demographic data from over 500 federal agencies.
- *Newsearch.* Daily index to over 2,000 news stories and other features from newspapers, popular magazines, trade and industry journals, complete press releases from PR Newswire, business and management journals, legal periodicals, and newspapers.
- *Health Planning and Administration.* Nonclinical literature summaries on all aspects of health care, facilities, and planning.

FIGURE 7-15
Examples of DIALOG's
on-line databases

- Business
- Law and government
- Current events
- Medicine
- Engineering
- Science and technology
- Environment
- Arts, education, and social sciences

A sample of some of DIALOG's on-line databases appears in Figure 7-15.

DIALOG contains only abstracts of articles. By contrast, the LEXIS on-line database provides the full text of legal documents. It is one example of a special-purpose on-line database that services lawyers. Another example of a special-purpose service is Questal, designed for chemical researchers. This on-line database service has over 45 databases of information on pharmaceutical and chemical manufacturers.

Search Services

Specialized software products, such as Pro-Search, illustrated in Figure 7-16, provide tutorials that simulate on-line database search sessions. They help users to plan actual search strategies. Planning is done on a personal computer,

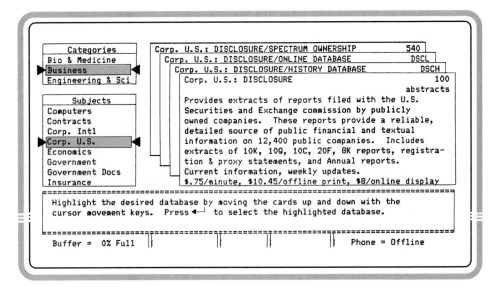

FIGURE 7-16
A simulated card catalog helps a user to develop an on-line database search strategy.

FIGURE 7-17

SAMPLE FEES FOR CONNECTING TO SEVERAL ON-LINE DATABASES ON PUBLIC COMMUNICATION SERVICES

Service	On-Line Database	Per Hour Cost (prime time[a])	Per Hour Cost (nonprime time[b])
Dialog	Donnelly Demographics	$ 60.00	$ 60.00
	EconBase	75.00	75.00
	Encyclopedia of Associations	99.00	99.00
	Harvard Business Review	96.00	24.00
HRIN	Conference Board Abstract Database	90.00	70.00
	Daily Developments	80.00	60.00
BRS	Harvard Business Review	80.00	20.00
Dow Jones News Retrieval	Dow Jones News	112.00	17.40
Bechtel	Insiderline	110.00	110.00
MAID	Market Analysis and Information Database	195.00	195.00
Telescan	Telescan Financial Database System	36.00	18.00

[a]Usually from 7 A.M. to 6 P.M. weekdays
[b]Usually from 6 P.M. to 7 A.M. local time, and weekends and holidays

before any on-line charges are incurred. Fees can mount rapidly, as illustrated by the connection fees in Figure 7-17, until search techniques are perfected.

Services such as EasyLink from Western Union give subscribers easy access to a host of other vendors' on-line database services. Users do not have to subscribe separately to each desired service and need not learn new and different commands to work with each service.

On-Line Database Alternative

Providers of CD-ROM (compact disk read-only memory) databases offer an alternative to pay-as-you-go on-line database use. **CD-ROM databases** are provided on a CD-ROM disk that allows a user to browse through information at leisure without worrying about on-line charges. Some available CD-ROM databases are

- News Digest
- Census Bureau Disc
- Physician's Desk Reference
- Shakespeare on Disc

This alternative is viable for those able to afford the initial investment of a CD-ROM player and the disks.

TELECOMMUNICATION SOFTWARE EVALUATION

A checklist to help evaluate telecommunication software is given in Figure 7-18. Most of the listed items have already been covered. Others include

- **Error correction:** This is a built-in method of catching and correcting errors in file transfers. Errors can be caused by static on telephone lines. Popular methods of detecting and correcting errors are called the *Xmodem, Ymodem, Kermit*, and *Zmodem protocols*. Error detection and correction occur "under the hood." A user is not aware of the process.

FIGURE 7-18

TELECOMMUNICATION SOFTWARE EVALUATION CHECKLIST

Are file transfers possible?
Can file transfers be checked for transmission errors?
Can a remote computer be dialed automatically?
Is remote computing possible?
Is there an unattended automatic answer capability?
Can a log-on response be reduced to a single keystroke?
Can more than one telecommunication session be conducted at a time?
Is there a programming language to automate telecommunication applications?
Is it possible to set up one or more private functions, like electronic mail, bulletin boards, and computer conferencing?

(Figure 10-9, General Software Evaluation checklist, is necessary to complete this evaluation.)

- **Programming language:** This allows a user to create a so-called *script file* of procedures to automate a telecommunication task. One example is a script file that logs a user on to a favorite telecommunication service and enters the commands that get the user into the offering desired, such as a stock quotation service.
- **Multiple sessions:** This feature provides an ability to conduct more than one telecommunication session at a time.

LOCAL-AREA NETWORKS

The second major focus of this chapter concerns local-area networks. **Local-area networks (LANs)** consist mainly of connected personal computers and serve as the backbone of an *automated office*. They facilitate private group communication services in small companies and departments of large companies.

Automated Office

Many arguments exist for why an organization should automate office procedures. One generally accepted premise is that 80 percent of the information generated by an organizational group is used only within the group. This figure motivates progressive small organizations, and departments within large organizations, to install local-area networks. They recognize a fundamental need to exchange local information quickly, easily, and reliably. They may also have a cost-cutting motive to share expensive computer hardware, like disk drives, printers, and graphic plotters.

Figure 7-19 shows typical local-area network cabling that runs through an

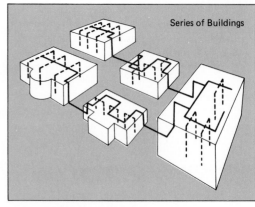

FIGURE 7-19
Local-area networks cabled throughout an office building and through a series of buildings in a campuslike setting

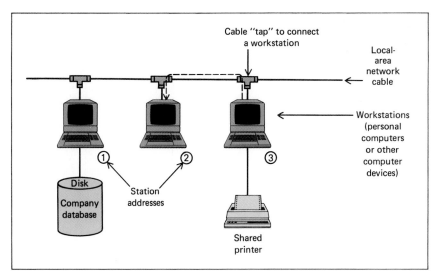

FIGURE 7-20
In this local-area network, workstation 3 sends electronic mail to
workstation 2's diskette.

automated office. The most common environment is a single building. But local-area networks can extend throughout an industrial park, university, or other campuslike setting. Data traffic flows over the cable and is accessible to any personal computer or other device linked to the cable. Devices linked to the network are often called **workstations** or **nodes**.

Printers and hard disks attached to personal computers can be shared, as shown in Figures 7-20 to 7-22. But some local-area networks do not allow a personal computer to share their resources. Instead, they attach separate devices that are called *servers*. Database servers, for example, provide access to central database files for all workstations, or "clients," on a local-area network. The computing industry refers to this arrangement as adhering to a *client/server architecture*. Printer servers are also common on networks, as shown in Figure 7-23.

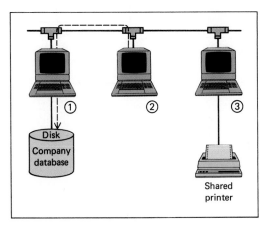

FIGURE 7-21
Workstation 2 sends a new record to the company's database, which is stored on a hard disk.

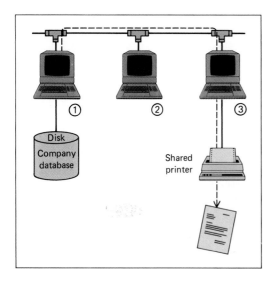

FIGURE 7-22
*Workstation 1 sends a letter to be
printed at the shared printer attached
to workstation 3.*

FIGURE 7-23
*Connected local-area networks
with separate dedicated servers*

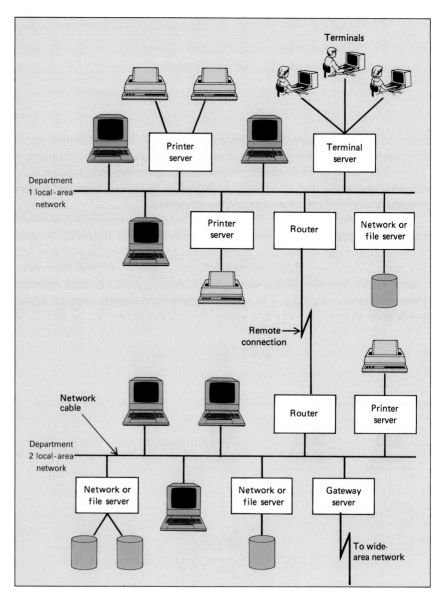

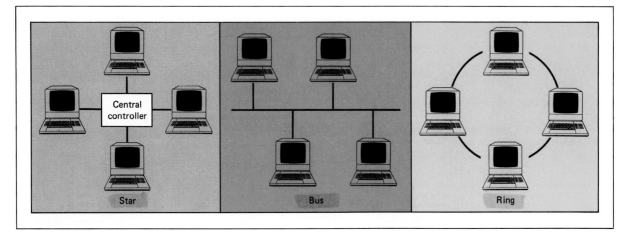

FIGURE 7-24
Three local-area network layouts

HOW A LAN WORKS

Every device on a network has a unique address. It enables one workstation to send a message or transfer a file to another attached device. Figures 7-20 to 7-22 illustrate how users on a local-area network

1. Exchange electronic mail

2. Share database information

3. Share hardware

Exchange Electronic Mail.   In Figure 7-20, user 3 creates a word-processed letter. It is essential that user 2 review a copy of the letter before it is circulated to others. By addressing users 2's workstation, the letter is sent as a file over the cable with a simple COPY statement.

Network software in each personal computer executes the file transfer. User 2 can interact with the letter as if it were created locally. The received file can be modified, and a copy saved, before being returned to its originator.

Share Database Information.   In the second example in Figure 7-21, user 2 adds a new customer record to the company's database. It is stored on a shared hard disk. Users access the company database according to privileges granted to them, such as the authorization to read, change, add, or delete records.

Share Hardware.   In the third example in Figure 7-22, user 1 prints a letter on the shared printer attached to workstation 3. An address followed by the PRINT command suffices to accomplish this task.

Diskless personal computers or **workstations** may be found on local-area networks. They are desktop computers without local diskette storage. They retrieve all working files from the hard disk of a network file server. Because a diskless workstation user has no facility to make copies of files, a company's database is less vulnerable to network security breeches.

Choices

There are three main LAN layouts. As diagrammed in Figure 7-24, they are the star, ring, and bus.

195

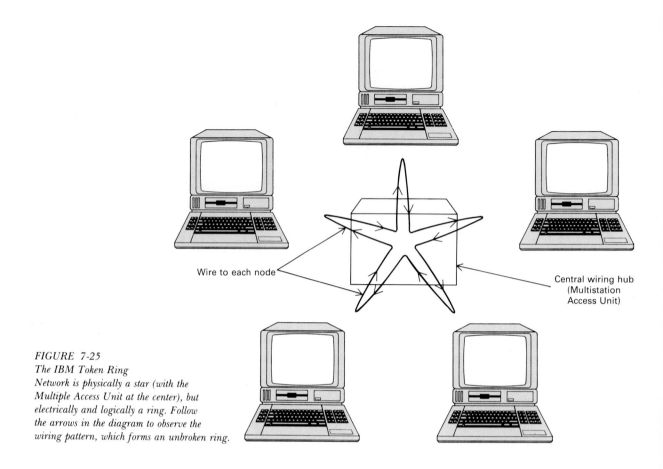

Wire to each node

Central wiring hub
(Multistation
Access Unit)

FIGURE 7-25
The IBM Token Ring
Network is physically a star (with the
Multiple Access Unit at the center), but
electrically and logically a ring. Follow
the arrows in the diagram to observe the
wiring pattern, which forms an unbroken ring.

A **star network** has workstations clustered around a computer that acts as a central controller, or "switch." To communicate, a workstation must be switched, or temporarily connected at the controller, to the other workstation. If the central controller fails, the network is down. Usually duplicate parts are built into central controllers to avoid such a disaster.

In a **ring network**, workstations are linked in an unbroken chain. One ring network, when it is all wired, looks very much like a star, as shown in Figure 7-25. A *central wiring hub* functions as the network's safety net if problems occur. As an example, if one workstation goes down, the central wiring hub immediately senses the problem, disconnects the problem workstation, and skips over it. To keep the logical ring "alive," it automatically attaches the two workstations on either side of the "dead" one. This restores the ring and keeps the network "up."

Data are transmitted in a ring network using a scheme called **token passing**. When the network is idle, a message called a *token* is circulated around the ring from station to station. To send a message, a workstation

- Captures the token when it is empty
- Changes it to indicate a message is on the way
- Sends its information

A user is completely unaware that token passing is occurring at lightning speed under the hood. In a well-designed network, a user cannot detect a difference between using a personal computer as a stand-alone unit or using it as a networked unit.

The third local-area network layout is a bus, much like the one in Figure 7-

23. In a **bus network**, workstations are linked to a single cable, called a **bus**, and contend with each other to transmit a message. It works like a party-line telephone. If the line is not busy, a workstation is free to transmit its message. This method is variously called *Ethernet*, *CSMA/CD*, or *contention* transmission. Like token passing, it works under the hood at lightning speed and is completely unobservable and unobtrusive from a user's vantage point.

Local-area networks come in variations other than the common ones described here. All have their unique advantages and disadvantages. Each type should be evaluated to compare

- Transmission speed
- Number of possible workstation attachments
- Ease of adding a new workstation
- Ability to continue working if workstation failure occurs
- Ability to transmit data, voice, and full-motion pictures simultaneously
- Ability to guarantee workstations specific access time

Connections and Evaluation

Workstations in a local-area network can be connected by a number of transmission media. **Twisted-pair wire** is easily recognizable as the line that connects a telephone to the wall jack. It is economical and easy to install.

Coaxial cable is often the same cable used to install home cable television. It is more expensive than twisted-pair wire, but it can handle higher data transmission rates over longer distances.

As in other communication areas, **fiber-optic cable** is the leading edge of transmission technology. It offers the highest data transmission rates possible. It is also immune to electromagnetic interference, which makes it desirable for local-area networks that wander through factories or other heavy-duty work areas.

Many organizations hire a consultant who specializes in local-area networks to assist in the evaluation and implementation of a local-area network. Some of the network evaluation criteria are listed in Figure 7-26. Some of the products considered are listed in Figure 7-27.

FIGURE 7-26

LOCAL-AREA NETWORK EVALUATION CHECKLIST

Is the total cost reasonable and within budget?

Does it meet specific requirements?

Is it possible to start small, at a low financial risk, and gradually expand to meet more and more requirements?

Is it designed to prevent total network failure?

Does it interface with equipment supplied by more than one vendor?

Is it easy to install, maintain, interconnect to other networks, switch hardware around, and reset software controls without impacting other hardware and software?

(Figure 10-9, General Software Evaluation Checklist, is necessary to complete this evaluation.)

A SAMPLER

3Com 3+
Apple Computer Appletalk Personal Network
Banyon VINES
DECnet
IBM Token Ring Network
Novell Netware
Xerox Ethernet Network

FIGURE 7-27
Examples of local-area network products

FIGURE 7-28
A large organization's distributed processing network

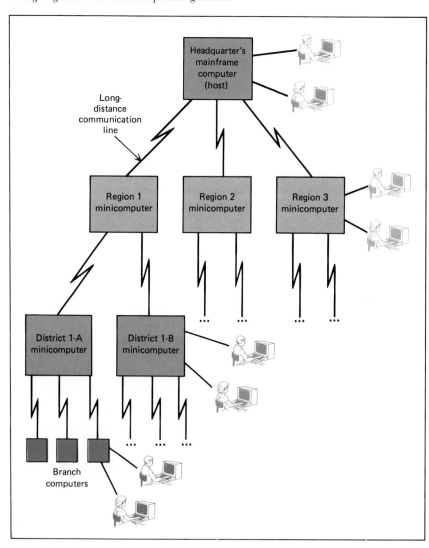

WIDE-AREA NETWORKS

This final section of the chapter covers wide-area networks. **Wide-area networks (WANs)** are characterized by using modems and the established telephone system to communicate over greater distances than are possible with local-area networks. Organizations often lease communication lines from companies like AT&T to make wide-area connections, such as those diagrammed in Figure 7-28.

Distributed Processing

A wide-area network supports an organization's distributed processing. In **distributed processing**, computers are located throughout an organization to satisfy local computer processing needs.

The diagram in Figure 7-29 illustrates the basic components in a common wide-area, distributed processing network. A **host computer**, typically a headquarters' central computer, is linked by various interconnected communication lines to subordinate computers. The host computer is comparable to any public service computer that provides users with electronic mail, on-line databases, or other services.

FIGURE 7-29
Basic components in a wide-area communication network

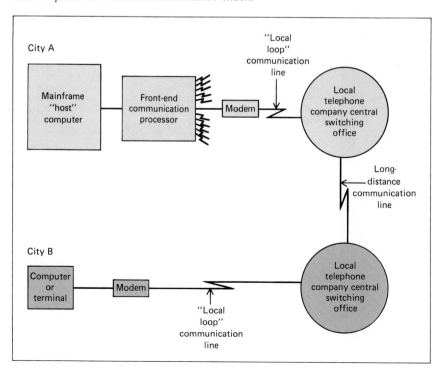

FOCUS ON: *EDI: Putting the Muscle in Commerce and Industry*

Electronic Data Interchange (EDI)—the direct computer-to-computer exchange of standard business documents such as invoices and purchase orders—holds out the promise of streamlined daily business routines. As a result, supporters claim, companies can save time and money.

"Doing business without EDI will soon be like trying to do business without the telephone," said Edward E. Lucente, an IBM vice president.

According to Lucente, IBM's 37 worldwide plants will be doing EDI with over 2,000 of the company's largest suppliers. He says IBM believes that implementing EDI will save it $60 million over the next 5 years.

The savings and the speed of doing business are just two selling points that customers are hearing from suppliers. Sometimes, the message comes through loud and clear, as in General Motors' letter that gave its suppliers an ultimatum to get on-line with EDI or go off-line with GM. More

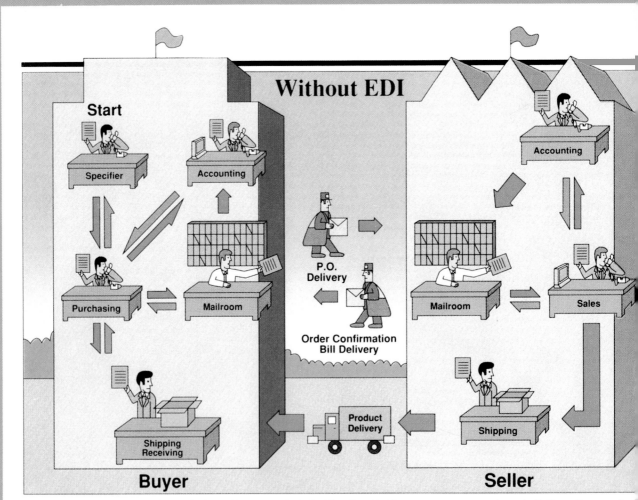

Without EDI, the real power—either at the Buyer Company or the Seller Manufacturing Company—may seem to be vested in the mail room and wi

(*SOURCE:* Datamation, *March 15, 1988. Copyright © 1988 Cahners Publishing Company. Reprinted with permission.*)

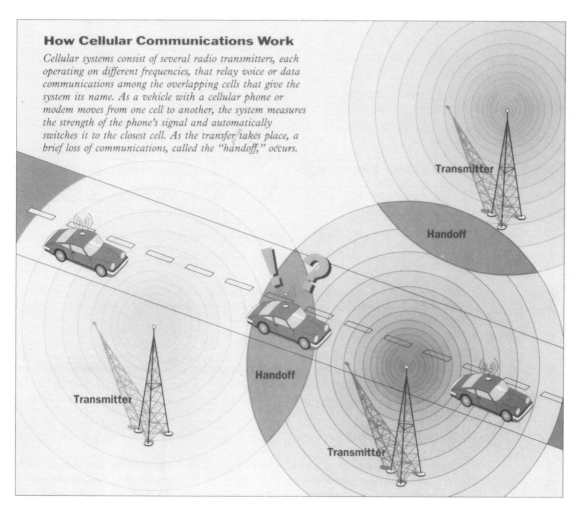

How Cellular Communications Work

Cellular systems consist of several radio transmitters, each operating on different frequencies, that relay voice or data communications among the overlapping cells that give the system its name. As a vehicle with a cellular phone or modem moves from one cell to another, the system measures the strength of the phone's signal and automatically switches it to the closest cell. As the transfer takes place, a brief loss of communications, called the "handoff," occurs.

FIGURE 7-34
How cellular communications work

Car phones are one popular application of cellular radio. Another is wireless portable computers. They have built-in radio modems to provide data communication for people on the move. Journalists, repair people, and sales people, among others, are finding applications for them.

Large organizations put together private networks using a variety of communication media.

TELECOMMUNICATION CARRIERS

Organizations go to a **telecommunication carrier** like AT&T, or any of thousands of independent companies that provide transmission services. Some carriers specialize in surface cables, satellite, microwave, or other kinds of transmission.

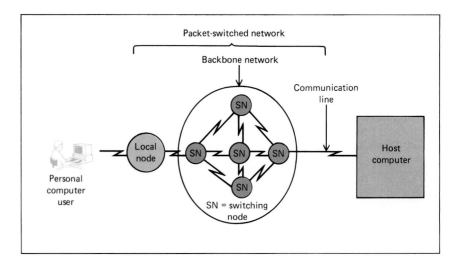

FIGURE 7-35
A packet-switched network has many local nodes in many cities that feed the backbone network which services various public and private host computers.

Customers lease or rent bandwidth from a carrier. **Bandwidth** is the bits-per-second transmission capacity of a line. Carriers sell bandwidth as a commodity, in varying capacities.

Packet-Switched Service

Another telecommunication carrier alternative is a *packet-switched service*, such as Telenet, Tymnet, and Uninet. The diagram in Figure 7-35 shows how these packet-switched networks operate. They have many *local nodes* in many cities to link users to a connected host computer. The host pays for a permanent attachment to the network. The host is then billed by the packet-switching company for all calls to it.

Inside the **packet-switched network**, data are routed in groups of characters called a *packet*. All user packets time-share the same backbone network provided by the carrier. Packets are "switched" from one node to another to reach their destination.

Many large and small companies have permanent connections with packet-switched networks. It is a convenient way to have an instant telecommunication network. It is an alternative to which more organizations turn rather than develop their own wide-area network.

TRANSMISSION RULES

Both ends of a communication line, such as the one illustrated in Figure 7-29, must follow the same transmission rules to communicate. An alternative to the asynchronous, character-by-character transmission protocol is called the *synchronous protocol*. Many mainframe-oriented organizations use this.

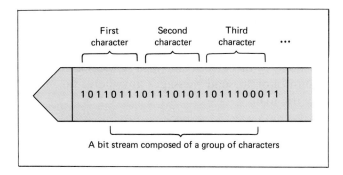

FIRST character   Second character   Third character   •••

1011011101110101101100011

A bit stream composed of a group of characters

FIGURE 7-36
Synchronous communication

The diagram in Figure 7-36 shows how it works. In **synchronous communication**, characters are sent in groups as a single bit stream. The bit stream follows a precise timing pattern that is set or "synchronized" by a master system clock.

Typically the front-end communication controller assumes a "master" function and *polls* the computing devices on the line, one after the other, to see if they have traffic. All this happens under the hood at lightning speed without a user ever being aware of it.

If a device answers yes to a poll, the controller releases an entire bit stream of characters. Meanwhile, others on the line have to group characters until the poll arrives. Only one computing device is given permission to use the line at a time.

INDUSTRY GOALS

The future of telecommunications is related to two computer industry goals:

- To have voice, data, and video flow simultaneously worldwide over the same public communication lines.
- To allow any computing device to "talk to" any other computing device.

One emerging technology that promotes these goals is metropolitan area networks. **Metropolitan area networks** or **MANs** are designed for high-speed data exchange over a minimum distance of 50 miles. This network can handle voice and video transmission in addition to data.

Metropolitan area networks are precursors to a worldwide network intended to carry simultaneous voice, data, and full-motion pictures. Communications engineers call this ideal network *Integrated Services Data Network (ISDN)*. International committees are at work developing standard rules, or protocols, to make this networking possible.

While international networks may help to "bring the world together," there are problems. One is the lack of firm standards. **Standards** are specifications intended to facilitate data exchange between computers. Another is the lack of uniform pricing structures. In addition, political and security concerns cause some countries to restrict the flow of data outside their borders.

International standards are already in place for connecting to public packet-switched networks. The rules of connection are called the *X.25 standard* or *protocol*. It is part of a seven-layer structure for interconnecting telecommunication devices established by the *International Standards Organization (ISO)*.

The *X.400 standard* promises to connect electronic mail services around the world. It will enable a communicator to send messages anywhere, no matter what service is used to initiate the mail.

CASE STUDY #1: *Securing a Network*

Implementing the right security for a telecommunication network requires planning. Says Peter Stephenson, a consultant on networking, the basic issue is "How much can I afford to lose and how likely am I to lose it?"

A small local-area network, where all the users know each other and where a week's worth of data can be replaced in half a day, is a low-risk, low-exposure network, Stephenson says. An example of a high-risk, high-exposure network would be a large telecommunication system that spans cities and updates thousands of database records an hour, such as at a major bank. This network requires more security measures.

"The biggest threat to security in the large organization is the disgruntled employee," says Stephenson. "That is absolutely the number-one threat to malicious data loss." To guard against such damage, he recommends changing passwords, among other measures, when an employee leaves.

The bad news is that nothing is 100 percent effective against intruders who are both determined and skilled. "If somebody wants to break into a computer system and they're good, they'll do it," Stephenson says. "What you're trying to do is to erect enough barriers so it becomes more trouble to get at the data than the data is worth."

For that reason, it's important that the security solution provide a record of use. "It allows seeing if someone is trying to get on your system, or if a user who is allowed to is trying to access data that he or she is not permitted to," says Paul Palmer, vice president of Fischer International Systems Corporation.

If an intruder is capable of getting to the actual data on a computer system, one way to secure the data is to encrypt them. Data encryption simply means garbling the data so an intruder can't understand or use them.

DISCUSSION QUESTIONS

1. Discuss measures a company can implement to secure a telecommunication network system.
2. In addition to disgruntled employees, what else can you think of that can be a security threat to a computer network? Discuss measures that can be taken to limit the risks of these threats.

CASE STUDY #2: *Furor Erupts from Computers in Politics*

For more than a year, the mayor of a major midwest city read the electronic messages about city business that members of the city council sent to one another from portable computers at their homes. All messages were available to him on a centralized computer in the city office.

The mayor has defended his actions, saying he monitored the council members' messages at the central computer because he was concerned that they were using the system to hold illegal caucuses. Under their state's law, city council business, with a few exceptions, must be conducted at public forums.

The mayor's ability to monitor the messages was curtailed after several council members became curious about his knowledge of issues discussed on the computer. The city manager decided the messages were as private as telephone calls and should therefore be read only by those to whom they were addressed. He ordered a stop to making copies of the messages.

The mayor confirmed that he had been reading the messages by complaining to the council later that his access to them had been cut off.

The mayor said he believed that messages should be open to the news media as well to make sure the council was complying with the state law on conducting business in public. He also believed that information on the computer, including the council members' messages, should be accessible to the public.

Public Versus Private Conflict. The disclosure of the mayor's mail perusal has not only touched off a bitter political dispute in the city but also has put a spotlight on problems in reconciling advances in computer technology with laws on open meetings, public records, and personal privacy.

"It's serious," said Marc Rotenberg, national director of the Computer Professionals for Social Responsibility, an advocacy group. "Users of electronic mail systems should have a fundamental expectation of confidentiality. When that expectation is breached, the value of the network is undermined and a chilling effect on future use is likely to result."

The law requires operators of public electronic communications systems to protect the privacy of messages on their systems. The law distinguishes between public systems and those that are for private use. Violations carry a maximum penalty of 5 years in prison.

The city attorney is now reviewing the city's policy regarding the use of the electronic mail system. He does not believe that the mayor's actions violated the communications privacy law. But legal experts said it was possible the law had been violated.

DISCUSSION QUESTIONS

1. With whom would you be inclined to agree, the city attorney or the legal experts? Defend your answer.

2. Do you agree with the statement "People are going to worry that if they plug into these systems it will be like bringing Big Brother into their households."? Defend your answer.

CHAPTER SUMMARY

- A *modem* modulates digital signals from a computer into analog, or telephone, signals to communicate data.
- *Asynchronous* communication is the most common way in which personal computers communicate. Single characters are transmitted with a random idle period between characters.
- *Protocol* is a set of rules or procedures established and followed by cooperating devices. To telecommunicate successfully, transmitting and receiving computers must follow the same protocols.

- *Public communication services* might offer, among other options, electronic and voice mail, bulletin board systems, computer conferencing, and on-line databases.
- *Electronic mail* is the transfer of messages by electronic methods.
- *Uploading* is sending a file to another computer. *Downloading* is receiving a file into one's own computer.
- In voice mail, a *voice digitizer* measures voice sound frequencies and assigns them values that can be

stored as 1's and 0's. In playback, a *voice synthesizer* reads digital signals and converts them back to sound.

- An electronic *bulletin board system (BBS)* makes messages available to any logged-on communicator.
- *Computer conferencing* or *teleconferencing* is a restricted form of a bulletin board system.
- *Videoconferencing* allows conferees in different locations to meet interactively with both sound and picture.
- *On-line database services* provide collections of information, called *on-line databases*, which are stored in computer files and available to subscribers for a fee.
- A *local-area network* (LAN) consists mainly of linked personal computers and serves as the backbone of an automated office.
- A *star network* has workstations clustered around a computer that acts as a central controller, or "switch."
- A *ring network* has workstations linked in an unbroken chain. It uses *token passing* transmission.

- A *bus network* has workstations linked to a single cable, called a *bus*. It uses a party-line transmission scheme.
- LAN workstations are connected by *twisted-pair wire, coaxial cable,* and *fiber optic cable.*
- *Wide-area networks* (WANs) use modems and the telephone system to communicate over greater distances than are possible with local-area networks.
- A *front-end communication processor* off-loads the telecommunication task from the mainframe.
- Noncable communication media include *microwave, satellite,* and *cellular systems.*
- A *packet-switched network* sends communication in groups of characters called a *packet*. Packets time-share the service's backbone network.
- In *synchronous transmission*, groups of characters are sent as a single bit stream that is timed, or synchronized, by a master system clock.
- *Standards* are specifications intended to facilitate the exchange of data between computers.

SELECTED KEY TERMS

Asynchronous communication
Bandwidth
Bulletin board system (BBS)
Bus network
Cellular system
Coaxial cable
Computer conferencing
Downloading
Electronic mail (E-mail)

Fiber optic cable
Front-end communication
   processor
Local-area networks (LANs)
Modem
On-line database service
Packet-switched network
Protocol
Public communication service

Ring network
Standards
Star network
Synchronous communication
Twisted-pair wire
Uploading
Videoconferencing
Voice mail
Wide-area networks (WANs)

REVIEW QUESTIONS

1. Compare the following:
   a. Asynchronous versus synchronous communication.
   b. Electronic mail versus electronic bulletin board systems.
   c. Digitizing versus synthesizing voice.
   d. Uploading versus downloading.
   e. Local-area network versus wide-area network.
2. Identify the following:
   a. Public communication service.
   b. Front-end communication processor.
   c. Packet-switched network.
   d. Cellular system.

3. What is a modem?
4. Describe some uses of electronic mail.
5. What is videoconferencing?
6. What are on-line databases? Give two examples.
7. Describe three ways to use a local-area network.
8. What are three types of local-area networks?
9. Describe three transmission media used to connect LAN workstations.
10. Identify three ways to telecommunicate that do not involve cabling.
11. What are standards?

EXERCISES

1. Visit your school or local public library to learn if any on-line database services are available for reference purposes. Find out who can use the services and what the restrictions are to use the service. If possible, use the service yourself to research a term paper topic or to help supply information for the next exercise.

2. Prepare a research report that compares the features offered by three data communication software packages. Recent articles about packages should be available in the computer periodicals section of your library.

3. Find out what public electronic bulletin board systems are available in your local area and the types of services they provide. Your local computer store or computer user group should be able to give you some guidance. Try to arrange a demonstration of how to use one.

4. Find out if there is a local-area network installed in school or at work. If you find an installation, ask the network manager for a demonstration of how a user

- Sends a word-processed document to a printer on the network.
- Stores a word-processed document on a network file server.
- Accesses an on-line database at a public communication service.

Ask the network manager to demonstrate

- How a user workstation is added to the local-area network.
- How a workstation is removed from the network.

5. Locate three recent articles on local-area networking. Prepare an oral or written report on the products described and the advantages and disadvantages of each.

6. Locate articles that discuss the use of fiber optic cable as a communication medium. Prepare a report on the reasons why so many communication carriers are now installing fiber optic lines for wide-area communications.

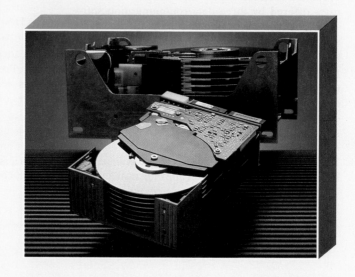

8

Multiuser Hardware

AFTER READING THIS CHAPTER, YOU SHOULD BE ABLE TO

- Discuss differences between single-user microcomputer and multiuser mainframe computer hardware
- Identify hardware typically found in mainframe computer installations
- Identify other types of computers, such as minicomputers and supercomputers

The cost of MIPS (millions of instructions per second) at a desktop microcomputer is almost three orders of magnitude less than the cost of MIPS at a mainframe. The issue is to get some of those desktop MIPS to take over work the mainframe has been doing at much higher cost. This will let the mainframe do what it does best, which is handling vast quantities of data.

Splitting an application between the desktop and mainframe would work like this. The desktop computer would get a transaction from a user, edit the accuracy of the data, arrange the data into a format the mainframe expects to see, and ship off the neatly packaged transaction. The mainframe then has only to validate the source of the transaction, revalidate the data to assure integrity, and process the data.

The real benefit of distributing an application in this way is that the desktop computer can spend much more of its time working on a transaction than it now does. Its machine cycles can be allocated to "prevalidating" everything, checking certain data against local storage (for example, there is no branch #77 because this bank has only 30 branches), giving the user help as required, and more. Tens of millions of instructions can be expended on these tasks.

By comparison, spending that kind of time at the mainframe for a single transaction from a single user, as traditionally done, is hideously expensive and wasteful of resources.

Mainframe computers and minicomputers provided organizations with all their computing power before the emergence of the personal computer or microcomputer. Internally all these computers work the same. But the larger computers are far from personal. They handle the processing needs of many users all at once.

Mainframes excel at handling large processing tasks such as producing volumes of telephone, gas, and electric bills. At banks, mainframes as well as minicomputers process teller transactions and customers' automated teller machine transactions.

This chapter explores mainframe hardware by taking a tour of a bank's computer center. Mainframe input, processing, and output hardware are contrasted with comparable hardware on a personal computer. Also covered are other classifications of computer systems, including minicomputers and supercomputers.

MAINFRAME COMPUTER ENVIRONMENTS

National Bank is a large organization that has both domestic and international operations. It is typical of a company that operates within a mainframe computer environment.

Terminals

A visit to the bank's offices finds many *terminals* on the employees' desks. They look much like the one in Figure 8-1.

While a **terminal** resembles a personal computer, it does not have a system unit. Without the system unit, it has no independent processing capability. It cannot process computer programs on its own.

FIGURE 8-1
A typical modern terminal that can also have a printer attached

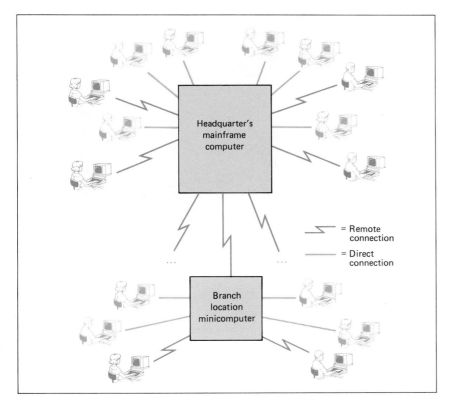

FIGURE 8-2
Distant branch offices are linked to the mainframe computer.

All the processing capability is housed in the mainframe computer on another floor of the headquarters' building. The bank's mainframe processes computer tasks for many users at once. All share the centralized computer. Bank branch offices also are linked into the central computer, as shown in Figure 8-2. Distance is no barrier to user access to the bank's mainframe computer.

Some professionals at the bank elect to use personal computers instead of terminals. Personal computers can *emulate*, or act like, a terminal whenever desired.

Special-Purpose Terminals.   Special-purpose terminals are designed for specific jobs, like bank teller terminals, automated teller machines, and point-of-sale terminals.

Tellers at the bank use *bank teller terminals* to process deposit and withdrawal transactions, post savings account passbooks, and print checks or receipts right at their workstations.

Other special-purpose terminals stand in the bank's lobby. These are **automated teller machines**, like the one shown in Figure 8-3. Using them, customers can

- Withdraw cash from personal accounts
- Inquire about account balances
- Take care of other bank business without teller assistance

The bank's benefits from using automated teller machines include

FIGURE 8-3
A bank's automated teller machine

- Providing 24-hour service without increasing employee and related costs
- Experiencing fewer errors because of less manual processing

Some customers dislike the dehumanization of teller operations. Another negative aspect of using automated teller machines includes the possibility of computer failure. A machine could also run out of money when a customer wants a cash withdrawal. Because they contain cash, automated teller machines are vulnerable to theft and other abuse.

To use an automated teller machine, a user inserts a plastic bank-issued card into a card slot. The machine asks or *prompts* for the user's secret password or *personal identification number*, called a PIN. If the password is correct, money can be withdrawn or simply transferred, say, from a savings to a checking account. Such a money transfer is one example of many types of **electronic fund transfers** possible in the banking industry.

An automated teller machine is a variation of some special-purpose terminals used in retail operations. **Point-of-sale (POS) terminals** capture data at the point a sale is transacted. Like the example in Figure 8-4, they usually include

- A keyboard for data entry
- A display to show prices
- A printer to provide a customer receipt
- A cash drawer

Some point-of-sale terminals, such as those at many retail department stores, feature optional light-sensitive wand readers for reading and recording product codes.

Some of the bank's data collection operations first go into a minicomputer before they end up on mainframe disk storage. The delay is normal in batch operations.

Batch versus Transaction Processing

Batch processing occurs whenever large amounts of data are saved and input at one time, in a *batch*. Usually data originate on some kind of *source document*, such as customer account application forms or deposit slips.

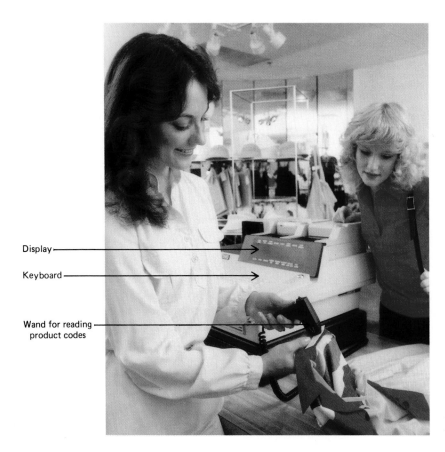

Display

Keyboard

Wand for reading
product codes

FIGURE 8-4
A point-of-sale terminal

At National Bank, mailed-in deposits or dropped-off deposits left in the bank's lobby deposit box are processed in a batch. At night, bank personnel open the deposit envelopes and keyboard transactions all in one batch session.

Batch processing contrasts with **transaction processing**. In transaction processing, data are not collected or saved before entering. They are entered directly into the computer that processes it, immediately as a transaction occurs. Both the bank teller and the automated teller machines handle transaction processing.

Computer professionals often refer to transaction processing as **real-time processing**, where results occur quickly enough to influence an event. As an example, if a customer asks to withdraw $1,000 but has only $500, the outcome of the event is altered immediately.

Computer professionals also refer to transaction processing as **on-line processing**. The terminal is "on a line," directly connected to the computer responsible for processing the entire transaction. No intermediate steps or storage intervene to delay a transaction's progress to completion.

Almost all organizations use a mix of transaction and batch processing.

Related Hardware

Converting printed characters into electronic signals that can be processed by a computer is accomplished by **optical character recognition**, or **OCR**, equipment. The banking industry uses a special optical character recognition technique, called **magnetic ink character recognition (MICR**, pronounced "miker").

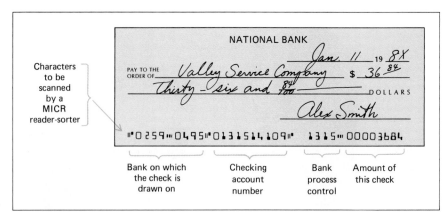

Characters to be scanned by a MICR reader-sorter

NATIONAL BANK

Bank on which the check is drawn on

Checking account number

Bank process control

Amount of this check

FIGURE 8-5
A check with MICR characters

A device called a MICR reader-sorter reads the coded line at the bottom of a check, as shown in Figure 8-5. It is printed by the bank in special magnetic ink using a MICR inscriber. The reader-sorter processes 2,600 checks a minute using a technique called **scanning**. *Scanning* refers to technology that rapidly "reads" documents and converts them into binary digits for storage.

A familiar nonbank use of scanning devices is at supermarket checkout counters, as shown in Figure 8-6. Universal product code (UPC) scanners read alternating fields of black and white bar-code bands. Various band widths represent the item's name, price, stock number, and other information. These data

FIGURE 8-6
A computerized universal product code scanner speeds checkout in
supermarkets (left); samples of universal product codes (right).

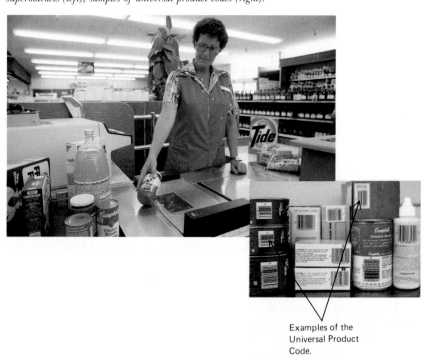

Examples of the Universal Product Code.

are processed by a central computer for stocking and inventory control. Two portable bar-code readers are shown in Figure 8-7.

A recent development may revolutionize how large institutions handle mountains of paperwork. The American Express credit card company has combined OCR technology with image processing to reduce the physical handling, storage, and retrieval of paper documents, as shown in Figure 8-8A.

An **imaging device** takes a picture of the credit card receipts and converts them to digital images. An OCR reader then scans the digital images for accuracy. The monthly bill is created from the images that are visible on screen and stored on optical disk. Figure 8-8B shows a sample of laser-printed credit card receipt images. This new procedure to process monthly statements reduced American Express's billing costs by 25 percent within the first months of operation.

A survey of large banking institutions indicates that 96 percent of senior bank managers expect to have check imaging systems in place by the mid-1990s.

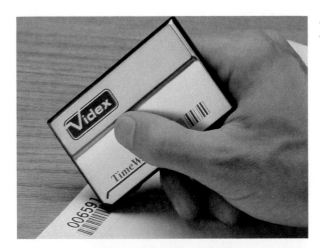

FIGURE 8-7
Examples of portable bar-code readers

(A)

(B)

(A) Methods of processing credit card receipts

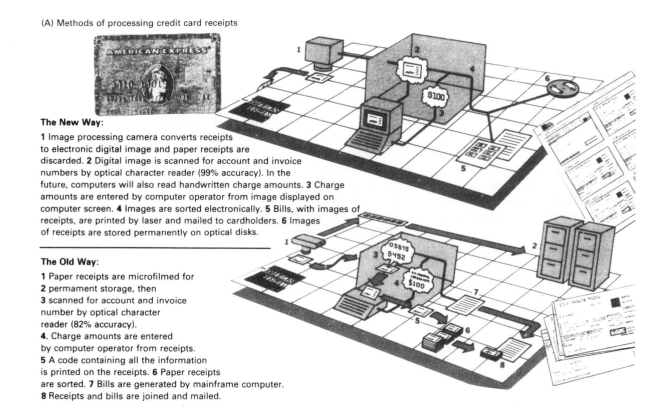

The New Way:

1 Image processing camera converts receipts to electronic digital image and paper receipts are discarded. **2** Digital image is scanned for account and invoice numbers by optical character reader (99% accuracy). In the future, computers will also read handwritten charge amounts. **3** Charge amounts are entered by computer operator from image displayed on computer screen. **4** Images are sorted electronically. **5** Bills, with images of receipts, are printed by laser and mailed to cardholders. **6** Images of receipts are stored permanently on optical disks.

The Old Way:

1 Paper receipts are microfilmed for **2** permamement storage, then **3** scanned for account and invoice number by optical character reader (82% accuracy). **4**. Charge amounts are entered by computer operator from receipts. **5** A code containing all the information is printed on the receipts. **6** Paper receipts are sorted. **7** Bills are generated by mainframe computer. **8** Receipts and bills are joined and mailed.

(B) A page of laser-printed images of charge card receipts

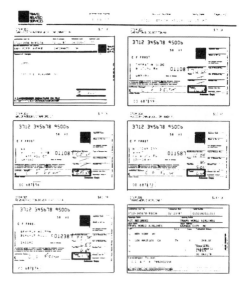

FIGURE 8-8
Image processing used for credit card billing

Page printer   Tape drive   One of several consoles to help monitor and control computer operation   Processor unit   Disk storage on direct access storage devices (DASDs)

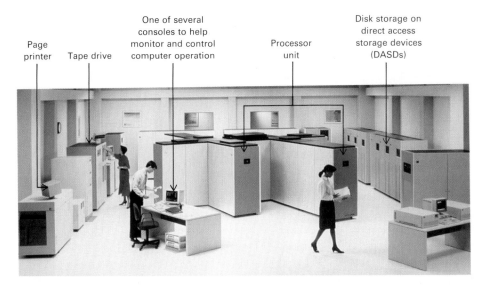

FIGURE 8-9
A mainframe computer

COMPUTER CENTER

The bank's **computer center** is a large room where the mainframe computer hardware is located. The mainframe is not one, but many, pieces of hardware, much like that shown in Figure 8-9. Many pieces are as big as a refrigerator and are completely boxed up. Only a few terminals, called *consoles*, show any signs of activity. **Consoles** silently monitor the hardware, and they display performance data on their screens. Remarkably few people actually work in the enormous room. It is as if the machines run themselves.

It is now possible for large organizations to have entire rooms or floors of mainframe computers operate without any human intervention. Some organizations refer to this phenomenon as a "lights out" operation, because the machines operate in literally blackened computer centers. The control console or consoles can be located in any room, which allows an operator to perform other duties. Warning signals indicate when human attention is required.

All the real activity occurs outside the computer center. Hundreds of terminal users like the bank tellers and automated teller machine users are pockets of computer activity.

The bank exercises tight security precautions for the computer center, as do most other large computer centers. For example, a security guard protects the floor of the building where the mainframe computer is housed. Only authorized personnel and guests are allowed entry.

Mainframe Computer

Major differences immediately distinguish mainframe from personal computers. One of the obvious things is the need for a special air-cooled, raised-floor room to house the mainframe hardware. Cooling keeps the circuitry from overheating and burning. The raised floor enables hidden cables that act as electronic roadways to be laid to connect peripherals, like disk drives, to the processing unit, as the diagram in Figure 8-10 shows.

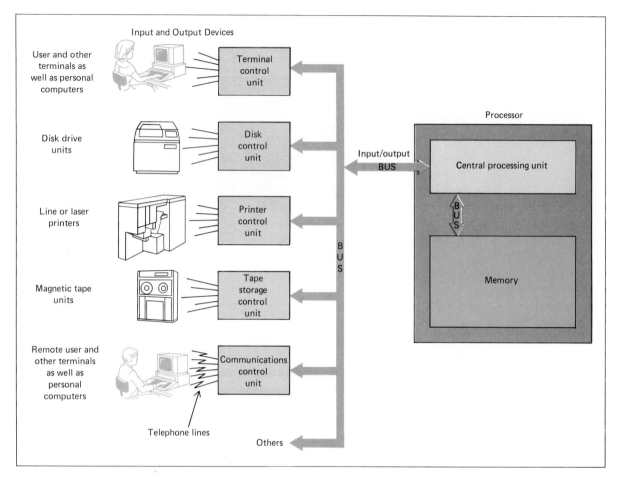

FIGURE 8-10
Relationship of a mainframe
processor to other hardware

Processor

The processor is the focal point of all computer hardware. Its size is enormous in a mainframe when compared to a desktop-size system unit. In mainframe systems, **processors** house only the central processing unit and memory. Separate **control units** handle input and output control.

Mainframe processors have a larger *word size,* as shown in Figure 8-11. **Word size** refers to the number of bits a processor handles at one time. The greater the word size, the faster the processing.

Because only one program instruction is executed at a time, speed is a relevant computer issue. It is especially relevant when hundreds of users must be serviced.

Computer operating speeds are measured in the following units:

- Millisecond = one thousandth of a second
- Microsecond = one millionth of a second
- Nanosecond = one billionth of a second
- Picosecond = one trillionth of a second

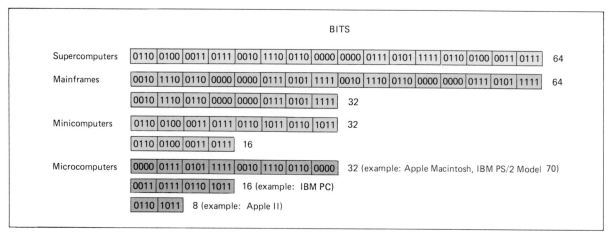

FIGURE 8-11
Width of one program instruction or
"word" handled by a computer's
central processing unit

National Bank's mainframe operates at the nanosecond speed. To give some perspective to how incredibly fast that is, it has been estimated that an average person taking one step each nanosecond could circle the earth about 20 times in 1 second.

Today's advanced microcomputers and minicomputers also operate at nanosecond speeds. Several nanoseconds are necessary to carry out a single program instruction. So computer processing speed is often also identified as a smaller number of **MIPS**, or **millions of instructions per second.**

While MIPS measure the rate at which a computer performs all types of instructions, *MFLOPS* or *millions of floating-point (arithmetic) operations per second,* measure the rate of performing only arithmetic instructions. The MFLOPS measurement traditionally was used to reference technical or scientific computers, such as supercomputers. It is now used to rate the performance of all computer classifications.

The diagram of the processor unit shown in Figure 8-12 helps explain how processing works. The processor works the same in a personal computer as in the bank's mainframe. The diagram shows two major components of a **mainframe processor**:

· **Central processing unit**, which consists of a control unit and an arithmetic/logic unit
· **Memory**, which temporarily stores programs and data

Both are connected by electronic circuitry or roadways known as *buses.*

Processing requires the operating system (equivalent to DOS on a microcomputer) to work in close coordination with the central processing unit. Inside the central processing unit the *control unit* carries out program instructions. The *arithmetic/logic unit* calculates and compares data when instructed by the control unit. Arithmetic operations are normal addition, subtraction, multiplication, and division.

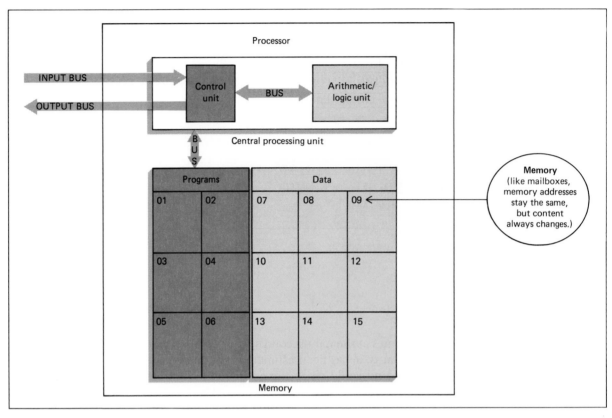

FIGURE 8-12
Inside a processor

Memory

The diagram shows how memory is sectioned off by the operating system into locations with addresses. *Memory addresses* are like mailboxes where the addresses never change, but content varies every time a new program is loaded and processed.

Programs typically are stored on disk and then are read into memory when needed. National Bank's check processing program is read into memory early in the day for use by tellers throughout the day. On the other hand, individual customer accounts, which are data, are brought into memory for only a brief time when needed by the check processing program.

Processing

Another diagram, shown in Figure 8-13, gives an example of how processing actually occurs. The example involves something done everyday during check processing: add a customer's deposit amount to their old balance. The example shows how a customer's new deposit of $200 is added to the old balance of $400. The example assumes that previous processing put the customer's old balance in the arithmetic/logic unit. The remaining steps to process the transaction are as follows:

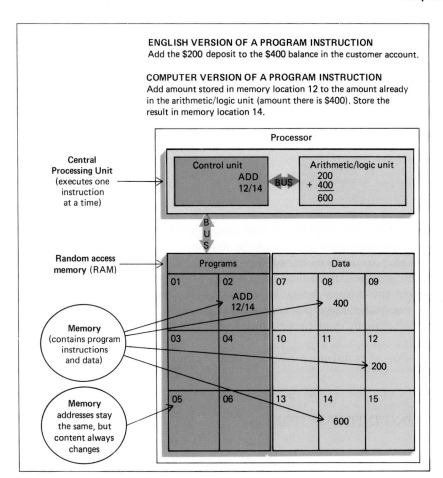

FIGURE 8-13
How a computer executes a program instruction

- First, a program instruction is brought by the operating system from its memory location and is temporarily stored in the control unit. In the example, the instruction is ADD, and the memory address 12 holds the data to be added.
- Next, data are brought by the operating system from memory location 12 and are temporarily placed in the arithmetic/logic unit. In the example, the value 200 is retrieved.
- Next, the central processing unit takes over to process the operation specified in the instruction, which is an "add" operation. In this example, the new amount in the arithmetic/logic unit is added to the amount already resident there.
- Finally, the result, 600 is transferred by the operating system to memory location 14.

A later program instruction makes the operating system store the data on an external disk for future reference and processing. This example is greatly simplified. In addition, all program instructions and data are really processed as strings of 1's and 0's, or on and off electronic pulses. Nothing would be understandable in English.

A SAMPLER	
Company	Product
Amdahl	5990 Series
Bull HN	DPS 8000 Series
IBM	ES 9000 Series
NCR	9800 Series
UNISYS	V Series

FIGURE 8-14
Examples of mainframe computers

The bank has more than one mainframe. Some handle special jobs, such as teller processing, and some act as backups in case of failure. The administrative computer is *plug compatible* with the teller processing computer. **Plug compatibles** are computer products that mimic other brands of computer products. In theory, if the plug of the original brand is removed and replaced with the plug of a compatible computer, the replacement will perform in an identical way. Usually plug-compatible mainframe processors cost less and are more powerful than the products they emulate.

A sampling of mainframe suppliers and products appears in Figure 8-14.

STORING INFORMATION

One report points out that the Bank of America requires 600 trillion bits of storage capacity annually for its checking transactions. Much of this mainframe storage is on hard disk, magnetic tapes, and optical disks. National Bank and other organizations use similar data storage devices.

Disk Storage

Mainframe disk storage units house hard disks that are larger, but essentially the same, as those in a personal computer. In mainframe jargon, hard disks are called *direct access storage devices (DASDs)*, as identified in Figure 8-9. They consist of large units holding multiple disk platters, and some can store 23 billion bytes of information. As with microcomputer storage, the trend is toward making units smaller so that they occupy less space.

Hard disks are the bank's main storage medium for information that must be instantly available. They are fast and allow data to be retrieved at random, which is called **random**, or *direct*, **access**. Random access is possible because all data are always available to the disk read/write heads, as shown in Figures 8-15 and 8-16. The device works like a musical record on a record player, where the player's arm can be deposited on any track to access the music there.

Data records on a computer disk can be erased and reused on the spot. This is important when a customer's current balance changes as a result of a withdrawal. The instantly updated balance provides a control for follow-up transactions the customer may initiate.

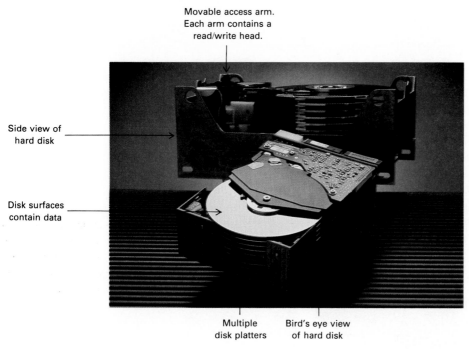

Movable access arm.
Each arm contains a
read/write head.

Side view of
hard disk

Disk surfaces
contain data

Multiple
disk platters

Bird's eye view
of hard disk

FIGURE 8-15
Two cutaway views of a hard disk

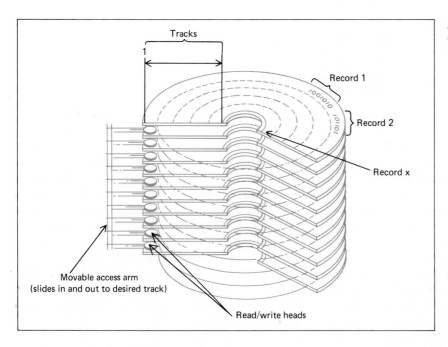

FIGURE 8-16
Cutaway diagram of a hard disk

Tracks

1

Record 1

Record 2

Record x

Movable access arm
(slides in and out to desired track)

Read/write heads

FOCUS ON: *Making Chips*

Scientists at dozens of laboratories in Europe, Japan, and the United States are shrinking the present generation of computers. New technology allows the complex circuitry of hundreds of integrated circuit chips to be etched onto a baseball-size, thin wafer which contains hundreds of tiny integrated circuit chips. The technique is known as *wafer-scale integration.*

The allure of wafer-scale integration is that it removes, in one fell swoop, a host of problems usually associated with the production of integrated circuit chips and their assembly into computers.

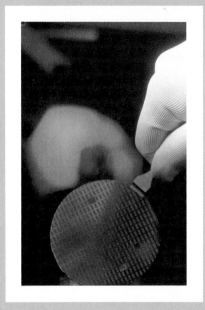

"You chop the wafer apart and then the first thing you do is put it back together," noted Dr. Robert R. Johnson, president of Mosaic Systems, Inc., a company in Michigan that is one of several companies developing the wafer-scale technology. "It's sort of nutty, but that's how the industry grew up."

Drawbacks

In a large computer, the big drawback is that all these separate chips slow things down tremen-

A single thin, baseball-size wafer contains hundreds of tiny integrated circuit chips.

Chip Manufacture

For years, the manufacture of integrated circuit chips has started with plain old sand, which is heated and formed into thin silicon wafers a few inches in diameter. In a complex series of steps, using light, chemicals, and special masks, not unlike tiny photographic negatives, the surface of these wafers is etched with "chip" patterns. These tiny chips are then tested, broken apart from the wafer, encased in carriers, hooked into printed circuit boards, and wired into the complex assemblages known as computers.

dously. It takes time for electrical signals to travel back and forth along the miles of electronic roadways that connect all the chips.

A single large wafer can eliminate this time lag, and several other problems as well. One is the huge expense of housing separate chips in a large computer cabinet and wiring them together, often by hand.

Approaches to creating a wafer range from the ambitious to the conservative. Whatever approach succeeds, researchers say that the active components of an entire supercomputer could eventually be etched on a single 5-inch wafer.

Other Storage

National Bank uses optical disks to back up current data for security purposes and to store data for historical record-keeping, or archival, purposes. One disk stores 2 billion bytes of information, which helps to keep storage space to a minimum.

The bank also uses **magnetic tape** for backup and archival purposes. Primary advantages of magnetic tape are that it is inexpensive, easy to store, and can be erased and reused.

Using computer magnetic tape is comparable to using an ordinary cassette tape recorder. It is a **sequential access** medium, as shown in Figure 8-17. If the last item on a tape is desired, the tape must be fast forwarded to its location. There is no way to randomly access the last item directly. This feature makes magnetic tape of limited day-to-day use in transaction-oriented computer systems.

A comparison of optical disks and other data storage media is given in Figure 8-18.

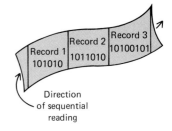

FIGURE 8-17
Record storage on a magnetic tape

PRINTING INFORMATION

The tour of the mainframe computer environment concludes with equipment used to print computer output. National Bank uses a heavy-duty laser printer and several line printers to service its printed output needs.

Occupying a large corner of the main computer center is a laser printer, like the one in Figure 8-19. High-production laser printers produce up to 200 pages per minute and produce professional-quality output.

FIGURE 8-18

	A DATA STORAGE SAMPLER	
MEDIA	TYPICAL STORAGE CAPACITY (IN CHARACTERS OR BYTES)	COMMENTS
Day-to-Day Use		
Floppy disk	.3 to 1.44 million	Small, inexpensive, and convenient for personal use.
Hard disk	7.5 billion	Fast, expensive, good for large volumes of instantly retrievable information.
Backup and Archival Use		
Optical disk	2 billion	Inexpensive, excellent for archival storage of information.
Magnetic tape	180 million	Inexpensive, good for archival storage of information.

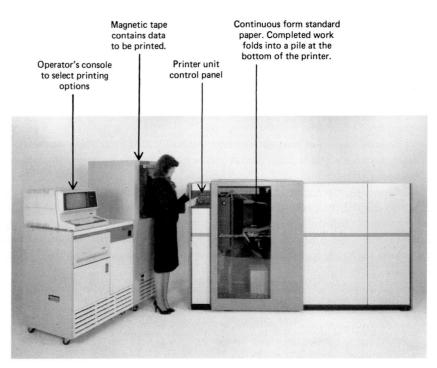

Magnetic tape contains data to be printed.

Operator's console to select printing options

Printer unit control panel

Continuous form standard paper. Completed work folds into a pile at the bottom of the printer.

FIGURE 8-19
A heavy-duty off-line laser printer

Line printers, like those in Figure 8-20, are housed in a very noisy and busy room. They clack away at about one-tenth the speed of a laser printer.

Line printers use hammer and inked ribbons to get characters on paper. They set up an entire line at one time, even though they print character by character. Printing happens so fast that it seems like an entire line is printed at once.

Several carbon copies can be produced. This is useful for reports that are distributed to several bank officers. But the poor print quality, combined with the noise, is steering the bank to replace the older line printers with high-speed dot-matrix and laser printers.

FIGURE 8-20
A line printer at a large mainframe installation

Printer unit control panel (start/stop button, jam light, etc.)

Glass window to observe printing progress

Cover to silence noise

230

DOWNSIZING COMPUTER SYSTEMS

Although mainframe computers have long been the data processing cornerstone of large organizations, their role is changing. Minicomputers and microcomputers now have the capabilities to take over some of the processing load.

Some organizations experience substantial savings by migrating down from a mainframe to a distributed network of personal computers in a local-area network. This shift of computing platforms from mainframes to PC-based networks is commonly called **downsizing**.

One downsizing option is a two-tiered strategy: a PC network linked directly to a mainframe. With such *client/server architecture*, the clients, or PCs on the network, and the server, or mainframe, work together to perform some task. For example, a PC in a travel office may ask a central mainframe for help in making an airline reservation.

Some companies advocate a third, middle tier, with a minicomputer. The minicomputer functions as a database server and adds processing power on the network. Regardless of hardware configuration, downsizing saves both operating and technical support costs. Applications can be built cheaper and faster on a local-area network than on a mainframe. One Fortune 500 company found that downsizing increased its computing capacity while cutting its data processing costs in half.

Figure 8-21 shows one way to classify computer hardware. As processing rates increase and prices fall, the lines separating these computer classes blur. For example, Sun Microcomputers is developing a high-end superminicomputer with processing power previously available only on supercomputers.

The next two sections examine minicomputers and supercomputer hardware.

FIGURE 8-21
Classification of computer hardware

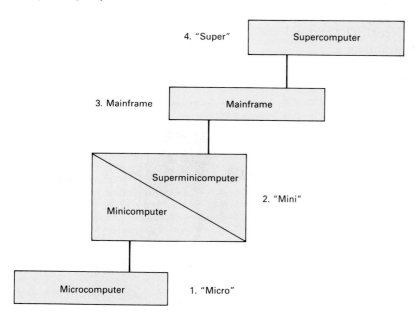

MINI AND RELATED COMPUTERS

Minicomputers, or *midrange computers*, such as the one shown in Figure 8-22, typically are smaller and cost less than mainframes. Their hardware is similar to that of mainframes. Most minicomputers do not require special air-cooled, raised-floor environments, as mainframes do. They can be installed almost anywhere and their computing power is evolving to rival low-end mainframes.

Minicomputers are suitable for many small- and medium-sized organizations, or departments of larger organizations. They function in every conceivable commercial environment:

- A Louisiana medical clinic that connects several user terminals to a mini. It provides patient records to doctors, nurses, and administrative personnel.
- A legal office that uses a mini to collect lawyers' time and charges for automatic client billing. It also is used for word processing, which saves an enormous amount of repetitive typing time.
- Numerous other small- and medium-sized businesses, as well as government and nonprofit organizations, do accounts receivable, accounts payable, and general ledger bookkeeping on minis.

The main minicomputer manufacturers are Digital Equipment Corporation (DEC) and IBM.

Threatening the minicomputer market is the microcomputer-based multiuser system. With such a system, users of microcomputers and inexpensive terminals share one host system, called a *supermicro*. Software and data are centrally shared and controlled in the supermicro and available to all users. Expensive hardware devices, such as printers and storage disks, are also shared among users.

Another threat to the minicomputer market are local-area networks which connect stand-alone microcomputers. They often provide equal or greater computing capabilities at a fraction of the cost of a minicomputer. For example, a NASA space flight center recently replaced its minicomputers with a network of microcomputers. The center documented productivity gains of 30 to 50 times over the minicomputers.

FIGURE 8-22
A large minicomputer like this could support banks, universities, and other high-volume processing facilities.

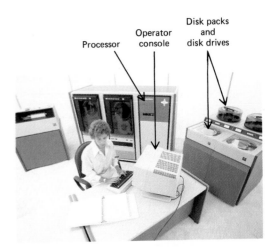

Processor   Operator console   Disk packs and disk drives

FIGURE 8-23
A superworkstation

The most powerful minicomputers are called *superminicomputers*. One of the fastest growing segments of superminis is high-performance workstations, or *superworkstations*, such as the one shown in Figure 8-23. The term *workstation* has come to designate a "power" user desktop, desk-side, or under-the-desk system. Workstations typically have large screens, for precision graphics, and advanced computing capabilities. Most use UNIX or other multitasking operating systems.

Such workstations are used, for example, by technicians who build computer hardware and software, as well as by engineers who construct electrical or mechanical computer-aided designs.

Some workstations use *RISC* (*Reduced Instruction Set Computing*, pronounced "risk") processors. A RISC processor may have only 30 to 50 instructions, while a conventional microprocessor chip may have 100 or more instructions. An instruction does such things as add two numbers in memory. To reduce its instruction set, the **RISC** processor eliminates seldom-used instructions and performs complex jobs using several of its simpler instructions. This results in increased processing speed.

Workstations are changing the way technicians and scientists conduct research. Processing that previously required a supercomputer can now be migrated down to a cluster of superworkstations. These implementations offer more convenience and cost a fraction of a supercomputer.

SUPERCOMPUTERS

Supercomputers do tasks that require massive amounts of data to be processed at extremely high speeds. Examples include petroleum and oil exploration, weather prediction, aircraft and automobile design, computer animation, and many areas of basic scientific research.

For example, aircraft designers typically build models or prototypes and require testing them in wind tunnels. It is more cost efficient to simulate the wind tunnel test using a supercomputer. As another example, the oil industry uses supercomputers to help pinpoint potential oil deposits, which avoids unnecessary drilling costs.

The Cray supercomputer, shown in Figure 8-24, uses several processor units

Supercomputer processing unit

FIGURE 8-24
A Cray supercomputer with a C-shaped processor unit

in parallel. Each processor is built in the shape of the letter C. It has many columns with vertical doors that open in order to check and replace defective controller boards. Hundreds of controller boards are layered in racks, the way a baker's oven layers racks of baked goods. They dwarf the single motherboard of a personal computer.

A list of major supercomputer manufacturers and products appears in Figure 8-25.

Parallel Processing

One way to obtain the processing power of a supercomputer without the cost is by harnessing less expensive processors to work together. **Parallel processing**, as shown in Figure 8-26, involves multiple central processor units working on various parts of the same job simultaneously.

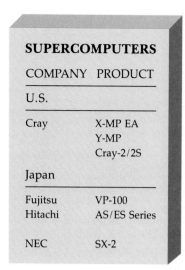

SUPERCOMPUTERS

COMPANY	PRODUCT
U.S.	
Cray	X-MP EA
	Y-MP
	Cray-2/2S
Japan	
Fujitsu	VP-100
Hitachi	AS/ES Series
NEC	SX-2

FIGURE 8-25

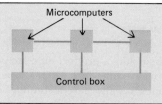

Coarse-grain architecture with a few powerful processors under the control of a central computer (the control box). Each processor can work alone on a job or with other processors.

Medium and fine-grained architecture with many processors. The laticelike arrangement is only one of several under commercial development.

FIGURE 8-26
Parallel processing systems

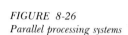

Parallel processing systems are used in technical applications, such as artificial intelligence, robotics, simulation analysis, chemical analysis, and aerodynamics. In addition, there is a growing commercial market for parallel processing computers. This includes retail credit authorization services, government and national security administration, international reservations systems, shop floor and inventory control, and on-line brokerage and banking services.

Some manufacturers produce **fault-tolerant computers** designed to be used in parallel. Their goal is not only added processing power, but also fail-safe operation. One vendor, for example, initially sells two processors to a new customer. More can be added as needed. The dual processors provide redundant components. If one fails, a duplicate component takes over without interruption. Transaction-oriented applications, like the bank's automated teller machines, depend on such uninterrupted computer service.

CASE STUDY: *Laser Device Could Be Key to Faster Computer*

Scientists at Bell Laboratories have introduced an experimental machine that uses pulses of light rather than currents of electricity to do calculations. Within several years, the new device, known as an optical computer, could reach speeds 1,000 times faster than the most powerful conventional computers.

Less than a foot high and about the size of a dining room tabletop, Bell Laboratories' new device has no counterpart in any other computer. There are no circuit boards or silicon chips. The machine consists of a network of lasers, lenses, and mirrors.

Unlike conventional electronic wires, light beams can intersect with no loss of data. In short, using pulses of light instead of electricity to perform calculations and to handle data is the computer equivalent of eliminating New York City's traffic jams by permitting cars and taxis to pass right through one another at intersections, rather than collide.

Optical computers could be used for tasks that require parallel computing, in which the processor simultaneously addresses millions of tasks. Among such tasks are image recognition—for example, discerning human faces in a security system, or acting as the

235

"eyes" for a robot assembling a product on a factory floor—and computing more easily the most difficult problems for which today's supercomputers are used.

These new machines will also have a stunning capacity to carry information. Future optical processors will be able to handle data equivalent to all the world's telephone conversations simultaneously. And an optical computer would be able to retrieve that data far more quickly than today's computers.

"It's the difference between going to a library and being able to read information from a single book versus being able to read all the books in the library at once," said Mr. Alan Huang, a leading optical computing researcher who heads the Bell Laboratories group. "It's like the Wright brothers," he said. "This is a technological milestone."

But other computer scientists point to the obstacles still faced by the optical computer. For example, the technology must be miniaturized so that millions of optical switches can be placed on a single small chip, as with semiconductors, so that they can be mass-produced inexpensively. Also, the programming of machines that can perform many tasks at once is still in its infancy.

DISCUSSION QUESTIONS

1. Discuss the advantages of optical over electrical computers. What are some obstacles faced by optical computers?

2. Discuss the impact optical computers could have on people and society.

CHAPTER SUMMARY

- Unlike a personal computer, a *terminal* has no system unit, or independent processing intelligence, and cannot process computer programs on its own.

- Special purpose terminals include: *bank teller terminals, automated teller machines,* and *point-of-sale terminals.*

- *Batch processing* occurs whenever data are saved and input at one time, in a "batch." *Transaction processing* occurs whenever data are entered directly into the computer that processes them, immediately as a transaction occurs.

- *Optical character recognition (OCR)* converts printed characters into electronic signals to be processed by a computer.

- A *magnetic ink character recognition (MICR)* device "reads," or scans, code printed in special magnetic ink and digitizes it for computer storage and processing.

- Some large organizations use *imaging devices* to take pictures of and digitize documents for processing and storage.

- A *computer center* is a large room where an organization's mainframe computer hardware is located.

- A *mainframe computer* consists of many pieces of hardware. *Console* terminals monitor the hardware and display performance data. Terminal users are outside the computer center.

- Some differences between a mainframe and a personal computer are: a mainframe handles multiple users, while a personal computer works with a single user; a mainframe needs a special air-cooled, raised-floor room to house the hardware, while a personal computer does not; a mainframe uses special *control units* to handle peripherals, while a personal computer uses controller boards to attach peripherals to the system board.

- The two main components of a *mainframe processor* are the central processing unit and memory. The *central processing unit* consists of a control unit and an arithmetic/logic unit. *Memory* temporarily stores programs and data.

- Hard disks allow data to be retrieved at random, which is called *random access.* This contrasts with magnetic tape, which is a *sequential access* medium.

- Laser printers and *line printers* handle large-volume printing required by mainframe organizations.

- *Minicomputers* are smaller and less costly than mainframes.

- A *workstation* is a "power" user system offering precision graphics and advanced computing capabilities.

- *Supercomputers* do tasks that require massive amounts of data to be processed at extremely high speeds.

- *Parallel processing* divides a processing job among multiple processing units.
- For fail-safe operation of critical applications, some companies use *fault-tolerant computers*. Dual processors ensure that if one fails, the other can take over.

SELECTED KEY TERMS

Batch processing	Magnetic ink character recognition (MICR)	Random access
Central processing unit	Mainframe computer	Sequential access
Computer center	Mainframe processor	Supercomputers
Console	Memory	Terminal
Control units	Minicomputer	Transaction processing
Fault-tolerant computers	Optical character recognition (OCR)	Workstation
Imaging device	Parallel processing	

REVIEW QUESTIONS

1. Compare a terminal with a personal computer.
2. Give examples of special-purpose terminals.
3. Compare batch and transaction processing.
4. What is the difference between a MICR and an imaging device?
5. What are some differences between personal computers and mainframe computers?
6. Identify the two main components of a mainframe processor.
7. What are common methods of storing mainframe computer data?
8. What kinds of printers handle large-volume printing requirements?
9. Compare a minicomputer with a mainframe.
10. What is a workstation?
11. What applications are appropriate for supercomputers?
12. What is parallel processing? Fault-tolerant computing?

EXERCISES

1. Investigate the hardware installed at your school's mainframe lab center, if one is available. Ask for assistance from a lab consultant to determine

   - The manufacturer of the mainframe and terminals
   - The word size of the processor
   - The data storage methods available
   - The types of printers used
   - The methods of data processing available, such as batch and on-line transaction processing.

2. Research current industry literature to prepare a report on methods of storing mainframe data. Include in your report the types of processing that are best suited for each storage method and the advantages and disadvantages of each. Do you foresee one method becoming dominant over the others in the future? Why or why not?

3. Special-purpose terminals, such as bank teller terminals, automated teller machines, and point-of-sale terminals, are rapidly becoming a part of everyday life. How have they served to make data collection and processing more efficient? What are their disadvantages, if any?

4. *Garner Industries Case.* Garner Industries is a large manufacturing firm that currently does all its data processing manually. The company is preparing to build two new plants, which will greatly increase its sales processing volume. The president of Garner has asked you to investigate the computer alternatives for the new plants and to make a recommendation. In your research, consider the following possibilities:

   - Mainframe
   - Minicomputer
   - Superminicomputer
   - Multiuser microcomputers

   Evaluate the advantages and disadvantages of each alternative and justify your recommendation.

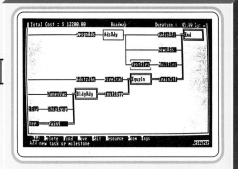

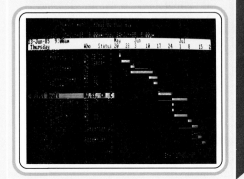

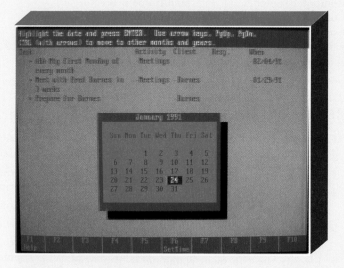

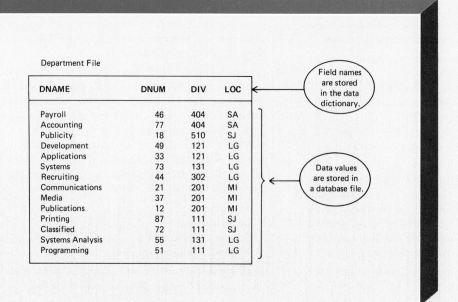

Department File

DNAME	DNUM	DIV	LOC
Payroll	46	404	SA
Accounting	77	404	SA
Publicity	18	510	SJ
Development	49	121	LG
Applications	33	121	LG
Systems	73	131	LG
Recruiting	44	302	LG
Communications	21	201	MI
Media	37	201	MI
Publications	12	201	MI
Printing	87	111	SJ
Classified	72	111	SJ
Systems Analysis	55	131	LG
Programming	51	111	LG

Field names are stored in the data dictionary.

Data values are stored in a database file.

9

Computer Systems
in Organizations

AFTER READING THIS CHAPTER, YOU SHOULD BE ABLE TO

- Identify types of computer system support found in organizations
- Give examples of three kinds of computer systems in organizations
- Describe software that supports workgroup activities in an organization

For many companies, the classic forms of corporate organizations no longer work very well. In the past, successful companies had a well-defined management hierarchy and a well-accepted way of assigning work tasks.

But the world changed. Partly as a result of widespread microcomputer and telecommunications use, the world has become more accessible, and change has become more rapid. Increasingly, competition has become global, markets have become deregulated, and new competitors have emerged.

The perfectly competitive organization of the future, according to some experts, will be an elaborate network of people and information, each exerting an influence on the other. A diagram of this network organization might show a small hub at the center surrounded by a widely dispersed network of resources.

Outside the hub, the network organization will carry on its functions of providing products and services. Inside the hub will be a small staff responsible for the strategic management of the company.

The traditional management hierarchy will be replaced by people who have the relevant information to contribute to the topic at hand. At the hub, the traditional division of labor will be replaced by a division of knowledge organized by new categories, such as setting goals and monitoring the results, and attracting resources.

Competitive advantage will rest increasingly in the way each network organization gathers and assesses information, makes its decisions, and then carries out those decisions.

One industry observer describes information as the "lifeblood" of business and computers as the "heart, the pump that keeps the blood flowing, nourishing the entire organization." Crucial to the management of information in every company is the structure of its computer-based systems.

This chapter provides an overview of the kinds of computer-based systems that support organizations of all sizes. It begins by examining "front-office," or mission critical, systems. These applications support the goals of an organization, such as facilitating service to customers at retail organizations or providing checking and savings services at a banking organization. Mission critical systems are becoming a competitive necessity as more and more organizations automate with computers.

While mission critical or front-office systems are unique to a company or to an industry, most types of organizations use similar "back-office" systems. They handle the routine payroll, accounts receivable, accounts payable, and other accounting-oriented activities of an organization. They are the most fundamental type of computer-based systems that pervade organizations of every size in every industry.

Many companies also use management and control systems, the third type of computer-based system looked at in this chapter. These systems provide managers with summary information to control organizational activities and do strategic planning.

This chapter walks through examples of each kind of computer-based system. It concludes by looking at a specialized category of software designed to support workgroup activities in organizations.

OVERVIEW OF ORGANIZATIONAL COMPUTER SYSTEMS

In modern organizations, computer-based systems, as identified in Figure 9-1, can be found to support three broad functional areas. For ease of understanding, this chapter will refer to these areas as

- Front-office support
- Back-office support
- Management and control support

Front-office, or **mission critical**, **computer systems** support the goals of an organization: what it does "over the counter in the front office" to fulfill its mission to customers, clients, or whoever is viewed as the target of the organization's critical reason for existence. In a bank, for example, the mission critical drive is to provide customers with money transaction services at a profit. Any of the bank's computer-based support systems that facilitate customer checking, savings, and loan transaction processing, therefore, are part of the organization's mission critical systems. Automated teller machines (ATMs), for example, are part of a bank's mission critical systems.

In an automobile company, for another example, the mission critical goal is to sell cars that customers desire at a profit. A computer-based system that supports selling or producing customized cars in time to meet a specified delivery date is a mission critical application.

Back-office, or **accounting-oriented**, **computer systems** support the handling

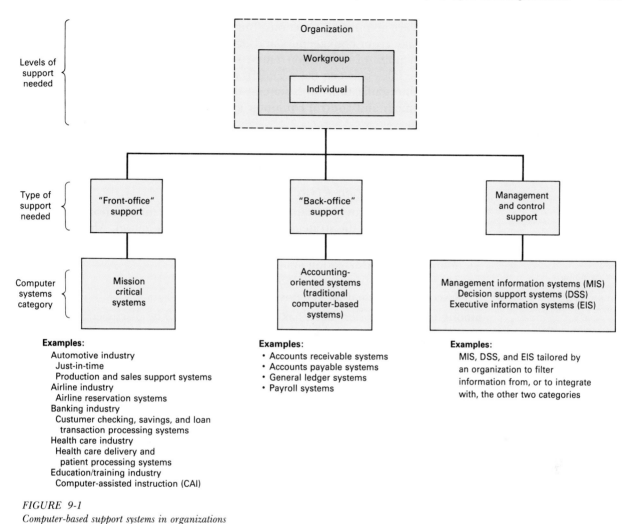

FIGURE 9-1
Computer-based support systems in organizations

of all the routine functions of any organization: what it does "behind the counter in the back office" to account for all daily transactions of the business activity.

Traditionally, accounting functions include the activities to record an organization's

- Accounts receivable (from customers)
- Accounts payable (to suppliers)
- General ledger bookkeeping (of income and expenses)

Many organizations today still function along traditional lines with clear distinctions between front- and back-office activities. At an automobile manufacturer, for example, the accounting information system records receipts for each car sold. It also records payments for raw materials used to manufacture cars.

Some automobile manufacturers have automated these back-office functions to a very sophisticated level. The FOCUS ON insert in "Telecommunications and Networking," Chapter 7, describes this trend.

In a bank, the activities to record a customer's loan payments or check withdrawals are accounting functions. But as computer automation moves these functions away from bookkeepers and data-entry clerks and closer to the customer's own point-of-transaction entry, such as through an automated teller machine, the lines between back- and front-office systems are blurring. This is a trend in all organizations with state-of-the-art computer-based systems.

Management and control computer systems pull together data from three sources:

- Front-office systems
- Back-office systems
- External sources that provide databases of information for a fee through a telecommunication service

This consolidation provides managers with summarized information to monitor, control, and plan for the strategic direction of the organization. Although these systems tend to be customized by organizations, they often are categorized as

- Management information systems (MIS)
- Decision support systems (DSS)
- Executive information systems (EIS)

among other categories. Each has a variation that will be discussed later in the chapter, but all have a common purpose to support management decision making.

Providing the foundation for all of an organization's systems are the database and telecommunication systems. These systems were discussed in detail in earlier chapters, and familiarity is assumed in this chapter.

The following sections detail the characteristics of the three types of support systems in organizations. The discussion begins with mission critical systems to support front-office activities.

MISSION CRITICAL SYSTEMS

Computers are beginning to be widely used for front-office support functions. It is these front-end, or *mission critical*, systems that will help organizations position themselves for doing business in the 21st century. And they may spell the difference between those companies who succeed and those who fail.

Mission critical applications address the goal, or "mission," of the organization. For service companies, mission critical systems most often directly involve the servicing of customers. Such systems usually improve customer service or extend it in some way. In manufacturing industries, mission critical systems often improve the production of some physical end product.

Some mission critical systems directly generate revenue for the organization. The classic example of a mission critical application is American Airlines' Sabre system, which is a computerized travel reservation system. It lists the flight schedules of every major airline in the world and automates booking procedures for travel agents.

American Airlines uses the Sabre system to gain a competitive edge in its industry. It offers the system, for a fee, to other airlines and travel agencies. This has generated millions of dollars for the airline and prompted its president to say, "We are now in the data processing as well as in the airline business."

A SAMPLER OF MISSION CRITICAL SYSTEMS

Coopers and Lybrand, a Big Eight accounting firm, specializes in tax planning and auditing for large organizations. In order to improve the quality and increase the speed of servicing clients, the firm uses a computer-based support program called ExperTAX. ExperTAX guides staff accountants through the tax audit information gathering process. Then ExperTAX analyzes the information using built-in knowledge accumulated from the company's experts. It identifies the client's basic tax issues and recommends the best tax choices. ExperTAX also serves as a teaching tool for field auditors.

The *Hospital of St. Raphael*, in New Haven, Connecticut, installed a computer-based system to improve its patient delivery services and to free nursing staff from paper shuffling. Nurses previously spent up to 25 percent of their day doing patient-related paperwork. Now all patient condition reports, prescription orders, notes, and other information are entered directly into a terminal in the patient's room. The hospital expects the patient care system to eliminate a major portion of its clerical and information processing labor costs.

American Airlines was forced to address the issue of aircraft maintenance demands as its fleet grew quickly over a 5-year span. American developed a computer-based system to ensure that every plane meets the Federal Aviation Administration's aircraft maintenance requirements. The system, called Maintenance Operation Control Advisor (MOCA), helps a human planner to make better maintenance scheduling decisions. MOCA is updated every 5 minutes from American's mainframe with flight changes which can affect maintenance planning. The system immediately analyzes all incoming data and makes recommendations for rescheduling. This gives planners more alternatives when scheduling aircraft maintenance and repairs.

Florida's 8th Judicial Circuit Court uses a network of computers to support the management and processing of criminal cases. The system, called the Criminal Justice Information System (CJIS), handles all of the calendaring, scheduling, and docketing for the circuit court. It facilitates the preparation of state-required forms and management reports of arrest, bail, and sentencing cases. Prior to the implementation of CJIS, one county was contemplating adding six more employees at a cost of $150,000 annually to keep up with paperwork demands. Now CJIS completes the documents in minutes.

Chrysler Service, a Chrysler Corporation unit that handles auto service contracts, needed a way to handle increased service center calls in the face of budgetary restraints. It installed a computer-based voice processing system to aid in processing service contracts and freeing service center agents for more productive work. The system allows agents from 5,500 dealerships nationwide to call the center 24 hours a day to check on customer service contracts. The voice processing system does the work of an average 9.9 agents and cuts in half the time required for an average service center call.

FIGURE 9-2

Merrill Lynch and Company, the stock brokerage firm, also developed a mission critical system that gave it a competitive edge. It used computers to create one of its most successful products ever: the cash management account (CMA). CMA combines information on a customer's checking, savings, credit card, and securities accounts into one computerized monthly statement. In addition, it automatically "sweeps" idle funds into interest-bearing money market funds. With this approach, Merrrill Lynch has lured billions of dollars of assets from other places, even though rivals now have similar offerings.

As such use of computer technology continues, every industry will be affected. But upstaging a rival today is no guarantee of superiority tomorrow. Often competitors respond in kind, bringing the situation back to normal. So aggressive organizations must keep innovating to maintain an edge. Often the beneficiary of these competitive thrusts is the customer, who gets faster service, a cheaper airfare, or a new product.

Examples of some other successful mission critical systems in organizations are given in Figure 9-2. The examples show that such systems do not have to give organizations a competitive edge. Instead, most mission critical systems have straightforward goals to improve whatever the organization does on a daily basis.

For example, one snack-food company uses a computer-based system to optimize truck routes. This enables drivers to make faster, more efficient deliveries to customers. It also reduces the amount of driving time and resources needed to fill each order.

FOCUS ON: *Reengineering in the 90s*

In a booming voice that needed no amplification, independent consultant Mike Hammer spelled out today's corporate agenda at a conference of executives: "Reengineering is the name of the game in the 90s. If you don't rebuild the business, you're dead, finished, over."

In simple terms, to reengineer a company is to recast the organization's operating units so they are more in line with its mission. Hammer's litany of companies engaged in corporate examinations included AT&T, IBM, Shell Oil Co., Xerox Corp., Deere & Co., Citicorp, Ford Motor Co., and many financial service firms.

Included on the list was Aetna Life and Casualty Co. The $19 billion Hartford, Connecticut, insurer reorganized its headquarters operations, a move that will lead to some major changes. The reorganization will wipe out a layer of middle management that has been rendered obsolete by computer and telecommunication technologies.

Facilitating Change

To facilitate change and to familiarize upper echelons with information systems, Aetna and other companies are sending executives back to school. Executives learn how they can exploit technology—in their daily routines and in their strategic thinking—for the business lines they manage.

Computer literacy training has been a must for Aetna executives since Ronald Compton became the company's president. Compton firmly believes quality suffers when systems are deployed by executives without hands-on computer experience.

"The major problem in the implementation of technology is not the technicians, nor the programmers, nor the systems analysts," he says. "The major problem is the businessperson who does not know what he or she wants and is unable to accurately communicate what little they can figure out."

Under the new structure, instead of 5 subordinates, managers will have as many as 10 to 15 people reporting to them. "It takes two things to do that," Compton says. "First, it takes the right people. Second, it takes technology."

ACCOUNTING-ORIENTED SYSTEMS

While mission critical systems present the greatest opportunities and competitive advantages, accounting systems are the most fundamental of computer-based applications. *Accounting-oriented systems* support back-office functions by doing the routine volume processing tasks in organizations. Another name for this type of system, especially in a mainframe environment, is a **data processing system**.

The specific accounting software to support back-office functions varies depending on the size of the computer used, as shown in Figure 9-3. Small- to

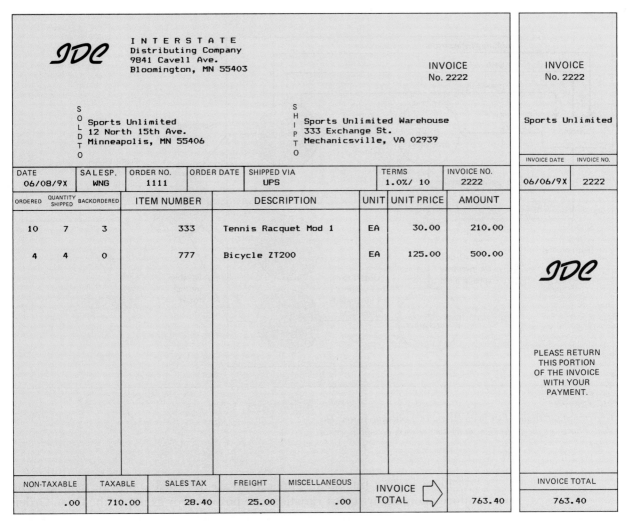

FIGURE 9-10
A computer-generated invoice using a preprinted form

They are by-products of entering the original order. Once order data are entered, they are reused to generate all required follow-up documents. All that is required to get any of these documents is to make a menu selection.

Overall, Interstate Distributing Company estimates that order processing productivity has improved about 50 percent over manual methods. Such increased efficiency is measurable throughout all of its newly automated functions.

Management Information Benefits

Interstate's sales manager often questions reasons for order shipping delays. The *Open Order Report*, shown in Figure 9-12, provides answers about which customers have unshipped orders. It also shows exactly what items are causing the backorder problem. The report is especially valuable

- To help avoid potential problems with customers
- To spot negative trends that may need reversing

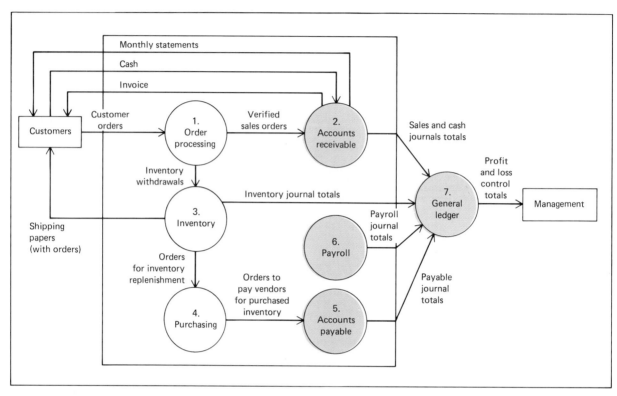

FIGURE 9-11
Overview of information flow in an integrated accounting system. The shaded areas are the applications at the core of every accounting-based system.

Because all of Interstate's applications are designed to provide management information, many report variations are possible. For example, the Open Order Report can be based on a select group of customers or a select item or group of items. In addition, it can be sorted in various ways, such as on customer ID or order status. Reports can also be displayed instead of printed. Most are available on a regularly scheduled or on an on-demand basis.

FIGURE 9-12
A daily report of unshipped orders by customer account

```
06/08/9X                          Interstate Distributing Company                              Page 1
                                    O P E N   O R D E R   R E P O R T

                    CUST    -------DATE-------     -----DESCRIPTION-----     QTY    -------QUANTITY/DOLLAR-------
  ORDER  STATUS     ID      ORDER  REQ'D  SHIP     ITEM NO.        PRICE    AVAIL    ORDERED  SHIPPED  BACKORDER

    214  PICKED     ABLE    05/24                  Ski-Rosner 190            510          8        0          0
                                                   420           200.00            1600.00        0        .00
   1114  BKORD      ABLE    06/06  06/15           Ski-Water Adult             2         10        0         10
                                                   666            50.00             500.00        0     500.00
                                                   ------------TOTAL-----------     2100.00        0     500.00


   1111  BKORD      SPRTSU  06/06  06/10  06/08    Tennis Racquet Mod 1        0         10        7          3
                                                   333            30.00             300.00   210.00      90.00
                                                   ------------TOTAL-----------      300.00   210.00      90.00
```

```
06/08/9X              Interstate Distributing Company              Page   1
                  S A L E S   H I S T O R Y  -  S U M M A R Y


      -----------CUSTOMER-------------
    ID            NAME              COST         SALES        PROFIT      %

  ABLE        Able Active Sports  26,120.25     37,252.80    11,132.55   29.9
  SPRTSU      Sports Unlimited     3,805.21      5,535.40     1,729.83   31.3


            G R A N D   T O T A L S  29,925.46   42,788.20   12,862.38   30.1
```

FIGURE 9-13
An on-demand Sales History Report that identifies profit by customer

The sales manager also finds a *Sales History Report* valuable. The report can be printed in summary form, as shown in Figure 9-13, or with detail for selected dates, up to one year. With this report he can analyze how his sales strategies are doing. He often sorts the report

- By item number: to identify products that are the most and least profitable. On examining this report, he asks, "Are sales efforts directed toward the most profitable products?"
- By product category: to identify groups of products that are the most and least profitable lines for the company to carry.
- By customer: to identify which customers are the most profitable. Using this summary he asks, "Does the sales staff presently spend the most time with these customers?"
- By salesperson: to identify which salespeople are the most profitable. The report answers the question, "Are the leading salespeople also the most profitable?"

Exception Reports

At Interstate Distributing Company, managers practice **management by exception**. The approach advocates spending time on exceptional conditions and not wasting valuable time on things that are performing as expected. To help support this style of management, most managers prefer **exception reports**. They list only the special, or exceptional, cases that require management attention or action. As an example, the sales manager might select the most and least successful people to appear on a salesperson report. While the most successful might be rewarded with incentives, the least successful might be scheduled for more training or other action.

The consequences of these sales reports are considerable. Managers adjust the company's marketing and other strategies based on answers the reports provide.

The higher up the management hierarchy a manager moves, the less detail ordinarily appears on reports. Instead, reports become focused on the so-called big picture. Management of the day-to-day operations is left to lower-level staff people.

In addition to prepared reports, Interstate's software provides an inquiry and report-generation capability. It is similar to the same capabilities described in Chapter 6, "Database Software."

While the software Interstate uses to run its business is not perfect, it provides relevant and timely information that the company never had before. It has enabled Interstate to make decisions that have reduced both customer bad debts and inventory costs. These decisions alone have more than paid for the investment in computer hardware, software, and training.

MANAGEMENT AND CONTROL SYSTEMS

Industry-specific packages as well as integrated accounting packages provide management and control information as a by-product of routine processing. These packages work primarily on microcomputer- and minicomputer-based systems.

In mainframe-based organizations, things can be different. Separate systems usually are custom-built to extract management and control information from accounting and mission critical systems. They are often categorized as one or more of the following:

- **Management information systems (MIS)**, which provide information to address recurring managerial issues, such as Which salesperson sold the most units? or How do current sales figures compare to the same quarter last year?
- **Decision support systems (DSS)**, which provide support for nonrecurring, often unstructured decision-making tasks, such as analyzing financial data for a possible takeover of another company.
- **Executive information systems (EIS)**, which provide top-level executives with highly filtered, summary information from internal company and external competitive intelligence sources. EIS support executives who are responsible for strategic management and control of the organization.

The following sections describe how each of these systems is used in organizations.

Management Information Systems (MIS)

Traditional management information systems are targeted at managers of all levels. At National Bank, for example, a management information system is used to answer operational management questions such as, Are new loans being processed in a timely fashion? as well as tactical management questions, such as, What proportion of loan payments are in default for 30, 60, 90, and 120 days?

In a management information system, many of the problems addressed can be anticipated in advance. They are often called *structured* problems. For instance, any time a loan manager at National Bank wants to know which accounts are delinquent, a standard set of data is examined. This includes delinquent customer name, date of last payment, and amount of last payment. Only the numbers change from one delinquent report to the next. This type of structured information is easily generated by the organization's management information system.

As evident from Figure 9-14, management information system is usually an

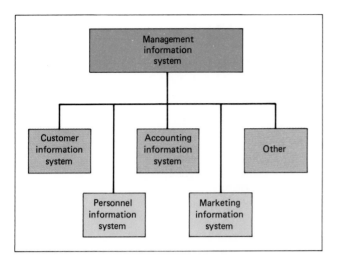

FIGURE 9-14
Subsystems function as components in a management information system.

umbrella term for a collection of more specific information systems. Large companies, like the bank, create these systems to supplement accounting-oriented, or data processing, systems that do not provide adequate management information.

One of the new systems developed by National Bank is an innovative type of management information system. It

- Delivers information primarily in a graphic, rather than textual or numeric, format.
- Focuses all information around the organization's strategic, or critical success, factors. Exceptions to acceptable performance are highlighted to act as an early warning of trouble.

The new system adds graphics and more refined information to the traditional management information system. Its goal is to communicate more clearly with decision makers.

Critical Success Factors

Critical success factors are the limited number of areas in which results, if they are satisfactory, will ensure successful competitive performance for an organization. As the examples in Figure 9-15 indicate, they are consistent with an organization's goals. After an organization identifies its critical success factors, information that is required to measure their success must be identified.

Information that decision makers require to evaluate performance varies by responsibility level, as identified in Figure 9-16. Sometimes it comes from extracting data from the corporate database. Sometimes it comes from purchasing databases of on-line demographic and competitive industry data. Whatever its source, usually *raw data* must be massaged through extraction, aggregation, regrouping, or reprocessing to give them added decision-making *information* value.

EXAMPLES OF CRITICAL SUCCESS FACTORS

TYPE OF ORGANIZATION	EXAMPLES OF GOALS	EXAMPLES OF CRITICAL SUCCESS FACTORS
Profit oriented		

Automotive industry	Improved:
	   Earnings per share
	   Return on investment
	   Market share
	   New product success
		Successful styling
		Good-quality dealer system
		Controlled cost
		Meet energy standards

Supermarket industry	(Same as above)	Successful product mix Optimized inventory Effective sales promotions Profitable pricing
Nonprofit oriented		
Hospital	Excellence of health care Meet future health care needs	Integration of health care with other regional hospitals Efficient use of scarce medical resources Improved cost accounting

FIGURE 9-15

FIGURE 9-16

INFORMATION REQUIREMENTS OF DECISION MAKERS

Management Level	Information Requirements

Strategic	External information on:
	   Customer actions
	   Competitive actions
	   Government actions
	   Availability of resources
	   Demographic trends
	Forecasts of long-term industry trends
	Results of previous analyses about long-term trends

Tactical	Information on:
	   Corporate historical patterns
	   Current performance
	   Exceptional performance trends (with both positive and negative impacts)
	Forecasts on short-term industry trends
	Results of previous analyses about short-term trends

Operational	Information on:
	   Recent past performance
	   Current performance
	   Exceptional performance (with both positive and negative impacts)

Decision Support Systems (DSS)

A *decision support system (DSS)*, a second type of management and control system, is used to analyze information for nonrecurring or unstructured decision-making tasks. In contrast to a management information system, many of the problems addressed with decision support systems cannot be defined and anticipated in advance. In addition, a good deal of data manipulation is expected of the user.

Any organization or individual with basic spreadsheet and database management system packages has the fundamental capabilities identified with a decision support system.

In an example case, the sales manager at Interstate is concerned about developing a new sales commission plan. He wants to explore alternative plans and their effect on next year's budget based on best- and worst-case sales year projections. The problem lends itself to asking "what if" type questions of information presented in a spreadsheet model.

At the center of every decision support system is some type of financial modeling software. As discussed in Chapter 5, it could be a spreadsheet package, a financial modeling package, or even a decision support system package, such as those identified in Figure 5-15. All these "tools" offer ways to model a problem to support a number-oriented decision-making task.

But not all nonrecurring, unstructured-type decision making is number oriented. Some is data oriented. So a decision support system package provides database inquiry capabilities, often by links to an organization's established database system.

An example case is when Interstate's sales manager had to query the company's database to explore the impact of the new sales commission plan. He searched for all salespeople who were at varying levels under and over their sales quota to date. He did averages, sums, and other calculations that provided numbers for planning purposes. Some of the numbers were plugged into his spreadsheet planning model for the commission problem.

In addition to basic database inquiry and modeling capabilities, more elaborate versions of packaged decision support systems include telecommmunication links to on-line database services. It is possible to think about such packaged systems as the glue that pulls together three familiar applications: spreadsheet, database, and telecommunications.

Executive Information Systems (EIS)

The third type of management-oriented system discussed here is *executive information systems (EIS)*. They provide top-level executives with effortless access to condensed information that helps with their strategic management of the organization. Executive information systems are primarily vehicles for tracking, analyzing, and displaying summary data about key or critical success factors for the organization and its competitors. They retrieve crucial data, filter it, and present it to managers in an easy-to-use and easy-to-understand, often graphical, form. Usually data manipulation is not a primary concern, as it is in a decision support system.

One analysis feature common to most executive information systems is called *drill down*. **Drill down** allows managers to examine particular data in as much detail as desired. Figure 9-17 illustrates how one executive uses this feature to analyze a company's performance. The executive chooses the "Investigate" icon

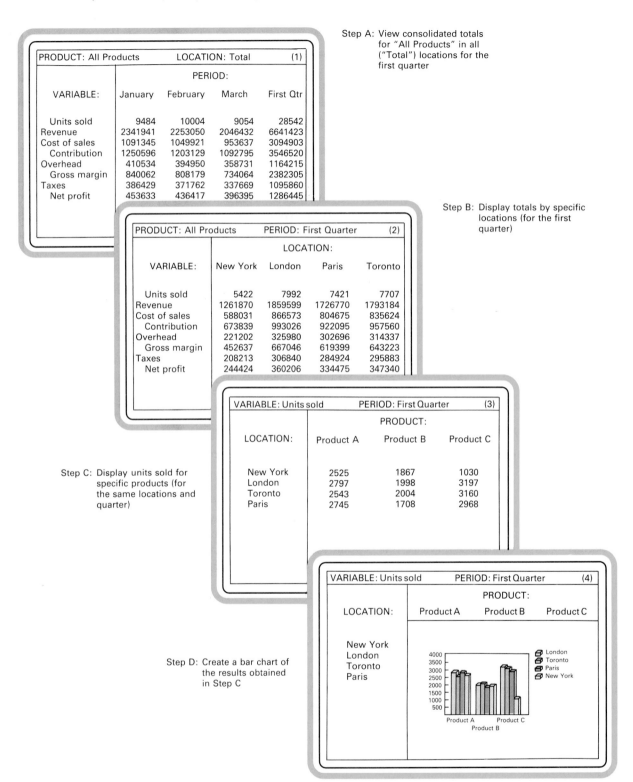

Step A: View consolidated totals for "All Products" in all ("Total") locations for the first quarter

Step B: Display totals by specific locations (for the first quarter)

Step C: Display units sold for specific products (for the same locations and quarter)

Step D: Create a bar chart of the results obtained in Step C

FIGURE 9-17
A drill-down example in an executive information system (EIS)

A SAMPLER

Microcomputer Packages

Command Center EIS
Commander EIS
Compete!
Encore EIS Toolkit
Executive Edge
Global EIS

Mainframe and Minicomputer Packages

Advanced Management Information System (AMIS)
Command Center EIS
Commander EIS
Executive Decisions
Executive Edge
Express/EIS

FIGURE 9-18
Examples of executive information
system (EIS) packages

on the main menu. The next screen shows first quarter financial data for the company's entire product line.

The executive "drills down" to obtain more information. He selects "LOCATION," and the next screen displays data by individual locations. It shows, for example, that New York is behind other locations in units sold and net profit. The executive drills down another level to look at product performance. The display shows the New York market is performing acceptably with Products A and B; the problem is with Product C.

This example illustrates how an executive information system enables probing to help identify potential problems. Drill down gives executives immediate feedback and the opportunity to take corrective action.

Executives often must look outside their own organizations for strategic information, especially about competition. This is why an important feature of executive information systems, as well as decision support systems, is telecommunication links to external database services.

A list of some available executive information system packages is given in Figure 9-18.

WORKGROUP SUPPORT

In most organizations, individuals belong to some functional workgroup, such as the sales order processing department, marketing department, or executive management team. These groups often need to share or develop ideas and be able to jointly manage schedules or documents and projects.

The class of software that facilitates the productivity of groups is called **workgroup computing software**, *computer-supported cooperative work*, or *group-*

A SAMPLER

Higgins
Lotus Notes
Office Works
Syzygy
The Coordinator
Together
Wordperfect Office

FIGURE 9-19
Examples of workgroup
support products

ware. This software includes modules for electronic mail, group scheduling, and group calendaring. Some products are listed in Figure 9-19.

The following example of how workgroup computing software supports group projects focuses on software not discussed elsewhere in this book.

A Workgroup Computing Example

In some modern organizations, workgroup members "meet" and converse electronically over networks using electronic mail, as well as a variety of other software applications.

One example of workgroup computing in action is at Secord Sports, a large bicycle manufacturer. Secord's vice president of marketing is project leader for a million-dollar new product introduction. She chooses workgroup members from the product development, publicity, marketing, and art departments. She then uses a variety of software applications on the company's local-area network to put together a product introduction proposal.

The first type of software the vice president uses is **project management software**. It helps with the formal planning and control of projects. It characteristically presents a project schedule as a chart, such as those shown in Figure 9-20. The vice president uses the software to help

- Divide a project into manageable units or tasks
- Assign resources (people, machines, materials) to each task
- Reassign resources to tasks as a situation changes

Project management packages are oriented for workgroups as well as for single users.

Next the vice president sets "Completion By," "Reply By," and "Remind Me" dates for the project tasks. She works with groupware scheduling software to enter these dates electronically into each participant's calendar.

To schedule an introductory face-to-face meeting, groupware scheduling software is again used. This time it helps to coordinate the time and activities of team members. It allows any group member to view the calendars of others for scheduling meetings and making appointments.

Most workgroup members have two calendars, one for group and one for personal use. **Personal information manager (PIM)** software handles a group member's personal calendar. It can also maintain lists of anything desired, such as "to do" lists. An example of a task list created with a personal information manager is given in Figure 9-21.

The vice president indicates whom she wants to attend the introductory meeting and types in the proposed time. The group scheduling software checks each attendee's calendar, flags any conflicts, and tentatively schedules the meeting. The software notifies each group member to send an electronic mail note to confirm their attendance.

The project begins with the face-to-face meeting to discuss project goals and member responsibilities. Then the group "meets" electronically each week to exchange progress reports and discuss problems. A computer conferencing program records the typed comments, or "conversations," so that team members can recall and review previous meetings.

Once members electronically post their final reports, one member pulls all the ideas together into a first draft of the proposal. The draft is electronically circulated among team members for comments. A *group writing tool* enables workgroup members to review the proposal and enter comments in the "electronic margins" of the draft without altering its original contents.

The vice president reviews the commented draft and okays changes. The final proposal is distributed to management over the local-area network.

PERT chart, shows
interrelationship
of tasks along the critical path (double lines).

FIGURE 9-20
Common project management software charts

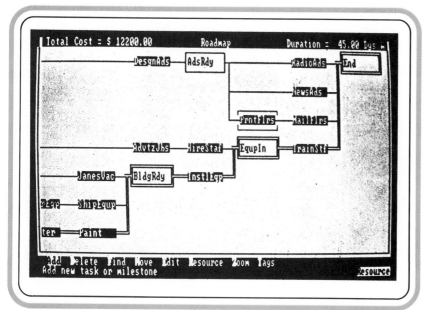

Gantt chart, shows task
beginning/ending times and sequence.

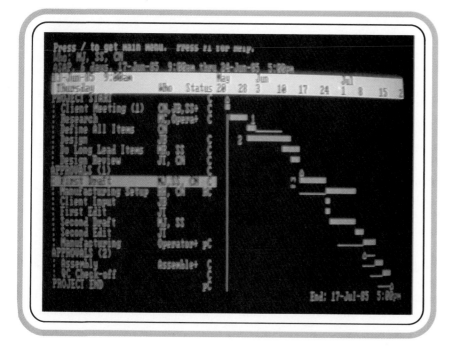

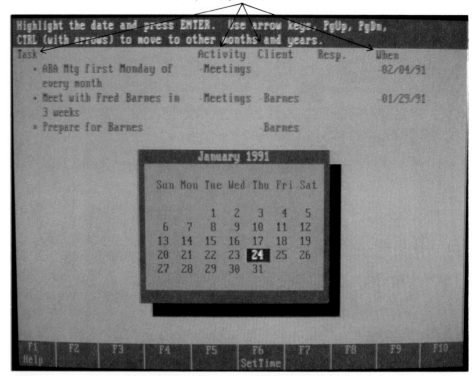

Information can be looked at by various "views," such as Task, Activity, Client, and so on.

FIGURE 9-21
A personal information manager (PIM)

Decision Rooms

A workgroup may gather in a specially engineered meeting facility called a **decision room**, or "war room." It may resemble the one shown in Figure 9-22. The participants who gather may use

- Electronic brainstorming software to support idea generation among group members
- Voting tools to provide questionnaires that allow members to cast ballots and accumulate results
- Group financial modelling software

among other automated tools. These tools may also be available in standard workgroup computing packages designed for local-area network use.

A decision room acts as a catalyst for debate and consensus building. For example, one marketing strategy session for a major personal care products

Small display monitors

Large display monitors

The central core of the conference table
has mounted personal computers that
can be lowered out of sight.

Users input
responses
with a mouse.

FIGURE 9-22
A decision room for workgroup meetings

company brought together the heads of four world regions. Their strategy required making complex decisions about setting priorities and funding for sales staff, advertising, research, and development.

Session participants entered ideas, votes, and other decision data directly into their computers. As an example, an on-screen questionnaire solicited their opinions on marketing issues. One question asked: "Currently 30 percent of sales are made through the sales staff. Should that change? To what percent?"

The cumulative responses were counted, and in some cases numbers were averaged, and eventually a financial model containing new figures was displayed at each computer, along with the original model. Differences were readily apparent. A debate ensued. Revised consensus data were entered into the financial model and its impact was again viewed and discussed.

This process continued for each key issue involved in developing the marketing strategy. By the end of the second day, the group reached a consensus on the key issues. A complete planning document was printed at the end of the session and distributed to participants.

Benefits of Workgroup Computing

Studies show that workgroup computing can reduce the time spent in face-to-face meetings and can enhance individual creativity. Group efforts can lead to shorter product development time, more effective marketing plans, and other benefits that help an organization gain a competitive advantage.

Other benefits realized from workgroup computing include

- Clearer intergroup communications
- Inclusion of a wide network of experts in project decisions
- Quicker decision making

In addition, there is a reduced need for support personnel to take messages and manage schedules.

CASE STUDY: *Automating the Sales Force*

The sales force is often one of the last areas to be automated. Yet sales is probably the most critical area within an organization where increased speed and efficiency result in increased revenues and profits.

A review of the sales figures at RealWorld Corporation, a business software firm in Concord, New Hampshire, showed that the numbers had become stagnant. The organization needed a way to generate increased revenues without increasing staff. Sales representatives needed a way to increase their volume of calls (and ultimately increase sales) and keep better track of existing proposals and accounts.

The Starting Point.   RealWorld started collecting information on sales management packages. Desirable features in any sales automation software were listed. They included tickler reports (automatic reminders to make certain calls or follow up visits), customer lists, calendars, personal notepads, activity reports, and especially the ability to generate proposals and orders. The package also had to be able to interface with the accounting system.

After an unsuccessful search for the ideal package, RealWorld decided to develop the system from scratch.

The new automated system ran concurrently with the manual system for several weeks. Because sales representatives were given time to become familiar with the automated system before completely giving up their paper systems, they were able to experience for themselves proof of increased productivity and improved control.

Enjoying the Rewards.   Since automating the sales force, RealWorld has observed many benefits. The volume of contacts, number of proposals, and dollar amount of sales have increased 10 to 20 percent. Leads are handled more rapidly and are no longer getting lost in the shuffle.

The order processing cycle is also much cleaner. The interface between the sales management and the accounting systems allows sales representatives to enter orders directly instead of writing them by hand and having someone else enter them. This eliminates wasted time and reduces errors—and also reduces customer service calls caused by billing mistakes.

DISCUSSION QUESTIONS

1. RealWorld experienced some initial resistance from its sales staff to the sales automation project. What do you think caused the resistance, and what arguments could you offer to counter the resistance?

2. Discuss the advantages of automated sales management from two viewpoints: the customer and the organization.

CHAPTER SUMMARY

- The three types of computer-based systems that support organizations are "front-office" or mission critical, "back-office" or accounting-oriented, and management and control computer systems.

- *Mission critical* systems support the goals of an organization, or the tasks performed to fulfill its mission to its customers or clients. An example is an automated teller machine system at a bank.

- *Accounting-oriented,* or *data processing, systems* support the back-office functions of an organization by performing the routine volume processing tasks, such as payroll and accounts receivable processing.

- A *stand-alone accounting package* performs one function, such as sales order processing.

- An *integrated accounting system package* combines several stand-alone accounting functions.

- An *industry-specific package* is tailored to automate procedures in one type of industry. Examples of industry-specific packages are a travel agency package, advertising package, and distributor management package.

- A *sales order processing application* allows orders to be entered into the computer as soon as they are received from a customer, with a minimal amount of typing effort.

- Two benefits of automated sales order entry procedures include automatic checks for item availability and customer credit limit.

- An *exception report* lists only special, or exceptional, cases that require management attention or action.

- *Management and control systems* pull together data from front-office and back-office systems, as well as external sources, to provide managers with summarized information to help monitor, control, and plan for the organization.

- Management and control systems are often categorized as management information systems, decision support systems, and executive information systems.

- *Management information systems (MIS)* provide information for recurring, structured problem-solving tasks. An example of output from this type of system is a delinquent loan accounts report or an open order report.

- A *decision support system (DSS)* is used to analyze information needed for solving nonrecurring or unstructured problems, such as determining the effects of alternative sales commission plans on next year's budget.

- *Executive information systems (EIS)* provide top-level executives with effortless access to condensed information that helps with their strategic management of an organization.

- A *drill-down* feature in an executive information system allows users to examine data items in as much detail as necessary.

- *Workgroup computing software* facilitates the productivity of groups by providing a means to share or develop ideas and jointly manage schedules, documents, and projects.

- Some software used in workgroup computing are electronic mail, project management, group scheduling, computer conferencing, and group writing tools. Individuals in a group often also maintain their own personal calendars in a *personal information manager (PIM)*.

- *Decision rooms* are specially designed facilities to expedite workgroup activities. They utilize workgroup software for brainstorming, voting on decisions, and other group activities.

SELECTED KEY TERMS

Accounting-oriented computer system
Data processing system
Decision room
Decision support system (DSS)
Drill down
Exception reports

Executive information system (EIS)
Industry-specific package
Integrated accounting system package
Management and control computer system
Management information system (MIS)

Mission critical computer system
Personal information managers (PIMs)
Project management software
Sales order processing application
Stand-alone accounting package
Workgroup computing system

REVIEW QUESTIONS

1. Identify three types of computer-based systems in organizations.

2. Give two examples of mission critical systems and explain how they help fulfill the goals of an organization.

3. What is a stand-alone accounting package? An integrated accounting system package?

4. What is a sales order processing application? Name some benefits from automated sales order processing.

5. What is an exception report?

6. Define the following management and control computer systems:
   • Management information system
   • Decision support system
   • Executive information system

7. What is a drill-down feature in an executive information system?

8. What is a workgroup computing system?

9. Identify three kinds of software used in workgroup computing.

10. Describe how a decision room is used to facilitate group decision making.

EXERCISES

1. Use recent computer periodicals to locate articles on any three industry-specific packages. Those identified in Figure 9-5 can serve as a guide to packages in this category. Prepare a report that summarizes what each application is designed to do for the industry it serves.

2. Investigate a company that uses workgroup computing systems. Prepare an oral report on how successful workgroup computing is at the company. Address issues such as: How long have they been using workgroup applications?; What specific type of hardware and software are they using?; Do users and management feel that there is an increase in productivity due to the workgroup environment?; How much training time was needed to learn to use the workgroup software?

3. Interview the user of a decision support system (DSS) or an executive information system (EIS). Determine the type of training required to use the system, the type of data manipulated or analyzed by the system, and the user's assessment of the system's worth, that is, does the user feel that the system aids in the decision-making process?

4. Try to arrange a demonstration of either a personal information manager or a project management package. As you run the software for the class, stress how the package can be used to increase an individual's and/or a group's productivity.

A SAMPLER

Directory of Software, Datapro Research

Software Catalog: Microcomputers, Imprint Software

Apple Software Directory, PC Telemart

IBM Software Directory, Bowker

Business Mini/Micro Software Directory, Bowker

Microcomputer Software and Hardware Guide, available on-line through Dialog

CHECKLIST FOR CONVERTING FROM OLD TO NEW SYSTEM

Training
  Orient managers about new system procedures.
  Train data-entry personnel to enter computer data.
Convert data
  Determine the source of computer data.
  Gather the data.
  Keyboard the data into the new system.
Parallel testing
  First, use the computer as a backup to manual processing.
  Next, use manual processing as a backup to computer processing.
  Cut over completely to the new system.

SELECTION SUMMARY WORKSHEET

	CANDIDATE SYSTEMS (scale: 1 = poor to 10 = excellent)	
Evaluation Items	ABC System	XYZ System
Satisfies all application "must have" requirements	8	9
General software evaluation	8	9
Hands-on test	7	8
Turnkey vendor evaluation	7	7
User satisfaction	7	8
Subtotal	37	41
Divide by 5 for average score	÷5	÷5
Total	7.4	8.2
Final ranking	2	1

10

Computer System Support Issues

AFTER READING THIS CHAPTER, YOU SHOULD BE ABLE TO
- Describe how an organization acquires a computer system
- Explain the hardware and other planning required to install and support a computer system
- Identify the support services provided by an organization's computer department

Developers of computer systems complain that they don't know what buyers want. Buyers very often *don't know either*—until they see it!

Defining what is wanted is hard enough for buyers, but living with those decisions can be even scarier. Because when an organization buys a few hundred copies of a packaged computer system, it makes a substantial commitment to that product and to its developer. The organization wants to be sure that software updates are coming to enhance the package, and it wants to make certain that support will be available 5 years from now. The organization also wants a guarantee that the software developer will be around to transfer the product to a new environment as computer industry standards evolve.

But all too often that wonderful new computer system isn't matched by wonderful support or continuing development. The developer goes under, and the package becomes an orphan. Or the package is sold at a bankruptcy court fire sale to a company that understands neither the software nor how to support its users. Either way, users are cut off from day-to-day support and from software updates.

The people who championed the purchase of the computer system are often in deep trouble. The sums involved here are not trivial. Say ABC Brands buys a hundred copies of the new computer system at a multiuser discount price of $3,500 for each workstation. That's $350,000 up front. It will cost at least that much again to distribute the system, install the software, train new users, and help them through their first, not-very-productive hours with it. So committing to the system costs at least $750,000. And organizations don't treat such purchases lightly.

M ost organizations need some kind of computer system to support their operations. These computer systems are mainly made up of software and hardware. The systems often need to be acquired, installed, and supported by existing staff who are not computer technicians. The main part of this chapter concerns the computer system support issues arising from such a typical scenario.

The concluding section of the chapter provides a contrasting scenario. It looks at the support services provided by the professionals who staff computer departments in large organizations.

COMPUTER SYSTEM ACQUISITION CHOICES

When a decision is made that a computer system, such as a sales order processing system, will help to support an organization's operations, the appropriate software and hardware must be acquired. Computer system acquisition choices, ordered in terms of the best investment of time and money, considering only software for the moment, are as follows:

- Buy a package
- Develop custom software using database software or other user-oriented development tools
- Develop custom software using traditional design and programming methods

Buy a Packaged System

Since application software costs less to buy than to program from scratch, most organizations buy it packaged. Most packaged software is sold "as is." Consequently, a major disadvantage of a packaged computer system is that it may not be an exact fit. Faced with such a situation, there are several possibilities. One advocates that if 80 percent of the package fits, use it and adjust the remaining 20 percent to make the package work. With most inexpensive retailed software, this is highly realistic.

For accounting-oriented and industry-specific packaged systems, there is another possibility. Software in these categories often can be modified to fit a user's needs better. With some packages, however, the cost of modifying that last 20 percent could cost more than building the software from scratch.

Develop Custom Systems

Many organizations choose to develop custom computer software using a variety of automated development tools. These include database management systems and other software development tools discussed next in Chapter 11, "Developing Business Computer Systems," and Chapter 12, "Programming."

Generally, large organizations maintain a staff of computer professionals to design custom computer systems from scratch for their unique support needs. Alternatively, an organization can contract with a freelance programmer-analyst or a "software house" to do the highly detailed technical development work required to develop a new computer system from scratch.

Customized computer software is usually very expensive compared to packaged software. But custom software is efficient since it is designed solely to please one organization. It is not encumbered with options designed to please a broad user population.

On the other hand, packaged computer software usually can be installed for use more quickly than can custom software. Also, no professional staff is required to install and run most packages, unlike with custom software.

A SYSTEMATIC APPROACH

Figure 10-1 identifies four steps in an orderly, systematic approach to buying any packaged computer system. It begins with specifying business requirements. This step actually sets the criteria that will be the basis for locating and evaluating software. Software is the primary ingredient of any computer system. Once software is selected, it often dictates the hardware required. Finally, purchased software and hardware are installed, used, and maintained.

Figure 10-2 illustrates these steps as a part of an infinite cycle. Because a business is a dynamic organization, it is a mistake to think of its computerized system as static or frozen in time. Changes occur in procedures, or new business opportunities arise that motivate a renewed look at the computer system.

While using a systematic approach to buying a computer system provides no guarantee of success, it very much reduces the chance of ending up with a disaster.

PROFESSIONAL SUPPORT

When Interstate Distributing Company decided to computerize, it went to a local business computer center for help. The store was different from a typical computer retail store, which is interested mainly in selling hardware. The busi-

FIGURE 10-1

A SYSTEMATIC APPROACH TO IMPLEMENT A PACKAGED COMPUTER SYSTEM

1. Specify requirements for
   Routine business automation
   Management information
2. Locate software that comes closest to meeting requirements
   Evaluate candidate software
   Select the best
3. Locate hardware that secures the most benefit from the software
   Evaluate candidate hardware
   Select the best
4. Install the new system

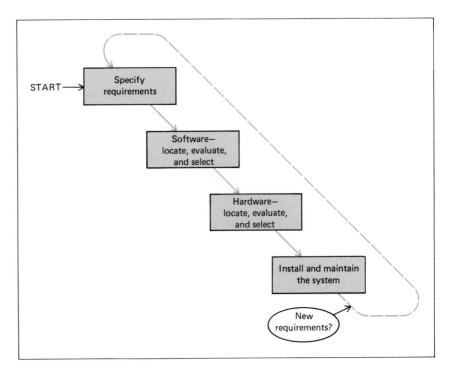

FIGURE 10-2
Cyclic nature of using packaged
computer systems

ness computer center, instead, is interested in selling consulting services. It specializes in helping local companies to set up computer systems.

The computer industry considers such business support–oriented stores to be a *value added reseller*. **Value added resellers (VARs)** combine hardware and software, often from various manufacturers, and resell them as a **turnkey system**. Theoretically, all a user has to do to use a turnkey system is to turn the key and go. It does require that the user organization first learn how to work the system.

Sometimes these resellers are called *independent system vendors (ISVs), system integrators*, and *turnkey vendors*. They are the computer industry's traditional distribution channel for accounting and industry-specific software.

A computer consultant typically begins with a *feasibility study*. A **feasibility study** is a formal term for analyzing a company's computing requirements.

SPECIFY REQUIREMENTS

To help specify Interstate's computing requirements, the consultant worked with its accountant and others in the organization, all of whom were professionals in areas other than computing. Together the team helped to prepare *requirements specification* lists, like the one in Figure 10-3. They identified the number of

REQUIREMENTS SPECIFICATION FORM
FOR AN INTEGRATED ACCOUNTING SYSTEM

General Ledger
\# General ledger accounts
\# Digits in largest balance
\# Accounting periods
\# Periods history retained (12, 24)
\# Companies

Order Processing
\# Orders/day
\# Line-items/order
\# Days until order filled
% Line-items backordered
\# Days on backorder
\# Prices for all items
\# Quantity breaks for all items
\# Price contracts
\# Sales history periods retained (12, 24)

Accounts Receivable
\# Customers
\# New customers added/year
\# Customer ship-to addresses
\# Invoices/day
\# Cash receipts/month
\# Days invoices unpaid

Inventory and Purchasing
\# Items
\# New items added/year
\# Product classes
\# Issues/month
\# Receipts/month
\# Adjustments/month
\# Purchase orders/month
\# Lines/purchase order
\# Warehouses
\# Warehouse transfers/month

Accounts Payable
\# Vendors
\# New vendors added/year
\# Invoices/month
\# Days invoices unpaid
\# Checks/month
\# General distributions/invoice

Payroll
\# Employees
\# Departments
\# Pay periods/year
\# States
\# Special deductions/employee
\# Unions

FIGURE 10-3

- General ledger accounts
- Accounting periods (per year)
- Orders prepared (daily)
- Customer accounts
- Invoices prepared (daily)
- Inventory items
- Employees
- Etc.

Such items are relevant to size the organization's needs with a suitable software package. In this case, the goal is to implement an integrated accounting system, such as one from the list in Figure 10-4.

Budget Guidelines

After helping to specify requirements, Interstate's accountant had to establish whether or not the company could afford the investment. Even if the firm had the funds, would it be a cost-justifiable purchase?

A SAMPLER

DacEasy Accounting
Great Plains Accounting Series
Macola Accounting
NewViews
Pacioli 2000
Peachtree Complete
RealWorld Accounting System
Solomon III

FIGURE 10-4
Examples of integrated accounting packages

Companies of all sizes use rule-of-thumb guidelines. Any company such as Interstate in the distribution business, as an example, budgets 1 percent or more of its annual gross sales on a computer system. The budget covers

- Hardware
- Software
- Supplies and related expenses

Service-oriented businesses tend to spend twice as much as distributing companies.

Supplies like extra disks and computer stock paper are needed. These supply expenses are ongoing expenses for the life of the system. Other expenses that might be involved in setting up a computer system are listed in Figure 10-5.

In many cases cost justification of a computer system shows a very swift payback. When Interstate installed its computer system, it was able to measure benefits such as

- Reduced clerical time (about 50 percent less) spent on all bookkeeping tasks
- Reduced debts from quicker billing after order shipment

FIGURE 10-5

EXAMPLES OF RELATED EXPENSES

Installation costs, including hardware delivery, new office furniture, extra cables and electrical outlets, and proper lighting
Renovation costs to prepare physical site for equipment installation
Conversion cost to enter information from the old system into the new system
Personnel costs, including hiring and training expenses
Security costs for affixing hardware to prevent theft, and for renting a safety deposit box or vault to store backup copies of files and sensitive printed documents
Supplies expense for disks, disk file containers, computer paper, printer ribbons, and equipment storage cabinet
Insurance for the computer system
Finance charges if a loan is involved
Hardware and software maintenance contracts
Consultant fees
Legal fees if advice is needed for vendor contracts and negotiations

- Improved customer service with automated and less error-prone order processing

Justifying the new computer system also included intangible benefits, such as improved employee morale and job satisfaction.

LOCATE SOFTWARE

Interstate decided to proceed with the computer investment, based on its cost-justification review of the project. It triggered the next step, which was to locate an appropriate software package.

Computer professionals locate industry-specific packages through

- Contacting other consultants
- Contacting knowledgeable associates, as well as industry-specific professional organizations
- Looking through *software directory* listings of package information, such as those identified in Figure 10-6
- Attending industry-specific trade shows and seminars
- Studying computer and industry trade magazines for advertisements and articles related to the software of interest

Any user or organization can check software directories for a do-it-yourself packaged computer system. **Software directory** listings contain information about available packaged software, including

- Details about what the software does
- Hardware requirements
- Number of current users
- Price
- Contact information
- Geographic area serviced by the software vendor

These directories list a host of software categories. This is evident from the sample list of subject categories given in Figure 10-7.

In many cases, packaged software in these directories can be *customized*. **Customizing** a package is introducing program modifications to tailor a package for an organization. It is done for a fee.

Alternatively, computer retail stores often carry microcomputer accounting and some industry-specific software for the do-it-yourself organization or user.

SOFTWARE EVALUATION TESTS

Once appropriate software is located, it must be evaluated. Does it meet all the application requirements specified?

In Interstate's case, the consultant reads all the literature supplied with the package to do an initial evaluation. More checklists, like the order processing example in Figure 10-8, guide this more detailed evaluation.

FIGURE 10-6
Examples of software directories

A SAMPLER

Directory of Software, Datapro Research
Software Catalog: Microcomputers, Imprint Software
Apple Software Directory, PC Telemart
IBM Software Directory, Bowker
Business Mini/Micro Software Directory, Bowker
Microcomputer Software and Hardware Guide, available on-line through Dialog

SUBJECT CATEGORY INDEX

100 Productivity

ACCOUNTING-FIXED ASSET	1
ACOUNTING-GENERAL LEDGER	8
ACCOUNTING-INTEGRATED SYSTEMS	35
ACCOUNTS PAYABLE/CHECKWRITING	72
ACCOUNTS RECEIVABLE	94
BUSINESS FORMS	115
COMPUTER TUTORIALS	120
FINANCIAL	134
FINANCIAL FORECASTING/ MODELLING	149
FONTS/IMAGES	167
GRAPHICS	233
GRAPHICS (COMMERCIAL ART)	271
GRAPHICS SUPPORT	278
HUMAN RESOURCE MANAGEMENT	289
INTEGRATED PRODUCTIVITY	307
INVESTMENT MANAGEMENT	338
INVOICING/ORDER ENTRY	367
MAILING LISTS	384
MARKETING SALES	400
MISCELLANEOUS PRODUCTIVITY	419
PAYROLL	438
PROJECT MANAGEMENT	461
PURCHASING/INVENTORY	503
SPREADSHEET SUPPORT	531
SPREADSHEETS	544
STATISTICS	556
TAXES	590
TIME MANAGEMENT	608
TIME/CLIENT BILLING	618
TYPING TUTORIALS	624
WORD PROCESSING	634
WORD PROCESSING SUPPORT	670

200 Education

ADDITION/SUBTRACTION	696
ADMINISTRATION	705
APTITUDE TESTING/COUNSELING	740
COGNITIVE DEVELOPMENT	764
COMPOSITION/GRAMMAR	790
COMPUTER LITERACY	832
CURRICULUM DEVELOPMENT/ AUTHORING	854
DECIMALS/FRACTIONS/PERCENTS/ RATIOS	884
EARLY CHILDHOOD DEVELOPMENT	902
ENGLISH AS A SECOND LANGUAGE	928
FOREIGN LANGUAGE (MISCELLANEOUS)	933
FRENCH	944
GEOGRAPHY	959
GERMAN	979
GOVERNMENT/ECONOMICS	985
HISTORY	998
HUMANITIES	1020
LIBRARY MANAGEMENT/REFERENCE	1029
MATH (ADVANCED)	1042
MATH (BASIC, GENERAL)	1083
MISCELLANEOUS EDUCATION	1138
MULTIPLICATION/DIVISION	1171
READING/VOCABULARY	1177
SCIENCE	1294
SOCIAL SCIENCE	1398
SPANISH	1409
SPECIAL EDUCATION	1422
SPEED READING	1434
SPELLING	1435
VOCATIONAL/BUSINESS SKILLS	1452

300 Industries

AEROSPACE	1486
AGRICULTURE	1506
AUTOMOTIVE	1528
AVIATION	1533
CHEMICAL	1539
COMPUTER-AIDED DESIGN (CAD)	1542
COMPUTER-AIDED MANUFACTURING (CAM)	1576
CONSTRUCTION/CONTRACTING	1579
ENERGY (OIL, GAS, ALTERNATIVE, ETC)	1604
ENGINEERING (CIVIL/STRUCTURAL)	1617
ENGINEERING (ELECTRICAL/ ELECTRONIC)	1692
ENGINEERING (MECHANICAL)	1721
ENGINEERING (MISCELLANEOUS)	1757
INVENTORY INDUSTRIES	1773
LUMBER	1780

FIGURE 10-7
Subject categories available in a software directory

Code	Category	Code	Category	Code	Category
1784	MANUFACTURING		600 Sciences	2369	SERVICES/MISCELLANEOUS PROFESSIONS/SERVICES
1810	MINING	2122	ASTRONOMY	2383	SERVICES/NON-PROFIT/ASSOCIATIONS
1811	MISCELLANEOUS INDUSTRIES	2127	BIOLOGY	2398	SERVICES/PHARMACEUTICAL
1823	SURVEYING	2132	CHEMISTRY	2401	SERVICES/PUBLIC UTILITIES
1827	TRANSPORTATION	2138	EARTH	2405	SERVICES/PUBLISHING/PRINTING
	400 Personal	2149	ENVIRONMENTAL	2413	SERVICES/REAL ESTATE/PROPERTY MANAGEMENT
1839	ASTROLOGY AND DIVINATION	2150	MATHEMATICS	2441	SERVICES/RECREATION
1850	CAREER DEVELOPMENT	2177	MISCELLANEOUS SCIENCES	2444	SERVICES/RETAIL/WHOLESALE
1862	COOKING AND DIET	2188	NUCLEAR	2469	SERVICES/VETERINARY PRACTICE
1876	ELECTRONIC PUBLICATIONS	2189	PHYSICS		800 Systems
1878	FINANCIAL/LEGAL		700 Professions	2471	ARTIFICIAL INTELLIGENCE/EXPERT SYSTEMS
1891	GAMBLING	2194	SERVICES/ARCHITECTURE/INTERIOR DESIGN	2482	ASSEMBLERS
1902	GENEALOGY/FAMILY HISTORY	2199	SERVICES/BANKING	2496	COMMUNICATIONS/SYSTEM EMULATION
1906	HEALTH/SELF-IMPROVEMENT	2220	SERVICES/COMMUNICATIONS/MEDIA	2589	COMPILERS/INTERPRETERS/LANGUAGES
1921	HOBBIES	2232	SERVICES/CPA	2635	CONVERSIONS/CROSS COMPILERS
1929	HOUSEHOLD MANAGEMENT	2237	SERVICES/FOOD/RESTAURANT	2648	DATA ENTRY
1933	MISCELLANEOUS PERSONAL	2245	SERVICES/GOVERNMENT/MUNICIPALITIES	2651	DATABASE MANAGEMENT SYSTEMS (ADVANCED)
1947	MUSIC	2258	SERVICES/HOSPITAL MANAGEMENT	2682	DATABASE MANAGEMENT SYSTEMS (BASIC)
1984	SPORTS	2275	SERVICES/HOTEL/MOTEL	2698	DEVICE/UTILITY CONTROLLERS
1995	TRAVEL	2279	SERVICES/INSURANCE		
	500 Entertainment	2288	SERVICES/LEASING/RENTAL		
1997	ADULT	2291	SERVICES/LEGAL		
1998	ADVENTURE	2305	SERVICES/MEDICAL (DIAGNOSIS/ANALYSIS)		
2028	ARCADE/SIMULATION	2336	SERVICES/MEDICAL/DENTAL (OFFICE MANAGEMENT)		
2062	ANIMATION/DRAWING/MOVIE MAKING				
2070	MISCELLANEOUS ENTERTAINMENT				
2081	SPORTS GAMES				
2093	STRATEGY				

FIGURE 10-7 (continued)

277

DETAILED ORDER PROCESSING REQUIREMENTS CHECKLIST

Type
Prebilling
Postbilling
Cash/counter sales
Multiuser

Capacities
Customers
Ship-to addresses/customers
Items
Branches
Warehouses
Companies
Orders
Line-items/order
Prices for all items
Quantity breaks for all items
Price contracts

Interfaces
Accounts receivable
Inventory
General ledger
Report writer
Other _____

Displays Provided
Open order inquiry
Backorder inquiry
Other _____

Order Entry
Check credit before accepting customer order
Hold order status
Ship-to multiple addresses
Accept:
    Noninventoried items
    Returned goods/credit memo
    Debit memo
    Direct shipped order
    Future orders
Suggest substitute for out-of-stock items
Add special charges to order
Modify or cancel order
Enter shipped quantities

Item Pricing Options
Item identification:
    Numeric only
    Any characters or numbers
Automatic by customer type
Automatic based on quantity ordered
Entered item price override
Base unit cost plus mark-up percent pricing
Contract pricing
Other _____

Discounting Options
Base unit-price minus discount depending on customer and/
    or item type
Line item discounts
Trade discount for entire order
Other _____

Backorders
Automatically filled when inventory is received by:
    Customer type priority
    Other _____
Manually filled by operator who releases selected backorders
    (system maintains and lists backorders)
Original order price retained to avoid customer penalty
Other _____

Printed Output Provided
Picking/packing slips
Preprinted forms
Prenumbered forms
Window envelope style
Open Order Report
    Options: _____
Order acknowledgment
Shipping labels

FIGURE 10-8

FOCUS ON: *Financial Systems Across Borders*

The company was no longer a sleepy little PC-networked tropical trucking operation. "Suddenly," recalls Ron Eisenberg, information systems manager for the distributor of Sunbeam appliances to Latin America, "we had the world." And until this year—when he finally found the right integrated international financial management system to match his new global responsibilities—Eisenberg was a busy fellow indeed.

For starters, his international customers recorded transactions and paid their bills in a multitude of languages and currencies. He needed an accounting system that could automatically compensate for these differences. Then it was necessary to log these international transactions in English and convert currencies to U.S. dollars at current exchange rates.

And that turned out to be the easy part. His customers were also using different fiscal calendars and accounting principles and had different national and local tax and financial reporting requirements. Eisenberg needed a whole new accounting software system that included extensive international capabilities.

Software Selection

The process of picking the right international financial software proved long. "We evaluated a lot of accounting software that claimed to be both integrated and international before eventually choosing one package," he says.

The key ingredients Eisenberg was looking for in a software package were "integration" and "international." Although many vendors offer integrated accounting packages, the roster of those software vendors with proven global capabilities as well is quite small. A growing number come from Europe, where international capabilities must be built into virtually every software package from day one.

What Is Needed

At the very least, the most successful international applications include the following capabilities:

- Multiple currencies
- Multiple languages
- Ability to handle, integrate, and report both locally and centrally on a wide variety of international accounting standards, tax codes, and legal requirements
- Consolidate financials into a single reporting standard

If a package meets detailed requirements, then a general checklist such as the one in Figure 10-9 is used for a follow-up. Part One of this General Software Evaluation Checklist helps to weed out unusable packages. It encourages

- A check of published reviews or articles. Often they shed revelatory insight on package performance and ease of use.
- A check with current users who can also provide valuable recommendations and insights.
- A check of the package's *User Guide* to be sure it includes helpful information such as an index and examples of use.

If the package passes the criteria in Part One of the checklist, it could justify a *hands-on test*. A **hands-on test** involves actually using the candidate software on a computer to check it firsthand. Part Two of the checklist guides the hands-on test.

Some software products are poorly designed, making them tedious and costly to use. Hands-on testing helps to avoid being encumbered with awkward software. It also helps to verify that the software does, or does not, work as advertised.

GENERAL SOFTWARE EVALUATION CHECKLIST

PART ONE: GENERAL CONDITIONS
(No computer needed)

Package

Are published evaluations and reviews available?
Are recommendations of others favorable?
Are hardware requirements satisfactory (like computer brand supported, minimum memory required, display required, number and type of disk drives required, printers supported)?
Are required add-on hardware/software available at a satisfactory cost?
Is the correct operating system available?
Are file exchanges with other software possible?

Documentation

Does the *User Guide* contain an index and procedures for start-up and disk backup?

After-Sale Support

Is service available from the purchase or package source?
Is a service charge, if any, appropriate?

PART TWO: HANDS-ON TEST
(Need a computer)

Ease-of-Use

Does overall operation feel comfortable or confusing?
Does data entry move along at a good speed (or are there unsatisfactory idle periods between entries)?
Do screen formats appear clear, uncluttered, and consistent?
Are HELP and EXIT routines provided?
Are ERROR correction messages understandable and solvable?
Do errors deadlock processing?
Are file or disk backup procedures complicated?

Support Tools

Are the disk-based tutorial and *User Guide* helpful?

Application Function

Does the software meet all the items identified as "must have" on the application Evaluation Checklist? (For example, see Order Processing Checklist in Figure 10-8, or Word Processing Checklist in Figure 4-14.)

FIGURE 10-9

VENDOR EVALUATION CHECKLIST

Part One: Vendor Questions

Business Background
How long has the company been in the computer business?
Are local customer references available?
What is the size of the technical support staff?
Is a recent financial statement available to validate company stability?
Is there any bankruptcy or computer litigation history?
Are contract terms negotiable?

System
What are charges for system installation, training, system maintenance, and custom programming?
What is the procedure to correct program errors?
Is the program code made available to users?
Are program change requests done by the developer who wrote the software?
Is a larger computer available to run the software package as is?
Is a list of hardware requirements available that identifies present use level and room for growth?

Part Two: User Questions

Would you buy the same system again today?
Would you recommend the vendor to others?
What level of technical knowledge is required to use and maintain the system?
Did you experience any unanticipated
  Expenses?
  Problems?
  Benefits?
  Operator turnover?
Are security controls adequate?

FIGURE 10-10

Interstate's consultant explains that a package should feel comfortable to use. If it feels confusing, or sluggish, it might never be used after purchase. To avoid a lost investment, especially of learning time, the hands-on test could prove invaluable.

Vendor Considerations

A Vendor Evaluation Checklist, such as the one in Figure 10-10, is used to evaluate the software vendor's background and any special package conditions. Most of the questions are answered directly by the software vendor.

One question on the list addresses program changes. Relatively inexpensive software can become costly if a user requires changes. With some packages, changes are impossible.

Since businesses operate in a dynamic environment, computer systems software must be changeable. Payroll software, as an example, is vulnerable to

SELECTION SUMMARY WORKSHEET

Evaluation Items	CANDIDATE SYSTEMS (scale: 1 = poor to 10 = excellent) ABC System	XYZ System
Satisfies all application "must have" requirements	8	9
General software evaluation	8	9
Hands-on test	7	8
Turnkey vendor evaluation	7	7
User satisfaction	7	8
Subtotal	37	41
Divide by 5 for average score	÷5	÷5
Total	7.4	8.2
Final ranking →	2	1

FIGURE 10-11

change, like adding a new tax. Business growth or new procedures inevitably require software changes. It is important to fix responsibility for who does changes and to determine what the costs are.

Many new companies in the computer business tend to be transient. To avoid being left with an unusable or incomplete system, the consultant closely analyzes the software vendor's company history and financial stability.

User Questions

A final evaluation effort is to ask current users if they would buy the same system again today. Their answers to this and other questions about software, hardware, and vendor support are informative.

Interstate's team rounds out the evaluation process by actually visiting some user sites. Seeing a candidate system in a production environment is worth the trip. On one visit, as an example, they observe an efficient order processing workflow arrangement. It is later successfully implemented at Interstate.

Selection

The consultant aims for an objective selection of the best software. Usually this involves giving numeric scores to evaluation results, as evident from the Selection Summary Worksheet in Figure 10-11.

The extra step from evaluation to selection involves combining simple or weighted scores from the various evaluations and comparing results. A final ranking identifies which package, from the analysis, appears to be the best choice. Interstate makes the final choice from the ranking and the consultant's recommendations.

HARDWARE PLANNING

Usually a company or a user buys whatever hardware that the software works on, if a good software package is located. The software that Interstate found most desirable worked on several brands of hardware, from microcomputers through large-scale minicomputers. The company's choice of hardware became highly influenced by such mechanics as

- The number of required **workstations**, or locations where computing would be carried out
- The volume of printing required
- The amount of disk storage space required

Workstations

Since all information entered into Interstate's computer system is key-boarded, the consultant had to do some planning to determine the number of workstations required.

As an example, one average order requires about 200 keystrokes. At 400 orders a day, that comes to 400×200, or 80,000 keystrokes. A simplified version of the keystroke planning worksheet is given in Figure 10-12.

Alternative solutions that the consultant proposed to Interstate for consideration were

- One order processing workstation with two work shifts
- One order processing workstation with overload work shared with the accounting or warehouse workstation
- Two order processing workstations with two operators on the same shift

With two workstations, one would be free several hours to process payroll, word processing, or whatever. The second workstation could also function as a backup should the other break down. Seasonal and other work patterns could influence workstation planning figures as well.

Disk Storage

To determine disk storage requirements, the consultant followed a standard formula:

1. List all the programs and data the company will use.

2. List the disk space programs and data occupy as a character count.

3. Sum the character counts.

4. Add an estimated growth factor to get total disk storage required.

A simplified worksheet example is given in Figure 10-13.

The consultant considers the critical step here to be translating the company's long-range plans into database expansion numbers. Is there to be a sales promotion to attract new customers? Is there a plan to increase inventoried items?

Estimating disk requirements also includes adding space for word processed

COMPUTER WORKSTATION PLANNING WORKSHEET

Keyboarded Transaction	Department Location	Characters in One Transaction		Daily Number of Transactions		Total Keystrokes
Order entry	Order processing	200	×	400	=	80,000
Inventory receipt	Warehouse	150	×	150	=	22,500
Cash payment	Accounting	100	×	100	=	10,000
Cash receipt	Accounting	110	×	300	=	33,000
						145,500

SUMMARY BY LOCATION

	Order Processing	Accounting	Warehouse
Total keystrokes	80,000	43,000	22,500
Add 10% overhead	8,000	4,300	2,250
	88,000	47,300	24,750
Divide by 10,000 (conservative keystroke estimate per hour)	÷ 10,000	÷ 10,000	÷ 10,000
Total hours of work required	8.8 Hours	4.7 Hours	2.5 Hours

FIGURE 10-12

FIGURE 10-13

DISK STORAGE PLANNING WORHSHEET

File Storage	Average Characters in One Unit		Number of Units		Total		Related Program Storage		Total Characters of Storage
1. *Company database records*									
Customer record	300	×	4,000	=	1,200,000	+	72,000	=	1,272,000
Accounts receivable record	100	×	16,000	=	1,600,000	+	64,000	=	1,664,000
General ledger record	100	×	500	=	50,000	+	84,000	=	134,000
2. *Other file storage*									
Word processing documents	3,000	×	400	=	1,200,000	+	170,000	=	1,370,000
Spreadsheets	3,000	×	400	=	1,200,000	+	160,000	=	1,360,000
3. *System software*							200,000	=	200,000
Subtotal									6,000,000
Allowance for growth and workspace									× 2
									12,000,000 characters

Disk storage space required

PRINTER PLANNING WORKSHEET

NUMBER OF PRINTED LINES

	Daily		Monthly	
	Letter Quality	Draft Quality	Letter Quality	Draft Quality
Invoices	6,000			
Invoice register		75		
Customer statements			3,200	
Aged trial balance				2,000
Characters per line	×80	×80	×80	×80
Printed Lines required	480,000	6,000	256,000	160,000

Most important planning figure

FIGURE 10-14

document and electronic spreadsheet storage. Document retention periods also must be established when several users share disk storage.

Printing

To determine Interstate's printing needs required listing every document printed. A simplified version of its printer planning worksheet is given in Figure 10-14.

Information for the worksheet comes from counting the number of lines on documents. Some things require estimates, such as on-demand management reports which can be lumped together and listed as a daily estimate.

Once daily print volume by location is known, alternative printer solutions can be evaluated. For example, a high-speed dot-matrix printer may output one day's business in 1½ hours. It may take a laser printer 40 minutes longer to print the same amount, but the output will be more professional looking.

The consultant ends the hardware planning task by considering questions such as What are major hardware firms planning to do that will influence, or even overwhelm, the computer industry with new standards?

INSTALLATION

The consultant worked with Interstate to prepare the physical site for installation of the new computer system. An initial six-month supply of computer paper, disks, and printer ribbons were on order. Then the focus turned to other phases, such as the following:

- *Conversion.* **Conversion** is the name given to the period when an organization changes from one system to another. Some recommend that a company begin with the least critical task first in order to give everyone

---

CHECKLIST FOR CONVERTING FROM OLD TO NEW SYSTEM

Training
  Orient managers about new system procedures.
  Train data-entry personnel to enter computer data.
Convert data
  Determine the source of computer data.
  Gather the data.
  Keyboard the data into the new system.
Parallel testing
  First, use the computer as a backup to manual processing.
  Next, use manual processing as a backup to computer processing.
  Cut over completely to the new system.

FIGURE 10-15

---

time to adjust to the new system. But Interstate decided to start with the most critical function, sales order processing. It began during a slow period in the business and followed the Conversion Checklist shown in Figure 10-15.

- *Training.* For data-entry personnel, training sessions consisted of discussions and demonstrations of the computer system's operation. Since some were involved in the evaluation and selection process, it helped training progress smoothly. Managerial training was handled on a private basis with each manager.

- *Converting data.* Converting files such as customer account records and inventory item records into computerized form is often a very trying period. Interstate hired temporary help for this project.

- *Parallel testing.* **Parallel testing** is the period when the manual and computer systems function together for comparison purposes until some time when it is appropriate to *cut over* completely to the new computer system.

After the consultant discontinued direct involvement with the computer system, Interstate did its own performance monitoring and security control. Security procedures included regular off-site storage of backup disks and rotating data-entry personnel and tasks.

When it looks as if automation might solve a new problem or create a new opportunity, Interstate begins a new cycle of specifying requirements, as shown in Figure 10-2.

INFORMATION SERVICES DEPARTMENT

Some organizations are large enough to have computer consultants and other computer professional support people on their payroll. The majority of them often are affiliated with the **Information Services (IS)** department. Another name for this function is the *Information Resource Management (IRM)* department. It is responsible for servicing all computer-based support needs of an organi-

- A *feasibility study* is a formal term for analyzing a company's computing requirements.
- A rule-of-thumb amount to budget for a computer system is 1 percent or more of annual gross sales.
- Tangible cost justification of a new computer system includes reduced expenses and improved customer service.
- Intangible benefits of a new system could be improved employee morale and job satisfaction.
- *Software directories* contain information about software packages, including: what the software does, the hardware supported, price, and contact information.
- *Customizing* a package is introducing program modifications to tailor a package for a user.
- A *hands-on test* of a computer package is actually using the candidate software to check it firsthand.
- A vendor evaluation should include checks on a vendor's business and financial background and how program changes can be implemented.

- Three mechanical requirements that influence hardware planning are workstation locations, disk storage requirements, and printing volume.
- *Conversion* is the term given to converting from one system to another.
- *Parallel testing* is a period when manual and computer systems function together for comparison purposes. When the test is over, there is a "cut-over" to the new system.
- An *Information Services (IS)* department is responsible for servicing the computer-based support needs of an organization.
- An *Information Center* provides computer technical support to nontechnical users.
- A *systems development* group creates new computer systems and maintains old ones.
- A *computer operations* center in a large organization is where the mainframes are located.

SELECTED KEY TERMS

Computer center operations	Information Center	System development group
Conversion	Information Services (IS) department	Turnkey system
Customizing	Parallel testing	Value added reseller (VAR)
Feasibility study	Software directory	Workstations
Hands-on test		

REVIEW QUESTIONS

1. Identify three computer system acquisition choices.
2. What are the steps in an orderly, systematic approach to implementing a packaged computer system?
3. What does a value added reseller sell?
4. What is a turnkey system?
5. What is a feasibility study?
6. What is a rule-of-thumb amount to budget for a computer system?
7. Give two examples of how to cost-justify a new computer system.
8. Give an example of an intangible benefit of a new computer system.

9. What can be learned from a software directory listing?
10. What is "customizing" a package?
11. What is a hands-on test?
12. Give three examples of things to look for in a vendor evaluation.
13. What mechanical requirements influence hardware planning?
14. What is conversion? parallel testing?
15. Describe the function of
    - Information Services department
    - Information Center
    - Systems development group

EXERCISES

1. *WMK Associates Case.* Mr. Kennedy, president of WMK Associates, a distributing company, wants to automate the company's accounting procedures. He wants you to research the availability of integrated accounting packages for the wholesale/distribution trade. Review software directories for listings. Report on the number of wholesale/trade distribution applications listed. For two listings report: name of application, geographic area served, hardware supported, operating systems the application runs on, number of clients/users, applications included, and price. Comment on how many

FIGURE 10-19

SIMULATED DIRECTORY LISTINGS FROM A PRODUCT-SPECIFIC PERIODICAL

PAYROLL #1
Handles 200 employees in 99 departments. Employees can work in multiple states under five different pay rates. Also handles vacation, sick, and nontaxable pay rates. Included are federal and state unemployment tax and six deduction fields. *(List Price: $495, manual and demonstration disk $50)*
Requires: 2Mb (other requirements not available).
Payroll #1 Company
P.O. Box M1047
Mountain View, CA 94043
(415)444-4444

PAYROLL #2
Stores 200 employee records on double-sided floppy disk. User manual included. Menu-driven. At additional cost, customizing is available. *(List Price: $49)*
Requires: 640K, one disk drive, printer.
Payroll #2 Company
3028 Silver Lane
Ann Arbor, MI 48106
(313)333-3333

PAYROLL #3
This payroll program provides for 300 employees distributed to a maximum of 15 divisions. Thirty deduction types and five taxable categories are available. Federal and state income taxes for all 50 states are built in through tax formulas. Updates are available at a modest charge. Printed output includes: checks, check register, W-2 forms, quarterly and summary reports. While it is written in UCSD Pascal, the UCSD Pascal system is not required. Hard disk compatible. *(List Price: $394)*
Requires: 2Mb, two disk drives, printer.
Payroll #3 Company
22 Hammel Dr.
Garden Grove, CA 92641
(714)777-7777

PAYROLL #4
Provides for 150 employees for every 100K of disk storage. This allows space to copy the master file on the disk if automatic backup is used. Details of each pay period are retained through a self backup feature.
Handles situations like reimbursing employees for out-of-pocket expenses, paying bonuses, keeping track of vacation time, loans, advances and repayments. Includes custom state and local tax calculation programming. Programs are designed for rapid reprogramming. Original commented program source code is included, along with the tax tables.
To eliminate errors, input data go through a double-keying procedure, if necessary.
Other features include: up to 10 department names per disk, up to five automatic fixed deductions with a different amount for each department, and up to five special pay amounts or deductions for each employee each period. *(List Price: $400)*
Requires: 1Mb, hard disk drive.
Payroll #4 Company
P.O. Box 735
Bellingham, WA 98226
(206)222-2222

PAYROLL #5
Designed for novice users, includes five modules: payroll, contractor, restaurant, farm and piecework. Prints checks and W-2 forms. Allows automatic posting to the Job Cost and General Ledger programs by the same manufacturer. Users maintain federal tax changes, FICA limits and percentage changes, FUTA limit changes, state unemployment limits, and state income tax changes. *(List Price: Each module $595)*
Requires: 2Mb, hard disk drive, 80-column monitor, 132-column printer.
Payroll #5 Company
P.O. Box 1301
Clearwater, FL 33575
(813)888-8888

specific items from Figures 10-3 and 10-8 are addressed in the product's narrative description.

2. *Yates Health and Beauty Care Supply Center Case.* Yates Health and Beauty Care Supply Center wants to implement a payroll application on a microcomputer. Mr. Cooper, the company's financial officer, located the payroll listings given in Figure 10-19 in a software directory. The listings seemed little more than product announcements. He had to request literature and documentation to learn if applications were candidates for further evaluation. His specific payroll requirements include: 75 employees, 6 department/divisions, 5 fixed payroll deductions, and multiple-state tax calculations. Based only on the information available in Figure 10-19

   a. Which payroll packages do you think should be examined further?

   b. Which package or packages address the following issues?
      Customization
      Source code availability
      Update

   c. If Mr. Cooper's long-term intention is to integrate payroll with the general ledger package, which product should be investigated further?

3. *WMK Associates Case.* Write to the companies identified in exercise 1. Ask for detailed information on their order processing package.

   When literature is available, prepare a written or oral report on the differences in package

   • Order entry types accepted
   • Backorder handling
   • Information displays provided
   • Printed output provided

4. Arrange to have a demonstration of a sales order processing package. Before the demonstration, read the *User Guide* to learn about

   • Setup tasks
   • Operating procedures
   • Printed and displayed output

   After the demonstration, make an oral or written report about how the first two items were handled. Attach copies of any printed output to the report.

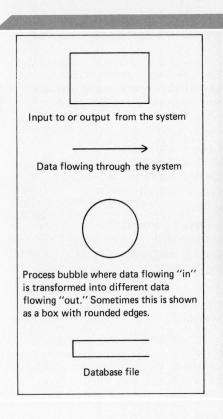

Input to or output from the system

Data flowing through the system

Process bubble where data flowing "in" is transformed into different data flowing "out." Sometimes this is shown as a box with rounded edges.

Database file

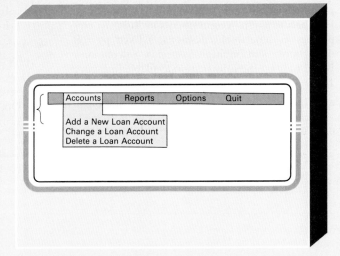

| Accounts | Reports | Options | Quit |

Add a New Loan Account
Change a Loan Account
Delete a Loan Account

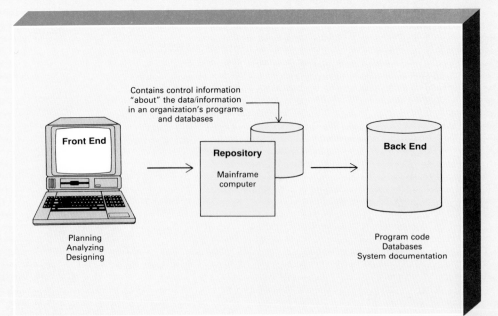

Front End

Planning
Analyzing
Designing

Contains control information "about" the data/information in an organization's programs and databases

Repository

Mainframe computer

Back End

Program code
Databases
System documentation

11

Developing Business Computer Systems

AFTER READING THIS CHAPTER, YOU SHOULD BE ABLE TO

- Describe how business computer systems are developed using the traditional approach
- Explain how modern tools automate system development
- Describe the advantages and disadvantages of user-developed systems

---

Yale University, in New Haven, Connecticut, is one place where the backlog of requests for new computer systems is much less of a problem than it used to be, says Richard Batza, associate director of management information services.

An important factor in reducing backlog, Batza says, is a well-trained user community willing to generate its own software for new computer system applications.

Batza's department handles the bulk of the school's administrative processing in alumni systems, personnel payroll, general ledger, and finance.

M ost organizations today count on computer-literate employees to develop some of the organization's new computer systems. But often major products are handled by an organization's computer department using conventional techniques. Figure 11-1 diagrams the steps widely associated with traditional system development efforts.

National Bank is an organization large enough to have its own in-house professional system development staff. This chapter focuses on how they analyze, specify, design, program, and install a new computer system. It follows their progress through each phase of a new business computer system development project.

Although smaller organizations buy packaged systems, someone first has to develop them. Often a professional software house does this using the system development life-cycle method described in this chapter. The method can be applied to microcomputer, minicomputer, or mainframe system development efforts.

The traditional method of developing a system is being challenged by newer methods. This chapter looks at two of them. One, called CASE, or *Computer-Aided Software Engineering*, automates part or all of the system development life cycle. The other bypasses the system development life cycle by allowing users to create their own systems.

TRADITIONAL SYSTEM DEVELOPMENT LIFE CYCLE

The computing industry formalizes the steps to create a new computer system into what it calls the **system development life cycle (SDLC)**. While Figure 11-1 shows one of many versions of the system development life cycle, Figure 11-2 gives a brief description of each step. Steps represent a formal set of guidelines and procedures for taking a system problem from beginning to end.

The investigation of *what* has to be done is commonly called the **system analysis** phase. The definition of *how* to do it is commonly called the **system design** phase.

Proceeding through the system development life-cycle steps represents a systematic approach to the initiation and follow-up of a new system project. Even a request to modify an old system follows the same systematic approach to completion, as indicated by the dashed line in Figure 11-1. In effect, new systems are born, developed, and die or are reborn through change.

National Bank's System Development group consists of professional **system analysts**. They are experienced in coordinating all tasks identified with the system development life cycle. In some cases they perform all the technical tasks themselves or work in teams with other professionals. A senior system analyst is assigned to be project leader for National Bank's new customer banking system.

One objective of the new system is to give customers a consolidated statement of all their bank accounts, like checking, savings, and loan accounts. Another objective is to give management the information it needs to track customer activity. Tracking will enable management to measure how it is meeting some of its critical success factors.

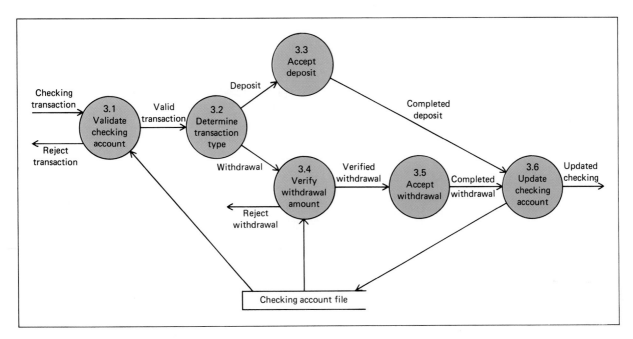

FIGURE 11-5
Data flow diagram—detail of bubble 3
from Figure 11-4

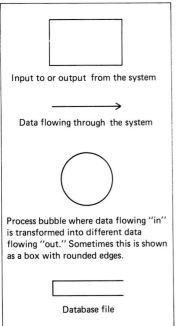

FIGURE 11-6
Data flow diagram symbols

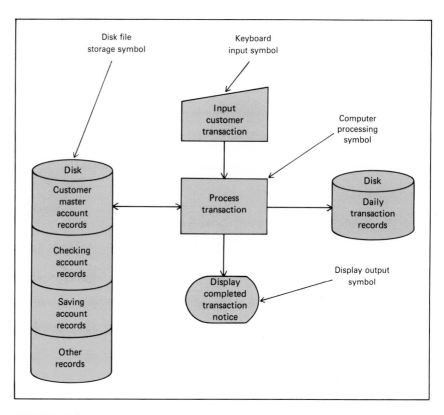

FIGURE 11-7
System flowchart of National Bank's customer transaction processing

The new system is modeled to have one customer master file and one file for each possible type of bank activity. In effect, the customer master file serves as a "lookup" file that is used by the other subordinate files.

The main advantage of this approach is that full customer information is entered only once into the system. All other files look up the full detail on a customer whenever required. This ensures that changes to a customer record will always be current whenever it is used.

Sometimes system analysts prepare two sets of data flow diagrams. The first is of the current or existing system. It helps to understand the old system better. The second set is to model the new system.

System Flowcharting

Some analysts prefer to use other techniques when specifying a new system. One older technique is *system flowcharting*. Figure 11-7 shows an example of a system flowchart. This technique requires the use of a specified set of symbols.

A **system flowchart** is a graphic model of the flow of control through a system. For example, in Figure 11-7 control passes from a keyboard terminal to a program that processes transactions. Some disk files are updated and a new transaction file is created.

Other graphic methods that can also be used in the system design phase are discussed in the next chapter on programming computer systems.

DESIGN

Once *what* will be done is specified, a system analyst concentrates on designing *how* it will be done. The design step in the system development life cycle moves toward creating a physical reality out of the paper (or logical) model. Output screens and printed reports, as well as input screens and database record content, are designed in this phase.

Output

The major output of any new system usually includes printed and displayed reports. The bank system's new output is mainly a printed consolidated customer statement, like the example in Figure 11-8. The statement design is considered a *custom form* because it has printing already typeset on it before the computer prints on it. Most companies use a custom format when a document goes to people outside the organization.

FIGURE 11-8
Output designed for printing on custom computer forms

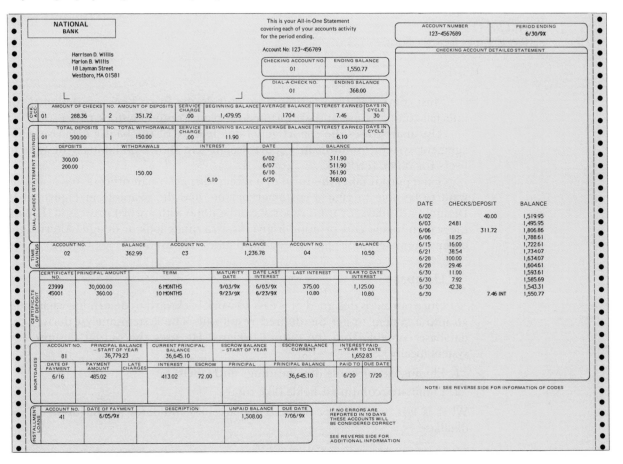

```
                    C U S T O M E R    P R O F I L E

Account No. 987-654321


                      Home: (609) 666-6921      Employer: K-Mart
Alan T. Phaser        Office: (609) 732-7776    Yrs-Emp  3    Income    17,000
Adrian R. Phaser      Homeowner
15 Pleasant St.       Married                    Employer-Spouse: TelCo
Delran, NJ 08075      Dependents  2             Yrs-Emp  3    Income    17,000


 Checking                    Over        Saving                        Int.
   Acct        Balance       Draft        Acct         Balance         Rate

    01         561.20          0           26         1,773.75         .065
    02          25.40          1


         ------Balance---           --Interest---       ----------Payments----------
 Loans   Old        Current    Payment  Rate    Paid    Number   Late   Last    Due

  41      785.00     582.75      35.00  .120    85.62     12       0    05-03   06-05
  42    2,200.00   1,871.50     136.00  .120   141.70     18       1    05-03   06-05
  81   39,500.00  38,500.00     398.00  .095 2,658.30    360       0    05-03   06-05
```

FIGURE 11-9
Output designed for screen display

Most computer reports do not go outside the firm. They are designed for internal company use and are printed on plain computer stock paper.

The analyst uses the report generator feature of the bank's database management system to automate report design. He shows preliminary designs to users for quick feedback.

Some output takes the form of a screen display. Loan officers, for example, want to be able to view a customer profile, like the example in Figure 11-9. Designing displays, or even reports, can be done with a word processor. Typing the screen image and printing it give users a quick look at design. Alternately, other automated tools, like screen formatters, are used.

Database

Once output is designed, it is easy to work backward to determine what must go into a system to get the desired result out. The system analyst derives the database content from the output designs. He uses the output designs and systematically

1. Eliminates constants (like headings and labels)

2. Eliminates computed fields (like totals)

What is left are primary fields. They are all candidates for inclusion in the database.

The bank's database administrator helps to organize data into records that will be stored in the database. The process followed to create records is similar to that described in Chapter 6, "Database Software."

Data Dictionary

All data that are stored in the organization's database must be recorded in a centrally controlled *data dictionary*. National Bank's database administrator authorizes all new entries that go into the automated data dictionary. A sample entry, for the new customer account number, appears in Figure 11-10.

Figure 11-10 shows how the problem of consolidating all the accounts owned by a customer is solved. It is done by creating one master account number with a variable two-digit suffix. The suffix identifies the various types of accounts a customer has with the bank.

FIGURE 11-10
Printout of a data dictionary page

```
                          DATA DICTIONARY


  Field Name:  Account Number

     Aliases:  Master Account Number, Account, Customer Number

 Description:  A unique number that identifies an individual bank customer
              and account.  The final two digits uniquely identifies
              different accounts a customer has open.

     Format:  999-999999-99
       Type:  Numeric
      Width:  11 digits

  Value and
    Meaning:  Digits      Valid Ranges          Meaning

              1-3            001-999      Branch number where the account is
                                         opened

              4-9       000001-999999     Unique sequential customer number
                                         originating from the branch's New
                                         Account Register

             10-11                        Suffix that uniquely identifies
                                         different accounts a customer may
                                         hold:
                             01-25       Checking
                             26-40       Savings
                             41-60       Installment loan
                             61-80       Commercial loan
                             81-98       Mortage loan
                             99          Other

  Where Used:  Consolidated Customer Statement
              Customer Master Display
              Daily Transaction Journal
              Cancelled Check Report
              Not Sufficient Funds Report
              Exception Report of Delinquent Loans
              Customer Profile Report

  Source and
 Maintenance:  An Account Number is assigned by the branch's New Account
              Register program whenever a customer opens an account with
              the bank.
              The Account Number is updated whenever a customer opens
              additional accounts or closes accounts.

     Storage:  Customer Master File
```

Input

After all files are designed, the next step is to design input. Input mainly concerns getting data into the database, usually through data-entry screens. The example in Figure 11-11 shows one of several data-entry screen designs. It gets a new account established in the customer database.

Similar fill-in-the-blank screens are designed to open savings, checking, and loan accounts. Regular bank teller and automated teller machine entry screens are also designed. They eliminate many customer account redundancies evident in the old system.

New menu screens, like the one in Figure 11-12, are also designed to simplify use of the new system. A special restricted menu now brings management information to the screen, such as customer service fees collected by category. Managers can also make random database requests if desired.

Structured Walkthrough

As a quality-control measure, **structured walkthroughs** are conducted. These are group meetings where analysts and prospective system users discuss the positive and negative points about a new system's design. The objective is to produce the best system product possible.

Design walkthroughs help to catch errors early in the system development

FIGURE 11-11
A screen designed for data input

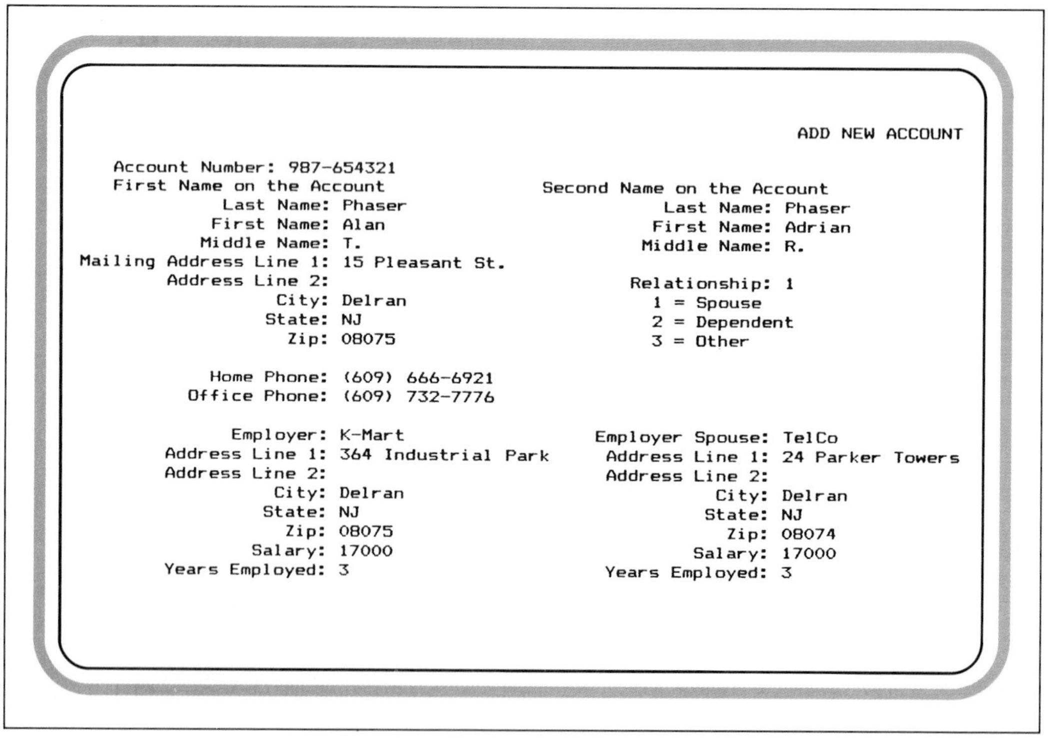

```
                                                          ADD NEW ACCOUNT
        Account Number: 987-654321
        First Name on the Account          Second Name on the Account
              Last Name: Phaser                     Last Name: Phaser
             First Name: Alan                      First Name: Adrian
            Middle Name: T.                        Middle Name: R.
 Mailing Address Line 1: 15 Pleasant St.
         Address Line 2:
                   City: Delran                  Relationship: 1
                  State: NJ                       1 = Spouse
                    Zip: 08075                     2 = Dependent
                                                   3 = Other

             Home Phone: (609) 666-6921
           Office Phone: (609) 732-7776

               Employer: K-Mart              Employer Spouse: TelCo
         Address Line 1: 364 Industrial Park   Address Line 1: 24 Parker Towers
         Address Line 2:                        Address Line 2:
                   City: Delran                          City: Delran
                  State: NJ                             State: NJ
                    Zip: 08075                            Zip: 08074
                 Salary: 17000                         Salary: 17000
          Years Employed: 3                      Years Employed: 3
```

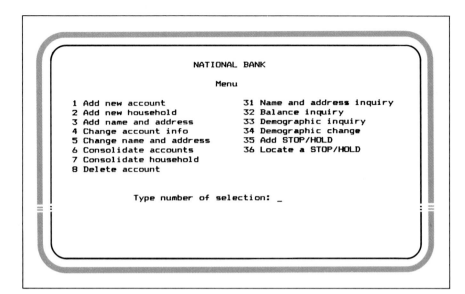

```
                    NATIONAL BANK
                        Menu
    1 Add new account           31 Name and address inquiry
    2 Add new household         32 Balance inquiry
    3 Add name and address      33 Demographic inquiry
    4 Change account info       34 Demographic change
    5 Change name and address   35 Add STOP/HOLD
    6 Consolidate accounts      36 Locate a STOP/HOLD
    7 Consolidate household
    8 Delete account


        Type number of selection: _
```

FIGURE 11-12
Menu screen design

life cycle. This helps to prevent cost overruns on new projects. The cost of finding and correcting errors increases with each successive step in the system development life cycle. Consequently, there is a financial advantage in early error detection and correction.

Hardware Specification

Early in the design phase, it may be necessary to specify and order hardware, if none is already available. National Bank has a separate group in the Information Services department charged with acquiring new mainframe computer hardware, if needed. The system analyst works with the head of this group to work out hardware requirements. It is important that the new system not overload the present hardware and degrade performance.

The bank retains computer professionals with special skills in mainframe hardware capacity planning. They calculate computer performance under various load conditions. With the addition of the new computer system, it is determined that increased demand from database management system services will overload present processing capacity. The options considered and being researched further include

- Acquire a larger mainframe processor with more memory and faster processing capability.
- Acquire another mainframe processor to split the workload with the current processor.
- Acquire a special dedicated database computer to off-load the database processing burden from the current mainframe processor.

Since some mainframe hardware takes a long time for delivery, decisions must be made early in the design phase.

PROGRAMS

At this point in a system development project, processing logic must be defined. Process logic is implemented in computer programs that must be organized into manageable modules. This phase is called *program design*. Program design, as well as program coding and testing, are discussed separately in the next chapter.

INSTALLATION

Installing the new system hardware and software, as well as maintaining them, follows a pattern similar to the one already described in Chapter 10. It involves setting up the physical computer and ordering supplies, training users and managers about how to run the system, converting data to computer format, running tests, and monitoring ongoing system performance.

Before anything can happen, there is a formal *acceptance test* of the new software. The test closely resembles the hands-on test commonly associated with packaged software. A difference is that with custom software, inaccuracy or performance flaws can be fixed.

The bank's technical writers prepare *User Guides* and training materials. They also polish and organize parts of the *system documentation*. As listed in Figure 11-13, it is a collection of all the documents created to develop and install the new system, plus a few others. It will be essential to the long-term maintenance of the system by others.

Converting data from the old system to the new system requires writing file conversion programs. All customer data already exist on files scattered throughout the various old systems. One conversion program takes customer data from all the old files and transfers it into the single new customer master file.

All file and program conversions occur in carefully orchestrated phases. First, both the old and the new systems run in parallel for a test period. Only one branch participates in the parallel test. After success of the new system is assured, a gradual conversion takes place on a branch-by-branch basis.

As new transaction types occur or as bugs emerge, program *modifications* to the existing systems are inevitable. A Program Modification Request form initiates changes. Essentially the form starts the system development life cycle all over again.

MODERN CASE TECHNOLOGY

Computer-Aided Software Engineering (CASE) uses computers to automate the system development process. It combines computers with structured methodologies to automate the work of people who develop computer systems.

**SYSTEM DOCUMENTATION
CONTENTS**

Management overview
Specification
   Data flow diagrams
Design
   Input forms
   Output forms
   Data dictionary
   Database definition
   Hardware and software requirements
Programs
   Organization or hierarchy charts
   Process logic descriptions
   Computer listing of program code
   Listing of test data
User Guide
   Overview
   Normal procedures
   Error procedures
   Sample input and output

FIGURE 11-13

The components of a complete CASE tool are shown in Figure 11-14. The "front-end" component facilitates performing the beginning steps of the system development life cycle. It is here that the developer plans, analyzes, and designs the new system. The "back-end" component generates executable program code, as well as databases and system documentation.

Both the front and back ends share a central **repository**, which is the heart

FIGURE 11-14
Typical integrated CASE architecture

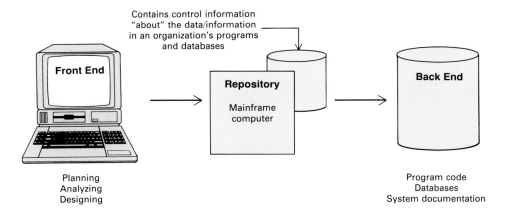

A SAMPLER

PRODUCT	VENDOR	HARDWARE
"Front-End" CASE Toolkits		
Analyst/Designer Toolkit	Yourdon, Inc.	Microcomputer
CA/Universe Prototype	Computer Associates	Mainframe
Excelerator	Index Technologies, Inc.	Microcomputer
"Back-End" CASE Toolkits		
APS	Sage Software	Micro/mainframe
CoFac	Coding Factory	Microcomputer
Neutron/CAP	Neutron, Inc.	Mainframe
Telon	Pansophic Systems	Micro/mainframe
Integrated (I-CASE) Tools		
Foundation	Anderson Consulting	Mainframe
Information Engineering Workbench (IEW)	KnowledgeWare	Micro/mainframe
Information Engineering Facility (IEF)	Texas Instruments	Micro/mainframe

FIGURE 11-15
Examples of computer-aided software engineering (CASE) products

of the CASE environment. The repository stores, protects, and manages all of the information concerning the organization's computer systems.

Integrated CASE (I-CASE)

An **integrated CASE** or **I-CASE** tool assists in *all* phases of software development.

One typical I-CASE tool includes three components:

- A "Planning Workstation" to help brainstorm user requirements.
- An "Analysis Workstation" to graphically describe the logic of a new system. Included is a data flow diagrammer that makes it easy to draw and change *what* the system will do.
- A "Design Workstation" to define *how* the new system will be built. Included are screen painters and database design aids.

These components all work on a microcomputer and have a common look and feel. They all work the same way, so once a designer learns one he or she knows them all. They all work with a common repository.

I-CASE is completed with a program code generator. It accepts information collected with the front-end tools and automatically generates the programs required to make the system work on a given computer.

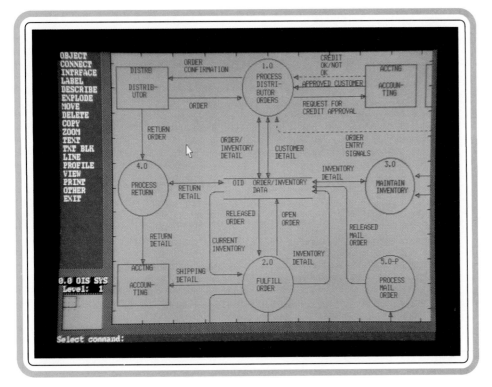

FIGURE 11-16
A data flow diagram created with a CASE tool

A sample listing of CASE products is given in Figure 11-15.

CASE Toolkits

The most common type of CASE product is a toolkit which automates only the front-end analysis and design phases of the system development life cycle. It usually contains data flow diagrammers, screen and report painters, and other tools. They support widely accepted methodologies, such as those defined in *Structured Analysis and System Specification* by T. DeMarco, or structured design, as defined in *Structured Design* by E. Yourdon and L. L. Constantine.

A data flow diagram created with one front-end microcomputer CASE toolkit is shown in Figure 11-16.

Back-end toolkits automatically produce program code from front-end design specifications. These tools eliminate the computer programmer's job. Another name for back-end CASE tools are **code generators**. They are most effective when they are integrated with a common repository. Then whenever requirements and specifications change, code can be regenerated by feeding the changes from the repository to the code generator.

Figure 11-17 shows an example of COBOL code produced by a code generator. Other back-end CASE tools design databases and prepare system documentation.

```
EDIT ---- CUSTPR.MKT.COBCICS(LTDLIST) - 01.03 ---------COLUMNS 001 072
COMMAND ===>                                          SCROLL ===> CSR
000135 000466 PROCEDURE DIVISION.
000136 000468 MAIN-MODULE SECTION.
000137 000470 LTD-MAIN-PARA.
000138 000472     PERFORM LTD-UPDATE-PARA
000139 000474         THRU LTD-UPDATE-PARA-EXIT.
000140 000476   IF TRANS-PROC-INVOKED
000141 000478       NEXT SENTENCE
000142 000480     ELSE
000143 000482         GO TO LTD-MAIN-PARA-001.
000144 000484
000145 000486         EXEC CICS RECEIVE
000146 000488             MAPSET( 'LTDMAP')
000147 000490             INTO(LTDLIST-RECORD)
000148 000492             MAP( 'LTDLIST') END-EXEC.
000149 000494         MOVE BIFFN TO LTD-BIFFN.
000150 000496         MOVE BITRNCODE TO LTD-BITRNCODE.
000151 000498
000152 000500 LTD-MAIN-PARA-001.
000153 000502     PERFORM LTD-NEW-PARA THRU LTD-NEW-PARA-EXIT.
000154 000504 LTD-MAIN-PARA-EXIT.
000155 000506     EXIT PROGRAM.
```

FIGURE 11-17
COBOL code automatically generated
by a CASE code generator

One class of tools to complement CASE technology is automated software to do *reverse engineering*. **Reverse engineering** is the automated restructuring of existing programs into more efficient and easily maintainable programs.

Most old programs that exist in organizations today were built by hand in an unstructured fashion. With a reverse engineering tool, these old programs are automatically regenerated as new CASE systems. Such reengineered systems can dramatically reduce the program maintenance bottleneck that exists in many organizations.

Benefits and Limitations

CASE tools have many benefits. Substantial productivity gains over traditional system development methods are reported. One major credit card company reduced the time required to complete a customer reporting system by three years, saving $6 million. Another company, a large chemical manufacturer, estimates productivity increases of 600 percent in its expanded CASE environment.

Another advantage of CASE is that blocks of program code can be reused. It can be recalled and modified as necessary for use in other systems. Code reusability greatly increases system development productivity and system maintenance.

Other benefits of CASE-developed over traditionally developed systems are

- A shorter system development life cycle, which decreases the time and costs of developing systems.

- Quicker development of *prototypes*, or rough versions, of systems. This allows end users to make improvement suggestions before substantial time and programming effort are invested.
- Higher quality, error-free program code that is automated and reusable.
- Ease of modifying and maintaining programs.

CASE has its drawbacks. For example, it is not easy to exchange information between various CASE products. One solution to this problem is umbrella products such as IBM's AD/Cycle (Application Development/Cycle). *AD/Cycle* is a set of plans, interfaces, and standards to allow various vendor's CASE tools to work together harmoniously.

Other disadvantages of CASE are

- Its steep learning curve. Even professional developers often need extensive training and experience to master the technology.
- Cost. In addition to buying CASE software, analysts need powerful, and expensive, graphics workstations. Also, the central repository may require a mainframe.

Expenses can easily add up to an investment of tens, or even hundreds, of thousands of dollars.

Application Generators

Like CASE tools, **application generators** are used to automate system development and to produce efficient program code automatically. But, unlike CASE products, application generators do not follow formal structured analysis and design engineering methodologies. Their less rigid requirements and user-friendly interfaces often make them usable by nontechnical developers.

One application generator, as an example, works with a fill-in-the-blanks technique. While sitting at a personal computer, a user is prompted to answer questions about screen layouts, dialogue flow, and file descriptions, similar to the example in Figure 11-18. A rough version of a new system can be up and running in just a few hours.

Application generator features are often built into modern database management systems. They are also available as stand-alone packages, especially for mainframe computers. Some example packages are listed in Figure 11-19.

FOCUS ON: *Do-It-Yourself Systems*

The earliest user-developed systems were designed by independent technical wizards, scientists, and academics who worked long and odd hours and spoke computerese. No longer the exclusive property of the academy, today's user-developed systems are created and maintained by mainstream corporate users. Often they have little or no support or control from their organization's computer or information services department.

Advantages

User-controlled systems have advantages. For

one, they fix responsibility for the system—bugs and all—with user departments. This is unlike traditional systems development, which the information services department attends to as one of its services. User-developed systems do not leave open the possibility for blaming the information services department when the system doesn't work. Users control the input, processing, and output of the system. If they want to reap benefits from the system, they must ensure that the system provides benefits.

Often users work independently, on their own time, to meet a portion of their own computing needs. This frees the information services department to work on more pressing problems. Even more important, user independence allows the organization as a whole to react faster and more effectively to opportunities. Novice developers usually design fairly simple applications and can get them running very quickly, given the proper tools to work with. It is a much more attractive proposition than waiting months or even years on the information services department's applications queue.

Staying out in front of the competition usually requires a fair amount of risk taking, which is a luxury many information service departments can't afford. User-developed systems, on the other hand, are generally smaller, isolated, and less expensive, thereby reducing substantially the risks of experimentation. Having limited its liability, an organization can still benefit from any important finds novice developers uncover. For users themselves, perhaps the most significant discovery is that they are, indeed, capable of mastering technology.

A Darker Side

Although there is much that is rose colored in user-developed systems, a darker side exists:

- User-developed systems divert employees from their primary responsibilities.
- Lack of central control can lead to duplication of effort.
- System overlap can cause infighting and increased costs.
- Novice developers often do not establish proper security and maintenance procedures.
- Inheriting a personal system can be a new manager's excuse for the department's other failings.

A Proper Balance

There are some steps managers can take to strike a proper balance. The first is to evaluate projects before they begin. Since management previews projects the information services department works on, it should do the same for user-controlled projects. Users should be asked to submit an estimate of the project costs and benefits.

Managers should also demand that user-developed systems be projected. In fact, system design is incomplete until procedures for documentation, backup, and security have been established.

USER-DEVELOPED SYSTEMS

User-developed systems are computer-based systems developed by end users for their own benefit. Because they help reduce the backlog of application requests, companies like National Bank encourage user-developed systems. They are done through the Information Center staff of computer professionals who work directly with users.

Prototyping

When assisting in end-user application development, the Information Center staff usually creates a quick **prototype**, or rough version, of a system. The *prototyping approach* involves working with users, showing them interim results, and

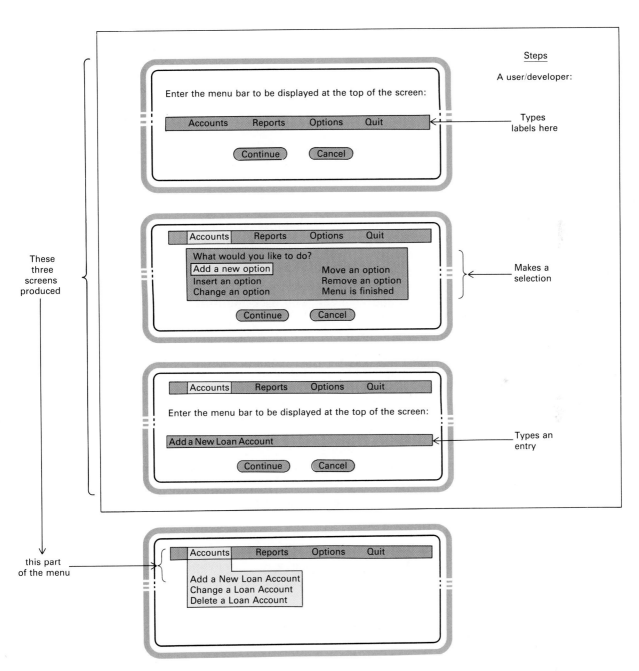

FIGURE 11-18
Creating a menu with an application
generator

A SAMPLER

Software	Vendor
dBASE IV	Ashton-Tate
DMS	IBM Corp.
FOCUS	Information Builders
NOMAD 2	Must Software International
ORACLE	Oracle Corp.
Paradox	Borland International
R:base	MicroRim

FIGURE 11-19
Examples of stand-alone and database
management application generator packages

refining a system until they are happy. It avoids rigorous adherence to the system development life cycle.

In one case, an Information Center specialist at National Bank worked with the chief financial officer to build a decision support model in under one week. After observing the working prototype, the executive provided feedback for improvements and changes. The back-and-forth process continued until the chief financial officer was content with the new system.

Prototyping is used for most decision support applications at the bank because it

- Gets the applications into operation quickly.
- Provides more precise definition of user requirements, since a user actually works with the application.
- Controls user expectations because of their involvement in actually building the application.
- Eliminates user training.
- Has a low-risk, high-payoff benefit to the organization.

A prototype of a system can be created from 10 to 50 times more efficiently than using conventional development methods.

Experienced user-developers sometimes build their own prototypes without any technical assistance. The finished prototype is then expanded into a full-blown system by the user or, if the application is complicated, with help from the Information Center. In some cases, a prototype system is used as the model for a system that is rebuilt using the rigorous system development life cycle approach.

CASE STUDY: *CASE—Virginia Power, Full Steam Ahead*

For Virginia Power Co., the adoption of computer-aided software engineering (CASE) is bringing about a major cultural change. Managers strive to sell application developers on a new way of working.

"When you tell people that the new tools will help them be more productive and improve the quality of their work, they believe they are being told they aren't doing a good job," explains Jeff Boyle, an information-resource specialist at Virginia Power.

But, says Boyle, that's not the reason for the change. Corporate management believes that CASE will speed development of new systems and control development costs.

Virginia Power is training 130 system analysts and programmers to use CASE tools. For help in making the move, the company turned to Arthur Young's Information Systems consulting group of Washington.

State-of-the-art CASE workstations were installed for system analysts and programmers to use. At the core of the hardware is KnowledgeWare Inc.'s Information Engineering Workstation (IEW) software, a CASE tool. It automates application planning, analysis, and design.

The workstations will be used to develop new corporate systems. Two large marketing systems are planned that will help the utility gain competitive advantages.

DISCUSSION QUESTIONS

1. Computer professionals at Virginia Power, as well as other companies, exhibit some initial resistance to using CASE technology. What arguments can managers use to help staff accept new software development tools?

2. Implementing CASE technology requires an investment. Discuss.

CHAPTER SUMMARY

- The *system development life cycle* is a formal series of steps to create a new computer system. It consists of five phases: analyze requirements; specify requirements; design input, output, and processing; program; and install the system.

- The *system analysis* phase is an investigatory phase into *what* has to be done. The definition of *how* to do it is commonly called the *system design* phase.

- A *system analyst* coordinates all tasks identified with the system development life cycle. In some cases a system analyst performs all technical tasks or works in a team with others who do them.

- Three methods used to analyze a company's requirements are interviewing, observing procedures, and examining documents.

- A *feasibility report* spells out the economic, technological, and operational feasibility of developing a requested system.

- A *data flow diagram* is a graphic model of a system.

- *Structured methods* begin by looking at the "big picture" and become systematically decomposed into more and more refined detail.

- A *system flowchart* is a graphic model of the flow of control through a system.

- Output design in a system development project usually includes printed reports and displayed reports.

- Design *structured walkthroughs* are a quality control measure to catch errors early in the system development life cycle and to prevent cost overruns.

- Installation of a computer system involves preparing hardware sites, ordering supplies, training users and managers, converting data, running a parallel test, and monitoring ongoing system performance.

- *System documentation* is mainly a collection of all the documents created to develop and install a new system, like data flow diagrams, input forms, output forms, program listings, and the *User Guide*.

- *Converting data* from one computer system to another involves writing file conversion programs to take data from old file formats and re-creating them into other file formats.

- *Computer-aided software engineering (CASE)* software uses computers to automate the development of new computer systems.

- *Integrated CASE (I-CASE)* tools assist in *all* phases of software development.

- "Front-end" CASE toolkits automate the analysis and design phases of the system development life cycle. "Back-end" CASE tools, or *code generators*, automate the programming and testing of new systems.

- *Application generators* automate system development and produce efficient program code automatically. Application generators do not follow formal analysis and design methodologies, as do CASE products.

- *User-developed systems* are developed by users for their own benefit.

- A *prototype* is a rough version of a system. It is usually created by a technical support person while working with a user to refine results until the user is happy.

SELECTED KEY TERMS

Application generator
Code generator
Computer-aided software engineering (CASE)
Data flow diagram
Feasibility report
Integrated CASE (I-CASE)

Prototype
Requirements analysis
Structured methods
Structured walkthrough
System analysis
System analyst

System design
System development life cycle (SDLC)
System flowchart
User-developed systems

REVIEW QUESTIONS

1. Identify the phases in the system development life cycle.

2. Identify the basic difference between the system analysis and system design phases.

3. What is the job responsibility of a system analyst?

4. What three methods are used when analyzing a company's requirements?

5. Identify three kinds of feasibility addressed in a feasibility report.

6. What is a data flow diagram?

7. What is the main characteristic of structured methods used in system development work?

8. What is a structured walkthrough?

9. List at least four items that make up system documentation.

10. Give an example of how data is converted from one computer system to another.

11. Compare front-end and back-end CASE toolkits.

12. How do CASE tools differ from application generators?

13. What is a user-developed system?

14. What is the purpose of a prototype?

EXERCISES

1. *Mystic Gift Shop Case.* The Mystic Gift Shop is a mail-order company which sells an extensive line of novelty items. The company has hired you to design a computer-generated customer invoice form. It may be helpful to look at existing invoices from other similar businesses to determine what information is typically included on an invoice. Mystic also wants you to design a sales activity report which summarizes a month's sales by item. This report may include such information as item number, item description, unit price, quantity sold,

and total. For both the invoice and the report be careful to make the layout readable and informative.

2. Conduct a requirements analysis for a small, existing manual system. Interview users and management to determine what they would need from a computerized system and observe the current manual operation. Examine all available documentation from the manual system. Conclude the investigatory stage with a feasibility report. NOTE: If you are unable to complete this exercise using

a real company, devise a fictitious one. Imagine what the needs of the users and management would be in this fictitious company.

3. Research recent computer periodicals and prepare a report on CASE software. Compare the features available in three packages. What features are common to all of the packages? How do they differ? Pick one package that you feel stands out among the rest and defend your choice.

4. There are many versions of the system development life cycle. Consult system analysis and design references to investigate several life cycles different from the one covered in this chapter. What common steps, if any, are characteristic of all versions? What are the differences? Do you feel that any one version is superior to the others? Why?

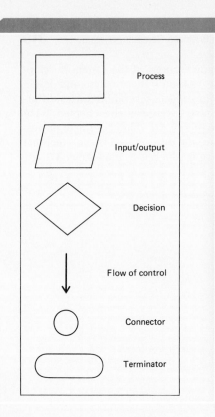

Process

Input/output

Decision

Flow of control

Connector

Terminator

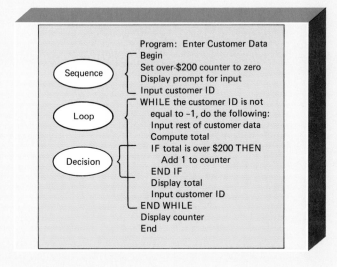

Sequence

Loop

Decision

Program: Enter Customer Data
Begin
Set over-$200 counter to zero
Display prompt for input
Input customer ID
WHILE the customer ID is not
equal to –1, do the following:
Input rest of customer data
Compute total
IF total is over $200 THEN
Add 1 to counter
END IF
Display total
Input customer ID
END WHILE
Display counter
End

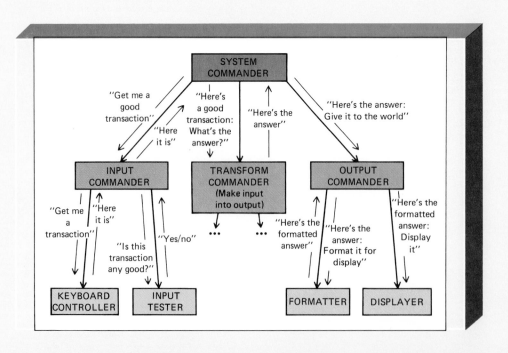

12

Programming

AFTER READING THIS CHAPTER, YOU SHOULD BE ABLE TO

- Identify the steps involved in writing a computer program
- Describe the benefits of structured programming methods
- Identify characteristics of computer program languages

Creating computer programs through evolution rather than by programming them "is a radical approach," said Esther Dyson, an industry analyst.

Scientists have produced computer programs that can actually evolve into more powerful programs through their own interaction. They can merge to create a new generation—a Darwinian process similar to that of biological organisms.

Through the computerized equivalent of the survival of the fittest, a computer runs thousands of programs simultaneously. Then a specially tailored master program selects those that most efficiently accomplish a given task. Then the programs produce a next generation that is even better in accomplishing the task. Such evolution could produce software more reliable than that designed by human programmers.

Said Danny Hillis, a computer scientist who is cofounder of Thinking Machines Inc., maker of a supercomputer, "The dream is to 'evolve,' or breed, useful programs that do things that we want."

T hat future where programs can "evolve" from one another on their own is still a long way off. The overwhelming majority of programs today are still created by human programmers using techniques described in this chapter or the previous one.

Programming a computer system is a multistep process, as shown in Figure 12-1. First, a system's overall program structure and logic must be designed. Then the coding of the program begins. Usually there are several programs in one computer system. Coded programs must then be "debugged" to remove errors. Finally, programs must pass tests for performance accuracy.

The steps outlined in this chapter are valid whether programs are coded in BASIC, C, COBOL, or another program language. They guide the development of all professionally produced software.

This chapter describes the programming languages in common use. It also outlines the four generations through which computer languages have evolved.

FIGURE 12-1

PROGRAMMING IS A MULTISTEP PROCESS

Common Term	Step	Visible Result
Program design	1. Design the overall program structure.	Program "hierachy" or organization chart
	2. Design the detailed processing logic.	Process logic specifications prepared using pseudo-code, program flowcharts, Warnier-Orr diagrams, Nassi-Schniderman diagrams, or some other technique
Coding or programming	3. Write the code in COBOL, C, BASIC, or another program language that will make the computer execute the logic desired.	Handwritten program code
		Often these two steps are combined by programmers who write code while sitting at a personal computer or terminal.
	4. Type the code into the computer using the COBOL, C, BASIC or another language processor.	Computer printed lists or displays of program code (examples are given in Figures 12-9, 12-11, 12-12, 12-14, 12-15, and 12-17).
Testing or debugging	5. Remove code errors ("debug" the program).	Progress from problem to error-free program execution
	6. Test the program.	Correctly printed reports, displays, or any input/output programmed

Throughout the chapter, modern structured methods of programming are emphasized.

PROGRAM DESIGN

Program design is the general name given to the first two steps in the programming process. These two steps involve organizing a program's structure and describing its processing logic. In the case of developing a new system at National Bank, a senior programmer-analyst performs both design steps. She is assigned to be the lead programmer of the new customer transaction system. Some companies retain professional *software engineers* to perform the program design task.

Hierarchy Charts

The lead programmer uses an ordinary hierarchy chart to represent the design of what a system's program structure should look like. The chart resembles a typical company organization chart. One prepared for a program that prints a new customer report appears in Figure 12-2. The chart follows the input-processing-output logic that influences all computer system operations.

A **hierarchy chart**, such as the one in Figure 12-2, specifies the overall architecture of one or more programs. Several charts are used to represent a large system that is structured in a top-down fashion from the "big picture" to successively more refined detail.

When the lead programmer passes the hierarchy charts to other members of the project's programming team, the charts serve as a guide to program

FIGURE 12-2
The flow of processing through a program as diagrammed in a hierarchy chart

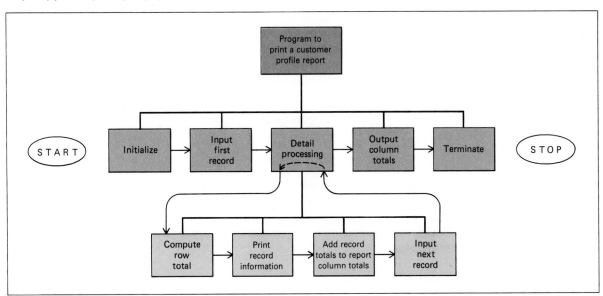

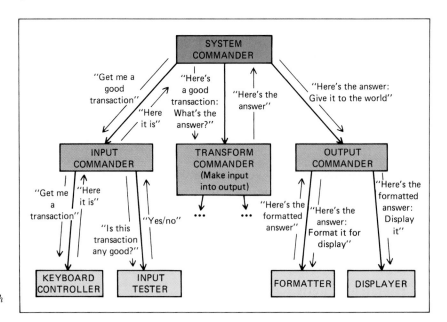

FIGURE 12-3
A "structured" program's analogy with
a military organization

coding. Each box, called a **program module**, will be represented by a block of program code.

Figure 12-3 illustrates an alternative way to draw a hierarchy chart. It illustrates the analogy **modular programs** have with the units of a military organization. Both obey rigid superior-subordinate rules. Each module has its own job, which it performs only when given orders from above. It communicates only with its superior officer and with its subordinates, to whom in turn it will issue orders.

This rigid structure produces programs that are easily changeable over their lifetime. Separate modules, such as checking, savings, or loan transactions, can be extracted, modified, and reinserted, without causing chaos in the rest of the program code.

When the lead programmer is done designing all the hierarchy charts, she can show anyone on the project team where within the programs any logic task is performed. The charts become a permanent part of the system's documentation. They will serve as guides or maps to maintenance programmers who must examine programs at a later time to implement change requests.

PROCESS LOGIC DEFINITION

Some of the processing logic inside a program module is not self-evident. In such cases, the lead programmer describes the **process logic**, or detail of what a program should do, on a separate sheet. She uses several methods to describe the detailed logic. Among them are *decision trees* and *tables*, and *pseudocode* descriptions.

A. Decision tree

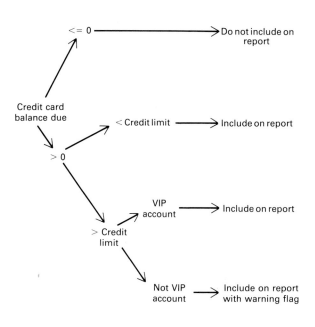

The symbol < means less than; the symbol <= means less than or equal to; the symbol > means greater than.

B. Decision table

Credit Card Table	1	2	3	4
Conditions:				
Balance less than or equal to 0	Y	N	N	N
Balance greater than 0 and less than card limit	N/A	Y	N	N
Balance greater than 0 and greater than card limit and cardholder is a VIP account	N/A	N/A	Y	N
Balance greater than 0 and greater than card limit and cardholder is not a VIP account	N/A	N/A	N/A	Y
Actions:				
Do not include on report	X			
Include on report		X	X	
Include on report with a warning flag				X

Decision Rule Numbers

(Y = Yes, N = No, N/A = not applicable)

FIGURE 12-4
A decision tree and a decision table

Decision Trees and Tables

A **decision tree**, or a **decision table**, like the examples in Figure 12-4, are graphic ways to represent the detailed programming logic in a program. The examples show the processing logic to create a Credit Card Report. It is a new report that National Bank's managers want.

Bank managers intend to use the report to learn the charging patterns of the bank's VIP (Very Important Person) and non-VIP customers. It will also help identify those credit card accounts that are consistently over their credit limit. These customers will be further investigated to see if their credit limit should be increased or their card should be revoked.

Pseudocode

Figure 12-5 gives an example of how **pseudocode**, also called structured English, is used to describe program process logic.

Pseudocode is fairly free-form, except for four key words which each design team picks and reuses religiously. They are the words that describe the beginning and end of repetitive, or loop, processing and the beginning and end of decision processing. The words the bank's program designers use are

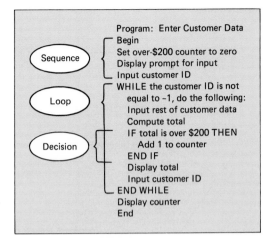

FIGURE 12-5
Pseudocode is another way to describe the logic that must be coded into a program.

Key Words	Rule
WHILE and END WHILE	Used to mark the boundaries of a looping process
IF and END IF	Used to mark the boundaries of a decision

If process logic is neither a loop nor a decision, it must be sequential, or "do one right after the other," logic.

Every program is made up of only three **control structures**:

- *Loop* (repetition)
- *Decision* (alternative paths)
- *Sequence*

One structure can be nested inside another. Figure 12-5, for example, has a decision nested inside a loop structure. Any program logic that uses only these three control structures is called a **structured program**.

Other Methods

Many other methods exist to describe program logic. Examples, most in outline form, of some of these other methods appear in Figure 12-6. They are

- *Program flowcharts*
- *Warnier-Orr diagrams*
- *Nassi-Schniderman diagrams*

A more detailed example of a program flowchart appears in Figure 12-7. Flowcharts generally use only the six basic program flowchart symbols illustrated in Figure 12-8. The flowchart symbols are easily drawn using a stencil of cutout symbols called a *template*.

When the program hierarchy charts and process logic are in place, the lead programmer conducts a **structured walkthrough**. It parallels the structured walkthroughs conducted during the earlier design phase. This one is a formal meeting designed to catch design problems as early in the programming process as possible. Other objectives are to see where program design can be improved, and to coordinate the efforts of project team members and programmers.

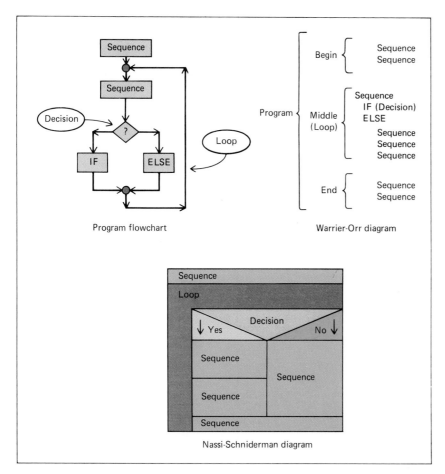

Program flowchart

Warrier-Orr diagram

Nassi-Schniderman diagram

FIGURE 12-6
Other methods used to describe program
process logic

PROGRAM CODING

Program coding is the next major step in the programming process. But coding usually can begin as soon as the main program's hierarchy chart, or structure, is in place.

Program coding is writing computer programs using the code and rules of a chosen program language. The code instructs the computer to carry out the logic design. Examples of program code appear in Figure 12-9.

To code a program, first a programmer studies the program hierarchy charts and logic descriptions. Then the programmer writes the code in one of several program languages, like COBOL, C, or BASIC, that instructs the computer to carry out the logic design.

Many people incorrectly think coding is all there is to programming. But coding cannot occur without a program plan and without knowing what the logic is that must be coded. Program coding and designing are separate and distinct jobs.

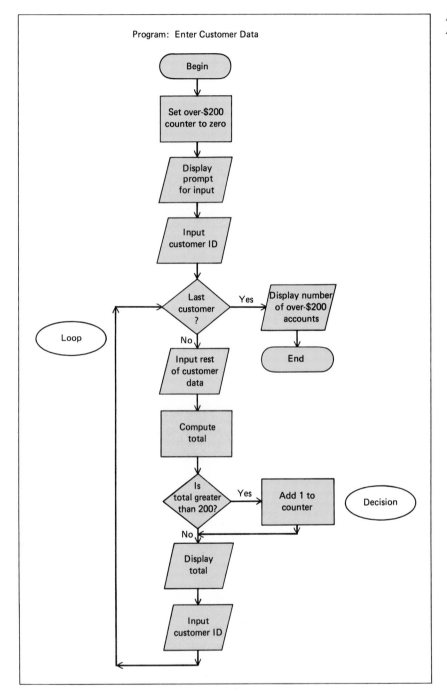

Program: Enter Customer Data

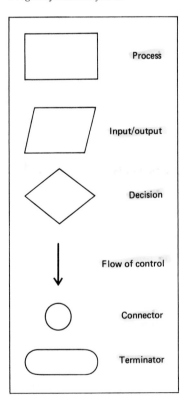

FIGURE 12-7
A program flowchart

FIGURE 12-8
Program flowchart symbols

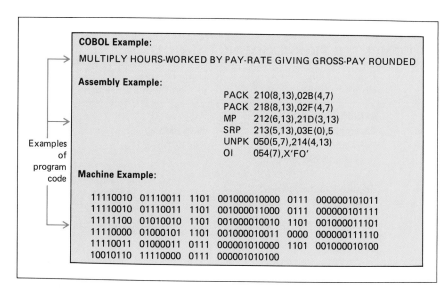

FIGURE 12-9
*A single line of COBOL program code
compared with two other programming
languages*

In some smaller organizations, a single person performs all program design and coding work. Sometimes the same person also performs the preliminary analysis and design work for the entire system.

PROGRAMMING LANGUAGES

Program languages, like COBOL, C, or BASIC, are coding systems with formal syntax and rules that instruct a computer to carry out logical procedures, which are collected into a *program*.

The programming language used to code programs depends on the project. National Bank's customer transaction project is a routine business production system. Most of it is to be programmed in COBOL. **COBOL** is an acronym for *CO*mmon *B*usiness *O*riented *L*anguage. Most existing mainframe transaction processing programs are in COBOL.

Assembly Language

Critical sections of the code may be programmed in *assembly language*. Assembly language programs execute much faster than COBOL programs. Assembly language requires an enormous amount of specialized programmer skill. As Figure 12-10 indicates, **assembly language** is a second-generation programming language and is older than COBOL, a third-generation language. The four generations of computer languages that have endured are called machine, assembly or assembler, third-, and fourth-generation languages.

Machine Language

As Figure 12-10 also shows, assembly language is only one step removed from first-generation *machine language*. **Machine language** is like talking to a computer in its native language of 1's and 0's, or off and on electronic pulses.

COMPUTER PROGRAMMING LANGUAGES

Generation	Examples of Program Languages	Units of Time to Complete a Program
First generation	Machine Language	500 to 1,000
Second generation	Assembly Language	50 to 100
Third generation (*High-Level Language*—HLL)	COBOL, C, BASIC, FORTRAN, PASCAL, PL/1	5 to 10
Fourth generation (*Very-High-Level Language*—VHLL)	dBASE, Paradox, FOCUS, NOMAD	1

FIGURE 12-10

Figure 12-9 gives an example of machine language. Programming in machine language can be a nightmare to do or correct. Imagine a programmer finding a single 1 among thousands that should be a 0.

To make programming the computer a more humane task, program languages evolved. As they became more readable by humans, they became less readable by hardware. The translation process from a human-readable language to a machine-readable language takes time. The higher the language, the less efficient it is in terms of processing speed. More translation steps must go on to reduce higher-level languages into 1's and 0's.

Language Processors

The program that accepts a programmer's code and translates it into 1's and 0's, or machine language, is technically called a **language processor**. Language processors use two methods to translate code. They either interpret or compile it. These methods give language processors their more common names of interpreters or compilers.

An **interpreter** takes human-readable program code and changes it into machine code during the actual step-by-step execution of a program. If the program is run seven times a day, the program code is reinterpreted seven times. Ordinary microcomputer BASIC is usually interpreted BASIC.

From 4 to 50 times faster than interpreted code is compiled code. A **compiler** takes programmer-created, human-readable statements, called **source code**, and goes through the language translation stage once. The translation stage is called *compiling the program*. The resulting machine code image is saved as a program file ready for execution any time desired. The executable program file is called the **object code**. COBOL is one example of a compiled language.

BASIC

BASIC is one of the most popular languages used with microcomputers. The term **BASIC** is an acronym for *Beginner's All-purpose Symbolic Instruction Code*. For people with no programming experience, BASIC is very easy to learn.

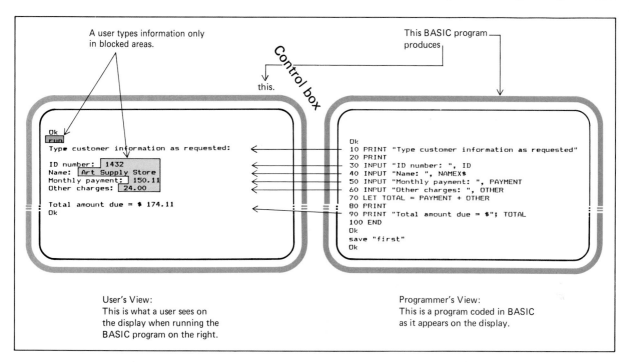

FIGURE 12-11
A BASIC program shown from the user and programmer views

An example of a BASIC-coded program appears in Figure 12-11. The example is comparable to a program that a beginning BASIC student might prepare.

As Figure 12-11 implies, a programmer types coded statements into a computer using a BASIC language processor. The "OK" on the programmer's display is a signal that the BASIC language interpreter is prepared to respond to the programmer's bidding. First, each line of program code is typed. Lines must precisely follow rules of the program language used. Some BASIC language program characteristics are shown in Figure 12-12.

After typing lines of program code, which are called **program statements** or **instructions**, a programmer has several options. In the example, the programmer chooses to SAVE the program. It becomes a disk file that will be called "First" for "first" exercise. Typing SAVE "FIRST" is all that it takes to store a BASIC microcomputer program on a disk as a program file.

To execute the program, a programmer or user simply types RUN. The RUN command executes the program immediately.

To get a computer-printed copy of the program statements, called a **program listing**, a programmer types LLIST. A listing is the only human-readable evidence and documentation that a program exists. Otherwise, the real executable program exists as magnetic fields of 1's and 0's stored on the disk. To prevent a disaster, programmers make a copy of their program onto another safety or backup disk.

Figure 12-11 shows how the BASIC program requires a user to interact with the program during execution of lines 30 to 60. Whenever a user interacts with a program during execution, the program is called an *interactive* program.

Most BASIC programs are interactive, except those that print reports. When-

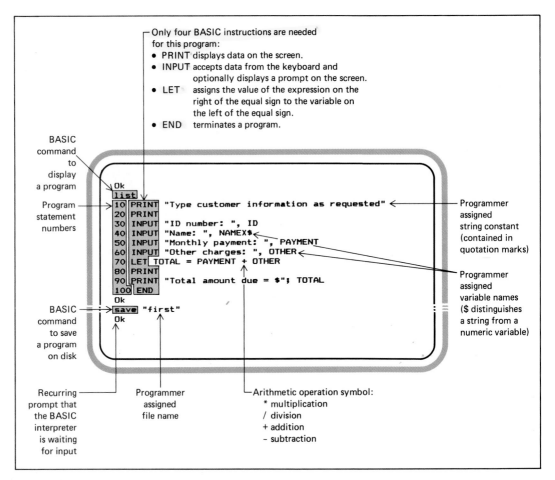

FIGURE 12-12
BASIC program characteristics

ever a user does not have to interact, as in report printing, the program is called a *batch* program. The term comes from early computer systems when everything was done in *batches*, without any user interaction whatsoever.

COBOL

COBOL is the most widely used program language for business applications on large computers. By contrast, **FORTRAN**, for *FOR*mula *TRAN*slation, is the most widely used program language for scientific applications on large computers.

Commercial small computer applications usually are not done in these languages. They are mainly done in assembler, C, BASIC, and Pascal. A brief review of these and other programming languages is given in Figure 12-13. Examples of some of these languages are shown in Figure 12-14.

SEVERAL PROGRAMMING LANGUAGES AND THEIR MAIN CHARACTERISTICS

Ada. Developed in 1980 under the sponsorship of the U.S. Department of Defense and (named for Lady Augusta Ada Byron, considered the world's first programmer) intended to be a standard language for weapons system, although it also has commercial applications.

ALGOL (ALGOrithmic Language). Introduced in 1960 for scientific and mathematical projects. Its programs tend to be easy to read, but it has limited input/output capability. It is the forerunner of PL/1, Pascal, and Ada. It is widely used in Europe.

APL (A Programming Language). Introduced by IBM in 1968; is useful for processing large tables of numbers. There are many special characters in this language, and a special keyboard is required.

BASIC (Beginner's All-purpose Symbolic Instruction Code). Developed in 1964 at Dartmouth College. It is the most popular computer language and can be used by beginners as well as experienced people. BASIC is an interactive, procedure-oriented language that permits user and computer to communicate with each other directly.

C. A structured language developed by Bell Laboratories in 1972 as part of the Unix operating system. It is becoming increasingly important for microcomputer and system programming.

COBOL (COmmon Business-Oriented Language). Developed in 1959, it is the most frequently used programming language in business. Writing in COBOL is like writing a paper: one writes sentences that tell the computer which operations to perform. COBOL has several advantages: (1) It is easy to understand—even more so than BASIC. (2) It is self-documenting. (3) It can be used for almost any business programming task. COBOL also has some disadvantages: (1) It is wordy. (2) It is not well suited for mathematics. (3) It is not as speedy as other languages.

FORTRAN (FORmula TRANslation). Introduced by IBM in 1954 as the first high-level language. It is the most widely used scientific-mathematic language. FORTRAN has several advantages: (1) It is more compact than COBOL. (2) It is very useful for processing complex formulas. (3) Many application programs for scientists and engineers have been written in FORTRAN. It also has some disadvantages: (1) It is not as structured as COBOL. (2) It is not as able to handle large amounts of input and output data. (3) It is more difficult to read, understand, and maintain.

LISP. Developed at the Massachusetts Institute of Technology in 1958 to write programs for artificial intelligence applications. It processes characters and words rather than numbers.

Logo. Developed at the Massachusetts Institute of Technology as a dialect of LISP and is known as *turtle graphics*. It is used to command a triangular pointer, called a *turtle*, on a video screen to plot graphic designs. Logo is useful for teaching the fundamentals of programming, especially to children.

Modula-2. Developed in 1977 by Nicklaus Wirth, the author of Pascal. It combines the strengths of Pascal with the flexibility of C. It is designed to produce programs that work correctly the first time and that are easy to maintain.

Pascal (named after the seventeeth-century French mathematician and philosopher Blaise Pascal). Developed in the mid-1970s. It takes advantage of structured programming concepts. It is relatively easy to learn and it is frequently available on microcomputer systems. It is excellent for scientific and systems uses and has good graphics capabilities. Pascal's main drawback is that it has limited input and output capabilities.

PL/1 (Programming Language One). Introduced by IBM in 1964 as a language that combines the features of COBOL, FORTRAN, and other languages. PL/1's modular, general-purpose structure is very flexible, with few coding restrictions.

Prolog. Invented in France and is heavily used in artificial intelligence research projects.

RPG (Report Program Generator). Introduced by IBM in 1964. It is a problem-oriented language that is limited to generating business reports. RPG is very efficient for work on large files involving few calculations. However, its logic is not as complex as COBOL's or PL/1's, so it is not as powerful. It also has limited mathematical capability.

Smalltalk. Invented by Xerox Corporation and designed to support an especially visual computer system. It is one of the first object-oriented programming environments and is considered to be a prime tool for learning object-oriented programming.

FIGURE 12-13

An example of a COBOL program appears in Figure 12-15. A programmer wrote the code following the rules of the COBOL language. The sample COBOL program has over 100 statements, or lines of code. More realistic business COBOL programs have several hundred to several thousand lines of code.

The example program in Figure 12-15 prints a simple report. It requires no user interaction and is typical of a batch program. National Bank's new system requires batch processing to print customer statements and interactive processing to input customer transactions. This is representative of the normal distribution of programs in most modern-day computer systems.

FIGURE 12-14
A sampler of code from five
programming languages

```
01 COUNTR = 0.0
02 TOTAL = 0.0
03 READ (1,04,END=09) SCORE
04 FORMAT (F6.2)
05 COUNTR = COUNTR+1.0
06 TOTAL = TOTAL+SCORE
07 WRITE (2,04) SCORE
08 GO TO 03
09 AVRAGE = TOTAL/COUNTR
10 WRITE (2,11) COUNTR,AVRAGE
11 FORMAT (1X,F10.2,F6.2)
12 STOP
13 END
```
FORTRAN

```
PROGRAM averagescore {infile,outfile};
VAR  score, sum, average, count : real;
        infile, outfile : text;

BEGIN
     sum: =0.0; count:0.0;
     REPEAT
       READ {INFILE,SCORE};
       sum:=sum + score;
       count: = count + 1.0
     UNTIL eof {infile};
     average: =sum/count;
     write {outfile, 'Average score is',  average}
END.
```
PASCAL

These programs compute the
average (arithmetic mean) of
a group of numbers.

PL/1

```
AVERAGE: PROCEDURE OPTIONS {MAIN};
      /* PROGRAM FOR AVERAGE OF STUDENT SCORES */
      /* END OF SCORES IS INDICATED BY A NEGATIVE NUMBER */

      DECLARE {AVERAGE, TOTAL, VALUE, SCORE, COUNTER}
      FIXED DECIMAL;

        COUNTER = 0;
        TOTAL = 0;
        GET LIST {SCORE};
        DO WHILE {SCORE> =0};
          COUNTER = COUNTER + 1;
          TOTAL = TOTAL + SCORE;
          GET LIST {SCORE};
        END;
        AVERAGE = TOTAL/SCORE;
        PUT LIST {'AVERAGE  SCORE IS', AVERAGE};
      END AVERAGE;
```

```
/*   This program reads two numbers
     and displays their sum
*/

#include "stdlib.h"

main ()
{
char num1[60], num2[60];

printf("Enter the first number: ");
gets(num1);
printf("Enter the second number: ");
gets(num2);
printf("Sum is: %ld",atol(num1)+atol(num2));
}
```

This "C" program
adds two numbers.

```
MODULE Main; (* Modula - 2 source *)

  MODULE RandomNumbers;
     IMPORT TimeOfDay;
     EXPORT Random;
     VAR Seed : Interger;

     PROCEDURE Random : INTERGER;
     BEGIN
        Seed := ( ( Seed * 21) + 13)
              MOD 256);
        RETURN Seed;
     END Random;

  BEGIN
     Seed := TimeOfDay;
  END RandomNumbers;

BEGIN ( * Main * )

  WriteInt (Random,3);

END Main.
```

This "Modula 2" program
generates a random number.

This "RPG" program shows only two of several
forms necessary to code a payroll program.

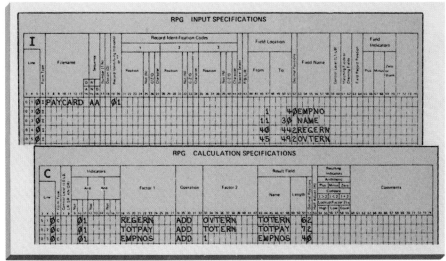

FIGURE 12-14
Continued

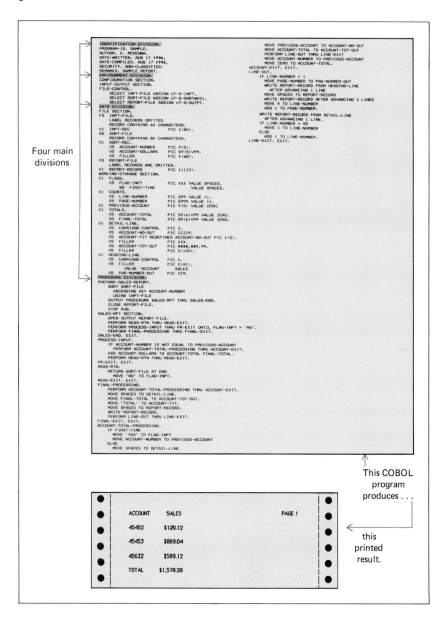

FIGURE 12-15
Sample COBOL program and resulting
output

C LANGUAGE

The **C** program language was originally developed at Bell Laboratories to write operating system and related software. Over time, this powerful language has proven efficient for writing application software as well. It has replaced the use of assembly language for many tasks. Figure 12-14 shows an example of a simple C program.

Much of the appeal of C is its portability. It is independent of any computer hardware architecture. Consequently, C code can execute without change on a variety of computers. C compilers exist today for almost every hardware category.

Another program language, C++, enhances the original C language. It represents a new direction in program languages, object-oriented programming. **Object-oriented programs (OOPs)** work with units called *objects*, which contain information about the data in the object as well as the procedures performed on that data. Each object exists as a separate module that can be reused as needed. One of the greatest benefits of the object-oriented programming approach is that it produces reusable code. It is quickly emerging as a programming method of choice for many tasks. Additional characteristics of object-oriented programming are discussed in the FOCUS ON feature in this chapter.

HIGHER-LEVEL LANGUAGES

A current trend is toward even higher level computer programming languages. The trend is being bolstered by increasingly fast computer hardware. More important, the trend is being supported by a computer industry need to boost human programming productivity.

The productivity goal is being met in part by **fourth-generation languages (4GLs)**, also called *very-high-level languages (VHLLs)*, which are many times more efficient to program with than third-generation languages. Generally, these languages are found in

- Database management system packages (described in Chapter 6)
- Decision support system packages (described in Chapter 9)
- Application generator packages (described in Chapter 11)

Figure 12-16 gives an example of the fourth-generation language called FOCUS. It is similar to all the other database inquiry languages examined earlier in Chapter 6. The FOCUS code could replace the entire COBOL program in Figure 12-15. Both produce the same output shown on the bottom of Figure 12-15.

```
TABLE
> SUM SALES AND COLUMN-TOTAL
> BY ACCOUNT
> END
```

FIGURE 12-16
This fourth-generation FOCUS inquiry produces the same result as the COBOL program in Figure 12-15.

FOCUS ON: *Object-Oriented Programming*

Like handcrafted furniture, software has traditionally been a customized task more like artistic work than engineering. Now, software is increasingly being written in the form of prefabricated pieces that can be reused in different combinations. It is much like plumbing systems that can be tailored for each house yet still be built out of standard pipes, valves, and joints.

The computer industry is flocking to the technique, which is known as object-oriented programming (OOP).

"I call it the software industrial revolution," said Brad J. Cox, founder and chief technical officer of the Stepstone Corporation in Sandy Hook,

being used to their full advantage. The data processing departments at many large corporations, for example, have 2- to 3-year backlogs of programs they need to write.

The Object-Oriented Method

In object-oriented programming, the data and the instructions are combined into a single module of software, called an object. In the case of a credit card application, for example, a customer object would contain both the data on the customer's purchases and the techniques for calculating the customer's balance.

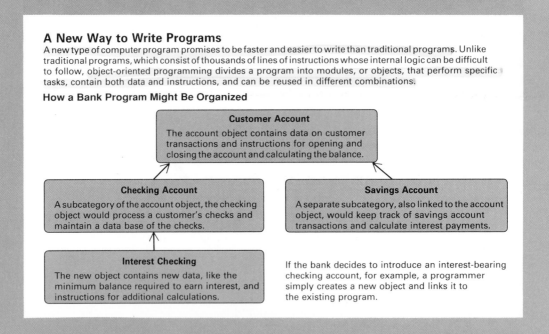

A New Way to Write Programs

A new type of computer program promises to be faster and easier to write than traditional programs. Unlike traditional programs, which consist of thousands of lines of instructions whose internal logic can be difficult to follow, object-oriented programming divides a program into modules, or objects, that perform specific tasks, contain both data and instructions, and can be reused in different combinations.

How a Bank Program Might Be Organized

Customer Account
The account object contains data on customer transactions and instructions for opening and closing the account and calculating the balance.

Checking Account
A subcategory of the account object, the checking object would process a customer's checks and maintain a data base of the checks.

Savings Account
A separate subcategory, also linked to the account object, would keep track of savings account transactions and calculate interest payments.

Interest Checking
The new object contains new data, like the minimum balance required to earn interest, and instructions for additional calculations.

If the bank decides to introduce an interest-bearing checking account, for example, a programmer simply creates a new object and links it to the existing program.

Connecticut, which sells a language and other tools for the new kind of programming.

Such a revolution is sorely needed, experts say, because programs take so long to produce from scratch that they are preventing computers from

Objects pass messages to one another requesting information and giving instructions. Yet no object interferes with the internal workings of another. This makes it easy to reuse pieces of software.

Another principle of object-oriented programming allows one object to be defined as a subcategory of another. If the credit card company decided to create a class of customers—such as those with a gold card—it could create a new customer object merely by specifying the difference between the gold-card customers and the regular customers. Except for those differences, the gold-card customer object would automatically use the same procedures as used for the regular customers.

Advantages for Users

But object-oriented technology is not just for computer programmers. It is also making it easier for computer users to complete tasks that once required a programmer. For one thing, various companies have developed programming "construction sets." They guide the user in taking prefabricated objects and customizing them for their own use. At Bank of America, for example, financial analysts use an OOP construction set to make charts for managers in minutes. Formerly, that task would take hours and require a programmer.

Another advantage is the programs that users develop for one situation can easily be transferred and reused in other situations.

A Battle for the 90s

Despite its great promise, object-oriented programming has its drawbacks and detractors. Some critics say it is not all that easy to write programs from scratch using the technology. Also, similar modular programming can be accomplished with more conventional techniques.

The technique represents such a fundamental shift in thinking that programmers must be completely retrained. Programmers have long been trained to make sure that every detail of their program is correct and accounted for. To be told that they should trust objects without understanding their inner workings strikes some as heretical.

Object-oriented programs also tend to run more slowly than those written in traditional languages, and they can bog down a computer. That problem has prevented object-oriented programming from being widely used until recently, even though it was conceived over 20 years ago.

But now the tides are shifting. Computer hardware is becoming more powerful and less expensive, and software is now the expensive element.

In the comparison just made, the FOCUS language is used in its simplest form to generate a simple report. This is the so-called *nonprocedural* part of the FOCUS language and is meant for uncomplicated user-developed computer systems.

More advanced features of the language are *procedural*. They require programmer skill to write step-by-step code. The code spells out how a program should be executed. An example of an advanced FOCUS program appears in Figure 12-17.

Professional programmers as well as novices usually can learn a fourth-generation language in a few days. Applications can be developed up to ten times faster with fourth-generation languages than with such *third-generation languages* as COBOL, C, or BASIC. That is why organizations encourage the use of fourth-generation languages.

Natural language is emerging as the fifth generation of program languages. It expands on the natural language packages discussed in Chapter 6 that query databases in plain English. The goal of fifth-generation program languages is to be able to communicate with computers in an everyday language, such as English, Japanese, German, or another language. This is one of the most interesting emerging technologies in computers today.

```
DEFINE FILE BRANDS ADD
PTPYE/A3=IF PRODKEY CONTAINS '999' THEN 'POP' ELSE 'SHP';
DISTRICT/A20=EDIT(DISTRICT,'99999999999999999999');
END
MATCH FILE HOLD2
PRINT. AVESHP BY DISTRICT
RUN
FILE BRANDS
SUM CASES AS POP DIVISION BY DISTRICT
IF PTYPE IS POP  IF DATE IS 8103
AFTER MATCH HOLD OLD-AND-NEW
END
DEFINE FILE HOLD
CONSTANT/D8.2=&CONSTANT;
END
TABLE FILE HOLD
HEADING CENTER
"BRAND SIZE INFORMATION SYSTEM"
"REPORT 2"
"REPORTED ON & DATE AT & TOD"
"</2>"
PRINT AVESHP AND POP
AND COMPUTE
BDEV/D8.2=C1/C2;
AS 'BRAND,DEVELOP' AND CONSTANT AND COMPUTE
PEN/D8.2 =C3*C4;
BY DIVISION NOPRINT BY DISTRICT ON DIVISION SUMMARIZE
END
```

↑── This FOCUS program produces ──┐
                                   this printed output. ↓

PAGE 1

BRAND SIZE INFORMATION SYSTEM
REPORT 2
REPORTED ON 02/15/9X AT 09.51.40

DISTRICT	AVESHP	POP	BRAND DEVELOP	CONSTANT	PEN
BANGOR	2,796.67	138,000	.02	50.00	1.01
BUFFALO	2,534.33	142,000	.02	50.00	.89
CHICAGO	2,630.33	109,000	.02	50.00	1.21
DETROIT	2,285.00	45,000	.05	50.00	2.54
GREENBAY	2,668.00	115,000	.02	50.00	1.16
*TOTAL DIVISION NORTHERN DIVISION					
	12,914.33	549,000	.02	250.00	5.88
TOTAL	12,914.33	549,000	.02	250.00	5.88

FIGURE 12-17
A fourth-generation FOCUS language
program and resulting output

DEBUGGING

Programs prepared in BASIC, C, COBOL, or any programming language go through normal coding, debugging, and testing phases. To code a program, a programmer types lines of code into the computer. It is almost like using a word processor. Instead of typing sentences, however, a programmer types lines of program code, such as the lines of COBOL code shown in Figure 12-15.

When all the code is typed, it is saved in a disk file. The program file is then submitted to a compiler or interpreter for trial execution. It is normal for the execution to fail because of typos or other human error in the program. Programmers call cleaning up program errors **debugging** the program. They call errors *bugs*.

The story of the origin of the terms "bug" and "debugging" is part of computer folklore. In 1945, Grace Hopper, who spearheaded the standardization of the COBOL language, was asked to investigate why the computer she was working on had stopped. After looking inside the computer, she found a bug. It was a moth that had been beaten to death by an electronic relay signal. The moth was removed with tweezers. Since then, the process of isolating and correcting error, in both hardware and software, has been known as debugging.

Simple bugs in a COBOL program might include, for example, spelling PROCEDURE DIVISION as PROCDURE DIVISION. Such obvious so-called *syntax errors* are flagged by the language processor being used.

More difficult problems are *logic errors* which must be uncovered by a human. The program may accept, for example, 999 as a valid three-digit numeric transaction code. If only 001 to 777 are valid, however, a logic error exists that requires fixing. It is up to the programmer and program designer to catch and fix such errors.

TESTING

Programs that are coded from scratch must be tested to be certain that they operate correctly. Program **testing** checks that the program runs correctly and produces the expected results. Test data used in the program testing procedure include typical data as well as deliberately erroneous data. All test results are compared against manually computed results to verify that the program is correct.

One common method of program testing is *top-down testing*. This methodology starts with higher-level modules first, even before lower-level modules are coded or even designed.

Top-down testing ensures that the critical interfaces between major program modules function properly before continuing. It also avoids waiting until the end to discover errors in higher-level modules. Errors are more costly to correct the later they are found.

Another benefit of top-down testing is that users become testers. As users test programs, they also learn how to use the programs. This eliminates some or all of the user training required once a system is ready for use.

When all modules are complete, a user is expected to conduct a full test of the entire system. This is often called **acceptance testing**. When all parts work satisfactorily, the user usually *signs-off* that the programs work as ordered.

PROGRAM MAINTENANCE

Since programs exist in dynamic business environments, they must be viewed as ever-evolving or changing products. In addition, users request changes. Any change to an existing program is often called a **program modification** or maintenance request.

Requests for major changes, like the addition of a new transaction type, usually trigger a regeneration of the system development life cycle. These requests must be evaluated in terms of costs and benefits to the organization. Approved projects then go through normal system development life cycle phases.

Usually minor system enhancement requests and bugs are allowed to collect into a group. A *maintenance programmer* then handles the changes, or program modifications, to existing programs.

Since programmers move into and out of projects and jobs, it is vital that programs be maintainable by a new programmer without a lot of wasted effort. According to industry surveys, 50 to 80 percent of the work done by software developers involves modifying, converting, enhancing, or debugging programs *someone else* wrote! Satisfactory **program documentation** makes these tasks easier. Documentation maintained for each program typically includes

- Program hierarchy, or organization, charts
- Program process logic descriptions
- Computer listing of program code
- A list of data used to test the program and the result of the tests
- A guide for running programs

This documentation forms a part of the total documentation that accompanies any new system development effort.

Maintenance programming continues throughout the life cycle of most software products. At National Bank, 60 percent of all COBOL programmers are assigned to maintenance work. This leaves only 40 percent of the staff available to develop new systems. It has created a backlog of unfilled user requests that is being resolved with such approaches as user-developed systems.

CASE STUDY: *Teaching Computer Ethics*

Programmers have a moral and social obligation to ensure that their programs are thoroughly tested and as fail-safe as technically possible.

"If you give students an assignment to program a pacemaker, they are immediately aware that it is very important that it works," says Donald W. Gotterbern, a computer scientist at Allegheny College, explaining how he gets students to think about their professional responsibilities as programmers.

Other assignments get students to consider whether the use of computing is ethical in certain situations, he says. He recalls a program he asked students to write for a tracking device that would be attached to a person's leg. Students saw it as an unethical invasion of privacy when applied to adults, Mr. Gotterbern says. Yet students viewed it positively when applied as a potential method for finding missing children.

The Failure Problem.   Nancy Leveson, a computer scientist at the University of California at Irvine, cautions that instruction in computer ethics should not be seen as a way to prevent all computer malfunctions. Many of the problems have been caused by technical imcompetence.

"One of the principal causes for software failures, including catastrophic failures, is connected to the incomprehensibility of large systems," says Joseph Weizenbaum, a professor of computer science at the Massachusetts Institute of Technology. This results from the complexity of the technology, personnel turnover on the projects, and the speed with which programmers are required to work, he says.

"Generally speaking, people in software and hardware, whether educated at M.I.T. or anywhere else, may feel uneasy about [these practices], but they don't recognize the responsibilities that they have to do something about it," Mr. Weizenbaum says.

DISCUSSION QUESTIONS

1. What do you think people in software and hardware should do about the practices that make them "feel uneasy"?

2. Discuss this comment from James Martin, a computer industry leader: "Human beings can invent, conceptualize, demand improvements, and create visions. They can write music, start wars, build cities, create art, fall in love, go to the moon, and colonize the solar system, but they cannot write program code which is guaranteed.... Program coding is an inhuman use of human beings because it asks them to do something beyond their capabilities—produce perfect, intricate, complex logic."[1]

[1]James Martin, *System Design from Provably Correct Constructs*, Prentice Hall, Englewood Cliffs, NJ, 1985, p. 56.

CHAPTER SUMMARY

- *Programming* is a multistep process involving designing the overall program structure and logic, writing code, and debugging and testing programs.
- *Hierarchy charts* specify the overall architecture of one or more programs.
- A *modular program* obeys rigid superior-subordinate rules which makes it easily changeable over its lifetime.
- The *process logic*, or detail of what a program should do, can be described by using *decision trees, decision tables, pseudocode,* and *program flowcharts,* among other methods.
- A *structured walkthrough* is a formal meeting designed to catch design problems as early as possible.
- *Program design* is concerned with the overall structure and processing logic in a system. *Program coding* is concerned with writing code that instructs the computer to carry out the logic design.
- *Program languages*, like COBOL, C, or BASIC, are coding systems with formal syntax and rules that instruct a computer to carry out logical procedures, called a *program*.
- The four generations of computer languages are *machine, assembly, third-,* and *fourth-generation languages*.
- *Machine language* is the native language of a computer, represented by 1's and 0's, or off and on electronic pulses.
- *Language processors* accept program code and translate it into machine language. They are either interpreters or compilers.
- An *interpreter* takes human-readable program code

and changes it into machine code during the actual step-by-step execution of a program. A *compiler* goes through the code interpretation stage once.

- *BASIC* is one of the most popular languages used with microcomputers.
- Lines of program code are called *program statements*.
- A *program listing* is a computer-printed copy of program source code.
- *COBOL* is the most widely used language for commercial applications on large computers.
- *C* is a powerful program language used on all sizes of computers to write system and application software.
- BASIC, C, and COBOL are all examples of *third-generation languages*.

- *Fourth-generation languages* are many times more efficient to program with than third-generation languages.
- *Debugging* a program means cleaning up program errors.
- *Testing* ensures that a program runs correctly and produces the desired result.
- The objective of an *acceptance test* is to get a user to *sign-off* that the program works.
- *Program modifications* are any changes to existing programs.
- *Program documentation* is valuable because it helps programmers maintain old systems without a lot of wasted effort.

SELECTED KEY TERMS

Assembly language
BASIC (*Beginner's All-purpose Symbolic Instruction Code*)
C language
COBOL (*COmmon Business Oriented Language*)
Compiler
Debugging
FORTRAN (*FORmula TRANslation*)

Fourth-generation languages (4GLs)
Hierarchy chart
Interpreter
Language processor
Machine language
Maintenance programmer
Object code
Process logic
Program coding

Program design
Program documentation
Program languages
Program listing
Program modifications
Program statements
Programming
Structured walkthrough
Third-generation language

REVIEW QUESTIONS

1. Identify the steps in the programming process.
2. What is a hierarchy chart?
3. What is a modular program?
4. Describe three methods used to represent processing logic.
5. What is a structured walkthrough of a program?
6. Distinguish program design from program coding.
7. Identify characteristics of the four generations through which computer languages have evolved.

8. What is the difference between a language interpreter and a compiler?
9. What are the most common uses for BASIC and COBOL program languages?
10. What is a program statement? a program listing?
11. Define the following terms:
    - Debugging
    - Program testing
    - Acceptance test
    - Program modification
12. Why is program documentation valuable?

EXERCISES

1. Write the pseudocode for a simple payroll program. Assume that the input records consist of employee identification number (probably a social security number), number of hours worked per week, and hourly pay rate. For any hours worked over 40 hours, the employee receives time and a

half. You must also keep a count of the number of records processed through the program. Once completed, identify the three control structures: loops, decisions, sequences. Use Figure 12-5 as a guide.

2. COBOL was developed by Grace Hopper, a former commodore in the United States Navy and a computer program language pioneer. Trace the roots of COBOL or another widely used mainframe or microcomputer programming language, such as FORTRAN, BASIC, or C. Research the background of the person or institution re-sponsible for developing the language. Why was the language initially developed? What computing need, if any, did this language meet that its predecessors did not?

3. Determine what fourth-generation language systems are available at the computer lab at your school. Study the programming language and write a simple program using the language. Critique the language: how easy was it to learn, how English-like are the program commands, how simple was the program to debug?

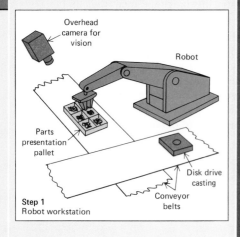

Overhead
camera for
vision

Robot

Parts
presentation
pallet

Disk drive
casting

Conveyor
belts

Step 1
Robot workstation

Artificial Intelligence

AFTER READING THIS CHAPTER, YOU SHOULD BE ABLE TO

- Identify the technologies that come from artificial intelligence research
- Describe how a simple knowledge-based system is built
- Describe how a robot performs useful tasks

A manager at Apple Computer, Harold Striepe, envisions artificial intelligence used in a number of ways. For example, he sees it used in a graphics program that could suggest ways to make a graphic look better, or a word processing program that "could ask basic questions to help structure your thoughts." A financial program could suggest investments that are appropriate for an individual's tax situation, recommend certain stocks to buy, or warn that cash flow does not look good. Such intelligence can be built into programs to help provide assistance when someone is using a computer.

This new software will not be billed as artificial intelligence. Rather, the artificial intelligence feature will be be built into many old and familiar applications—such as graphics programs, databases, spreadsheets, and word processors—making them more powerful, easier to use, and more flexible.

Increasingly, artificial intelligence technology is being seen as a tool that may help create the next generation of powerful new software.

A rtificial intelligence, often referred to as AI, is the branch of computer science that makes computers imitate human behavior. Other disciplines, among them psychology, linguistics, mathematics, business, education, and philosophy, contribute to AI's development.

AI is used as an umbrella term for the collective research that has produced, among other efforts

- Knowledge-based systems, which are also called "expert systems"
- Programmable robot systems
- Natural language systems

This chapter covers knowledge-based and robot systems. Natural language systems are covered in Chapter 6, "Database Software."

Knowledge-based systems act as assistants, colleagues, or even expert consultants to users in specialized areas. Examples explored in this chapter include a diagnostic system that helps locate machine failure and a classification system that helps match patients with appropriate health care.

Probably the most exotic of the systems explored here is programmable robots. The chapter concludes with a discussion of what they are and how they work. It also covers controversial issues related to robots in society.

KNOWLEDGE-BASED SYSTEMS

Knowledge-based systems capture, magnify, and distribute access to judgment. They function at the level of assistants, colleagues, or experts.

Some examples of established knowledge-based systems and the kind of assistance they provide are given in Figure 13-1.

Some systems are still at the beginning assistant level. Others have progressed over time to become expert systems. Progress comes from capturing more and more knowledge in the knowledge base.

FIGURE 13-1

SOME KNOWLEDGE-BASED SYSTEMS IN USE

CATS—Helps diesel locomotive repair engineers solve maintenance problems.

Authorizer's Assistant—Helps authorizers at American Express determine whether customer purchase transactions should be approved.

ExperTAX—Helps audit and tax staff at Coopers and Lybrand, a major accounting firm, perform client tax planning.

XCON—Helps order-fulfillment specialists assemble the minicomputer hardware components necessary to fill a customer order at Digital Equipment Corporation.

XSEL—Helps Digital Equipment Corporation salespeople assemble a minicomputer system for customer proposals.

Trader's Assistant—Helps financial securities traders assess the state of the stock market.

Mortgage Loan Analyzer—Helps loan specialists make decisions about residential mortgage loan applications.

PlanPower—Helps financial specialists prepare financial plans for high-income clients.

ACE—Helps AT&T's service staff resolve problems in telecommunication equipment.

GENESIS—Helps genetic engineers analyze DNA models.

PUFF—Helps doctors diagnose lung problems.

FOCUS ON: *Who Is Liable? Just Ask the Experts*

Here is a quick multiple choice test: If a knowledge-based or expert system in some way failed and caused personal or economic injury to an individual or organization, who would be the likely target of a liability lawsuit?

A. The vendor who created the system's shell

B. The expert who supplied the system's knowledge base

C. The user who placed too much faith in the system's output

D. All of the above and probably a number of others to boot

The correct answer is D, according to several legal experts.

Users can protect themselves to some extent by documenting the care they take in selecting a vendor's shell before putting it to use. That care should include a complete evaluation of the product and a reference check with current users of the shell.

Liability Issue

The vendor liability issue is a concern to the computer industry, says Larry Harris, founder and chairman of AI Corp. "It is not different than writing a medical book," Harris said. "I don't think that a doctor can sue the author of a medical book; it is still the responsibility of the doctor who makes the diagnosis."

Such disclaimers would probably not prevent a lawsuit or hold up in court, legal experts said. The vendor could be liable in ways never before imagined: Users could attempt to use the shell in unforeseen ways or simply decide not to take training courses offered by the vendor, for example. In either case, the vendor could be in court alongside the other defendants, according to legal opinion.

Legal experts say it is only a matter of time before a malfunctioning knowledge-based system triggers a lawsuit. When that happens, everyone involved in the creation of the knowledge-based system could face the prospect of legal action.

DEVELOPING A KNOWLEDGE-BASED SYSTEM

This section "walks through" the building of a sample knowledge-based system used by a Health Maintenance Organization, or HMO. HMOs are an alternative to more common fee-for-service medical facilities. They provide medical service to members in return for a prepaid fee.

At HMOs, as at all medical facilities, it is important that serious health problems obtain priority access to treatment over lower priority cases. A knowledge-based system is built to assist HMO personnel to make such screening decisions.

The criteria for treatment qualification are built into the rules in the system.

Personnel doing the screening can use the system as a guide through the approval-checking procedure. They answer questions asked by the knowledge-based system. Based on the answers it receives, the system makes a recommendation for the level of treatment to administer.

A fully developed system would cover all the standards established to determine the appropriate level of service support, given the seriousness of an individual's condition. Because this is only a small sample of a system, it concludes with the following selected recommendations:

Level of Support	Meaning
Level 1	Serious case
Level 2	Nonserious new case
Level 3	Nonserious follow-up case
Information—other	Inquiry or information only case
Nonmember	Nonmember services only

The application of knowledge-based system technology to the HMO problem provides the following potential benefits:

- It enables a consistent level of screening service to be delivered regardless of who is on duty.
- It allows extending decision making to personnel who were previously unauthorized to make decisions.
- It ensures that screening decisions are always made using the same set of criteria. The possibility of inappropriate concerns (for example, race, sex, political affiliation, etc.) are eliminated, and, in the event of a dispute, the criteria by which a particular decision was made can be proven.
- It can be used to train screening personnel, which frees more experienced staff for other duties.
- It can be copied for use wherever members are serviced, and the organization can be assured of a consistent level of service.
- It can be easily changed to reflect new or revised screening policies. Then the system can be quickly copied and distributed to implement the change uniformly throughout the organization.

These benefits are similar to those claimed by most organizations where knowledge-based system technology has been successfully applied to solve problems.

Step 1: Model the Problem

Step 1 in the development process is to create a model of the problem. It can be done using a so-called dependency diagram, as shown in Figure 13-6. A **dependency diagram** indicates the relationship (or dependencies) among all questions and recommendations made by the knowledge-based system. It serves as the paper model for how to write or code the actual knowledge base.

The model in Figure 13-6 identifies the three critical screening factors used for this small example:

- HMO status—Is the client entitled to member service?
- Reason—What is the reason for coming to the HMO facility? Is this a new case, follow-up case, information, or "other" purpose visit?
- Problem—How serious is the client's current condition? Is an abnormal temperature or other symptom present that requires primary-care service?

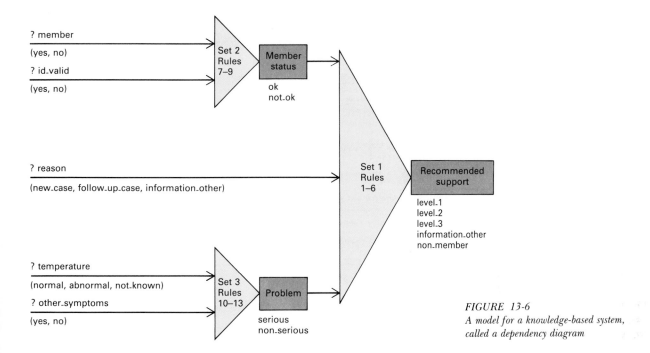

FIGURE 13-6
A model for a knowledge-based system,
called a dependency diagram

Step 2: Write IF-THEN Rules

Figure 13-4 shows all the rules written for this simple knowledge-based system.

If all the conditions in a rule are true, the THEN clause, or conclusion of a rule, passes, or is "fired." For example, consider this rule:

> RULE 6
> IF member = yes and
>   valid_id = yes
> THEN member_status = ok

This rule says, in effect, "IF, during a consultation, the value of 'member' is found to be 'yes,' AND the value of 'valid_id' is found to be 'yes,' THEN 'member_status' should be fired and assigned the value 'ok.'

Step 3: Construct the User Interface

Once the IF-THEN rules are written, the user interface elements of the knowledge base are constructed, as identified in Figure 13-7. In this case, the user interface refers to all the parts a user actually sees when running the knowledge-based system in a consultation session. At a minimum, this consists of the opening and closing messages, and the questions asked during the consultation session.

Once all elements that constitute the knowledge base are in place, as shown in Figure 13-8, they are typed into a computer file using a shell package. The example in Figure 13-8 was prepared for the VP-Expert shell package.

This entire job is not unlike the work a programmer does to create traditional

User
interface
elements

Opening
message

Questions
with
answer
choices

Closing
message

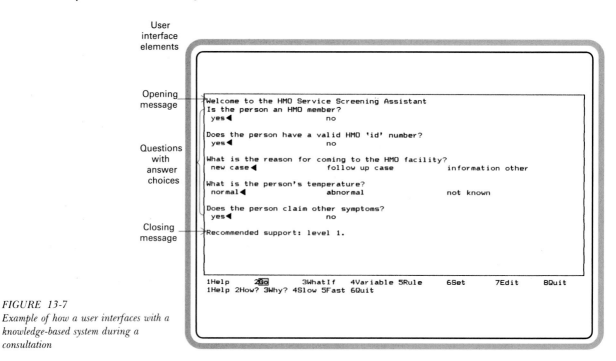

```
Welcome to the HMO Service Screening Assistant
Is the person an HMO member?
  yes◄                        no

Does the person have a valid HMO 'id' number?
  yes◄                        no

What is the reason for coming to the HMO facility?
  new case◄               follow up case          information other

What is the person's temperature?
  normal◄                   abnormal              not known

Does the person claim other symptoms?
  yes◄                        no

Recommended support: level 1.




 1Help        2Go       3WhatIf    4Variable 5Rule      6Set       7Edit     8Quit
 1Help 2How? 3Why? 4Slow 5Fast 6Quit
```

FIGURE 13-7
Example of how a user interfaces with a
knowledge-based system during a
consultation

new computer programs. The comparison is appropriate because a knowledge-based system fundamentally is just another type of computer program.

Generally, any knowledge-based system could be programmed in traditional programming languages such as C, BASIC, and COBOL. It often is more efficient, however, to program them in shell languages designed to optimize this type of application.

Finally, a knowledge-based system developer turns over a completed system to its users. They run so-called consultation sessions with it. In the HMO case, a consultation session resembles the example illustrated in Figure 13-7.

Still another type of shell, called an *induction system*, eliminates the need to write rules. It works on the premise that given enough example cases with solutions, it can "induce" the correct rules itself to reach the same conclusions. This type of shell automatically generates its own rules from the example cases given. Usually some program coding is still required to add user interface enhancements to the induced rules.

Additional Enhancements

There are many enhancements that can be made to the HMO sample system to make it more usable. These include

- Integrate the knowledge-based system with a database of HMO members. This would make the operation more efficient by eliminating a manual lookup of each client's membership status.
- Integrate the knowledge-based system with a spreadsheet file that keeps an easy-to-access summary record of the number and types of clients serviced each day. It could help the HMO manager spot trends and make adjustments to avoid potential service bottlenecks.

With shell packages, it is fairly easy to make these kinds of improvements.

Many computer industry observers believe that in the future, knowledge-based system segments will be built into or integrated with most computer programs. These enhancements will be used to help users navigate new programs without the use of guidebooks. Also, they will be used to add intelligence to

Structure
a knowledge
base

↓

ACTIONS
block

RULES
block

QUESTIONS
block

```
ACTIONS
    DISPLAY "Welcome to the HMO Service Screening Assistant"
    FIND support
    DISPLAY "Recommended support: (support)."
;

RULE 1
    IF member_status = ok and
       reason = new_case or
       reason = follow_up_case and
       problem = serious
    THEN support = level_1;

RULE 2
    IF member_status = ok and
       reason = new_case and
       problem = non_serious
    THEN support = level_2;

RULE 3
    IF member_status = ok and
       reason = follow_up_case and
       problem = non_serious
    THEN support = level_3;

RULE 4
    IF member_status = ok and
       reason = information_other
    THEN support = information_other;

RULE 5
    IF member_status = not_ok
    THEN support = non_member;

RULE 6
    IF member = yes and
       valid_id = yes
    THEN member_status = ok;

RULE 7
    IF member = yes and
       valid_id = no
    THEN member_status = not_ok;

RULE 8
    IF member = no
    THEN member_status = not_ok;

RULE 9
    IF temperature = normal and
       other_symptoms = yes
    THEN problem = serious;

RULE 10
    IF temperature = normal and
       other_symptoms = no
    THEN problem = non_serious;

RULE 11
    IF temperature = abnormal or
       temperature = not_known
    THEN problem = serious;

ASK member: "Is the person an HMO member?";
CHOICES member: yes, no;

ASK valid_id: "Does the person have a valid HMO 'id' number?";
CHOICES valid_id: yes, no;

ASK reason: "What is the reason for coming to the HMO facility?";
CHOICES reason: new_case, follow_up_case, information_other;

ASK temperature: "What is the person's temperature?";
CHOICES temperature: normal, abnormal, not_known;

ASK other_symptoms:  "Does the person claim other symptoms?";
CHOICES other_symptoms: yes, no;
```

FIGURE 13-8
Printout of the HMO knowledge base file

programs. This promises to simplify use and improve performance of future computer programs.

Edward A. Feigenbaum, Stanford University professor and a pioneer in the field of knowledge-based systems, says:

> Knowledge is power, and the computer is an amplifier of that power. Those nations that master new knowledge technology will have a cultural and political ascendancy. The information processing industry, which is destined to be the world's largest industry by the year 2000, exists to serve human information processing needs. But very few of those needs involve calculating numbers or storing and retrieving data. Most human work involves knowledge, reasoning, and thought.[1]

Organizations of all types are attempting to amplify their knowledge resources through knowledge-based systems. For example, Westinghouse provides customers with a knowledge-based system for its steam generators. It provides the benefit of continuous maintenance checks without added manpower for Westinghouse or the customer. The U.S. Bureau of Mines distributes a knowledge-based system to coal mine operators. It helps to teach them about dust and methane gas control, as well as ventilation techniques. This provides coal mine operators with expert instruction at their convenience, wherever they are located. The long-term effect of widespread distribution of such instruction is a healthier workforce.

The Army uses a knowledge-based system to help organize complex air cargo loads in minutes. This enables applying the best expertise the Army can bring to bear to help optimize any air cargo shipment anywhere it is needed in the world. Another knowledge-based system provides advice on the legal aspects of trade transactions between the United States and Canada. The availability of such specialized knowledge can enable more organizations to promote the kind of trade partnerships that will become more prevalent by the year 2000.

---

[1]Quoted in "PC World View," *PC World*, September 1984, p. 34.

FOCUS ON: *Neural Networks: Putting Brainpower in a Box*

Tasks that stump the most advanced supercomputer—recognizing a face, reading a handwritten note—are child's play for the 3-pound human brain. Most important, unlike any conventional computer, the brain can learn from its mistakes.

Researchers have tried for years to program computers to mimic the brain's abilities, but without success. Now a growing number of designers believe they have the answer: if a computer is to function more like a person and less like an overgrown calculator, it must be built more like a brain. The brain distributes information across a vast interconnected web of nerve cells.

Conventional versus Neural Approach

Conventional computers follow a chainlike sequence of detailed instructions. Although very fast, they perform only one task at a time. This lockstep approach works best in solving problems that can be broken down into simpler pieces. The processors in a neural-network computer, by contrast, form a grid, much like the nerve cells in the brain. Since these artificial neurons are interconnected, they can share information and perform tasks simultaneously. This approach works best at recognizing patterns.

Instead of programming a neural-network computer to make decisions, its maker trains it to recognize patterns by repeatedly feeding examples to the machine. The computer responds to each example by randomly activating its circuits to a particular configuration. The trainer elec-

tronically reinforces connections that produce a correct answer and weakens those that produce an incorrect one. After as many as several thousand trials, the computer activates only those circuits that produce the right answer.

Applications

Several organizations have already begun using neural networks in a variety of applications. For example, a bank "trains" a neural network by

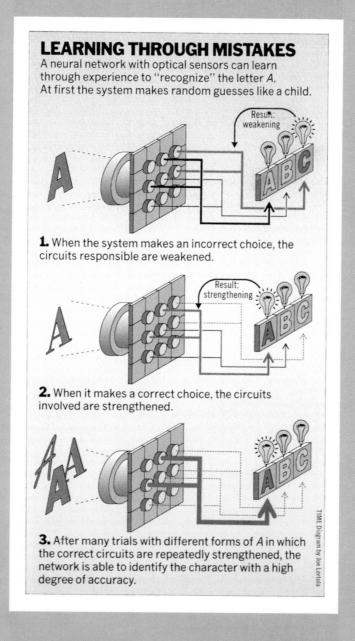

LEARNING THROUGH MISTAKES
A neural network with optical sensors can learn through experience to "recognize" the letter *A*. At first the system makes random guesses like a child.

1. When the system makes an incorrect choice, the circuits responsible are weakened.

2. When it makes a correct choice, the circuits involved are strengthened.

3. After many trials with different forms of *A* in which the correct circuits are repeatedly strengthened, the network is able to identify the character with a high degree of accuracy.

TIME Diagram by Joe Lertola

feeding it a large historical database of the characteristics of people who have defaulted on mortgage loans. The network then predicts whether a new applicant will default.

The intelligence community is another target for neural networking. One system is first trained to recognize certain words. The system then listens in on phone calls or taped conversations until it hears those keywords and then signals an operator.

"We're using neural networks to recognize certain problems in liver disease," says computer science professor Porter Sherman of the University of Bridgeport, Conn. "We used data and analyzed it two ways: using a statistical analysis program and a neural network to determine discrepancies between a normal and bad liver."

Sherman found that the neural network could be trained faster than the statistical analysis problem could be programmed. Also, the statistical method was accurate only between 77 percent and 84 percent of the time, while the neural network produced results with 86 percent to 90 percent accuracy.

Casey Klimasauskas, president of Neural-Works, suggests that "rather than a few blinding enhancements in neural networking technology, there'll be an evolutionary ooze, where thousands of engineers will solve the problems and push things a little bit further all the time."

ROBOT SYSTEMS

This final section of the chapter looks at robot systems. Robots are controlled by the smallest up to the largest types of computers.

By definition, a **general-purpose robot** is a mechanical device that can be taught to do a variety of complex jobs. A simplified illustration of one industrial robot appears in Figure 13-9. Its primary function is to pick a small part from a bin and place it in a hole on a disk drive's metal casting.

The program to control the robot's movements, which is summarized in Figure 13-10, reveals that

- All relevant actions must be programmed completely and unambiguously
- There is no intuitive knowledge present, such as that possessed by human workers

A human worker, especially one with experience in production-line assembly, can be instructed to do the task in a few minutes. A worker also knows, without further instruction, what actions to take for the unforeseen conditions that occur.

As shown, the steps in Figure 13-10 do not accommodate the many things that can go wrong. For example, what if the disk casting does not have a hole for the part to be inserted? The program also presupposes significant capabilities in the robot and its vision subsystem. They require that the vision subsystem and robot movements be synchronized.

FIGURE 13-9
Major structural components of a robot

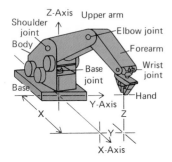

SENSORY SUBSYSTEMS

A robot's **sensory subsystems** allow it to sense its surroundings and modify its actions to carry out specified tasks. These sensory subsystems include

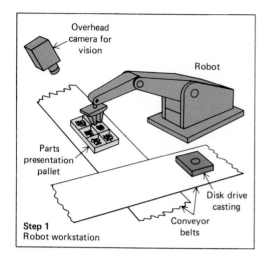

Step 1
Robot workstation

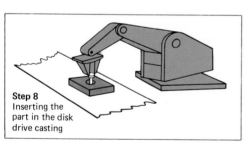

Step 5
A part has been
located and picked up.

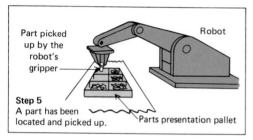

Step 8
Inserting the
part in the disk
drive casting

Summary of computer program steps

Step 1
Wait for a disk drive casting to enter the robot workstation.

Step 2
Take a photograph or image of the parts presentation pallet (an egg carton arrangement that separates parts). One or more overhead cameras photograph the egg carton to get an image.

Step 3
Locate a part in the image. A vision subsystem, often sold separately from the robot, does all image related work.

Step 4
If the egg carton is empty, move the empty carton to the stacking area and signal the conveyor belt controller to move a fresh egg carton into position. Go to step 2.

Step 5
A part has been located in the egg carton. Pick up the part and position it in the visual inspection station. Take a photograph to get an image of the part. Determine the orientation of the part.

Step 6
If an incorrect part is detected by the vision subsystem, deposit the part in the reject bin. Go to step 2.

Step 7
The part is correct. Adjust the robot hand angle according to the observed orientation of the part. Move the part to a point just above the insertion location on the disk drive casting.

Step 8
Insert the part in the disk drive casting, by moving it vertically downward while monitoring the force. When the vertical force reaches a specified value, stop the robot vertical motion.

Step 9
Check the vertical position of the robot hand when it stops moving. If it is at a height that indicates the part was inserted, release the part from the gripper and retract the robot hand.

Step 10
The part was not inserted correctly. Move the robot hand in the plane of the floppy disk casting by a small increment along a prescribed path. Go to step 8.

FIGURE 13-10
A robot's programmed sequence

- *Vision.* One manufacturer uses a three-dimensional vision-guided robot to weld parts together. Three-dimensional vision is obtained by mounting two cameras, 30 inches apart, on the robot arm, as shown in Figure 13-11. The cameras record and digitize images. But unlike a graphics digitizing system, this one analyzes the image for content. The analysis provides answers about an image's location, resting position, and quality. The answers are passed to the robot controller which activates the robot's movement.
- *Touch.* Touch subsystems complement vision subsystems in robot installations. The robot shown in Figure 13-12 attains a touch sensitivity almost equal to a human hand. Its sensors detect size, shape, and pressure.

Remote-controlled robots are being designed to repair satellites 22,300 miles

Twin cameras

Welding robot

Programmer

Teach pendant

FIGURE 13-11
A robot equipped with two cameras for three-dimensional vision

in space. Armed with a sensory-feedback system, they will make repairs with a human partner. The human partner, who may be an astronaut based at a space station or on a shuttle, will manipulate the teleoperated robot. This remote-controlled technique is called **telepresence**.

Telepresence has more down-to-earth applications. Surgeons envision a day when they will be able to slip on a pair of special gloves connected by remote control to a pair of mechanical hands. The teleoperated hands will be able to perform surgery in a hospital hundreds of miles away.

Some robots are also outfitted with senses that no human being has: the perception of infrared light and ultrasonic sound. One breed of **homebots**, or personal robots, typically have ultrasonic transmitters/sensors. To determine where objects are located, a robot's sensor sends out an ultrasonic wave signal

FIGURE 13-12
A visual-tactile sensing robot handles objects as fragile as eggs.

and detects its feedback. Then it sends a second sensor signal. By computing the time taken for individual signals to go out and return, the robot can determine where objects are located. Such a sonar sensor is used with great effect during demonstrations of "follow me," where a personal robot automatically rolls behind its demonstrator who walks from room to room.

FACTORY OF THE FUTURE

General Motors' highly flexible and completely **computer-aided-manufacturing (CAM)** facility in Michigan uses computers to streamline the manufacturing process. It allows making adjustments to parts of different sizes in minutes. The emphasis is on manufacturing that accommodates rapid design changes and product customization. It has abandoned the old concept of long production runs of one component, and only one component, at a time.

The plant produces not one but a family of axles for different models of cars. In its pilot phase, 50 robots move parts within 40 manufacturing and *assembly cells*. Driverless robot-driven carts move parts between cells and transport products to shipping areas.

The robots in this flexible environment are mainly general-purpose robots. A general-purpose robot can be *taught* a task through programming. Once a task is learned, the robot can repeat it endlessly. But should a new task be required, the same robot can easily be reprogrammed to do the new task. Theoretically, a general-purpose robot programmed to assemble axles could easily be reprogrammed to assemble TV sets, or electric motors, or just about anything.

TEACHING ROBOTS

Teaching a robot its task refers to the process of

- Leading a robot through a sequence of moves.
- Recording the coordinate geometric and other data necessary to reproduce the movement sequence.
- Including the known data in the robot controller program.

As an example, to teach the robot how to function in the disk drive assembly operation, a programmer uses a **teach pendant** like the one in Figure 13-11. The device allows taking a robot through movements by pushing appropriate buttons to

- Move robot joints
- Adjust movement speeds
- Record coordinate locations

During the teaching phase, the teach pendant is attached to the robot controller program. Only those motions and coordinates that the robot programmer selects are recorded.

Robot programming languages are proprietary, and each robot manufacturer supports its own language. Most require skilled programmers.

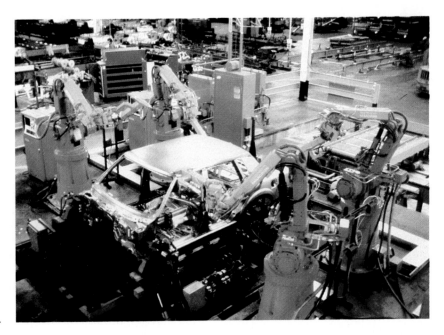

FIGURE 13-13
Robots measure openings for
windshields, doors, and lights.

COST JUSTIFICATION

The factors driving a decision to modernize a facility are often labor related. At a Ford Motor plant, shown in Figure 13-13, robots measure openings for windshields, doors, and lights. They work ten times as fast as humans and require no fringe benefits.

At a U.S. Department of Energy plant, a robot works behind a 10-inch-thick concrete wall transporting reprocessed plutonium, one of the most toxic substances known to humans. Until now, this dangerous task has been done by humans in elaborate space suits. The $100,000 robot knows nothing about danger.

At the disk drive manufacturing facility, one operator oversees two robot systems. They do work that formerly required six people. The system is expected to pay for itself in 2 years.

The list in Figure 13-14 from *Business* magazine identifies the productivity advantages of robots over human workers. These advantages have been used to cost justify robots for such industrial applications as the following:

- Assembly
- Forging (example: removal of white-hot metal from a furnace)
- Inspection
- Materials transfer
- Packaging
- Parts sorting
- Product testing
- Quality control

**PRODUCTIVITY ADVANTAGES
OF ROBOT WORKERS OVER
HUMAN WORKERS**

Work more reliably:
  Set standards of 95% uptime.
  Can work three shifts.
  Take no vacations.
  Take no coffee breaks.
Work more consistently and accurately:
  Improve product quality.
  Reduce scrap rates.
  Make production more predictable.
  Contribute to higher capital utilization.
  Self-diagnose departures from efficiency.
  Can design improved work methods.
Work less expensively:
  Eliminate need for worker's compensation.
  Eliminate need for retirement plans and social security.
  Eliminate need for insurance programs.
Work in less controlled environments:
  Work in poor climatic conditions.
  Ignore noise.
  Do hazardous or dangerous jobs.
Work solely for the organization:
  Do not moonlight.
  Do not engage in industrial espionage.
  Do not sabotage operations.
  Do not become proselytized.
  Do not commit internal theft.

FIGURE 13-14

SOCIAL IMPACT

The impact of robots on a society can be measured in economic, personal, and psychological terms.

Economic

Research studies suggest that people will lose their jobs to robots in greater numbers in the future. Yet the argument is raised that if robots are not used, industries in the United States will not be able to compete with foreign producers. Then more jobs will be lost.

One observer suggests that for workers, a choice between robots or foreign competition is merely a choice between hanging and the electric chair. It is a problem society must resolve.

Others argue that the loss of jobs is not the most difficult economic challenge posed by robots. One robot expert claims that retraining is the major social problem created by robotization. He claims that massive retraining programs will be needed to prevent the creation of an oversupply of workers whose skills have become obsolete.

Personal

While robots are driving people out of work, people are bringing robots into their homes. One 2½-year-old child learned the alphabet from a 4½-foot robot, such as the one shown in Figure 13-15. The child considers the robot a companion and talks to it and kisses it. The parents fret when the child occasionally kicks it.

The father likes the robot to function as a house security guard. He bought security hardware components, including intrusion sensors, passive infrared detectors, and smoke sensors. Because he is a computer software developer, he uses the robot to develop his own programming skills. The robot has its own computer, keyboard, and display built into its head.

Computer industry experts believe that a typical consumer may be disappointed with a homebot. Most are still awkward pioneers, unlike fictional movie robots.

Psychological

Along with the fear of unemployment, robots trigger some odd anxieties at home. One mother feels her daughter would rather have the robot help her with homework than the mother. A child who has a robot feels neglected because

FIGURE 13-15
Personal robots, or "homebots"

his friends play with the robot more than him. Some psychologists firmly expect such outcomes when robots replace parents, friends, and teachers in people's affections.

There are, of course, more primordial fears, such as the apprehension over robot terrorism. Consider a scenario in which a mad electrician seizes control of the robots and marshals them into squadrons of killer troops guided by a central computer. Most experts view such an eventuality as highly improbable. They base their opinion on the fact that robots really behave like severely retarded children that require continuous attention from their parents to solve or deal with the most trivial problem.

CASE STUDY: *Campbell's Keeps Kettles Boiling with Personal Consultant*

At Campbell Soup Company plants around the country, soup is "cooked" in giant product sterilizers—commonly called cookers. Plant operators and maintenance personnel handle day-to-day cooker operations, but on occasion, difficulties arise that require the attention of an expert—someone thoroughly versed in the design, installation, and operation of the equipment.

Unfortunately, there just aren't enough experts to go around. So, when problems arise, the cookers can be shut down for long periods of time while an expert is flown in. To ease that time pressure while freeing the experts for design improvements and other work, company officials decided to try a knowledge-based system. They wanted the system to diagnose possible problems and recommend specific solutions. And they wanted it to help train new maintenance personnel.

Because the company wanted a system in each plant, it decided to try personal computers. The system picked was the Texas Instruments (TI) computer.

Campbell and Texas Instruments agreed to work together to produce a system using a knowledge-based system shell. Campbell provided the experts, and TI provided the knowledge engineer to enter that expertise in the computer.

System development took about 6 months, with a cooker expert and knowledge engineer getting together for 3 or 4 days each month at Campbell.

TI developed the prototype system with about 30 rules. Although this system didn't have much depth to its knowledge, it served to uncover a wealth of knowledge about the cooker which the human expert had not previously considered relevant.

The system was enlarged and refined over the next several months. Each revision produced more refined questions and new steps in the rules. The complete system has 150 rules plus start-up and shut-down procedures for the cookers. It has been demonstrated to plant personnel, and has been well received. The system is now being installed in Campbell plants for use in diagnosing problems.

DISCUSSION QUESTIONS

1. Describe the motivations for developing a knowledge-based system.

2. Originally the Campbell cooker expert was reluctant to have a computer program capture his knowledge. His resistance was slowly overcome after he saw positive system results. What suggestions can you make about how to deal with experts who are reluctant about transferring their knowledge to knowledge-based systems?

CHAPTER SUMMARY

- *Artificial intelligence*, or *AI*, is the branch of computer science that makes computers imitate human behavior. Many disciplines contribute to AI's development.

- AI is used as an umbrella term for, among other things, knowledge-based systems, programmable robot systems, and natural language systems.

- *Knowledge-based systems* capture, magnify, and distribute access to judgment. They can function as assistants, colleagues, or experts.

- Classic examples of knowledge-based systems include CATS, XCON, ExperTAX, and PUFF.

- The three main parts of a knowledge-based system are the knowledge base, inference engine, and explanation facility.

- A *knowledge base* is a stored collection of facts and rules about a specific area of knowledge.

- *Heuristics* are rules-of-thumb about a task at hand. One expert calls heuristics the knowledge of good judgment.

- *Knowledge engineers* have special skills to mine heuristics from human experts and to transfer them into a computerized knowledge base.

- An *inference engine* handles the logic processing inside a knowledge-based system. It knows when and how to retrieve rules from the knowledge base and ask user questions.

- LISP and PROLOG are two common programming languages used for knowledge-based systems.

- An *explanation facility* reports how a knowledge-based system arrived at a given conclusion or line of reasoning.

- A *shell* package contains an inference engine without a knowledge base. It is the predominant way to develop knowledge-based systems on microcomputers.

- A *dependency diagram* indicates the relationship among all questions and recommendations made by a knowledge-based system. It serves as a paper model of how to write the program code for the system.

- A *general-purpose robot* is a mechanical device that can be taught to do a variety of complex jobs.

- A *sensory subsystem* allows a robot to sense its surroundings and modify its actions to carry out specified tasks. Examples are vision and touch subsystems.

- *Telepresence* is the remote control of robot functions. An example is an astronaut controlling a robot arm to repair a satellite in space.

- A goal of *computer-aided manufacturing (CAM)* is to streamline manufacturing processes, such as at an automobile manufacturing factory.

- *Teaching* a robot involves leading it through its task with a *teach pendant* and recording coordinates and other data to reproduce the movement sequence.

- Advantages used to cost justify robots for industrial applications include the following: they work faster than humans, they require no fringe benefits, and they do dangerous tasks.

- Robots have an economic, personal, and psychological impact on society. For example, they can put people out of jobs, they can enter the home as companions and pets, and they can replace parents, friends, and teachers in people's affections.

SELECTED KEY TERMS

Artificial intelligence	Heuristics	LISP
Computer-aided manufacturing (CAM)	Homebot	PROLOG
Dependency diagram	Inference engine	Sensory subsystem
Explanation facility	Knowledge base	Shell
General-purpose robot	Knowledge-based system	Teach pendant
	Knowledge engineer	Telepresence

REVIEW QUESTIONS

1. What is artificial intelligence?
2. List three examples of classic knowledge-based systems.
3. Describe the three parts of a knowledge-based system.
4. What does a knowledge engineer do?
5. Describe the purpose of an inference engine.
6. What are two common programming languages used for knowledge-based system development?
7. What is an explanation facility in a knowledge-based system?
8. What is a shell package? How is it used?
9. What is the reason for creating dependency diagrams when developing a knowledge-based system?
10. What is a general-purpose robot?
11. What is a sensory subsystem? Give two examples.
12. What is telepresence?
13. Explain the goal of computer-aided manufacturing (CAM).
14. How is a robot taught to do useful tasks?
15. List three advantages used to cost justify robots for industrial applications.
16. List three impacts of robots on society.

EXERCISES

1. Identify a situation you think would benefit from a knowledge-based system. Write a report that describes the situation and justifies the benefit of having a knowledge-based system. Include a section that addresses problems that might arise. Describe how the problems could be handled if the system were implemented.
2. Locate articles on three knowledge-based system shell packages. The articles will probably call the software "expert system" shells or development packages. Prepare an oral or written report that compares the packages.
3. Prepare a report on the impact of robots on society. Give specific examples of robots both succeeding and failing in areas such as manufacturing and science. Include a discussion of robots for educational and recreational purposes. Do you think that, in general, robots have had a positive or negative impact? Defend your answer.

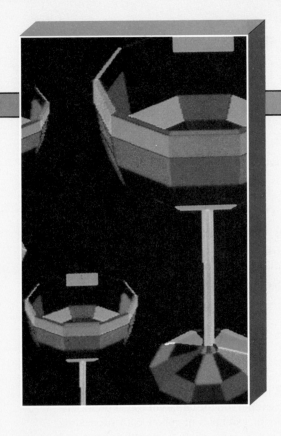

14

History, Society, and Careers

AFTER READING THIS CHAPTER, YOU SHOULD BE ABLE TO

- Identify historical milestones that led to today's information society
- Give examples of how computers affect society
- Identify computer career opportunities

Linked by telephones, fax machines, and computers, a new breed of information worker is reorganizing the landscape of America. These workers are free to live almost anywhere, and more are deciding to live in small cities and rural areas. The new electronic heartland they create is spreading throughout developed countries around the globe.

The new electronic heartland is peopled by individuals who are not location-dependent. They are artists, composers, stock and bond traders, transcribers and translators, software programmers, and writers of every stripe who can do what they do anywhere and look for agreeable places to do it. Computer-based technology makes it possible.

We do not have to cluster together in cities or suburbs to get our work done, as we did during the industrial era.

This chapter first looks at historical milestones in computing that led to the present information society. It then examines ways computers affect society, including education and health care areas, among others. Social issues that concern a computer-based society, such as employment, privacy, crime, and ethics, are addressed.

The last part of this chapter looks at computer careers.

COMPUTING MILESTONES

Computers, as we know them, were born in early 1940 with the so-called ABC computer. John V. Atanasoff, a mathematics professor at Iowa State University, required a calculating device to perform mathematical operations. With an assistant, Clifford E. Berry, he designed and named the machine the *Atanasoff-Berry Computer*, or the **ABC Computer**, as shown in Figure 14-1.

The design of the ABC Computer influenced the design of the **ENIAC** (*Electronic Numerical Integrator And Computer*), shown in Figure 14-2. Built in the 1940s by John W. Mauchly and J. Presper Eckert, Jr., of the University of Pennsylvania, it was the first large-scale computer.

Also in the 1940s, another University of Pennsylvania pioneer, John von Neumann, developed the **stored program concept** of reading a program into memory for processing. Although reading programs into memory is standard today, it was different on the ENIAC. The ENIAC was *hard-wired*. All its circuitry was wired to perform one specific job. If the job changed, wires had to be changed. Loading and storing a new program in memory for execution, instead of rewiring the computer, was a major computing milestone.

First Generation of Computers

With the ENIAC began what is traditionally thought of as the four generations of computers. **First-generation computers**, built from 1946 to 1959, were characterized by bulky **vacuum tubes**. They resemble slim light bulbs in size and shape, as shown in Figure 14-3, and register on and off electronic pulses. The ENIAC, which weighed 30 tons and required the floor space of a house, contained 18,000 vacuum tubes.

During this time, Dr. Mauchly and Mr. Eckert built the first commercial-use computer. The **UNIVAC I**, shown in Figure 14-4, was used to predict the outcome of the 1952 presidential election.

FIGURE 14-1
The Atanasoff-Berry Computer (or ABC Computer)

FIGURE 14-2
The ENIAC computer with its coinventors, J. Presper Eckert, Jr. (front, left) and John W. Mauchly (center)

Vacuum tubes used in first-generation computers (1 tube equals 1 circuit element)

Transistors used in second-generation computers (1 transistor equals 1 circuit element)

FIGURE 14-3
The shrinking size of computer electronic circuitry

Integrated circuits on a silicon chip used in third- and fourth-generation computers (1 chip equals over 15,000 circuit elements)

FIGURE 14-4
The first commercial-use computer,
the UNIVAC I, predicted the winner
of the 1952 presidential election.

First-generation hardware was programmed using *machine language*, which consists of only 1's and 0's. It is difficult for humans to read as well as to write machine language programs.

Second Generation

FIGURE 14-5
Computer program language pioneer Grace Hopper, retired U.S. Navy

In the **second generation**, 1959–1964, computers became faster, smaller, and less expensive than first-generation machines. Vacuum tubes were replaced with smaller, more reliable **transistors** for the controlling circuitry. The second generation of computing witnessed an immense growth of computer use by industry and government agencies.

Efforts were also made during this period to simplify programming. Languages like FORTRAN (*FOR*mula *TRAN*slation) and COBOL (*CO*mmon *Busi*ness *O*riented *L*anguage) were developed.

Grace Hopper, a commodore in the United States Navy, was a pioneer in the field of computer languages. She was a member of the committee that explored solutions to the problem of transporting programs written for one computer to another, different computer. The result was a standardized COBOL for which Dr. Hopper, who is shown in Figure 14-5, wrote the first practical program.

Third Generation

In 1964, IBM announced its System 360, a large mainframe computer shown in Figure 14-6. It launched the **third generation** of computing, from 1964 to 1970. These computers used **integrated circuit** technology, which is still used

FIGURE 14-6
The IBM System 360, a third-generation computer

today. In this technology, on and off circuit elements are first etched, then burned, into a *silicon chip*. Figure 14-3 shows a silicon chip.

With integrated circuits, computer companies began to introduce smaller computers. Among them, Digital Equipment Corporation (DEC) opened the *minicomputer* market by introducing the DEC PDP-8, the first successful mini-computer.

Software companies began to emerge, and software made substantial advances. The interactive BASIC (*Beginner's All-Purpose Symbolic Instruction Code*) program language allowed nontechnical people, like students, to program computers. Operating systems were developed to help manage new input and output devices and to improve the speed and efficiency of computers.

Fourth Generation

The period from 1970 to the present is referred to as the **fourth generation** of computing. The IBM System 370 mainframe computer used integrated circuit chips that contained over 15,000 circuit elements on a single chip. The chips are called **LSI** (for **large-scale integration**) chips. Earlier third-generation integrated circuits had as few as 22 circuits on a chip.

In 1971, Intel Corporation introduced the first **microprocessor** chip. It contained all the major logic circuitry of a computer on one chip. The first commercial *microcomputer*, which had a microprocessor as its "brain" or "engine," appeared in 1974. It was offered in kit form and was called the Altair.

By 1977 Apple Computer, Radio Shack, and Commodore were selling completely assembled microcomputers, also called *personal computers*, such as the one in Figure 14-7. The inventors of the Apple computer, Steve Jobs and Steve Wozniak, were members of the Homebrew Computer Club in California. Club members, impressed with their assembled computer, wanted to buy a copy. So the two entrepreneurs borrowed money and assembled the first Apple computers in a garage.

Microcomputers did not attract business users until 1979, when the first electronic spreadsheet program, **VisiCalc**, appeared. The idea for VisiCalc came from Dan Bricklin, a Harvard student who had a complex business analysis assignment that required lots of calculations. He developed VisiCalc with a friend, Bob Frankston. The program ran only on the Apple II microcomputer.

FIGURE 14-7
One of the earliest completely assembled
microcomputers, the Apple II

It was the first time a software program was responsible for the sale of computer hardware.

The 1970s saw many other computer firsts, including local-area networks, supercomputers, and commercially used knowledge-based or expert systems.

The Apple personal computer lost its dominance in the early 1980s because of the rise of the IBM Personal Computer (IBM-PC). Today there are many brands of personal computers, but the standards established by the IBM-PC continue to dominate new, evolving hardware standards.

The mid-1980s saw the microcomputer eclipse the mainframe and minicomputer in market dominance. Hardware, in turn, is being eclipsed by software dominance.

Most agree that a *fifth generation* of computing is not far away. Work is underway in the United States, Japan, and elsewhere to produce more powerful machines with parallel processors. Many believe that the next generation of computers will also be more "intelligent," which is one of the goals of artificial intelligence researchers.

COMPUTERS IN SOCIETY

The second section of this chapter looks at computers in society. Computers, especially personal computers, have become a part of almost every aspect of modern society. This section contains "snapshots" of how computers are used to support efforts in health care, environmental studies, education, and a variety of other areas.

Health Care

Doctors use a computerized robotic arm, as Figure 14-8 shows, to remove tissue samples from suspected brain tumors that are difficult to reach by conventional means.[1] The robotic arm's great accuracy

---

[1]Sandra Blakeslee, "A Robot Assists in Three Brain Operations," *New York Times*, June 25, 1985, p. C1.

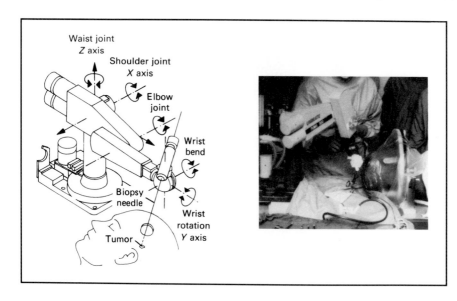

FIGURE 14-8
A robot arm assists in a brain operation.

- Eliminates the need for general anesthesia
- Reduces trauma to the brain
- Allows patients to go home the day after brain surgery, instead of a week or more later

In the future, the device is expected to repair blood vessels, guide laser beams to tumors, and help orthopedic surgeons repair ruptured discs and torn ligaments.

At the Mayo Clinic/Foundation, a program helps doctors "practice" brain surgery.[2] As shown in Figure 14-9, practice is done using three-dimensional images from a patient's X-rays and other tests. The program alerts surgeons to any unusual conditions they may encounter in an actual operation.

In the future, telecommunications, combined with robotic technology, is expected to enable physicians to perform long-distance surgery. This could have a positive impact on the health of Third World nations. These nations could also benefit from knowledge-based, or expert, systems, which could be used to help paramedics diagnose medical problems.

Environmental Studies

Environmental researchers with the U.S. Geological Survey team use computers to help monitor potential earthquakes and volcanoes.[3] Their old minicomputer system cost $100,000 for every site studied. The new microcomputer one costs about $5,000. It is now possible to make life-and-death disaster predictions in high-risk, poverty-stricken communities that previously could not afford it.

At Chicago's Brookfield Zoo, a microcomputer helps with a different kind of environmental work.[4] It controls a database system called ARKS (Animal

---

[2]Maura J. Harrington, "Taking Surgery to a New Dimension," *Computerworld*, May 21, 1990, p. 16.

[3]Patrick Honan, "How We Explore the Universe," *Personal Computing*, October 1989, pp. 177ff.

[4]Janet Goldenberg, "Animal Trackers," *PC World*, June 1983, pp. 266-74.

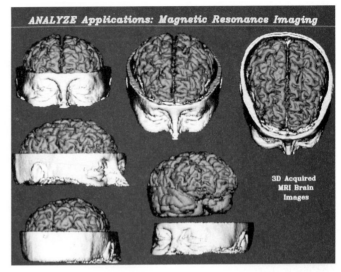

A three-dimensional display and manipulation of the brain

FIGURE 14-9
Screens from a program that enables
doctors to "practice" brain surgery

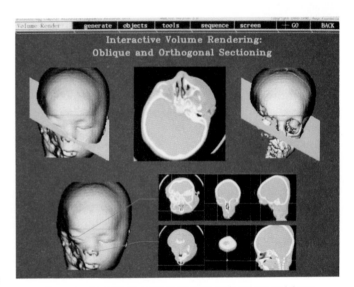

Example of a sectioning tool to research brain tumors and tissue

Records Keeping System). It links, through telecommunication lines, into another database of 70,000 zoo animals worldwide. The databases help promote breeding programs that seek to preserve and replenish the planet's endangered species.

Education

The variety of ways that computers have changed education and training are evident everywhere.

The computer has changed some of the ways students learn. Computer-based videodisc courses, as an example, allow a student to

- Select subjects from a display menu
- Follow a video image and sound presentation on a TV set

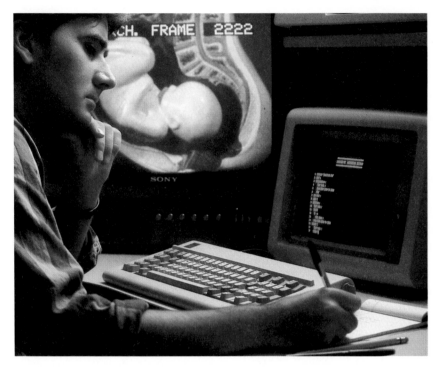

FIGURE 14-10
Nelson Whitney creates an interactive
video display lesson that combines
text and graphics.

- Interact with the video through computer keyboard input or touch-sensitive displays

Developers claim that the method is a more effective way to learn than with traditional methods.

Figure 14-10 shows an educator creating a videodisc lesson for a biology course.[5] The course is prepared with an **authoring system**. This software allows nonprogrammers to create, or "author," computer-based instruction programs. When students take the course, they will be experiencing **computer-assisted instruction (CAI)**, which

- Asks questions
- Keeps track of answers
- Adjusts its presentation to a student's demonstrated knowledge and experience

Some educators use a computer to teach subjects such as anatomy and genetics. One program requires a student to act like a scientist breeding cats in order to discover the principles of genetics.

Many company training programs also depend on computers. For example, airlines use computers to train pilots and mechanics.

Self-education is also possible to anyone who has access to a personal computer. Programs are available for remedial or accelerated subjects including reading and math study. They are aimed at everyone, from preschoolers through college or continuing studies students.

---

[5]Wayne Parker, "Interactive Video: Calling the Shots," *PC World*, October 1984, pp. 99-108.

Other Areas

Computers have become part of many other areas in today's society. Selected examples include:

- *Special Services.* Hundreds of adaptive computer devices include Braille keyboards and printers, as well as programs that read aloud whatever appears on a display screen. They make computers usable by a wide spectrum of society.
- *Children Services.* One program used nationwide develops "aging" photographs of missing children to help identify them. At an adoption center, a minicomputer helps to match prospective parents with hard-to-place children.
- *Home.* Household budgeting and tax planning are done with home computers. Some use telecommunication lines to access services for home shopping, airline ticketing, banking, and encyclopedia referencing.
- *Entertainment.* Arcade-style computer games are familiar to everyone. More sophisticated games can put a user in the seat of a jet fighter, as shown in Figure 14-11. Other games recreate the stock, real estate, and commodities markets.
- *Sports.* Most major league teams in all professional sports use computers to compile player and team statistics. Some coaches also use a computer to develop game strategies.
- *Music and Art.* Using a personal computer with music software and a synthesizer, anyone can listen to Mozart or a top-40 hit. Artists turn out images like those shown in Figure 14-12, that are as sharp as photographs, yet as free from the bounds of reality as animated cartoons.

FIGURE 14-11
This flight simulator puts the user in the cockpit of an F-15 fighter jet.

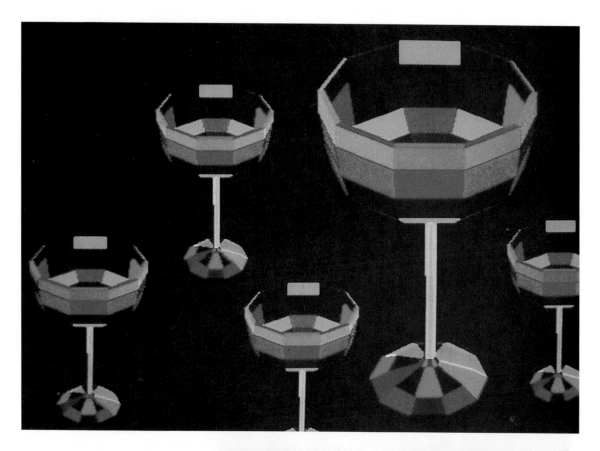

FIGURE 14-12
Computer art

FOCUS ON: *When the Dead Are Revived*

"It was a moment of exploding consciousness," recalls James Charlesworth, professor of New Testament languages at Princeton Theological Seminary. "You dare not hope, and then—bingo!—it springs into view. Whole sentences, paragraphs. Right from the time of Jesus!"

Charlesworth's enthusiastic reaction was understandable, for the text he was examining was not just any scrap of parchment. It was one of the known copies of Old Testament scriptures.

But the scroll containing a narrative version of the book of *Genesis* had deteriorated so badly that scholars despaired of ever uncovering its ancient secrets. That is, until the American team that included Charlesworth arrived in Jerusalem. The team hoped to analyze the aged parchment with sophisticated computer-based image-enhancement techniques.

Dr. Bruce Zuckerman at camera looking at Dead Sea Scroll.

original seven rolls of inscribed sheepskin known as the Dead Sea Scrolls—and the only one whose contents were still largely unread. Unearthed in 1947 by shepherds from rocky caves only 15 miles from Jerusalem, the Dead Sea Scrolls are considered by biblical archaeologists to be the greatest manuscript discovery ever made. Their texts, set down in Hebrew and Aramaic some 2,000 years ago, include long-lost originals of dozens of celebrated religious works, as well as the oldest

The scroll, ravaged by moisture, had deteriorated further than they feared. A breakthrough came when the document was lit from behind and shot with a special Japanese-made infrared film.

Pixels and Smudges

The scholars used a process known as *digitization* to put the pictures into a form suitable for computer analysis. In this procedure, a video cam-

Dead Sea Scroll unrolled

much like the process by which old Hollywood black-and-white movies are colorized.

But instead of assigning colors to each pixel, the computer assigns each dot a number according to how light or dark it is. So on a scale of one to ten, a dark smudge or scratch might be assigned a nine or ten, while a lighter stroke becomes a five or six.

These numbers can then be manipulated to filter out noise and bring out hidden features in the text. For example, all the pixels with high numbers can be changed to zeros to make them disappear, while the lighter pixels representing parts of actual letters can be darkened by boosting their values from five or six to ten.

A total of about 4,000 images were shot. Only a few dozen have been developed so far, but they shed new light on the customs of the ancient Jews and the cultural backdrop against which Christianity developed.

era is used to feed an electronic representation of each black-and-white photo to a special circuit board inside a personal computer. The circuitry divides each picture into tiny dots called *pixels*,

SOCIAL CHANGES

As society beomes more computerized, changes occur that create issues related to the work environment, privacy, and crime. They are discussed next.

Work Environment

In a computer-based economy, some workers are no longer bound to the traditional office. The term **telecommuting** has been used to describe home-bound workers who report to the office through a personal computer and a modem.

Some companies that have successfully used telecommuting claim that it

- Increases employee productivity, quality of life, and morale
- Reduces office operating costs and automobile pollution

In California, where commuter pollution is a major problem, air-quality regulations force organizations to adopt telecommuting. Other states have similar plans.

But for telecommuters and others who sit at a computer many hours a day, there are possible health risks. Some recommended ways to prevent or minimize any negative effect of computer use are

- Take a 15-minute break every 2 hours.
- Look up from the screen periodically and focus on a distant object. Blink often.
- Use an adjustable display with an antiglare screen, a chair with lower-back support, and lighting that is not focused on the screen.

Privacy

Privacy is a concern of many in a computer-based society. This is especially so because of all the databases that exist about U.S. residents, such as

- *Department of Health, Education, and Welfare:* Maintains records on recipients of Social Security, social services, medicaid, medicare, and welfare benefits.
- *Civil Service:* Maintains records of government employees or applicants for government jobs.
- *Department of Transportation:* Maintains records on all motorists whose licenses have been withdrawn, suspended, or revoked by any state.

Laws that help individuals to control the information in such databases include

- *Freedom of Information Act* (1970): Allows anyone access to any federal agency records kept about them.
- *Fair Credit Reporting Act* (1970): Allows anyone access to credit bureau records kept on them. It also allows a person to challenge the records if they are inaccurate.

The potential for misuse of computer-based information, nonetheless, is a serious problem for any society devoted to freedom.

Computer Crime and Ethics

Related to the misuse of computer information is *computer crime*. **Computer crime** refers to all uses of computers to

- *Steal money or goods*—such as using knowledge of a bank's computer system to embezzle money from inactive customer accounts.
- *Steal information*—such as using a computer list of customer names for personal profit-making purposes.
- *Steal computer time*—such as using a company's computer to run a side business.
- *Steal software*—such as copying a friend's or company's software for private purposes. This is typically called **piracy**.

Computer criminals usually are people employed in positions of trust. They have no prior record and are well educated. Their profiles superficially make them desirable employees.

Young people who find penetrating someone else's computer a challenge may be called *hackers*. But the slang term **hacker** means anyone whose hobby is studying how computers work. Some do not see themselves as criminals, although they are aware of the malicious nature of their intent.

One student, for example, released a *virus* program that jammed more than 6,000 computers nationwide. Computer **viruses** are programs that can copy themselves and spread from computer to computer, stealing processing power and destroying files. This particular virus raised an awareness of how a virus cripples a computer network.

Federal and state laws are emerging to deal with computer crime. Penalties currently range up to $250,000 or 5 years in prison.

Professional organizations in the information industry, such as the Data Processing Management Association, require members to maintain and support ethical behavior. Since computing has spread well beyond computer professionals, an ethical attitude toward computing concerns a much greater population. All computer users must consciously monitor and assess their own actions to prevent criminal behavior.

COMPUTER CAREERS

This last section of the chapter examines career opportunities in computers, which include

- Jobs in user areas of an organization
- Jobs in the Information Services Department
- Jobs in other areas of the computer industry

In User Areas

Figure 14-13 gives a brief list of computer users and examples of how they apply computers to their jobs. The list gives evidence that the greatest variety of computer use opportunities exists in user areas. Most of the people who provide these examples have enhanced career options because of their computer skills.

The users on the list fall into two main groups. One group, on their own initiative, began to use computers in their jobs. They seized the opportunity to make computers support their work. The other group has jobs that already require computer use.

The first group of users are the innovators. The lawyer who uses an outline processor to help prepare his legal briefs is one example. While he was not trained in computer use, he started to use a personal computer because he thought it could help him to be more productive.

For the other type, computer use is a required part of their job. Bank tellers, for example, are expected to execute a major part of their job responsibilities on a computer. Even top management is expected to interact with the decision support and executive information systems in many organizations.

Opportunities exist for innovative computer use in most organizations. To exploit these opportunities, individuals must bring a knowledge of computers to their jobs. Those who can often experience greater career mobility than others.

In Information Services Departments

Large organizations have in-house staffs of computer professionals. They develop, deliver, and service all computing resources within the organization. While Chapter 10 covers the functions this department performs, this chapter examines the computer careers available.

A SAMPLER OF COMPUTER USERS—THEIR JOBS AND RELATED COMPUTER APPLICATIONS

Job Title	Computer Application	Chapter for Further Reference
Advertising agency partner	Uses a graphics painting package to create ads	5
Airline reservation specialist	Uses a mission critical computer-based travel reservation system	9
Apartment building owner	Uses a database package to produce rent bills and maintain tenant files	6
Automotive engineer	Uses a computer-aided design package to design engine parts	5
Bank teller	Processes customers' bank deposit and withdrawal transactions	8
Chief financial officer, bank	Works with an Information Center staff member to build a decision support model	11
Cooker-maintenance specialist	Uses a knowledge-based system to help solve equipment problems	13 Case Study
Dairy specialist, food broker	Uses spreadsheet and graphics packages to create sales presentations	5
Delivery person, snack food company	Uses a hand-held computer to enter customer orders	3 Focus On
Doctor	Uses a robotic arm to perform brain surgery	14
	Uses a knowledge-based system to help diagnose patient problems	13
Financial analyst, bank	Uses an object-oriented programming "construction set" to make financial charts	12 Focus On
Illustrator	Uses a desktop publishing system to scan images and create drawings	4
Lawyer	Uses on-line databases to do legal research	7
Legal secretary	Uses word processing to prepare legal materials	8
Loan officer	Uses a spreadsheet template to calculate customer loans	5
	Uses a management information system to examine delinquent accounts	9
Medical college instructor	Uses a hypertext application to help teach premedical students	4
Medical products manufacturer	Maintains a private bulletin board service for customers to call for information and ask questions	8
Nurse	Uses a patient care system to input patient information directly into a computer	9

FIGURE 14-13

A SAMPLER OF COMPUTER USERS—THEIR JOBS AND RELATED COMPUTER APPLICATIONS—continued

Job Title	Computer Application	Chapter for Further Reference
Oil industry scientist	Uses a supercomputer to analyze seismic data and model reservoirs	8
Orchard owner and manager	Uses an agricultural cost accounting package to help manage several profit centers	10 Case Study
Order taker, wholesaler	Uses an order processing package to expedite new order entry	9
Prison health personnel	Uses videoconferencing to contact medical personnel outside of the prison to help treat inmates	7
Purchasing manager	Uses a file manager package to store suppliers' names	6
Railroad personnel	Uses a pen input system to record train information	3
Retail sales clerk	Processes point-of-sale transactions using a special-purpose terminal	8
Sales manager, sporting goods distributing company	Uses electronic mail to send and receive information to the sales staff	7
	Uses a decision support system to explore the impact of a new sales commission plan	9
Software vendor	Uses sales management software to automate its salesforce	9 Case Study
Supermarket checkout person	Uses a universal product code scanner to speed customer checkout and automatically update inventory	8
Telecommuter	Uses telecommunications to do paid work at home	14
Trainer, consumer electronics company	Uses a slide show feature in a graphics package to train employees	5
Typist	Uses word processing software	4
University professor	Uses a text-based data management package to organize research notes	4
Vice president, bicycle manufacturer	Uses workgroup software to help prepare a new product introduction	9

FIGURE 14-13 Continued

Figure 14-14 shows a chart of typical computer jobs found in an organization's computer or **Information Services** department. The department may be called different things in different companies, like **Information Resources**, **Data Processing**, **Management Information Services**, or **Management Information Systems** department.

The jobs also carry a variety of titles. One common breakdown of titles appears in Figure 14-15. Figure 14-16 provides examples of the type of work

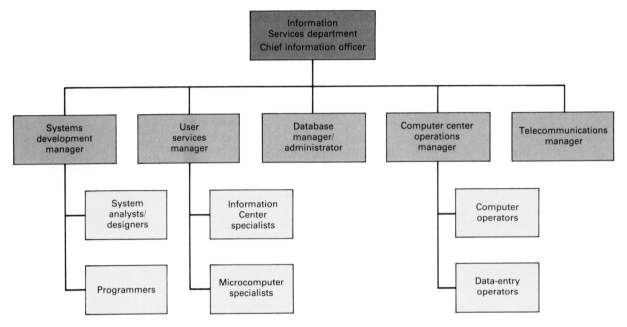

FIGURE 14-14
Jobs that can be found in a large organization's Information Services
department

associated with some of these computer jobs. The most familiar ones in this group are

- **Programmer:** Writes computer programs. As evident from Figure 14-15, two programming career paths are possible. An **applications programmer** writes user-oriented business programs, while a **system programmer** works on operating system, utility, telecommunications, and other more technically oriented service programs. Other types of programmer positions include program *maintenance programmer, spreadsheet programmer,* and *database programmer.*
- **System Analyst:** Analyzes, designs, and implements new computer systems. Programming is a usual stepping stone to a career as a system analyst. Some organizations combine the two jobs as system analyst/programmer.
- **User Services Manager:** Helps employees become self-sufficient computer users. The typical kind of job concentrations found in an organization's User Services group may be
  - **Information Center specialist:** Concentrates on helping users with computer access, use, and programming.
  - **Microcomputer specialist:** Concentrates on researching the latest microcomputer hardware and software trends and introducing useful microcomputer technology into the organization.

These specialists are expected to have good skills working with others and to be good communicators.

A SAMPLER OF SALARIES FOR COMPUTER JOBS

Job Title	Average Yearly Salary in Dollars
Corporate Staff	
Vice President of Information Services	85,089
Director of Data Processing/Management Information Systems	65,816
Information Center/Data Center Manager	50,778
System Analysis	
Manager	52,178
Senior System Analyst	45,048
System Analyst	39,411
Junior System Analyst	30,285
Applications Programming	
Manager	51,959
Applications Programmer	29,722
Junior Applications Programmer	26,122
Operating System Programming	
Manager	56,052
Senior System Programmer	44,318
Intermediate System Programmer	37,427
Database Administration	
Manager	53,426
Database Administrator	46,680
Telecommunications	
Manager	52,228
Analyst	48,174
Network Administrator	33,077
Computer Center Operations	
Manager	43,356
Shift Supervisor	33,542
Computer Operator	21,090
Microcomputer/Workstation Manager	38,974
Data Entry	
Supervisor	23,341
Operator	20,040
Office Automation	
Microcomputer User Services Specialist	29,560
Word Processing Supervisor	28,000
Word Processing Operator	22,418

FIGURE 14-15

A SAMPLER OF COMPUTER JOBS

Job Title	Example of Work	Chapter for Further Reference
Computer center specialist	Handles the day-to-day operations of an organization's mainframe computers	10
Computer dealer	Sells computer hardware and software	3 Case Study
Computer scientist	Develops experimental laser computers that are 1,000 times faster than conventional computers	8 Case Study
Consultant	Provides computer expertise to clients	10
Database administrator	Designs and coordinates an organization's database content, use, and security	11
Decision support center specialist	Helps managers to construct and program financial models	10
Information Center specialist	Provides technical support to nontechnical computer users	10
Knowledge engineer	Mines heuristics from human experts and transfers them into a computerized knowledge base	13
Maintenance programmer	Removes "bugs" or otherwise modifies the code of existing programs to maintain their usefulness	12
Programmer/analyst	Performs the detailed technical development work and programs computer systems	10, 12
Robot programmer	Programs a robot's movements	13
Senior programmer	Writes computer programs and possibly helps to design them	12
Spreadsheet programmer	Programs spreadsheet templates for use by others	5
System analyst/designer	Designs computer systems	11
Technical writer	Prepares *User Guides* and training materials for computer systems	11
Value added reseller	Combines hardware and software for resale to customers	10

FIGURE 14-16

- Two technical management jobs in large organizations include
  - **Database manager/administrator:** Designs as well as controls use of and access to an organization's database files.
  - **Telecommunications manager:** Designs and implements an organization's telecommunications network.
- **Computer Center Operations Manager:** Manages an organization's mainframe computer. In a large organization, that involves the work of
  - **Computer operators:** Work in shifts to keep the mainframe computers and other equipment in the computer center running.
  - **Data-entry operators:** Keyboard batches of raw data into computers for processing.

MAIN COMPUTER CAREER TYPES

(Business)   (Science, research, and engineering)

	Computer information systems	Computer science or engineering
Formal training or college degree →	**Computer information systems**	**Computer science or engineering**
Training or course work emphasis →	• Business • Applying computers to end-user needs	• Mathematics • Electronics • Building computer hardware and operating system–level software
Example of traditional career possibilities →	• Applications or business programmer • System analyst • Information center specialist • Computer consultant • Value added reseller • Sales representative, computer hardware, software or services • Computer information systems teacher	• Systems or scientific programmer • Hardware designer • Operating system software designer • Artificial intelligence researcher • Computer science teacher

FIGURE 14-17
Main computer career types

Figure 14-17 gives a breakdown of training required for some of these jobs. Some computer center jobs require only a high-school or vocational school diploma to start. From there, on-the-job training and other education provide career advancement opportunities.

Most programmer jobs require formal programming education. It can range from vocational school to a college degree with a computing concentration. Generally, the larger the organization, the more formal the education requirements.

Entry-level jobs are possible in the Information Center, especially for people proficient in specific software products required by an organization.

In general, job and career opportunities vary by company size. Smaller companies offer great job variety, which provides broad computing and management training. Large companies offer the opportunity to specialize and advance within a specialty area.

In Other Computer Industry Areas

Not all computer careers are in computer departments in organizations. Other opportunities exist in the computer industry, as identified in Figure 14-18. The main jobs within the computer industry categories are

- *Hardware:* To design, manufacture, and sell computers and related equipment.
- *Software:* To design, program, and sell computer packages and other software. Large **software developers** hire programmers and system analysts to create new software packages for resale.

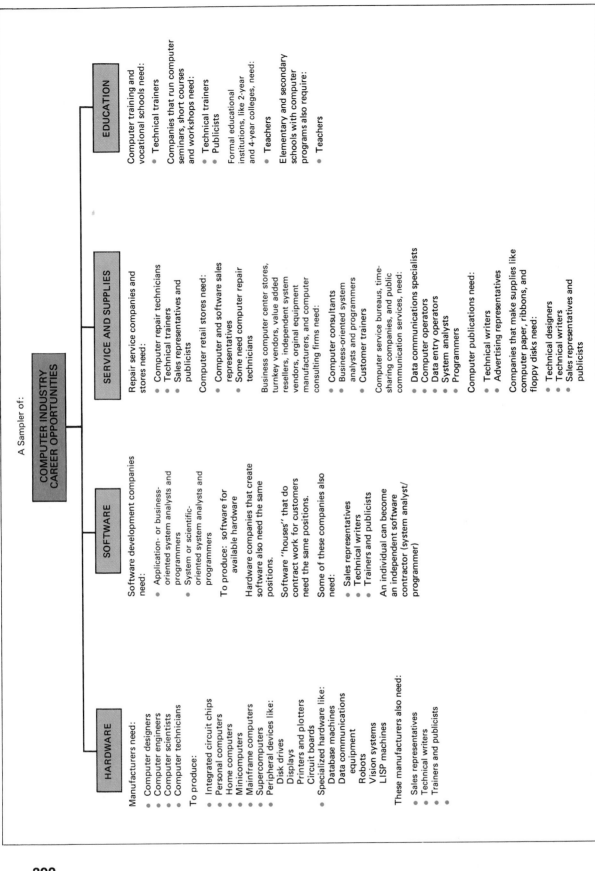

FIGURE 14-18
A sampler of computer industry opportunities

Freelance programmers or system analysts work on their own or through a broker. The broker locates software development jobs and gets a percentage of the contract fee.

Other career opportunities in the software area include technical writers, trainers, and publicists.

- *Services and Supplies:* To deliver computer related services, such as hardware repair or consulting, and supplies, such as diskettes and computer printer paper.
- *Education:* To provide computer training and education through traditional educational institutions or private organizations.

The variety of job possibilities in the computer industry is as rich and varied as the people in them. One computer store owner, as an example, has only a high school diploma. By contrast, some jobs in hardware design require doctoral degrees.

Continuing Education

Rapid changes in the computer industry make continued education a necessity for those who want to advance professionally.

Continued education can be achieved by

- Attending workshops, seminars, and continuing education courses.
- Joining one or more professional organizations, such as those listed in Figure 14-19, and attending their meetings and conventions.
- Regularly reading computer magazines, journals, and books.

FIGURE 14-19

A SAMPLER OF COMPUTER PROFESSIONAL ORGANIZATIONS

Association for Computing Machinery (ACM). The ACM is the largest association for computer professionals. It sponsors computer seminars and conferences on almost all computer topics. Special interest groups, called SIGs, exist within the organization for members to concentrate their activities on, for example, artificial intelligence, graphics, database systems, microcomputers, and computer education. It has a technology and computer science emphasis.

Data Processing Management Association (DPMA). The DPMA's emphasis is on the management of computer information services in user organizations. Its members include managers of computer centers and information services departments, as well as educators, vendors, and others in the computer industry. Like the ACM, the DPMA has student chapters at various colleges.

Association for Systems Management (ASM). The ASM is dedicated to the advancement and continuing education of system analysts and system development managers.

Computer Society of the Institute of Electronic and Electrical Engineers (IEEE-Computer Society). Computer Society members are devoted to computer engineering and science.

Institute for Certification of Computer Professionals (ICCP). The ICCP administers voluntary tests to certify computer professionals. The Certificate in Data Processing (CDP) and the Certificate in Computer Programming (CCP) give formal recognition for competence and experience in computing. Guides and courses are available to help candidates pass the certificate examinations.

Some companies encourage continuing education by sponsoring in-house courses and self-paced tutorial programs. They even offer to pay for computer courses taken at colleges and other institutions.

CASE STUDY: *Let the Customer Do It*

Today, companies are using technology to get customers to do their work for them.

Examples of do-it-yourself point-of-sale technology are becoming more common. In addition to using the automated teller machine (ATM), travelers can do self-ticketing of airline flights. You can also design your own deck or price a new car, all by keying in your requirements. Fully automatic gas stations enable you to pump your own gas and pay by credit card—without a human attendant.

Yet the idea of letting the customer do transaction processing is not new. Users have been dialing telephone calls without operator assistance since the 1920s.

Two major factors are driving the rapid growth of self-service systems: improved technology and business pressures. Today's technology allows capturing transactions at the point of sale and integrating them electronically with billing and order-replenishment systems.

Not Just an Option. Letting the customer do it may be more than just an option. Research company American Demographics points out that a fast-growing elderly population, declining numbers of young adults, and a record low population growth rate will put the nation in a demographic vice in the 1990s. Nationally, the 20-to-29 age group is projected by the U.S. Census Bureau to drop 12.5 percent during the next decade. With continued growth of a service-oriented economy, there may not be enough people to satisfy the demand for retail clerks and service attendants.

These demographic shifts are forcing retailers, financial service providers, and other firms that deal directly with consumers to take a hard look at customer self-service systems. The approach could become a key determinant of survival for some industries.

Checkrobots: New Wave Market. A different twist on customer self-service systems is the Automated Checkout Machine (ACM) System, a product of Checkrobot, Inc. It enables shoppers to check out their own merchandise before paying a centrally located cashier. It incorporates a security system to ensure that each item departing the store has been scanned and paid for. Laser scanning, local-area networks, and database management systems are combined to interface with the store's central computer.

Checkrobot claims that its system offers the perception of improved customer service because it is easy to use, decreases shopping time, and increases customer control over the shopping environment. The system is also claimed to provide a high return on investment, primarily because of decreased labor costs. While the current target market is supermarkets, the company plans to expand to retail organizations in general.

DISCUSSION QUESTIONS

1. Discuss the technological improvements and demographic trends behind the idea of "letting the customer" do transaction processing.

2. Discuss the benefits of "letting the customer" do transaction processing from two viewpoints: the customer and the company that uses such transaction processing.

CHAPTER SUMMARY

- Computers, as we know them today, began in early 1940 with the *ABC Computer*. It influenced the design of *ENIAC*, the first large-scale computer ever built.

- The *stored program concept* is to read a program into memory from processing. Early computers were *hard-wired*. If their job changed, wires had to be changed.

- *Vacuum tubes* provided the electronic circuitry in *first-generation* computers.

- The first business-use computer was the UNIVAC I.

- *Second-generation* computers used *transistors* instead of vacuum tube circuitry. They were faster, smaller, and less expensive than first-generation computers.

- During the 1950s, programming languages like *COBOL* and *FORTRAN* were developed.

- The first *microcomputer* appeared in the 1960s.

- *Third-generation* computers used *integrated circuit* technology, which is still in use today.

- The use of *large-scale integration* (LSI) chips marked a *fourth generation* of computers.

- A *microprocessor* chip contains all the major logic circuitry for a computer on one chip. It served as the "brain" of the first *microcomputer*, which appeared in 1977.

- *VisiCalc*, an electronic spreadsheet program, was the first software responsible for the sale of computer hardware.

- An *authoring system* allows nonprogrammers to create computer-based instructions, sometimes used for *computer-assisted instruction (CAI)* courses.

- *Telecommuting* has been used to describe home-bound workers reporting to the office through their personal computer and a modem.

- People are concerned about the misuse of computer-based information held about them in *data banks*. Laws help individuals to protect their privacy.

- *Computer crime* includes stealing information, computer time, and software. Illegally copying software is called *piracy*.

- A *hacker* is anyone whose hobby is studying how computers work.

- Computer *viruses* are programs that can copy themselves and spread from computer to computer, sometimes destroying files.

- Career opportunities in the *computer profession* include jobs in an organization's computer department or in the computer industry.

- The most familiar jobs in an organization's computer department are *system analyst* and *programmer*.

- An *applications programmer* writes user-oriented business programs, while a *system programmer* works on operating systems, utility, telecommunications, and other technically oriented programs.

- *User Services* jobs help users to access, use, and program computers as well as introduce useful microcomputer technology into an organization.

- Two technical management jobs in large organizations include *database manager* or *administrator* and *telecommunications manager*.

- Computer center jobs include *computer operator* and *data entry operator*.

- Computer hardware industry jobs include those to design, manufacture, and sell computer hardware and related equipment.

- *Software developers* hire programmers and system analysts to create new software packages for resale.

- Anyone in the computer industry can stay professionally up-to-date by attending workshops and seminars, taking continuing education courses, and participating in professional organizations.

SELECTED KEY TERMS

ABC Computer
Applications programmer
Computer crime
Database manager/administrator

End-user support specialist
ENIAC
First-generation computers
Fourth-generation computers

Hacker
Information Services Department
Integrated circuit
Piracy

Programmer
Second-generation computers
Software developer
Stored program concept

System analyst
System programmer
Telecommunications manager
Telecommuting

Third-generation computers
Transistors
Vacuum tube
VisiCalc

REVIEW QUESTIONS

1. When were computers, as we know them, first developed?

2. What provided the electronic circuitry of the first computer?

3. Why was the invention of the *stored program* concept significant?

4. What marked the emergence of second-generation computers?

5. What marked the emergence of third-generation computers?

6. When did assembled microcomputers, or personal computers, first appear?

7. What was the first type of software program that was responsible for the sale of computer hardware?

8. Give one example of how computers are used for each of the following:
   - Health care
   - Environmental studies
   - Education

9. Identify one social issue related to the impact of computers in each of the following areas:

   - Workplace
   - Privacy
   - Crime

10. Give an example of an innovative computer user and describe how the computer is applied to the user's job. How does it enhance the user's career?

11. Describe the two most familiar jobs commonly found in an organization's Information Services department.

12. What is the difference between an applications and system programmer?

13. Describe two different concentrations for a specialist in an organization's End-User Support department.

14. What are two technical management jobs often found in an organization's Information Services Department?

15. Identify two computer center jobs.

16. Give examples of how a computer professional remains technologically up-to-date.

EXERCISES

1. Examine your local newspaper and clip any computer articles. After doing this for two weeks, prepare an oral or written report that summarizes each social issue addressed. Each summarized issue should be followed by your own analysis and opinion about the issue addressed.

2. Research how personal computers are being used in your community. Select one example to do a researched written or oral report that answers the following questions:
   - Who uses the computer?
     What is it being used for? (Provide specific examples and even computer printouts, if available.)

   - When is it used?
   - Where is it used?
   - Why is it used?
   - What hardware is used? How much did it cost?
   - What software is used? Where did it come from? Did someone program it? What language was used to program it?
   - What training was necessary to use the hardware and software?
   - What problems have been experienced?
   - What benefits have been experienced?
   - How has the computer changed the way things are done?

   Include anything else that would be relevant to

"flesh out" your report. This could include profiles of the computer users and their reaction to learning about and using computers.

3. Careers in a large organization's Information Services department include systems development, programming, end-user support management, database management and operations (see Figure 14-14). Choose one of these five categories and research it in depth. Use current computer periodicals to determine such information as the upper and lower salary ranges, the current market demand for the specialty skill, and the predicted future market for the specialty skill. Do you foresee this specialty becoming more important or less important as computer technology continues to advance? Why?

4. Computers have had a huge impact on noncomputer professions. Explain the importance of obtaining at least minimal computer training for students who are not planning to major in the computer field. Can you think of any other professions that are affected by computers, other than those mentioned in the text?

Appendix A

Number and Code Systems

How does the computer do arithmetic when all it works with are 1's and 0's? This appendix examines the characteristics of the binary, or base 2, number system. It looks at how *binary* dig*its*, or "bits," perform addition and are converted to decimal numbers. It covers the same topics again with the hexadecimal number system. It concludes with a review of computer code systems.

BINARY NUMBER SYSTEM

The binary number system that does all the calculation inside a computer can be thought of as the collection of lights diagrammed in Figure A-1. Each light can be turned "on" or "off." When a light is "on," it is a signal to use the number, or value, equal to its position.

As an example, look at the binary representation for a number 7. It consists of three "on" signals. Reading from right to left, it is interpreted as follows:

Column Position	Positional Value
1	1
2	2
3	4

The sum of positional values is $1 + 2 + 4 = 7$.

Conventional form uses the shorthand symbol of "power" or "exponent" to express position. A power is shown as a raised number next to a base number, like 2^2, which represents 4.

Although the binary system is built on a base of 2, it only uses the numbers 0 and 1. It is similar in concept to the familiar decimal system, which has a base of 10 but uses only the numbers 0–9.

As Figure A-2 shows, both the decimal and binary number systems use positional values. Some decimal system positions follow:

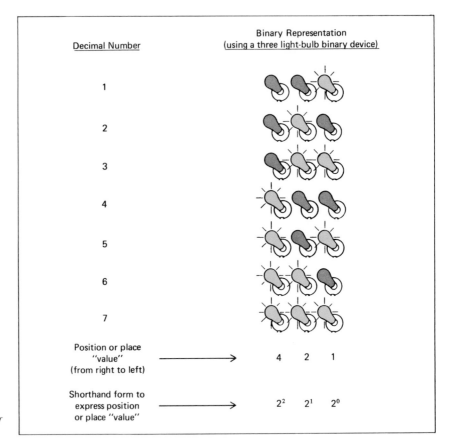

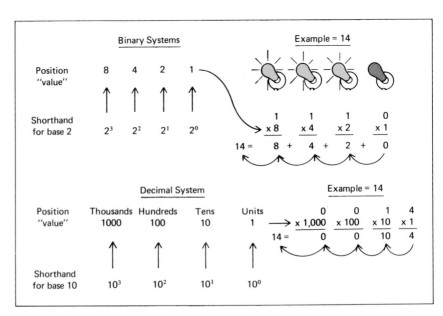

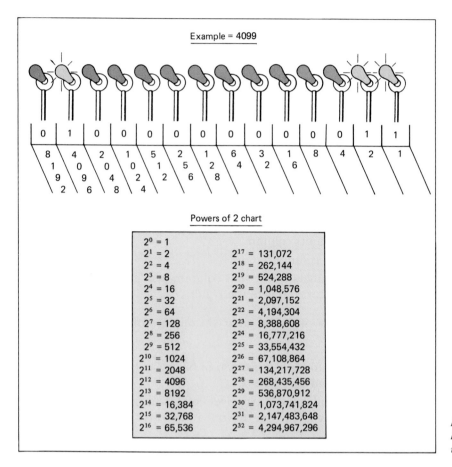

FIGURE A-3
Incremental positional values in the binary number system

Position	Position Value
1	Units
2	Tens
3	Hundreds
4	Thousands

The decimal number 14, as an example, consists of 4 unit values and 1 tens value.

By contrast, to represent the number 14 in the binary system requires that positions 2, 3, and 4 be "on." The sum of the positional values is $2 + 4 + 8 = 14$. Figure A-3 identifies, in more detail, some positional values associated with the binary number system.

Binary Addition

Some binary arithmetic processes, like the addition shown in Figure A-4, are similar to decimal arithmetic. But the binary addition may look confusing because there are no symbols beyond 1 and 0 to use.

To see how addition works in the binary number system, it helps to review the ordinary process of decimal addition. As an example, to add $7 + 7$, which is 14:

BINARY ADDITION IS SIMILAR TO DECIMAL ADDITION

Binary Addition		Equivalent Decimal Addition
111	→	7
+111	→	+7
1110	→	14

1. Put down the 4 in the units column.

2. Carry the 1 to the tens column.

3. Since there are no numbers in the tens column, just "bring down" the 1 that is "carried over" to complete the result.

To apply the same process to the binary example, work from the right to the left column and

1. Add 1 + 1, which is 2 and is represented in binary as 10. Put down the 0 in the first column and carry the 1.

2. Add 1 + 1, which is 2 plus the "carry over" of 1, which results in 3 and is represented in binary as 11. Put down a 1 and carry the other 1.

3. Repeat step 2.

4. Since there are no numbers to add the last "carry-over," just "bring down" the 1 that is "carried over" to complete the result.

The binary example in Figure A-2 provides evidence that the binary addition answer in Figure A-4 is correct.

While this provides an example of how binary arithmetic works, it does get more complex. Even having more than two numbers to add can prove confusing for humans. Fortunately, humans do not have to do binary arithmetic to work effectively with computers.

Decimal Conversion to Binary

To convert a decimal number to a binary number, the "remainder method" can be used, as shown in Figure A-5.

The "remainder method" requires dividing a decimal number by 2 through several iterations. When no more answers are left to divide by 2, the process is finished. The binary value is made up of the collection of "remainders" that result. The most significant digit of the binary value is the final remainder.

This "remainder method" is useful to convert decimal numbers to any other number system. It requires only changing the number system base as the divisor. Some other number systems that computer professionals work with are octal (base 8) and hexadecimal (base 16).

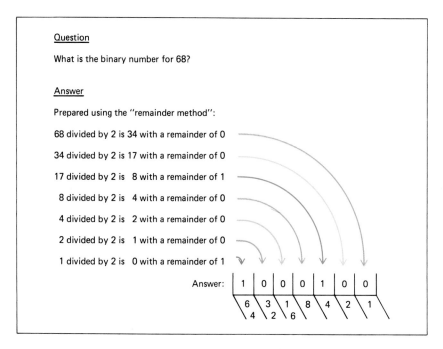

FIGURE A-5
Converting a decimal to a binary number

HEXADECIMAL NUMBER SYSTEMS

Humans are not as good as computers when working with page after page of all 1's and 0's. Computer scientists and others prefer to work, instead, with the hexadecimal number system. It has a base of 16, as shown in Figure A-6.

Hexadecimal numbers range from 0 to 9 and then switch to the alphabet at decimal 10. Ten to 15 are conveniently represented by a single alphabetic character.

The hexadecimal number system is often encountered when examining a snapshot of memory, called a *memory dump*. It is a printed listing of the computer's memory at any given moment of time. It is often used to investigate processing problems. The printout consists of row on row of hexadecimal numbers. As the example in Figure A-7 implies, one 8-bit byte of memory is represented on a memory dump as two hexadecimal numbers. This represents a 4 to 1 reduction of data, which makes the investigation into memory problems more manageable.

Consulting a chart, similar to the one in Figure A-6, is a convenient way to convert groups of four binary digits to hexadecimal equivalents.

Hexadecimal Arithmetic

To solve memory dump problems often involves adding and subtracting hexadecimal numbers. An easy way to do this:

1. Convert the hexadecimal value to decimal.

2. Add or subtract in decimal.

3. Convert the answer back to hexadecimal.

FIGURE A-6
Binary-to-hexadecimal conversion

Decimal Number	Hexadecimal (Base 16) Equivalent	Binary Equivalent
0	0	0000
1	1	0001
2	2	0010
3	3	0011
4	4	0100
5	5	0101
6	6	0110
7	7	0111
8	8	1000
9	9	1001
10	A	1010
11	B	1011
12	C	1100
13	D	1101
14	E	1110
15	F	1111

Binary digits in memory → 1 1 1 0   4 digits

Decimal equivalent   1 4

Hexadecimal equivalent   E   1 digit

Binary numbers are easier to interpret if they are separated into groups of four digits and then converted to a hexadecimal equivalent.

FIGURE A-7
One byte requires two hexadecimal numbers.

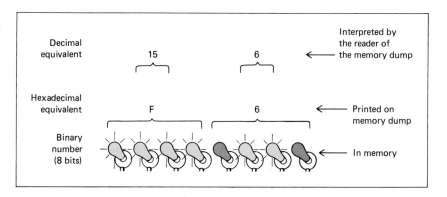

Some examples are given in Figure A-8. The first addition example is fairly straightforward, using the chart in Figure A-6 as a reference:

· Hexadecimal B converts to decimal 11.
· Hexadecimal 4 converts to decimal 4.
· Adding 11 + 4 results in decimal 15, which the chart shows is equivalent to hexadecimal F.

In the second addition example, each column is treated separately. When hexadecimal C(11) and B(12) are added, the result is 23. For any number above 15, the procedure is to

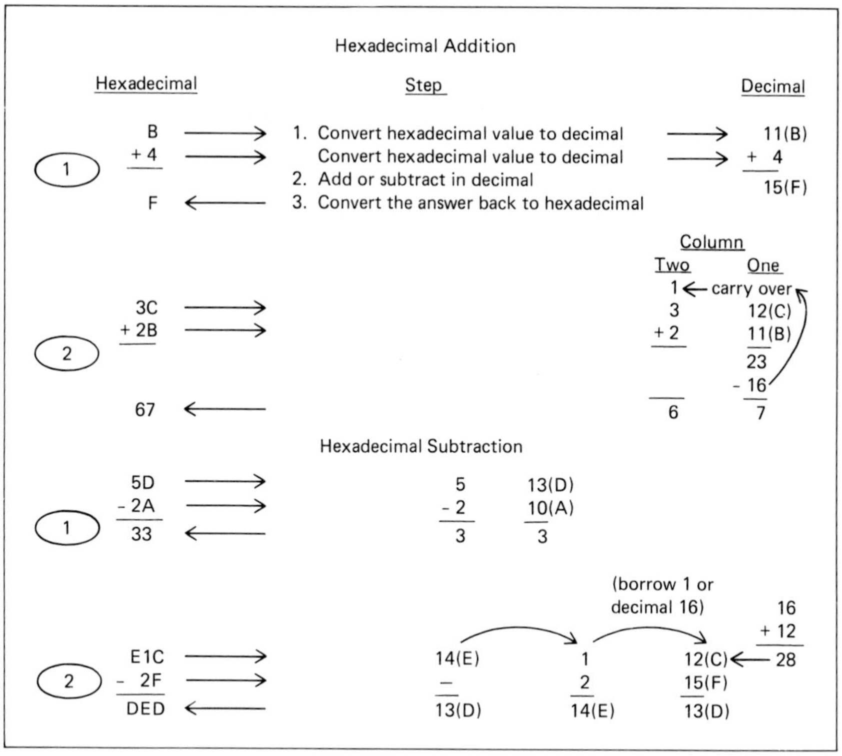

FIGURE A-8
Hexadecimal addition and subtraction

Hexadecimal Addition

Hexadecimal	Step	Decimal

①
B ⟶ 1. Convert hexadecimal value to decimal ⟶ 11(B)
+ 4 ⟶   Convert hexadecimal value to decimal ⟶ + 4
   2. Add or subtract in decimal   15(F)
F ⟵ 3. Convert the answer back to hexadecimal

Column
Two   One
1 ⟵ carry over

②
3C ⟶   3   12(C)
+ 2B ⟶ + 2   11(B)
            23
           − 16
67 ⟵   6   7

Hexadecimal Subtraction

①
5D ⟶   5   13(D)
− 2A ⟶ − 2   10(A)
33 ⟵   3   3

(borrow 1 or
decimal 16)   16
              + 12

②
E1C ⟶ 14(E)   1   12(C) ⟵ 28
− 2F ⟶ −   2   15(F)
DED ⟵ 13(D) 14(E) 13(D)

1. Subtract 16, which is the base of the hexadecimal number system, from the sum (in this case, it is $23 - 16 = 7$)

2. Place the answer, in this case 7, in the column and carry a 1 to the next column

Each column is treated in the same way.

    Subtraction is similar, as the examples indicate. The second subtraction example shows that when a "borrow" occurs, it is for the decimal value 16, the base of the hexadecimal number system.

Contrast to Code Systems

    Generally, numeric data are processed in memory using the binary number system. But some numbers never have arithmetic operations performed on them. An example may be a zip code like 12491. This zip code is stored in memory as an *alphanumeric* character, and not a number.

    Programmers tell the computer how to treat numbers. Using the BASIC programming language as an example, a programmer might indicate the following data for computer entry:

BASIC Data Name	Actual Data
ZIP.CODE$	Zip Code
TAX.AMOUNT	Taxes

In BASIC, the $ symbol in a data name tells the computer that the actual data, like zip code, are to be stored as "character" data. The data will not be used for arithmetic operations.

By contrast, the absence of a $ symbol in a data name tells the computer that the actual data, like taxes, are to be used in arithmetic calculations. Such data are stored as binary numbers ready for all arithmetic operations.

The two most common code systems that computers use to store "character" data are the following:

Code System	Description
ASCII (pronounced AS key)	American Standard Code for Information Interchange. It is a 7-bit code scheme that adds an eighth check bit to get a regular 8-bit byte (pronounced *bite*). Personal computers and most data communications use the ASCII code to represent character data.
EBCDIC (pronounced eb SEE dick)	Extended Binary Coded Decimal Interchange Code. It is an 8-bit code scheme developed by IBM and is used mainly on IBM mainframe computers.

Examples of binary bit patterns for both coding systems are given in Figure A-9.

FIGURE A-9

COMPUTER CODE SYSTEM BIT PATTERNS

Character	ASCII 7-Bit Code	EBCDIC 8-Bit Code	Character	ASCII 7-Bit Code	EBCDIC 8-Bit Code
A	1000001	11000001	T	1010100	11100011
B	1000010	11000010	U	1010101	11100100
C	1000011	11000011	V	1010110	11100101
D	1000100	11000100	W	1010111	11100110
E	1000101	11000101	X	1011000	11100111
F	1000110	11000110	Y	1011001	11101000
G	1000111	11000111	Z	1011010	11101001
H	1001000	11001000			
I	1001001	11001001	0	0110000	11110000
J	1001010	11010001	1	0110001	11110001
K	1001011	11010010	2	0110010	11110010
L	1001100	11010011	3	0110011	11110011
M	1001101	11010100	4	0110100	11110100
N	1001110	11010101	5	0110101	11110101
O	1001111	11010110	6	0110110	11110110
P	1010000	11010111	7	0110111	11110111
Q	1010001	11011000	8	0111000	11111000
R	1010010	11011001	9	0111001	11111001
S	1010011	11100010			

REVIEW QUESTIONS

1. How are the binary and decimal number systems similar?

2. Explain the process of binary addition, using 101 + 111 as the example.

3. How is the "remainder method" used to convert a decimal number to a binary number? Use 67 as the example.

4. What is the base of the hexadecimal number system?

5. What is a memory dump used for? What number system is it printed in?

6. What is a convenient way to convert binary numbers to hexadecimal equivalents, or vice versa?

7. Explain the process of hexadecimal arithmetic, using 2A + 3C as an example, and hexadecimal subtraction, using D1C − 2E as an example.

8. How are character data different from numeric data in a computer's memory? Write your first name using first the ASCII and then the EBCDIC code systems. The table in Figure A-9 should be used for guidance.

Appendix B

ASCII Code Chart

ASCII Code	Character	ASCII Code	Character	ASCII Code	Character	ASCII Code	Character
000	Null	032	(space)	064	@	096	
001		033	!	065	A	097	a
002		034	"	066	B	098	b
003		035	#	067	C	099	c
004		036	$	068	D	100	d
005		037	%	069	E	101	e
006		038	&	070	F	102	f
007	beep or bell	039	'	071	G	103	g
008		040	(	072	H	104	h
009	tab	041	)	073	I	105	i
010	line feed	042	.	074	J	106	j
011		043	+	075	K	107	k
012		044	,	076	L	108	l
013	carriage return	045	–	077	M	109	m
014		046	.	078	N	110	n
015		047	/	079	O	111	o
016		048	0	080	P	112	p
017		049	1	081	Q	113	q
018		050	2	082	R	114	r
019		051	3	083	S	115	s
020		052	4	084	T	116	t
021		053	5	085	U	117	u
022		054	6	086	V	118	v
023		055	7	087	W	119	w
024		056	8	088	X	120	x
025		057	9	089	Y	121	y
026		058	:	090	Z	122	z
027		059	;	091	[	123	{
028	right ⎫	060	<	092	/	124	|
029	left ⎬ cursor	061	=	093	]	125	}
030	up ⎪ move-	062	>	094	V	126	~
031	down ⎭ ment	063	?	095	—	127	⌂

The ASCII, American standard code for information interchange, character set shown with its three-digit so-called "decimal" code, which is a "shorthand" for the seven-bit binary representation of each character.

Appendix C

HANDS-ON EXERCISES—TELECOMMUNICATIONS

The following hands-on exercises provide a simulated experience of what it is like to log-on to a telecommunication service and then use each of the five service offerings: News, Sports, Entertainment, Bulletin Board, and Electronic Mail.

Some of the exercises require you to print (on the printer) an image of what is on your display screen. In computer jargon this is called a "screen dump." To do this, press two keys simultaneously, the shift key and the PRTSC key. Some computers require pressing only the PRTSC key, so experiment to discover what works in your situation.

The following exercises assume that the disk accompanying this book is loaded on your system and that you arrived at the main menu by typing

A>HANDSON [Enter]

Then type the following sequence:

Keystrokes	Comments
[Enter]	To continue past the "Hands-on Exercises" welcome screen
[Enter]	To select the first Main Menu item, "Telecommunications"
[Enter]	To move past the "Telecommunications" welcome screen

Follow the on-screen instructions to experiment with all the options. This will prepare you to do the following exercises.

1. Log-on
   A. What happens after three attempts to enter the wrong User ID?
   B. Why do you agree or disagree with what happens?
2. General
   A. Examine the first three Main Menu selections available from the telecommunications information service. Which ones have sub-categories and what are they?
   B. What news items are covered in Computer News? Identify the source and date of the news items.
   C. Why do you agree or disagree with the last computer news item?
3. Bulletin Board
   A. Identify the Forums presently available on the Metro Bulletin Board Service (MBBS) and those expected to be added.
   B. Leave a message on the Forum of your choice. The message should be appropriate for the Forum chosen. Check the chosen Forum to verify the addition of your message (only the most recent is saved). Get a "screen dump" of your addition to turn in to your instructor.
4. Electronic Mail

A. Send an electronic mail message to your instructor. Assume your instructor's E-mail ID # is 33. A copy of your message is automatically saved in your electronic mailbox.
B. Read the saved message and get a "screen dump" of it to turn in to your instructor.
C. Examine the electronic mail send/read procedure and compare it with the bulletin board message send/read procedure.

HANDS-ON EXERCISES—ACCOUNTING

The following hands-on exercises provide a real, but scaled-down, experience of what it is like to use accounting-oriented software. You will experience what it is like to enter detailed "transactions." Transaction data entry is the heart of any so-called back office "accounting-oriented" or "data processing" system. You will also explore both operational benefits and management information benefits that follow from the automated accounting procedures.

The following exercises provide for saving data. You must have a formatted 5¼-inch or 3½-inch diskette available for saving data, or a hard disk.

Some of the exercises require printing (on the printer) an image of what is on your display screen. In computer jargon this is called a "screen dump." To do this, press two keys simultaneously, the shift key and the PRTSC key. Some computers require pressing only the PRTSC key, so experiment to discover what works in your situation.

The exercises assume that the disk accompanying this book is loaded on your system and that you arrived at the main menu by typing

A>HANDSON [Enter]

Then type the following sequence:

Keystrokes	Comments
[Enter]	To continue past the "Hands-on Exercises" welcome screen
[down arrow]	To move the highlighted selection bar down and select "Accounting" from
[down arrow]	the Main Menu
[Enter]	
[Enter]	To continue past the "Accounting" welcome screen

1. For this accounting exercise, assume that you prepared the student budget shown in Figure C-1, then
A. Select "Setup a budget" from the Accounting Main Menu.
B. Indicate the disk drive for saving data.
C. Using Figure C-1 as a guide, enter the three Income account names from column A, rows 5-7 (shorten the name on row 6 to "Savings.") Also enter the corresponding total amounts from column D. Then enter the five Expense account names from column A, rows 12-16. Also enter the corresponding total amounts from column D. Use the Tab key to move around the "Budget Information Screen" for making changes. (Alternately, use the up and down arrow keys, or the "shift/tab" key combination to move around the screen.) When done, press the F2 function key.

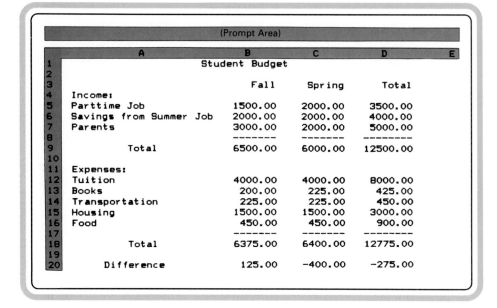

FIGURE C-1
A student budget prepared
with a spreadsheet program

D. Select "Enter transactions" from the Main Menu and "Begin a new transaction file" from the Transaction Menu. When asked to enter a filename, type MYDATA and press the [Enter] key.

Enter the following transaction. For category, select "Parttime Job" from the drop-down menu.

Date	Description	Income or Expense	Category	Amount
9/1	Paycheck	I	Parttime Job	100

Press the F2 function key. Press Y for yes to save the transaction and Esc for the Escape key to return to the Main Menu.

E. Examine the effect of entering the $100.00 paycheck. Select "Reports" from the Main Menu. Then select "Budget Report" from the Reports Menu. Press the [Enter] key to select the transaction file named MYDATA and examine the report. What information can you learn from the "Budget Report?"

Press Esc for the Escape key twice to return to the Accounting Main Menu.

2. Enter the following transactions to the MYDATA transaction file. Begin by selecting "2. Enter transactions" from the Accounting Main Menu. Select option "2. Use an existing transaction file" from the Transaction Menu. Select the MYDATA.TRN (transaction) file then make the following entries on your own. Press the F4 key after each transaction to clear the screen for the next transaction.

Date	Description	Income or Expense	Category	Amount
9/1	R&L Realtors	E	?	250.00
9/8	Check from Dad	I	Parents	2500.00

Date	Description	Income or Expense	Category		Amount
9/10	Tuition balance	E	Tuition	?	2000.00
9/16	Shoprite	E	Food		63.00
9/21	Textbooks	E	Books		135.00

Press the F2 key when done. Press Y for yes to save the transactions. Examine the effect the transactions have on the two reports.

A. Print out a "screen dump" of the Transaction Listing to give to your instructor.

B. Print out a "screen dump" of the Budget Report to give to your instructor.

3. You discover that you input the wrong amount for one transaction. The correct amount for the "Textbooks" transaction is $105, not $135.

To correct the error, select "Enter transactions" from the Accounting Main Menu. Choose "Change existing transactions" from the Transaction Menu. Press the [Enter] key to choose the MYDATA.TRN (transaction) file. Press the F4 function key until the expense transaction appears on the screen. Repeatedly press the [Enter] key to get to the Amount item and enter the correct amount, 105.00. [*Note:* Alternately, the Tab key, or the up or down arrow keys, or the shift/tab key combination move the cursor to a previous item.] Press the F2 function key and save the changed transaction file. Examine the effect the change has on the reports.

4. Compare your "student budget" accounting experience with the "sales order processing" example discussed in the chapter.

A. What "Operational Benefits" follow from the automated accounting procedures?

B. What "Management Information Benefits" follow from the automated accounting procedures?

5. If you examine Figure C-1, you see that the student budget illustrated there was prepared with spreadsheet software.

A. Explain why you would use spreadsheet software to do a student budget.

B. Explain why you would use accounting-oriented software to do student budget accounting.

6. Develop an Income/Expense budget situation of your own. Enter the budgeted amounts and several transactions. Print out a "screen dump" of your Budget Report and Transaction Listing to give to your instructor. Ideas to consider using are your own personal budget situation, or one from your workplace, or an organization you belong to. Other ideas are a video rental store or a college book store situation.

HANDS-ON EXERCISES—KNOWLEDGE-BASED (EXPERT) SYSTEMS

The following hands-on exercises provide a real experience of what it is like to use knowledge-based (expert) system software. An expert system asks questions, then based on the answers, provides a recommendation.

Some of the exercises require that you print (on the printer) an image of what is on your display screen. In computer jargon this is called a "screen dump." To do this, press two keys simultaneously, the shift key and the PRTSC key. Some computers require pressing only the PRTSC key, so experiment to discover what works in your situation.

The following exercises require a color display/monitor or a monochrome display with a color graphics controller card. They assume that the disk accompanying this book is loaded on your system and that you arrived at the main menu by typing

A>HANDSON [Enter]

Then type the following sequence:

Keystrokes	Comments
[Enter]	To continue past the "Hands-on Exercises" welcome screen
[down arrow]	To move the highlighted selection bar down and select "Knowledge-based
[Enter]	(Expert) Systems" from the Main Menu
[Enter]	To move past the "Knowledge-based Systems" welcome screen
[Enter]	To select "Go" from the menu bar at the bottom of the screen

1. The first example is a small "prototype" or model for a larger system designed for a foreign tourism authority. It provides "expert" guidance to a user who consults it for help in planning a vacation to Thailand.

For this exercise, use the on-screen instructions and the following as a guide for response entries:

Outdoor activities
Water sports
By car
Standard

Any time you want to change your mind about an entry, first use the DEL delete key to cancel a selection, then use the right or left arrow keys to move to another selection and press the Enter key. Changes can only be done before the End key is pressed.

[*Note:* Ignore the bottom-of-the-screen prompts. They are inactive for the consultation. If used, the system may dead end. Just start over again if a dead end occurs.]

A. Get a screen dump of the recommendation.
B. Answer "Yes" to see further information. What categories of information are provided?
C. Run another consultation and enter different responses. Record the responses entered. Get a screen dump of the recommendation and compare the results observed from the two consultations.

[*Note:* To return to the Hands-on Main Menu after you are done running consultations, press the F4 Quit key.]

2. This exercise looks at an "industrial strength" knowledge-based system that concerns tax preparation. It determines whether a person can be claimed as a dependent for tax purposes. Frequently students are claimed as dependents on their parents' tax forms.

This system must be loaded from the DOS prompt, for example:

A>VPXRUN DEPENDEN

Enter the following responses to explore how the system works. [*Note:* This system was designed to *not* require pressing the End key to move to the next entry.]

> [Enter] key to select GO
> John Doe
> Nancy
> 18
> 3000
> Married
> Separate
> Over half
> No
> United States
> United States
> Yes

A. Get a screen dump of the conclusion to the consultation.
B. Experiment by running another consultation with different responses. Record the responses entered. Get a screen dump of the conclusion to the consultation and compare the results observed from the two consultations.

3. One of the features of knowledge-based (expert) systems is the ability to ask "why" a question is being asked. This "explanation" feature is handled differently by each system and system developer. For example, in the Thailand system, the developer determined users would not need such a feature, so it is inactive in that system. In the DEPENDEN system, the developer also disabled this feature. But the DEPENDEN system does provide a kind of summary of why questions were asked in its "recommendation" screen.

In order to get a sample of how this feature works, another small prototype is provided on the disk. This system advises users about which industrial cleaning solvents to use to clean different types of industrial equipment.

To find out why a particular question is being asked, enter "/W" once the question appears on the screen, before responding with your answer. An explanation will appear in a pop-up window. Press any key to return to the consultation session.

This system must be loaded from the DOS prompt, for example:

A>VPXRUN SOLVENT1

A. For the first consultation, experiment by using the following:

Keystroke(s)	Description
Enter	Select GO
Enter	Begin the consultation
/W	Ask why the first question is being asked
Enter	Continue
Enter/End	Select "Stainless Steel"
/W	Ask why the second question is being asked
Enter	Continue
→	Move the highlight bar over "Fair"

User
interface
elements

Opening
message

Questions
with
answer
choices

Closing
message

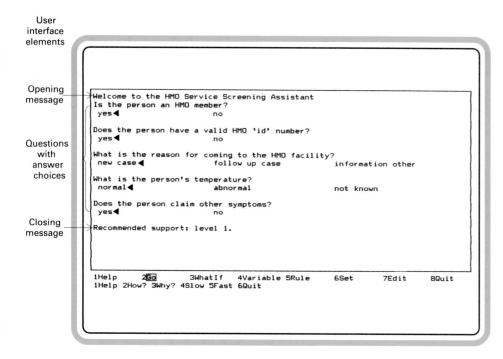

```
Welcome to the HMO Service Screening Assistant
Is the person an HMO member?
 yes◄                   no

Does the person have a valid HMO 'id' number?
 yes◄                   no

What is the reason for coming to the HMO facility?
 new case◄              follow up case          information other

What is the person's temperature?
 normal◄               abnormal              not known

Does the person claim other symptoms?
 yes◄                   no

Recommended support: level 1.




1Help      2Go       3WhatIf   4Variable 5Rule    6Set      7Edit     8Quit
1Help 2How? 3Why? 4Slow 5Fast 6Quit
```

FIGURE C-2
Example of how a user
interfaces with a knowledge-
based system during a
consultation

Enter/End	Select "Fair"
/W	Ask why the third question is being asked
Enter	Continue
→	Move the highlight bar over "No"
Enter/End	Select "No"

Get a screen dump of the consultation. Turn it in to your instructor with the responses underlined that gave the recommendation.

B. Run a second consultation using different responses and ask "why" each question is asked. Observe the "explanations" given. Compare them with the "explanations" given during the first consultation.

4. This exercise enables you to see the system discussed in the chapter, and shown in Figure C-2, come alive! Although it is a very small prototype, consisting of only 11 rules, it does demonstrate how the HMO system would work—which is the purpose of a concept-testing "prototype."

This exercise also examines the HMO prototype from the "user's viewpoint." At the DOS prompt, type VPXRUN HMORUN, for example:

A>VPXRUN HMORUN

Enter any responses desired. Another version of the same 11-rule system is available by typing, for example:

A>VPXRUN HMOUSER

Run this system and enter any responses desired. Compare and contrast the two versions of the 11-rule system. If you were a potential user of the full-blown HMO system, which version would you prefer? Why?

Glossary

ABC Computer The Atanasoff-Berry-Computer from 1940, the forerunner of the first large-scale computers.

acceptance testing Checking of a completed program by users.

accounting-oriented computer system A "back office" computer system used to support the handling of routine functions in organizations, such as payroll and accounts receivable systems.

add-ins *See* add-ons.

add-ons Packages created to add value to other, more widely used packages; also called add-ins.

alternate key A key (called ALT) often found on a personal computer keyboard used in conjunction with other keys to perform various functions.

analog graphics standard A color display standard characterized by an ability to display a large range of colors simultaneously.

analog signals The signals sent over normal telephone lines.

analytic graphics Use of graphics for personal data analysis.

animation Continuous movement graphics.

application generator Software to automate system development and produce program code.

application software Software that makes hardware perform a specific user task, such as word processing or sales order processing.

applications programmer Writes user-oriented business programs.

architecture The design and construction of a computer that shows how it handles its input-processing-output functions.

arithmetic/logic unit A component of the central processing unit that calculates and compares data when instructed by the control unit.

arrow key *See* cursor control key.

artificial intelligence Term used for computer systems that mimic human behavior, such as knowledge-based systems, robot systems, and natural language systems.

ASCII American Standard Code for Information Interchange, a 7-bit code system that dominates microcomputer hardware.

assembly language A second-generation computer language; also called symbolic language.

Association for Computing Machinery (ACM) Largest organization for computer professionals.

asynchronous communication Communication in which characters are transmitted with random idle periods between characters.

authoring system (1) Software package permitting nonprogrammers to create instructional programs. (2) Software used to create a multimedia presentation.

auto-answer A feature of telecommunication software which allows a computer to accept incoming data communications.

auto-dial The capability of telecommunication software to automatically dial a phone number listed in its dialing directory.

automated office An office with linked computers that facilitates the exchange of information.

automated teller machines A type of special-purpose terminal used for customer transactions such as cash withdrawals, account balance inquiries, and other bank business not needing teller attention.

backup The process of copying a file or an entire disk so that data are not lost when a disk is damaged.

backup copy A duplicate copy of a file, disk, or other media.

backward compatibility *See* downward compatibility.

bandwidth The bits-per-second transmission capacity of a telecommunication line.

bank teller terminals A type of special-purpose terminal designed for specific jobs such as deposit and withdrawal transactions.

bar chart A graphical tool used in systems analysis to control development projects; also called a Gantt chart.

BASIC Acronym for Beginner's All-purpose Symbolic Instruction Code, a popular microcomputer language developed in the 1960s.

batch processing A data processing system in which input data are stored and processed all at one time.

baud rate The bits-per-second (bps) transmission rate of data over a telecommunication line.

binary system A two-state system.

bit One binary digit.

bit-mapped images Images stored by painting packages; the location of each dot making up the image is recorded, allowing for the individual manipulation of the pixels.

bits-per-second (bps) A measure of the information that can be transmitted by a telecommunication device.

block function A word processing function used to define or mark a block of text.

bootstrap program The part of a system that operates when the computer is first turned on.

bugs Errors in a computer program.

built-in function Prepared formulas, like sum, average, and count, that are built into spreadsheet software.

bulletin board system (BBS) A telecommunication system that makes messages available to any logged-on computer user.

bus (1) A single cable which links workstations in a bus network. (2) The electronic roadways that are etched into a controller board.

business graphics Analytic and presentation graphics.

bus network A local-area network layout which links workstations to a single cable; normally workstations must contend with each other for use of the transmission line.

byte A group of 8 bits creating the fundamental unit with which a computer works.

C language A programming language popular for its portability to many different computer architectures.

carrier (1) Plastic unit that houses integrated circuit chips. (2) Characteristic high-pitched sound produced by a modem.

cathode-ray tube (CRT) The display technology used by color and monochrome monitors; it is the same technology that is used in ordinary television sets.

CD-ROM databases Databases provided on a CD-ROM disk that allow users to browse through information at leisure without incurring telecommunication connection charges.

cell The intersection of a column and a row on a spreadsheet; also called coordinate.

cell pointer A visual indication of which cell is currently activated.

cellular system A telecommunication system that divides a geographic region into cells, each with its own antenna and radio frequency for transmitting information.

central database A database maintained by a widely distributed organization in a single, self-contained location.

central processing unit (CPU) The "brain" of a computer that works on, or processes, input and generates output; it consists of a control unit and an arithmetic/logic unit.

central wiring hub A component of a ring network which functions to keep the network "up" by detecting problems with connected workstations.

certainty factor Margin of confidence included in a conclusion derived by a knowledge-based system.

character-based user interface A style of interacting with a computer which typically requires a user to type commands on a keyboard (*see* graphical user interface).

client/server architecture A network of computers where some provide database services to other "client" computers.

clip art Prestored symbol libraries used in preparing graphics.

clone *See* compatible computer.

coaxial cable A high-frequency transmission cable.

COBOL (COmmon Business Oriented Language) A third-generation programming language widely used for business applications on large computers.

code generator Software tools that automatically produce program code from design specifications; another name for "back-end" CASE tools.

cold boot A term for starting a personal computer that has been off.

command An instruction to a computer to perform a function.

command mode (1) The absence of menus in a software application. (2) A database search style that requires a user to type programlike instructions to produce any desired result.

compatibility The capability of application programs written for old operating system versions to be used on newer versions.

compatible computer A personal computer that mimics the PC standard; also called clone.

compiler One type of language processor; it translates source code into machine language.

computer-aided design (CAD) A type of program used to create and manipulate precision-drawn objects.

computer-aided manufacture (CAM) Production of goods by robots that can accommodate rapid design changes and product customization.

Computer-Aided Software Engineering (CASE) Software designed to automate part or all of the phases of the system development process.

computer-assisted instruction (CAI) Instruction in which students learn with the aid of computer programs.

computer center Usually a mainframe computer facility that serves as the central processing center.

computer center operations manager Manages an organization's mainframe computer center's operations.

computer conferencing A restricted form of a bulletin board system for informal exchanges between conference participants; also called teleconferencing.

computer crime Stealing data, computer time, or software through illegal access to or manipulation of a computer system.

computer operators Those responsible for keeping hardware running.

computer-supported cooperative work *See* workgroup computing software.

computer system A group of interrelated items considered as a unit, consisting of hardware, software, people, and procedures.

console A terminal used to run and monitor mainframe hardware which displays performance data.

consolidation A spreadsheet feature that allows for combining several spreadsheets to get a "master" or summary spreadsheet.

constant data Items, like headings on a report, that do not change from report to report.

contention protocol *See* ethernet.

context-sensitive help A software feature which provides assistance appropriate to the action the software "senses" is causing a user to seek help.

control key A key (called CTRL) often found on a personal computer keyboard which is used in conjunction with other keys to perform various functions in word processing and other applications.

controller A hardware device designed to off-load certain processing tasks from the central processing unit (CPU).

controller board A web of electronic components and pathways designed to perform one or more functions, such as a display controller board; the common way to attach devices to the system unit.

control structures Processes within a program including loops, decisions, and sequences.

control unit (1) The component of the central processing unit that carries out program instructions. (2) An input and output device control on a mainframe.

conventional memory Memory locations on an IBM-PC or compatible microcomputer ranging from 0 to 1 million bytes. Most programs reside in conventional memory.

conversion Changing from one system to another.

coordinate *See* cell.

copy (1) A program feature that duplicates information in one location to another location. (2) Another name for text and graphics in desktop publishing.

critical success factors The limited number of areas in which satisfactory results will ensure successful performance for an organization.

CSMA/CD (Carrier Sense Multiple Access with Collision Detection) *See* ethernet.

cursor A tiny underscore on the screen which indicates the position where the next typed character will appear.

cursor control key A key that moves the cursor around the current display; also called arrow key.

customer statement A listing of a customer's unpaid invoices. Statements are usually generated once a month by a sales order processing application.

customizing Introducing program modifications to tailor a package for a user.

cut over The switch to a new system at the end of the parallel testing period.

database Collection of related files.

database administrator An individual in charge of overseeing all of a large organization's database activity.

database management system (DBMS) File management package that can work on several files at one time.

data dictionary Stores descriptions of everything in a database.

data entry operator Keyboards raw data into computers for processing.

data file A file usually created by using a program. An example is a file containing a business letter created with a word processing program.

data flow diagram A graphic model of a computer system.

Data Processing department Department in an organization in charge of all computerized information services.

Data Processing Management Association (DPMA) Organization for computer managers and educators.

data processing system Computer-based system that does the routine volume processing tasks in a mainframe organization.

debugging The process of correcting programming errors.

decision One of the three control structures in a structured computer program.

decision room A specially engineered meeting facility used by workgroups; contains individual personal computers and large display monitors for presentations.

decision support system (DSS) Software that provides support for nonrecurring or unstructured decision-making tasks.

decision support tool Applications such as financial modeling and spreadsheet packages which provide information to decision makers.

decision table A graphic representation of complex aspects of the logic underlying a computer program.

decision tree A graphic representation of the detailed programming logic in a program.

defaults Preselected choices that simplify data entry.

demodulation The process of converting analog signals to digital signals.

dependency diagram A model to represent the relationship (or dependencies) among the parts of a knowledge-based system.

desktop publishing The use of microcomputers and other hardware, as well as appropriate software, to produce documents for publication purposes.

dialing directory Stores the auto-dial phone numbers in telecommunication software.

digital graphics standard A color display standard characterized by a display of a small number of colors.

digitizing Recreating an image into a series of computer-readable dots.

direct access A method of storing information in a computer system that allows it to be accessed in a random order.

direct access storage device (DASD) Computer jargon for hard disk storage devices used by mainframe computers.

directory A listing of all the files on a disk.

diskcopy A utility command which allows the user to make backup disks of programs and data.

disk drive A hardware component that houses, and physically provides access to, disks during use by a program.

diskette A small portable disk used to store information in a microcomputer.

diskless workstation Desktop computers without local diskette storage.

disk operating system (DOS) Special software that manages a microcomputer, preparing the hardware to accept programs, among other things.

disks Magnetic storage media for data and programs.

display TV-like screen or monitor.

distributed processing A system in which computers are located throughout an organization to satisfy local data processing needs.

distributed or local databases Databases maintained by an organization in several locations.

dot-matrix printer A printer that arranges dots to form characters.

downloading Transmitting a file from a remote computer into one's own computer.

downsizing The shift from mainframe to personal computer networks in organizations.

downward compatibility The ability of newer model computers to run software which was designed for older standards.

drill down A feature in an executive information system which allows a user to examine data in as much detail as desired by "drilling down" into successive levels.

drop-down menu *See* pull-down menu.

EBCDIC (Extended Binary Coded Decimal Interchange Code) The 8-bit coding scheme used in mainframes.

editing The process of revising or correcting a document.

electronic funds transfer Using a bank's computer system to automatically withdraw money from accounts and transfer funds between accounts, among other transactions.

electronic mail (E-mail) The transfer of messages by electronic methods.

encryption A security measure that disguises information by processing it through an elaborate mathematical formula.

end user *See* user.

ENIAC Acronym for Electronic Numerical Integration And Computer, the first large-scale computer.

error correction A built-in method of catching and correcting errors in data that are transferred between modems.

ethernet protocol The transmission protocol used in a bus network.

exception reports Reports that call a manager's attention to information that falls outside specified parameters.

executive information system (EIS) Software that provides top-level executives with highly filtered summary information for strategic decision-making tasks.

Expanded Industry Standard Architecture (EISA) A computing standard that processes information with a 32-bit data bus and is also compatible with the older Industry Standard Architecture (ISA) standard.

expansion slots Places on a system board for inserting controller boards that attach peripherals to the computer.

explanation facility Part of knowledge-based system that explains the line of reasoning behind conclusions.

export A file conversion function that transports a copy of a file in a format for use on foreign software.

extended memory The name given to memory on an IBM-PC or compatible microcomputer that extends above 1 million bytes.

facsimile system A device that can transmit text and graphics over ordinary telephone lines.

fault-tolerant computers Computers designed for fail-safe operation. Dual processors provide redundant components; if one fails, a duplicate component takes over without interruption.

fault-tolerant computing A feature of newer PC architecture which kicks in a duplicate hardware component the instant a failure is detected in a primary component.

feasibility report A formal, written report that details the economic, technological, and operational feasibility of a proposed development project.

feasibility study Formal analysis of a firm's computing requirements.

fiber optic cable A cable immune to electromagnetic interferences used to transmit data at extremely high speed over a network.

field Slot in a record to hold data; one data element of a record.

file A collection of one or more similar records about one subject.

file and database management programs Software to help users set up, maintain, and manipulate data.

file conversion *See* translation.

file linking A spreadsheet feature that automatically updates multiple spreadsheets with common linked cells.

file locking A feature which prevents users, except the file owner, from destroying a file.

file manager software A microcomputer data management package that can work on only one file at a time.

financial modeling package Software used to handle problems that have more dimensions and complex formulas than can easily be handled by spreadsheet packages.

first-generation computers The earliest computers, including the ABC computer and ENIAC; characterized by vacuum tubes.

flat-panel display A monitor that lies flat rather than stands upright; usually found on small portable microcomputers.

font A complete set of characters in one typeface and size.

footnote tie-in A word processing feature that controls footnote placement to ensure that a footnote appears on the page where it is referenced.

format (1) To partition a disk into sectors and tracks. Blank disks are not usable until they have been formatted. (2) In many software packages, the physical appearance of work, such as in a spreadsheet package the way a spreadsheet is displayed or printed with specified column widths or decimal places.

formatting The process of specifying a document's final appearance on the printed page.

form generation A feature of database software that produces custom forms without programming.

FORTRAN (FORmula TRANslation) A high-level computer language developed in the 1950s; widely used in scientific and mathematical applications.

fourth-generation computers Computers developed in the early 1970s; they use chips that can contain over 15,000 circuits each.

fourth-generation language (4GL) Very-High-Level Language (VHLL) used in database management systems, decision support systems, and application development packages; programming language resembles normal English.

front-end communication processor A computer that off-loads the communication task from the mainframe.

full-duplex transmission A transmission mode that allows two computers to transmit data simultaneously.

function keys Keys in a separate part of the keyboard that are programmed to perform various tasks.

Gantt chart A tool used in systems analysis that graphically illustrates schedules; also called a bar chart.

general-purpose robot   A mechanical device that can be programmed to perform a variety of jobs.

global change   A change made in a word processing document that is made throughout the entire text; also used in other applications.

goal-seeking   A financial modelling feature which allows a user to indicate a desired result and then identify the numbers that can and cannot be manipulated in order to achieve the goal.

grammar checker   Software that spots errors that would be ignored by a spelling checker, such as redundancies, incorrect forms of words, and so on.

graphical user interface (GUI)   A way for a user to interact with a computer using symbols and a mouse selection device instead of typing commands on a keyboard.

graphics controller board   A separate controller board required by digital displays.

graphics program   Software that can make images for presentations, often by converting spreadsheet numbers into charts.

graphics standards   Specifications that define the graphic capabilities of a computer.

groupware   *See* workgroup computing software.

hacker   One whose hobby is studying how a computer works; can involve illegal access to others' systems.

half-duplex transmission   A transmission mode that allows only one computer to send data at a time.

hands-on test   Using candidate software on a computer to check that it is appropriate for the intended use.

hard copy   A printed copy of computer output.

hard disk   A rigid metallic disk encased in a sealed box and used for data storage; also called fixed disk.

hardware   The physical part of a computer.

hard-wired   Wired to perform one specific job, as the ENIAC. A new program required rewiring.

heuristics   Rules-of-thumb used to solve problems.

hierarchy chart   A diagram specifying the overall architecture of one or more computer programs.

homebot   Personal robots, often designed to perceive ultrasonic sound.

horizontal package   An accounting package that is generalized enough to be used by many industry types.

host computer   A central computer linked by various telecommunication lines to subordinate computers or other devices.

hypertext   An electronic system for organizing and presenting information nonsequentially.

icons   Symbols used to indicate program settings and commands.

imaging device   A device that "reads" and digitizes entire documents.

imaging software   Software that allows for digitization of a photograph or any printed (or live) images.

import   A file conversion function that retrieves an exported file and converts it into its native format to make it available for use.

independent system vendor (ISV)   *See* value-added reseller.

index file   (1) A file created by database software that speeds up queries in a master file. (2) A file by means of which a specific record can be located.

induction system   A knowledge-based system shell or feature that automatically constructs rules from examples.

industry-specific package   Software that is geared to a specific industry, such as a medical patient profile system or a hotel management package.

Industry Standard Architecture (ISA)   Another name for the IBM-PC/AT standard architecture which processes data in 8-bit or 16-bit blocks.

inference engine   A program that handles the logic processing inside a knowledge-based system.

Information Center   A center through which the user services group provides computer technical support to nontechnical computer users.

Information Center specialist Helps users with computer access and with programming.

Information Resources Management department *See* Information Services department.

Information Services (IS) department The department responsible for servicing all computer-based support needs in a large organization.

ink-jet printer A printer that projects drops of ink to the surface of the paper.

input Computer jargon for putting something into a computer as well as a name for anything put into the computer.

installation The process of setting up a new computer system; includes data conversion, training, parallel testing, and security and performance monitoring.

integrated accounting system package The name given to a package consisting of several stand-alone accounting functions.

integrated CASE (I-CASE) Software that automates all the phases of the system development life cycle.

integrated circuit A circuit etched onto a silicon chip; also, the technology that makes use of this technique. The use of integrated circuits marked third-generation computers.

integrated circuit chips A computer device consisting of miniaturized electronic components etched onto a silicon surface.

integrated services data network (ISDN) A communication network that carries simultaneous voice, data, and full-motion pictures.

interactive Method of computer use in which a user interacts with the computer.

internal modem A special-purpose controller board that fits into a personal computer's expansion slot and is connected directly to the telephone wall outlet by a cable.

International Standards Organization (ISO) Organization which sets rules for international telecommunication.

interpreter One type of computer language processor; it translates source code into machine language during program execution.

invoice A customer bill.

keyboard The hardware unit of a personal computer with which a user most commonly enters and manipulates data.

keyboard oriented A data entry style that uses key strokes, often to select items on menu bars or to type commands (versus a mouse-oriented style, which is characteristic of a graphical user interface).

key field Any important lookup item in a record.

knowledge base A stored collection of facts and rules about a specific area of knowledge.

knowledge-based systems Software systems that capture, magnify, and distribute access to judgment.

knowledge engineers People who specialize in transforming rules-of-thumb (heuristics) and other kinds of knowledge into a computerized knowledge base.

language processor Programs that translate common programming languages, such as BASIC or COBOL, into machine language.

large-scale integration (LSI) 15,000 circuits or more etched on a single computer chip; marked the fourth-generation computers.

laser printer An extremely fast printer that uses photocopying techniques to produce high-quality text and graphic output.

layout A thumbnail sketch of possible arrangements of text and graphics on a page.

line items Lines of information which identify each actual item ordered on a sales order data entry screen.

line printer Used to handle large-volume printing required by mainframe installations. Line printers use hammers and inked ribbons to put characters on paper.

LISP A programming language used for knowledge-based systems, abbreviated from "List Processing."

local-area network (LAN) A network linking two or more personal computers and computerized devices which allows them to share software, hardware, and communication services.

local node   A connecting point in a packet-switched network that helps to link users to various public and private host computers.

lockout   *See* record locking.

logic errors   An error in a computer program that does not involve violation of language rules but which must be uncovered by the programmer.

log-on   A sequence that validates a communicator to a host computer.

loop   A process in a computer program designed to be repetitive.

machine language   First-generation computer language, consisting of only 1's and 0's to identify on and off electronic pulses.

macro   A block of program code or commands that allows a user to replace a series of keystrokes with far fewer keystrokes. Some packages automatically record macros from a series of keystrokes, save them, and play them back exactly as they were recorded. Macros are common in word processing and spreadsheet packages.

magnetic ink character recognition (MICR)   An optical character recognition technique whereby a scanner is used to read characters printed with magnetic ink.

magnetic tape   Flexible tape used as a backup or archival storage medium on mainframe computers.

mail merge   An application used to merge a form letter file and a data file to create personalized form letters.

mainframe computer   A large computer; also known as a mainframe.

mainframe processor   The processor in a large computer system which houses the central processing unit and memory.

maintenance programmer   A specialist who refines and improves existing computer programs.

management and control computer system   A generic term for all software in organizations which pulls together information from front- and back-office systems and external sources and provides managers with summarized information to monitor, control, and plan organizational strategy.

management by exception   A management approach which advocates spending time on exceptional conditions and not wasting valuable time on things that are performing as expected.

management hierarchy   The three levels of management—operational (lowest), tactical (middle), and strategic (upper)—found in most organizations.

Management Information Services (or Systems) department   *See* Information Services department.

management information system (MIS)   Computer software designed to provide management and control information which is filtered from other internal and external computer-based systems.

markup copy   A copy of a style-checked document with comments and suggestions inserted throughout.

master pages   In a page composition package, used to set column widths, margins, and any other items that appear in each left or right page.

memory   (1) One of two major components of the mainframe processor unit, used for temporary storage of data and programs. (2) *See* random access memory.

memory address   A unique number in a computer's memory which identifies a storage location.

menu bar or line   A line of menu items on the screen that are selected by using a mouse or by pressing selected keys.

menu pointer   Used to highlight one of several command choices on a display.

metropolitan area networks (MANs)   Telecommunication networks designed for high-speed data exchange over a minimum distance of 50 miles.

Micro Channel Architecture (MCA)   A microcomputer architecture which allows other processors, besides the central processing unit, to coexist and perform various processing tasks.

micro channel connectors The expansion slots in the PS/2 microcomputer which tether various physically separated components to the system unit.

microcomputer A small computer with a central processing unit contained on a single microprocessor chip; also called a personal computer.

microcomputer specialist Researches latest microcomputer hardware and software and introduces new technology into a firm as appropriate; usually works in a company's Information Center.

microprocessor A miniature central processing unit on a single integrated circuit chip.

microwave A telecommunication medium that transmits radio signals and relies on antennas rather than cables.

millions of instructions per second (MIPS) A measure of the rate at which a computer performs instructions.

minicomputer Smaller, less powerful, less costly computers than mainframes. Usually do not require special rooms and can be installed anywhere. Considered a medium-sized computer between a smaller microcomputer and a larger mainframe.

mission critical computer system A front-office system that supports the goals of an organization. An example is a computer-based support system for savings and checking transaction processing at a bank.

modem A device that modulates digital signals from a computer into analog, or telephone, signals to telecommunicate data.

modular program A program that obeys rigid superior-subordinate rules of construction, allowing changes to be made easily.

modulation A process that takes discrete digital computer signals of 1's and 0's and gives them sound to go through telephone lines.

monitor *See* display.

monochrome display A monitor that presents data or graphics in one color.

motherboard *See* system board.

mouse A device used to control the movement of an arrow pointer around a screen; usually involves pointing to selections on a pull-down menu.

mouse oriented A data entry style that uses a mouse and pull-down menus (versus a keyboard-oriented style).

MS-DOS A single-tasking operating system used on microcomputers; also called PC-DOS.

multimedia Presentations that combine computer text and graphics with audio and video, all of which are controlled by a computer.

multiplexer A device that bundles several slow-speed lines into one higher-speed line.

multiscan monitors Computer displays that accept a range of graphic standard scan rates from various display boards; also called multisync monitors.

multisync monitors *See* multiscan monitors.

multitasking operating system Allows several programs to be run simultaneously.

multiuser computer A computer supporting several people simultaneously.

multiuser operating system Provides services to many users who share one computer.

multiuser spreadsheet A centralized spreadsheet that allows many users access at once.

natural language Any language spoken by humans; distinguished from program language. User communicates with a computer in user's own language, English, for example.

natural language package Software that enables a user to ask search questions in plain English.

near-letter-quality printer A type of dot-matrix printer which produces both rough-draft and letter-quality output.

nodes *See* workstations.

nonprocedural language A language typically found in database management systems, characteristically used for uncomplicated user-developed systems.

normalizing files Rules used to create smaller, more manageable files from unorganized larger files.

numeric keypad Special keys designed to speed data entry in numerical-oriented applications.

object code The machine code image of compiled source code that is used to run, or execute, a program.

object library *See* symbol library.

object-oriented images Images produced by CAD packages and stored as formulas which are always sharp and clear when enlarged.

object-oriented programming (OOP) An approach to programming that combines data and instructions that act on that data in a single unit, called an object. OOP produces reusable code.

on-line database Files of information which a user can access with a computer, a modem, and communication software.

on-line database service Provides information over communication lines to subscribers for a fee.

on-line help A feature that provides aid to a user during program use.

on-line processing Another name for transaction processing which reflects that the terminal is "on a line," directly connected to the computer responsible for processing the entire transaction.

on-line spell checking A feature that catches spelling and typographical errors while a document is being typed; also called real-time spell checking.

Open Order Report A beneficial report generated by a sales order processing package which helps management to determine which customer orders have not been shipped and which items are causing backlogs.

operating environment *See* windows program.

operating system A special program that manages everything that happens inside a computer. It acts as a buffer between application programs and computer hardware.

Operating System/2 (OS/2) The multitasking operating system designed to optimize the performance of the IBM Personal System/2 line of microcomputers.

operational database Any central database that supports the day-to-day transactions and business activity of an organization.

optical character recognition (OCR) Converting printed characters into electronic signals that can be processed by a computer.

optical disk A high-capacity computer storage medium.

order header The data-entry screen in a sales order processing application which accepts all order data except line items.

outline processor An application used to organize elements on a screen in outline form.

output Computer jargon for getting something out of a computer as well as for what comes out.

overhead transparency Plastic sheets that contain data or illustrations that can be projected by an overhead projector.

override A program feature that allows a user to overwrite data which are automatically supplied.

packaged programs *See* packaged software.

packaged software Ready-made software.

packet A group of characters sent in a packet-switched network.

packet-switched network A system which sends data in groups of characters called "packets."

page composition package The main software ingredient in most desktop publishing systems which replaces a drafting table, scissors, and glue with the electronic assembly of text and graphics to create a page layout.

page description language (PDL) A system for coding document files to make them acceptable to laser printers, typesetters, or other devices. PDL coding is done automatically by most page composition packages.

page layout The composed page image created with a page composition package.

painting software Software that allows for creating free-form images.

parallel processing The ability to harness the power of several coprocessors for a single computing task.

parallel testing A period of time when manual, or old, and new computer systems function together for comparison purposes.

parity bit   Used to provide a low level of error checking.

PC-DOS   The industry standard single-tasking operating system; also known as MS-DOS.

pen input system   A keyboard alternative that uses an electronic "pen" or stylus to indicate user input on a specially coated display screen.

personal computer   A small, often desktop-sized, computer designed to be used by one person; technically called a microcomputer.

personal database   Database for a single individual's use.

personal identification number (PIN)   The number a user must enter into a computer for identification purposes.

personal information manager (PIM)   Software that handles a user's personal calendar as well as maintains lists of "to do" and other items.

Personal System/2 (PS/2)   The line of IBM personal computers which offer advanced processing capabilities over the Personal Computer (PC) line.

picking/packing slip   A document provided by an automated sales order entry procedure that is used in gathering (picking) order items as well as shipping (packing) them.

piracy   Illegal copying of software.

pixel   A term for one picture element.

plotter   A device used to print paper charts or transparencies.

plug compatibles   Computer products that mimic other brands of computer products.

pointer   A highlighted area on the screen which a user can move around, usually with a mouse, to make menu and other selections. A pointer is often shaped like an arrow.

point-of-sale (POS) terminal   A terminal used in a retail setting to act as a cash register; it captures the data at the point the sale is transacted and is connected to a central computer.

polling   A transmission procedure used with synchronous communication that allows only one terminal use of the line at a time.

presentation graphics   The use of graphics for presentation to others.

previewing   Permits a user to examine a document or graphic before printing.

primary data   Data that cannot be computed; the usual items included in a file.

print queuing   Allows several files, such as word processing documents, to be queued and printed in sequence, while other work, such as editing, can continue.

procedural language   A programmer-oriented language that requires specifying how a program should be executed.

processing   What occurs to transform input to output.

process logic   The detailed logic underlying a computer program.

processor   (1) A name for the centrally located main computer unit shared by multiple users. (2) A component of a mainframe computer that houses the central processing unit and memory.

program   A set of instructions for a computer, telling it what to do; another word for software.

program coding   The step in the programming process concerned with writing code that instructs the computer to carry out the logic design.

program design   The design of a program's overall structure and detailed processing logic.

program documentation   Written description of the operation and use of a program.

program file   Contains software often purchased from a computer store or other outlet. An example is a word processing program file.

program flowchart   A graphic representation of program logic.

program instructions   *See* program statements.

program language   Coding systems with formal syntax and rules that instruct a computer to carry out logical procedures which are collected into *programs;* examples are BASIC and COBOL.

program listing   A computer-printed copy of program statements.

programmers   Those who write computer programs.

programming A multistep process involving designing the overall program structure and detailed logic, writing code, and debugging and testing programs.

program modifications Changes in a computer program.

program module A box on a hierarchy chart that represents a block of code.

program statements Lines of program code; also called program instructions.

program testing Checking that a program runs correctly and produces expected results.

project management software Software that enables a user to oversee a project more effectively by dividing the project into manageable units, or tasks, assigning resources to tasks, and reassigning resources as a situation changes.

PROLOG A programming language used for knowledge-based systems, abbreviated from "Programming Logic."

prompts Messages that ask questions or give instructions to facilitate program operation.

proportional spacing A professional-class word processing feature that allocates printing space according to character size; for example, more room is allowed for an uppercase *M* than for a lower case *i*.

protected mode A mode of operation with the 80286 and higher microprocessors which makes multitasking possible.

protected spreadsheet A spreadsheet that has certain cells locked to prevent them from being changed.

protocol A set of transmission rules in telecommunications.

prototype A rough model of a user application.

prototyping approach When a systems developer works with a user to create a rough version of a computer system without adhering to the system development life cycle.

pseudocode A form of structured English used by computer programmers to describe the logic underlying a program.

public communication service Provides electronic mail and other types of telecommunication services for a fee.

public-domain software Software that is often distributed by user groups free, except for the cost of distribution.

pull-down menu A menu of command options that appear to "pull down" on a display once a main menu line command is selected.

query Database jargon for searching a file for records that meet specific criteria.

query by example (QBE) A database inquiry method characterized by filling inquiry conditions into empty slots under displayed field information.

random access File processing that allows records to be manipulated in a random order. It is the opposite of sequential access.

random access memory (RAM) A temporary storage area in the computer where programs and data must reside before they are processed by the central processing unit.

read-only memory (ROM) Permanent storage areas that contain utility programs.

real mode An operating mode supported by the 80286 and higher microprocessors which uses only the first 640 Kbytes of available memory. It is used for running traditional DOS programs because it mimics the old 8088 microprocessor memory addressing limitation.

real-time processing Another name for transaction processing where data are entered into the computer that processes them immediately as a transaction occurs.

real-time spell checking *See* on-line spell checking.

record The common unit of a file that is divided into slots, called fields, to hold data.

record locking or lockout Process whereby one user is put on hold if two users attempt to update one record at the same time.

Reduced Instruction Set Computing (RISC) processor A processor capable of increased processing speed by eliminating seldom-used instructions; common in workstations.

relational DBMS Database management system that links files to each other through a key field.

remote computing Linking two computers together so that both keyboards are active and both screens show the same thing.

report generation   A feature of database software that generates custom reports without programming.

report layout   An image of a desired report.

repository   A component of a computer-aided software engineering (CASE) tool that stores, controls, and manages all the information about an organization.

requirement analysis   The first step in the systems development life cycle, the investigatory stage.

resolution   The number of distinguishable points or dots on a display.

reverse engineering   The automated restructuring of existing programs into more efficient and easily maintainable programs.

RGB monitor   A monitor that uses a refined color separation technology to produce high-quality color images.

ring network   A local-area network layout which links workstations in an unbroken chain of many cable segments. Ring networks often use a token passing transmission protocol.

RS-232 cable   A cable that connects an external modem to a computer; also called serial cable.

Sales History Report   A report generated by a sales order processing application to help managers set marketing strategies.

sales order processing application   An application which allows orders to be entered into the computer as they are received from a customer.

satellite   A manufactured object launched into outer space that transmits radio signals around the world.

scanner   A computer input device that converts text, drawings, and photographs from a printed page to a form the computer can interpret and process.

scanning   Technology that rapidly "reads" documents and converts them into binary digits for storage.

screen painting   The process of designing a form or other graphics on a screen.

script file   A file created in some programmable telecommunication packages which holds procedures for automating tasks, such as logging on to a public communication service.

scrolling   Moving text up and down so that the desired portion of the text appears in the display.

search and replace   A function used to find a word or phrase in a word-processed document and replace it with another word or phrase.

secondary data   Any variable that can be computed from other variables.

second-generation computer   Faster and more reliable computer developed in the late 1950s and early 1960s that used transistors for its circuitry.

sensory subsystem   A part of a robot's design that enables it to perform activities that normally require human senses, for example, vision.

sequence   One of the three control structures in a structured computer program.

sequential access   File processing that begins with the first record and progresses sequentially through the entire file. Magnetic tape is an example of a sequential access medium.

serial cable   *See* RS-232 cable.

serial port   A port in the back side of a personal computer which provides the connection, via a cable, between the computer and an external modem or other serial device.

server   A device attached to a local-area network dedicated to performing one or more service functions, such as a file server.

shareware   *See* public domain software.

shell   A package containing an inference engine program without the knowledge base.

shift key   A key often found on a personal computer keyboard which is used in conjunction with other keys to perform various functions in word processing and other applications.

silicon chip   A chip on which circuits are etched. Its use marked the third generation of computers. *See* integrated circuit.

single-tasking operating system   Accommodates one user and is only used on microcomputers.

slide-show software   A program which allows personal computer users to create simulated "slides" for presentations.

soft copy   Display computer output.

software   The nonphysical part of a computer; the programs that run on a computer, telling the hardware what to do.

software developer   A person who creates new software packages, or a company that creates new software packages.

software directories   Contain information about software packages, including what the software does, hardware requirements, pricing, number of current users, contact information, and geographic area serviced by the supplier.

sort   Arranges records into any alphabetic and numeric order desired.

source code   Human-readable code.

spelling checker   Software used to match words in a document with words in its dictionary for mismatches. It displays suspect words and suggests corrections.

split screen   A feature that shows different sections of a project on a display.

spreadsheet   A convenient tool to explore problems that can be defined numerically in row and column format.

spreadsheet publishing   A feature that uses shading, boxes, lines, and different type styles to transform spreadsheets into high-quality presentation material.

stand-alone accounting package   A software application which performs one function, such as sales order or accounts receivable processing.

standardizing   Requiring everyone to use the same package, for example, a spreadsheet package. It occurs in multiuser environments to facilitate file exchange and to simplify training and maintenance support.

standards   Specifications intended to facilitate the exchange of data between computers.

star network   A local-area network layout with workstations clustered around a computer that acts like a central controller, or "switch."

storage   The keeping of data on disks rather than just in a computer's memory.

stored program concept   Concept of temporarily storing programs in a computer's memory.

structured methods   Methods used to analyze, design, and program computer systems; they start from an overview of the problem and then focus on increasingly smaller details.

structured query language (SQL)   A style of database inquiry characterized by typing inquiry commands in a structured format.

structured walkthrough   A formal meeting at which technicians attempt to catch design problems in computer programs.

style checker software   Used to spot errors that would be ignored by a spelling checker; also called a grammar checker.

style sheets   Prepared, or stored, formats that come with a word-processing package; some enable users to create custom style sheets.

supercomputer   A computer that does tasks that require massive amounts of data to be processed at extremely high speeds; used for advanced military, scientific, and other projects.

supermicro   A microcomputer with a processor unit that services multiple users.

superminicomputer   The most powerful type of minicomputer; it rivals a mainframe in power.

superworkstation   A high-performance workstation; a type of superminicomputer.

symbol library   A library of prestored symbols that can be used in the preparation of graphic presentations; also called an object library.

synchronous transmission   The transmission of data one byte after another in regular intervals synchronized by a master clock.

synonym finder   Software that performs the role of a thesaurus; also called electronic thesaurus.

syntax error   An error in a computer program that is flagged by the language processor.

system analysis   The investigative phase of what has to be done to develop a new application.

system analyst   A person who analyzes, designs, and implements computer systems.

system board   The main controller board of a personal computer on which the main chips reside.

system design Identifying how a computer system should be developed to serve a specific purpose.

system development life cycle (SDLC) The steps from initial analysis through implementation and maintenance involved in developing a new computer system.

system documentation A collection of all the documents created to develop and install a new system.

system flowchart A graphic model showing the flow of control through a computer system.

system integrator *See* value added reseller.

system programmer Writes operating system, utility, telecommunications, and other technically oriented service programs.

system unit A hardware component of a personal computer that houses the components that perform the actual processing.

systems development Creating new computer systems and maintaining old ones.

Systems Development department Consists of a group of computer professionals who create new computer systems and maintain old ones.

tape cartridge A common medium used for backing up files contained on hard disks.

teach pendant A device used to perform desired motions and coordinates of a robot.

telecommunication carrier An independent company that provides transmission services.

telecommunication program Software that enables using a telephone so that one computer can exchange information with another.

telecommunications manager An individual who designs and implements an organization's telecommunication network.

telecommuting Working at home and communicating with one's office or company through a computer and a modem.

teleconferencing *See* computer conferencing.

telepresence Remote control of robot functions.

template (1) A master spreadsheet without numbers or data. (2) A small plastic cut-out of memory jogger labels for the function keys.

terminal An input device connected to a central computer. Terminals resemble personal computers but have no system unit.

text-based data management A word processing feature or stand-alone package which allows a user to write notes marked with keywords for later search, retrieval, and organization.

text wrap To flow text around any obstruction on a page, such as a graphic image.

third-generation computer Computer developed in the 1960s that used integrated circuitry and silicon chips.

third-generation language Programming languages such as COBOL, C, and BASIC.

three-dimensional spreadsheet A spreadsheet that has rows, columns, and pages for display of three dimensions, for example, budget, time periods, and department.

titles A spreadsheet package feature which locks in a row or a column on the display.

token passing A method for controlling transmission in a local-area network.

top-down testing An ongoing procedure which ensures that critical interfaces between program modules function properly.

touch-sensitive display An alternative to a keyboard used on some personal computers that is activated by touching the screen and blocking light beams.

transaction processing Entry of data directly into the computer as the transaction occurs rather than saving them for entry at a later point.

transistors Devices that replaced vacuum tubes for computer circuitry and that marked the second generation of computers.

translation A spreadsheet feature that allows different packages to share files by importing and exporting them using file exchange formats; also called file conversion feature.

turnkey system A combination of hardware and software packaged for sale by a value-added reseller, theoretically ready to be turned on and used.

turnkey vendor *See* value-added reseller.

twisted-pair wire   The line connecting a telephone to a wall jack; the most economical transmission medium for local-area networks.

typeface   A designed set of characters with a name that is sometimes copyrighted.

typesetter   Machinery that uses photographic processes to produce a page image on photosensitive paper for reproduction; also called a phototypesetter or imagesetter.

type through   A word processing feature which enables a user to type directly to the printer.

unattended mode   A feature that allows a computer to run on "automatic pilot" for telecommunication tasks.

undo   A feature that restores the last deletion made in a word processing document; cancels a mistake or allows a change of mind.

UNIVAC   The first business computer, used in the early 1950s.

Unix operating system   A multitasking and multiuser operating system that works on many different vendors' hardware.

uploading   Transmitting a file from one's own computer to a remote computer.

user   An individual who uses computers.

user database   Centrally controlled database that supports the decision-making efforts of individuals in an organization. It often contains extracts from operational databases and external on-line databases.

user-developed systems   Computer systems that are custom-developed by the people who will be using them.

user groups   Formal or informal gatherings of computer users to share information, software, and other matters of interest.

User Guide   The part of a software package that contains instructions about how to use the software.

user interface   The communications that occur between a user and a computer.

user services manager   Manages computer professionals who help employees become self-sufficient computer users.

utilities   Programs that help perform disk housekeeping chores. They include format a disk, copy a disk, copy a file, and examine a file directory's content.

vacuum tube   A device for basic computer circuitry used in first-generation computers; resembles a slim light bulb.

value-added reseller (VAR)   Retailer who combines hardware and software, often from various manufacturers, for resale as a turnkey system.

variable data   Items that can be split into primary and secondary data and that can change each time a program is run.

vertical package   *See* industry-specific package.

videoconferencing   A telecommunication method that allows conferees in different locations to meet interactively with both sound and picture.

view   (1) Database file that contains only those fields that a user needs. (2) The original sort or search request (query) which is saved in a special query file.

virtual 86 mode   A mode of operation with the 80386 and higher microprocessors which allows a user to run many DOS applications at the same time.

virus   A computer program that can copy itself and spread from computer to computer, sometimes stealing processing power and destroying files.

VisiCalc   The first electronic spreadsheet program.

voice digitizer   A component necessary for voice mail service that measures voice sound frequencies and assigns them values that can be stored as 1's and 0's.

voice mail   A telecommunication system that uses a voice digitizer and voice synthesizer to transfer messages by sound.

voice recognition   A computer that operates by sound input rather than by a keyboard.

voice synthesizer   A component necessary in voice mail service that reads digital signals and converts them back to sound.

warm boot   Restarting a program with the computer already on.

war room   *See* decision room.

wide-area network (WAN)   A network that uses modems and the telephone system to communicate over long distances.

widow and orphan control A word processing feature which prevents one line from being separated on a page from the rest of the paragraph on another page.

wild card Characters, such as question marks, that are used, for example, in a search and replace process, to symbolize ambiguous characters.

window One area of a divided screen.

windows program A program that adds a new layer of software between a single-tasking operating system, such as DOS, and any application program. It enables a single-tasking operating system to function like a multitasking system.

word processing package A program that provides for the automated manipulation of words in a document. It helps the user to create, edit, and store text.

word size The number of bits a processor handles at one time. The greater the word size, the faster the processing.

word wrap A function that moves any word that crosses the right-hand margin to the next line.

workgroup computing software Software that facilitates the productivity of groups of individuals; includes electronic mail, group scheduling, and group calendaring, among others.

workstation (1) A device linked to a local-area network; also called a node. (2) A "power" user desktop computer system that typically has a large screen and advanced processing and graphics capabilities. (3) Location where computing is carried out.

WYSIWYG Acronym for "What you see is what you get." Software whose display shows exactly what a printed document will look like.

Xmodem protocol An example of a popular method of detecting and correcting errors in telecommunication.

X.25 Rules for connecting to public packet-switched networks.

X.400 A standard to connect electronic mail services around the world.

zoom function A painting software feature which improves graphic detail by causing an enlarged dot-by-dot pattern of a drawing section to be displayed.

Credits

Courtesy of *AI Interactions*, August 1985, Adapted with permission: Case Study 14

Courtesy of Aldus Corporation: Fig. 3-8

Courtesy of AMDEK Corporation: Figs. 3-15, 3-30

Courtesy of American Small Business Computers, Inc.: Fig. 5-37

Courtesy of Anaheim Publishing, G.B. Shelly and T.B. Cashman, COMPUTER FUNDAMENTALS, 1985: Fig. 12-14 (bottom)

Courtesy of Anderson Jacobson: Figs. 3-16, 7-2

Courtesy of Apple Computer, Inc.: Figs. 1-1 (top), 2-12 (top), 2-16, 3-5, 3-19, 3-22, 3-25, 14-7

Courtesy of Archive Corp.: Fig. 3-27

Courtesy of Ashton-Tate Corporation: Figs. 5-19 (top left), 6-6, 6-7, 6-8, 6-9, 6-10, 6-12, 6-13, 6-19, 6-21

Courtesy of AST: Fig. 4-22

Courtesy of Autodesk, Inc.: Fig. 5-36

Courtesy of Automatix: Fig. 13-11

Courtesy of Avalon Technology, Inc.: Fig. 2-7

Courtesy of Benjamin Cummings: Fig. 12-9

Courtesy of Borland International: Figs. 5-12, 6-17

Courtesy of Breakthrough Software Corporation, Time Line: Fig. 9-20 (bottom)

Courtesy of *Business* magazine: Fig. 13-14

Courtesy of *Business Week*, © 1991 by McGraw-Hill, Inc., Reprinted by special permission: Case Study Ch. 6 #2

Courtesy of Chinon America, Inc.: Fig. 3-11

Courtesy of Chorus Data Systems: Fig. 5-30

Courtesy of The Chronicle of Higher Education: Case Study Ch. 12

Courtesy of CMP Publications, Inc.: Figs. 7-12, 8-7 (bottom)

Courtesy of Compaq: Figs. 1-12, 3-17

Courtesy of CompuServe: Fig. 7-8

Courtesy of *Computerworld*: Focus On Ch. 3, Case Study Ch. 6 #1, Ch. Opening 11; Focus On Ch. 13 #1, Fig. 14-9

Courtesy of Comshare, Inc.: Figs. 3-9, 9-17

Courtesy of Control Data Corporation: Fig. 8-20

Courtesy of Cranston/Csuri Productions: Fig. 14-12 (bottom)

Courtesy of Cray Research, Inc.: Fig. 8-24

Courtesy of Datagraphix, Inc.: Fig. 8-19

Courtesy of *Data Management*: Fig. 12-10

Courtesy of Datamation, Cahners Publishing Company, Reprinted with permission: Focus On Ch. 7, Fig. 14-15

Courtesy of Datapro Research: Fig. 8-7 (top)

Courtesy of Datastorm Technologies, Inc.: Fig. 7-6

Courtesy of DecisionWare: Fig. 4-13

Courtesy of Digital Equipment Corp.: Figs. 7-19 (right), 7-23 (top), 8-22

Courtesy of *Edge*, from Sam Licciardi, Nov./Dec. 1990: Case Study Ch 9.

Courtesy of Elsevier Science Publishing Co., Inc.: Fig. 10-7

Courtesy of Execucom Systems Corporation: Fig. 5-16

Courtesy of Favert/Gamma Liaison: Fig. 13-15 (bottom)

Courtesy of General Electric Company: Fig. 13-3

Courtesy of Joel Gordon: Fig. 8-3

Courtesy of Grid Systems: Fig. 3-10

Courtesy of Gerry Gropp/SIPA Press: Fig. 3-10

Courtesy of GTE Spacenet & Dennis Raulin: Fig. 7-33

Courtesy of *Harvard Business Review*: Fig. 9-15

Courtesy of Harvard Graphics,® Software Publishing Corporation: Figs. 5-19, 5-23, 5-24

Courtesy of Harvard Software, Inc.: Fig. 9-20 (top)

Courtesy of Hewlett-Packard: Figs. 2-14 (top), 3-9, 3-17, 4-21, 5-21, Focus On Ch. 8
Courtesy of Hitachi America, Ltd.: Fig. 13-12
Courtesy of Index Technology: Fig. 11-16
Courtesy of Information Builders, Inc.: Figs. 12-15, 12-16, 12-17
Courtesy of Intel & Anderson Consulting: Fig. 5-33
Courtesy of International Business Machines Corporation: Figs. 1-1 (bottom), 2-13 (bottom left), 3-1, 3-4, 3-6, 4-3, 4-4, 5-32 (top), 6-11, 8-1, 8-15, 8-23, 14-3 (left), 14-6
Courtesy of Iowa State University: Fig. 14-1
Courtesy of Richard D. Irwin: Fig. 12-14 (top)
Courtesy of Lanier: Fig. 7-13
Courtesy of L.C. Technologies: Fig. 3-13
Courtesy of Lear Siegler, Inc.: Fig. 8-1
Courtesy of Levi Strauss & Co.: Fig. 8-7 (bottom)
Courtesy of Long Beach (CA) Memorial Medical Center: Fig. 14-8
Courtesy of Lotus Development Corporation: Figs. 5-4, 5-13, 5-18, 9-21
Courtesy of MacroMind: Fig. 5-32 (bottom)
Courtesy of MacWorld: Figs. 4-19, 5-8
Courtesy of MacWorld and F. B. Stinson: Fig. 3-28
Courtesy of Matrix Software: Fig. 11-18
Courtesy of MCI Communications Corporation: Fig. 7-9
Courtesy of Menlo Corporation: Fig. 7-16
Courtesy of MicroPro International Corp: Fig. 4-1, 4-5, 4-6
Courtesy of MicroProse: Fig. 14-11
Courtesy of Microscience International Corp.: Fig. 3-26
Courtesy of Microsoft Corp.: Figs. 1-7, 2-12 (bottom right), 2-15, 3-8, 4-8, 5-10
Courtesy of NCR: Fig. 8-4
Courtesy of *New York Personal Computer User's Group Newsletter:* Fig. 4-30
Courtesy of The *New York Times* Company, Copyright by The New York Times Company, Reprinted by permission: Case Study Ch. 7 #2, Case Study Ch. 8, Ch. Opening 9, Ch. Opening 12
Courtesy of OWL International: Fig. 4-19
Courtesy of Pacific Bell: Fig. 7-12
Courtesy of *PC Magazine:* Figs. 4-25, 4-27, 4-32, Ch. Opening 10
Courtesy of *PC Today:* Fig. 3-31, Case Study Ch. 7 #1
Courtesy of *PC Today,* Copyright © 1991 by Peed Corporation, Reprinted by permission: Case Study Ch. 7 #1
Courtesy of PC World: Figs. 4-14, 14-12 (top), 4-28, 5-9, 5-11
Courtesy of Peed Corp.: Fig. 3-31, Case Study, Ch. 7 #1
Courtesy of Polaroid Corporation: Fig. 5-26
Courtesy of Prentice-Hall, Inc.: Figs. 1-3, 5-2, 7-25, 12-3
Courtesy of Ralph's Grocery Company and Teri Stratford: Fig. 8-6
Courtesy of Raytheon Co.: Figs. 3-29, 14-3 (right)
Courtesy of Dr. Richard A. Robb, Mayo Foundation, May 22-25, 1990: Fig. 14-9
Courtesy of *Robotics Age:* Fig. 13-9
Courtesy of Ronin Development Corporation: Fig. 9-22
Courtesy of Sage Software: Fig. 11-17
Courtesy of Software Publishing Corporation: Figs. 5-19, 5-23, 5-24
Courtesy of Sperry Corporation: Fig. 14-4
Courtesy of George Steinmetz: Fig. 14-10
Courtesy of Symantic Corp.: Figs. 4-15, 9-20 (bottom)
Courtesy of Teri Stratford: Fig. 8-3
Courtesy of Texas Instruments: Figs. 3-12, 3-21
Courtesy of Tim Davis Photography: Fig. 1-13
Courtesy of *Time Magazine*: Fig. 13-13, Focus On Ch. 13 #2
Courtesy of Toshiba American Information Systems, Inc.: Fig. 1-12
Courtesy of UPI/Bettmaun Newsphotos: Fig. 14-2
Courtesy of U.S. Dept. of the Navy: Fig. 14-5

Index